The Law of Banking and Financial Institutions

2011 Statutory Supplement

EDITORIAL ADVISORS

Vicki Been
Elihu Root Professor of Law
New York University School of Law

Erwin Chemerinsky
Dean and Distinguished Professor of Law
University of California, Irvine, School of Law

Richard A. Epstein
Laurence A. Tisch Professor of Law
New York University School of Law
Peter and Kirsten Bedford Senior Fellow
The Hoover Institution
Senior Lecturer in Law
The University of Chicago

Ronald J. Gilson
Charles J. Meyers Professor of Law and Business
Stanford University
Marc and Eva Stern Professor of Law and Business
Columbia Law School

James E. Krier
Earl Warren DeLano Professor of Law
The University of Michigan Law School

Richard K. Neumann, Jr.
Professor of Law
Hofstra University School of Law

Robert H. Sitkoff
John L. Gray Professor of Law
Harvard Law School

David Alan Sklansky
Professor of Law
University of California at Berkeley School of Law

Kent D. Syverud
Dean and Ethan A. H. Shepley University Professor
Washington University School of Law

Elizabeth Warren
Leo Gottlieb Professor of Law
Harvard Law School

The Law of Banking and Financial Institutions

2011 Statutory Supplement

Richard Scott Carnell
Associate Professor of Law
Fordham University

Jonathan R. Macey
Deputy Dean and Sam Harris Professor of Corporate Law,
Corporate Finance, and Securities Law
Yale University

Geoffrey P. Miller
Stuyvesant P. Comfort Professor of Law and
Director, Center for the Study of Central Banks and
Financial Institutions
New York University

Copyright © 2011 Richard Scott Carnell, Jonathan R. Macey, and Geoffrey P. Miller.

Published by Wolters Kluwer Law & Business in New York.

Wolters Kluwer Law & Business serves customers worldwide with CCH, Aspen Publishers, and Kluwer Law International products. (www.wolterskluwerlb.com)

No part of this publication may be reproduced or transmitted in any form or by any means, electronic or mechanical, including photocopy, recording, or utilized by any information storage or retrieval system, without written permission from the publisher. For information about permissions or to request permissions online, visit us at www.wolterskluwerlb.com, or a written request may be faxed to our permissions department at 212-771-0803.

To contact Customer Service, e-mail customer.service@wolterskluwer.com, call 1-800-234-1660, fax 1-800-901-9075, or mail correspondence to:

> Wolters Kluwer Law & Business
> Attn: Order Department
> PO Box 990
> Frederick, MD 21705

Printed in the United States of America.

1 2 3 4 5 6 7 8 9 0

ISBN 978-1-4548-0827-5

About Wolters Kluwer Law & Business

Wolters Kluwer Law & Business is a leading global provider of intelligent information and digital solutions for legal and business professionals in key specialty areas, and respected educational resources for professors and law students. Wolters Kluwer Law & Business connects legal and business professionals as well as those in the education market with timely, specialized authoritative content and information-enabled solutions to support success through productivity, accuracy and mobility.

Serving customers worldwide, Wolters Kluwer Law & Business products include those under the Aspen Publishers, CCH, Kluwer Law International, Loislaw, Best Case, ftwilliam.com and MediRegs family of products.

CCH products have been a trusted resource since 1913, and are highly regarded resources for legal, securities, antitrust and trade regulation, government contracting, banking, pension, payroll, employment and labor, and healthcare reimbursement and compliance professionals.

Aspen Publishers products provide essential information to attorneys, business professionals and law students. Written by preeminent authorities, the product line offers analytical and practical information in a range of specialty practice areas from securities law and intellectual property to mergers and acquisitions and pension/benefits. Aspen's trusted legal education resources provide professors and students with high-quality, up-to-date and effective resources for successful instruction and study in all areas of the law.

Kluwer Law International products provide the global business community with reliable international legal information in English. Legal practitioners, corporate counsel and business executives around the world rely on Kluwer Law journals, looseleafs, books, and electronic products for comprehensive information in many areas of international legal practice.

Loislaw is a comprehensive online legal research product providing legal content to law firm practitioners of various specializations. Loislaw provides attorneys with the ability to quickly and efficiently find the necessary legal information they need, when and where they need it, by facilitating access to primary law as well as state-specific law, records, forms and treatises.

Best Case Solutions is the leading bankruptcy software product to the bankruptcy industry. It provides software and workflow tools to flawlessly streamline petition preparation and the electronic filing process, while timely incorporating ever-changing court requirements.

ftwilliam.com offers employee benefits professionals the highest quality plan documents (retirement, welfare and non-qualified) and government forms (5500/PBGC, 1099 and IRS) software at highly competitive prices.

MediRegs products provide integrated health care compliance content and software solutions for professionals in healthcare, higher education and life sciences, including professionals in accounting, law and consulting.

Wolters Kluwer Law & Business, a division of Wolters Kluwer, is headquartered in New York. Wolters Kluwer is a market-leading global information services company focused on professionals.

Contents

SELECTED PROVISIONS OF THE UNITED STATES CODE AND PUBLIC LAWS	1
Note on Federal Banking Statutes	3
Note on Statutory Headings	5

TITLE 5. GOVERNMENT ORGANIZATION — 6
Administrative Procedure Act — 6
  § 706. Scope of Review — 6

TITLE 11. BANKRUPTCY — 6
Bankruptcy Code — 6
  § 101. Definitions — 6
  § 510. Subordination — 7

TITLE 12. BANKS AND BANKING — 7
National Bank Act — 7
  § 1. Office of Comptroller of the Currency — 7
  § 2. Comptroller of the Currency: Appointment; Term — 8
  § 21. Forming a National Bank — 8
  § 22. Organization Certificate — 8
  § 24. Corporate Powers of National Banks — 9
  § 24a. Financial Subsidiaries of National Banks — 14
  § 25b. State Law Preemption Standards for National Banks and Subsidiaries Clarified — 18
  § 26. Commencing Business — 21
  § 27. Granting Charter — 21
  § 29. Holding Real Property — 22
  § 30. Changing Name or Location — 22
  § 35. Converting State Bank into National Bank — 23
  § 36. Branching — 23
  § 43. Interpretations Concerning Preemption of Certain State Laws — 26
  § 71. Board of Directors — 26
  § 72. Directors' Qualifications — 26

§ 81.	Place of Business	27
§ 83.	Loans by Bank on Its Own Stock	27
§ 84.	Lending Limits	27
§ 85.	Interest Rate on Loans	30
§ 86.	Usury	31
§ 90.	Depositaries of Public Moneys and Financial Agents of Government	31
§ 91.	Fradulent Transfers	31
§ 92.	Acting as Insurance Agent	32
§ 92a.	Trust Powers	32
§ 93.	Penalty for Violating This Act	33
§ 93a.	Authority to Prescribe Rules and Regulations	33
§ 191.	Appointment of Receiver	34
§ 203.	Appointment of Conservator	34
§ 206.	Conservator; Powers and Duties	34
§ 214a.	Procedure for Conversion, Merger, or Consolidation	34
§ 214d.	Prohibition on Conversion	35

National Bank Consolidation and Merger Act — 35

§ 215.	Consolidation of Banks Within the Same State	35
§ 215a.	Merger of National Banks or State Banks into National Banks	36
§ 215a-1.	Interstate Consolidations and Mergers	37
§ 215a-3.	Mergers and Consolidations with Subsidiaries and Nonbank Affiliates	37
§ 215c.	Mergers, Consolidations, and Other Acquisitions Authorized	37

Federal Reserve Act — 37

§ 241.	Federal Reserve Board	37
§ 250.	Independence of Financial Regulatory Agencies	37
§ 321.	Application for Membership	38
§ 335.	Underwriting and Dealing in Securities	38
§ 343.	Emergency Lending Through Discount Window	38
§ 347b.	Ordinary Lending Through Discount Window	39
§ 371.	Real Estate Loans	40
§ 371b-2.	Interbank Liabilities	40
§ 371c.	Banking Affiliates	40
§ 371c-1.	Restrictions on Transactions with Affiliates	47
§ 375a.	Loans to Executive Officers of Member Banks	49
§ 375b.	Extensions of Credit to Executive Officers, Directors, and Principal Shareholders of Member Banks	50
§ 378.	Deposit-Taking by Securities Dealers and Unregulated Firms	54
§ 484.	Limit [on] Visitorial Powers	55

Contents

§ 601.	Foreign Banking	55
§ 604.	Separate Accounts for Foreign Branches	56
§ 604a.	Foreign Branches May Have Usual Powers of Local Banks	56

Home Owners' Loan Act 56

§ 1462.	Definitions	56
§ 1463.	Supervision of Savings Associations	57
§ 1464.	Federal Savings Associations	58
§ 1467a.	Regulation of Holding Companies	63
§ 1467b.	Intermediate Holding Companies	75

Federal Deposit Insurance Act 77

§ 1811.	Federal Deposit Insurance Corporation	77
§ 1812.	Management	77
§ 1813.	Definitions	78
§ 1815.	Deposit Insurance	82
§ 1816.	Factors to Be Considered [in Granting Insurance]	83
§ 1817.	Assessments	83
§ 1818.	Enforcement	90
§ 1819.	Corporate Powers	106
§ 1820.	Administering Corporation	106
§ 1820a.	Examination of Investment Companies	111
§ 1821.	Insurance; Receivership	111
§ 1822.	Corporation as Receiver	151
§ 1823.	Investment of Corporation's Funds	152
§ 1828.	Regulations Governing Insured Depository Institutions	159
§ 1828a.	Prudential Safeguards	167
§ 1830.	Nondiscrimination	169
§ 1831a.	Activities of Insured State Banks	169
§ 1831c.	Assuring Consistent Oversight of Subsidiaries of Holding Companies	172
§ 1831d.	Interest Rate State Banks May Charge	174
§ 1831f.	Brokered Deposits	175
§ 1831i.	Agency Disapproval of Directors and Senior Executive Officers of Insured Depository Institutions or Depository Institution Holding Companies	177
§ 1831o.	Prompt Corrective Action	178
§ 1831o-1.	Source of Strength	188
§ 1831r.	Payments on Foreign Deposits Prohibited	189
§ 1831t.	Depository Institutions Lacking Federal Deposit Insurance	189
§ 1831u.	Interstate Bank Mergers	190

Contents

§ 1831v.	Authority of State Insurance Regulator and Securities and Exchange Commission	195
§ 1831w.	Safety and Soundness Firewalls Applicable to Financial Subsidiaries of Banks	196
§ 1831x.	Insurance Customer Protections	196
§ 1831y.	CRA Sunshine Requirements	200
§ 1831aa.	Enforcement of [Written] Agreements	203

Bank Holding Company Act of 1956 — 203

§ 1841.	Definitions	203
§ 1842.	Acquisition of Bank Shares or Assets	212
§ 1843.	Interests in Nonbanking Organizations	218
§ 1844.	Administration	236
§ 1846.	Reservation of Rights to States	242
§ 1848.	Judicial Review	242
§ 1850a.	Securities Holding Companies	242
§ 1851.	Prohibitions on Proprietary Trading and Certain Relationships with Hedge Funds and Private Equity Funds	245
§ 1852.	Concentration Limits on Large Financial Firms	250

Bank Holding Company Act Amendments of 1970 — 251

§ 1971.	Definitions	251
§ 1972.	Certain Tying Arrangements Prohibited; Correspondent Accounts	251
§ 1975.	Civil Actions by Persons Injured	253
§ 1976.	Injunctive Relief	254

Community Reinvestment Act of 1978 — 254

§ 2901.	Congressional Findings and Statement of Purpose	254
§ 2902.	Definitions	254
§ 2903.	Assessing Record of Meeting Community Credit Needs	255
§ 2906.	Written Evaluations	256
§ 2908.	Small Bank Regulatory Relief	258

Depository Institution Management Interlocks Act — 258

§ 3202.	Interlocks in Same Locality Prohibited	258
§ 3203.	Certain Interlocks Probhibited Nationwide	259
§ 3204.	Exceptions	259

International Lending Supervision Act of 1983 — 259

§ 3907.	Capital Adequacy	259

Contents

Dodd-Frank Wall Street Reform and Consumer Protection Act   261
    § 5301.   Definitions   261

TITLE I. FINANCIAL STABILITY ACT OF 2010   262
§ 5311.	Definitions	262
§ 5321.	Financial Stability Oversight Council Established	264
§ 5322.	Council Authority	265
§ 5323.	Authority to Require Supervision and Regulation of Certain Nonbank Financial Companies	267
§ 5325.	Enhanced Supervision and Prudential Standards for Nonbank Financial Companies Supervised by the Board of Governors and Certain Bank Holding Companies	270
§ 5327.	Treatment of Certain Companies That Cease to Be Bank Holding Companies	271
§ 5330.	Additional Standards Applicable to Activities or Practices for Financial Stability Purposes	272
§ 5331.	Mitigation of Risks to Financial Stability	273
§ 5342.	Office of Financial Research Established	273
§ 5343.	Purpose and Duties of the Office	274
§ 5363.	Acquisitions	274
§ 5365.	Enhanced Supervision and Prudential Standards for Nonbank Financial Companies Supervised by the Board of Governors and Certain Bank Holding Companies	275
§ 5366.	Early Remediation Requirements	276
§ 5367.	Affiliations	276
§ 5370.	Safe Harbor	278
§ 5371.	Leverage and Risk-Based Capital Requirements	278
§ 5374.	Rule of Construction	280

TITLE II. ORDERLY LIQUIDATION AUTHORITY   280
§ 5381.	Definitions	280
§ 5382.	[Appointment of Receiver;] Judicial Review	282
§ 5383.	Systemic Risk Determination	284
§ 5384.	Orderly Liquidation of Covered Financial Companies	289
§ 5385.	Orderly Liquidation of Covered Brokers and Dealers	290
§ 5386.	Mandatory Terms and Conditions for All Orderly Liquidation Actions	290
§ 5388.	Dismissal and Exclusion of Other Actions	291
§ 5389.	Rulemaking; Non-Conflicting Law	291
§ 5390.	Powers and Duties of the Corporation	291
§ 5392.	Prohibition of Circumvention and Prevention of Conflicts of Interest	305

Contents

§ 5394.	Prohibition on Taxpayer Funding	305
§ 5491.	Establishment of the Bureau of Consumer Financial Protection	306
§ 5611.	Liquidity Event Determination	306
§ 5612.	Emergency Financial Stabilization	307

TITLE 15. COMMERCE AND TRADE — 309

Sherman and Clayton Acts — 309

§ 1.	Combinations in Restraint of Trade Unlawful	309
§ 2.	Monopolization Unlawful	309
§ 18.	Acquisition by One Corporation of Stock of Another	309

Federal Trade Commission Act — 310

§ 45.	Unfair Methods of Competition Unlawful	310

Securities Act of 1933 — 310

§ 77b.	Definitions	310
§ 77c.	Classes of Securities Under This Act	311
§ 77d.	Exempted Transactions	314
§ 77e.	Prohibitions Relating to Interstate Commerce and the Mails	316
§ 77f.	Registration of Securities	317
§ 77k.	Civil Liabilities on Account of False Registration Statement	317
§ 77r.	Exemption from State Regulation of Securities Offerings	319
§ 77z-2a.	Conflicts of Interest Relating to Certain Securitizations	322
§ 77z-3.	General Exemptive Authority	322

Securities Exchange Act of 1934 — 323

§ 78c.	Definitions and Application	323
§ 78d.	Securities and Exchange Commission	333
§ 78j.	Manipulative and Deceptive Devices	333
§ 78l.	Registration Requirements for Securities	333
§ 78m.	Periodical and Other Reports	334
§ 78o.	Registration and Regulation of Brokers and Dealers	334
§ 78o-3.	Registered Securities Associations	337
Note to § 78c on the Definition of "Identified Banking Product"		339

Investment Company Act of 1940 — 340

§ 80a-2.	General Definitions	340
§ 80a-3.	Definition of Investment Company	346

Contents

§ 80a-4.	Classification of Investment Companies	351
§ 80a-5.	Subclassification of Management Companies	351
§ 80a-6.	Exemptions	352
§ 80a-7.	Transactions by Unregistered Investment Companies	352
§ 80a-8.	Registration of Investment Companies	353
§ 80a-10.	Affiliations of Directors	354
§ 80a-12.	Functions and Activities of Investment Companies	355
§ 80a-13.	Changes in Investment Policy	357
§ 80a-15.	Investment Advisory and Underwriting Contracts	357
§ 80a-16.	Changes in Board of Directors	358
§ 80a-17.	Transactions of Certain Affiliated Persons and Underwriters	359
§ 80a-18.	Capital Structure	363
§ 80a-20.	Circular Ownership	366
§ 80a-21.	Loans	366
§ 80a-22.	Distribution, Redemption, and Repurchase of Redeemable Securities	366
§ 80a-23.	Distribution and Repurchase of Securities: Closed-End Companies	367
§ 80a-34.	Unlawful Representations and Names	368
§ 80a-35.	Breach of Fiduciary Duty	368
§ 80a-37.	Rules, Regulations, and Orders	369
§ 80a-46.	Validity of Contracts	369

Investment Advisers Act of 1940 — 369

§ 80b-2.	Definitions	369
§ 80b-3.	Registration of Investment Advisers	371
§ 80b-3a.	State and Federal Responsibilities	372
§ 80b-4a.	Prevention of Misuse of Nonpublic Information	374
§ 80b-5.	Investment Advisory Contracts	374
§ 80b-6.	Prohibited Transactions by Registered Investment Advisers	375
§ 80b-11.	Rules, Regulations and Orders of Commission	376
§ 80b-15.	Validity of Contracts	377
§ 80b-18a.	State Regulation of Investment Advisers	377

McCarran-Ferguson Act — 378

§ 1011.	Declaration of Policy	378
§ 1012.	Nonpreemption	379

Fair Credit Reporting Act — 379

§ 1681.	Congressional Findings and Statement of Purpose	379
§ 1681a.	Definitions; Rules of Construction . . .	379
§ 1681b.	Permissible Purposes of Consumer Reports	383

Contents

§ 1681c.	Requirements Relating to Information Contained in Consumer Reports	385
§ 1681c-1.	Identity Theft Prevention; Fraud Alerts	387
§ 1681c-2.	Block of Information Resulting from Identity Theft	388
§ 1681d.	Disclosure of Investigative Consumer Reports	388
§ 1681e.	Compliance Procedures	390
§ 1681f.	Disclosure to Governmental Agencies	391
§ 1681g.	Disclosures to Consumers	391
§ 1681i.	Procedure in Case of Disputed Accuracy	394
§ 1681j.	Charges for Certain Disclosures	399
§ 1681k.	Public Record Information for Employment Purposes	400
§ 1681*l*.	Restrictions on Investigative Consumer Reports	401
§ 1681m.	Requirements on Users of Consumer Reports	401
§ 1681n.	Civil Liability for Willful Noncompliance	403
§ 1681o.	Civil Liability for Negligent Noncompliance	403
§ 1681q.	Obtaining Information Under False Pretenses	404
§ 1681r.	Unauthorized Disclosures by Officers or Employees	404
§ 1681s.	Administrative Enforcement	404
§ 1681s-2.	Responsibilities of Furnishers of Information to Consumer Reporting Agencies	405
§ 1681s-3.	Affiliate Sharing	409
§ 1681t.	Relation to State Laws	410
§ 1681x.	Corporate and Technological Circumvention Prohibited	412

Gramm-Leach-Bliley Act   412

§ 6701.	Operation of State Law	412
§ 6711.	Functional Regulation of Insurance	419
§ 6712.	Insurance Underwriting in National Banks	419
§ 6713.	Title Insurance Activities of National Banks and Their Affiliates	421
§ 6714.	Expedited and Equalized Dispute Resolution for Federal Regulators	422
§ 6715.	Certain State Affiliation Laws Preempted for Insurance Companies and Affiliates	422
§ 6801.	Protection of Nonpublic Personal Information	423
§ 6802.	Obligations with Respect to Disclosures of Personal Information	423
§ 6803.	Disclosure of Institution Privacy Policy	425
§ 6804.	Rulemaking	427
§ 6805.	Enforcement	427
§ 6821.	Privacy Protection for Customer Information of Financial Institutions	429

Contents

Selected Provisions of the Code of Federal Regulations		431
12 C.F.R., Part 1—Investment Securities		433
§ 1.1.	Authority, Purpose, Scope, and Reservation of Authority	433
§ 1.2.	Definitions	433
§ 1.3.	Limitations on Dealing in, Underwriting, and Purchase and Sale of Securities	436
12 C.F.R., Part 32—Lending Limits		438
§ 32.1.	Authority, Purpose, and Scope	438
§ 32.2.	Definitions	439
§ 32.3.	Lending Limits	443
§ 32.5.	Combination Rules	447
§ 32.6.	Nonconforming Loans	450
§ 32.8.	Temporary Funding Arrangements in Emergency Situations	450

The Law of Banking and Financial Institutions

2011 Statutory Supplement

SELECTED PROVISIONS OF THE UNITED STATES CODE AND PUBLIC LAWS

Selected Provisions of the United States Code

NOTE ON FEDERAL BANKING STATUTES

Over the years, Congress has enacted thousands upon thousands of pages of banking legislation. How is this material organized, and how do people keep track of what is current law?

When a bill becomes law, it first appears as a "public law," which consists simply of the statutory text passed by both houses and signed by the President (or enacted over the President's veto). Public laws are numbered sequentially according to the Congress than enacted them. Thus, for example, the 102nd public law enacted by the 106th Congress would be Public Law No. 106-102. Most significant modern public laws bear congressionally enacted "short titles," which despite the appearance of informality have official standing. Thus Congress specified that Public Law No. 106-102 can be cited as the "Gramm-Leach-Bliley Act."

At least two major systems exist for organizing federal banking statutes in more comprehensive fashion. Both systems use statutory sections—the basic building blocks (or organizing principles) of federal legislation—but they organize and number those sections in different ways. The first system uses the section numbers in title 12 of the United States Code, which codifies "general and permanent" federal banking statutes. The second system uses the section numbers within particular Acts of Congress.

Thus, for example, 12 U.S. Code § 1818 authorizes the appropriate federal banking agencies to take administrative enforcement action against FDIC-insured depository institutions that violate laws or commit unsafe or unsound practices. The forerunner of this section became law as section 8 of the Federal Deposit Insurance Act. One can thus refer to this section both as 12 U.S. Code § 1818 and as section 8 of the Federal Deposit Insurance Act.

Banking law practitioners rely primarily on the first system, based on 12 U.S. Code. The textbook and this supplement also follow that approach. That approach has the advantage of more rigorously organizing statutory provisions by subject-matter. After all, although public laws usually focus on a particular subject, they may include all sorts of extraneous provisions and thus may not be a particularly convenient way to access or to refer to statutes.

But when Congress enacts, repeals, or amends banking statutes, it relies primarily on the second system, based on the internal numbering of certain prior Acts of Congress. It uses title 12 only as a supplemental means of identifying the statute in question. Thus, for example, legislation amending subsection (e) of the enforcement statute just discussed would begin:

> Section 8(e) of the Federal Deposit Insurance Act (12 U.S. Code 1818(e)) is amended to read as follows. . . .

Why this roundabout approach? Why not rely exclusively on the numbering in 12 U.S. Code? Congress has never enacted title 12 into law. Instead, title 12 is a restatement created in 1926 by two legal publishing companies working under the auspices of the House and Senate Committees on Revision of the Laws. So title 12 stands on a different legal footing than those U.S. Code titles formally enacted into law, such as title 5, which deals with government organization; title 11, bankruptcy; title 17, copyrights; title 18, crimes and criminal procedure; title 26, the Internal Revenue Code; title 28, judiciary and judicial procedure; title 31, money and finance; and title 35, patents. In amending banking statutes, Congress uses title 12 references for identification but relies primarily on the section numbering of the prior Act that is being amended. Moreover, title 12 is not integrated and systematized to the same extent as some of those other titles. Different Acts codified within 12 U.S. Code often read as if they were freestanding Acts rather than part of an integrated whole.

Here are some additional examples of statutory numbering under the two systems:

STATUTORY NUMBERING: TWO SYSTEMS

12 U.S.C. §	Official Name	Subject
371c	Section 23A of the Federal Reserve Act	Transactions between banks and affiliated firms
371c-1	Section 23B of the Federal Reserve Act	Transactions between banks and affiliated firms
375b	Section 22(h) of the Federal Reserve Act	Loans to a bank's executive officers, directors, and principal shareholders
378	Section 21 of the Banking Act of 1933	Deposit-taking by securities dealers
1821	Section 21 of the Federal Deposit Insurance Act	FDIC's powers as receiver for failed banks
1831o	Section 38 of the Federal Deposit Insurance Act	Prompt corrective action
1842	Section 3 of the Bank Holding Company Act of 1956	Acquiring banks
1843	Section 4 of the Bank Holding Company Act of 1956	Nonbanking activities of bank holding companies
5323	Section 113 of the Dodd-Frank Wall Street Reform and Consumer Protection Act	Requiring regulation of systemically significant nonbank financial firms

Selected Provisions of the United States Code

NOTE ON STATUTORY HEADINGS

In this book we seek to make it easy for readers to navigate federal statutes governing banks and other financial institutions. We include a running header showing the Act and U.S. Code section number. We add headings to many provisions that would otherwise lack them. We also clarify, correct, and remove clutter from headings written by code compilers rather than Congress.

In old statutes these unenacted headings are too often wordy and unclear. Consider the heading for 12 U.S.C. § 461(b): "Additional Definitions; Required Amounts of Reserves Maintained Against Transaction Accounts; Waiver of Ratio Limits in Extraordinary Circumstances; Supplemental Reserves; Reserves Related to Foreign Obligations or Assets; Exemption for Certain Deposits; Discount and Borrowing; Transitional Adjustments; Additional Exemptions and Waivers." Had we included § 461(b), we would have made the heading shorter and more to the point: e.g., "Reserve Requirements; Additional Definitions." Unenacted headings are sometimes also misleading. Section 1818 governs most types of administrative enforcement action, including cease-and-desist orders, removal orders, and civil money penalties. Yet the unenacted heading refers only to terminating deposit insurance ("Termination of Status as Insured Depository Institution"). We modify unenacted headings as needed to promote clarity, accuracy, and brevity, without specifically noting the changes.

Only rarely do we modify congressionally enacted headings—and in such cases we indicate the changes with brackets, ellipses, or both. The heading of 12 U.S.C. § 36(g) refers to "State 'Opt-in' Election to Permit Interstate Branching Through De Novo Branches," even though the Dodd-Frank Act eliminated any need for states to opt in. To avoid confusion, we make the heading ". . . Interstate Branching Through De Novo Branches."

TITLE 5—GOVERNMENT ORGANIZATION

ADMINISTRATIVE PROCEDURE ACT

§ 706. Scope of Review

To the extent necessary to decision and when presented, the reviewing court shall decide all relevant questions of law, interpret constitutional and statutory provisions, and determine the meaning or applicability of the terms of an agency action. The reviewing court shall—

    (1) compel agency action unlawfully withheld or unreasonably delayed; and

    (2) hold unlawful and set aside agency action, findings, and conclusions found to be—

        (A) arbitrary, capricious, an abuse of discretion or otherwise not in accordance with law;

        (B) contrary to constitutional right, power, privilege, or immunity;

        (C) in excess of statutory jurisdiction, authority, or limitations, or short of statutory right;

        (D) without observance of procedure required by law;

        (E) unsupported by substantial evidence in a case subject to §§ 556 and 557 of this title or otherwise reviewed on the record of an agency hearing provided by statute; or

        (F) unwarranted by the facts to the extent that the facts are subject to trial de novo by the reviewing court.

In making the foregoing determinations, the court shall review the whole record or those parts of it cited by a party, and due account shall be taken of the rule of prejudicial error.

TITLE 11—BANKRUPTCY

BANKRUPTCY CODE

§ 101. Definitions . . .

    (31) "insider" includes—

        (A) if the debtor is an individual—

            (i) relative of the debtor or of a general partner of the debtor;

            (ii) partnership in which the debtor is a general partner;

            (iii) general partner of the debtor; or

            (iv) corporation of which the debtor is a director, officer, or person in control;

        (B) if the debtor is a corporation—

            (i) director of the debtor;

(ii) officer of the debtor;
(iii) person in control of the debtor;
(iv) partnership in which the debtor is a general partner;
(v) general partner of the debtor; or
(vi) relative of a general partner, director, officer, or person in control of the debtor;
(C) if the debtor is a partnership—
(i) general partner in the debtor;
(ii) relative of a general partner in, general partner of, or person in control of the debtor;
(iii) partnership in which the debtor is a general partner;
(iv) general partner of the debtor; or
(v) person in control of the debtor;
(D) if the debtor is a municipality, elected official of the debtor or relative of an elected official of the debtor;
(E) affiliate, or insider of an affiliate as if such affiliate were the debtor; and
(F) managing agent of the debtor. . . .

§ 510. Subordination . . .

(c) [A]fter notice and a hearing, the court may—
(1) under principles of equitable subordination, subordinate for purposes of distribution all or part of an allowed claim to all or part of another allowed claim or all or part of an allowed interest to all or part of another allowed interest; or
(2) order that any lien securing such a subordinated claim be transferred to the estate.

TITLE 12—BANKS AND BANKING

NATIONAL BANK ACT

§ 1. Office of Comptroller of the Currency

(a) **Office of the Comptroller of the Currency Established.**—There is established in the Department of the Treasury a bureau to be known as the "Office of the Comptroller of the Currency" which is charged with assuring the safety and soundness of, and compliance with laws and regulations, fair access to financial services, and fair treatment of customers by, the institutions and other persons subject to its jurisdiction.

(b) Comptroller of the Currency.—

(1) In general.—The chief officer of the Office of the Comptroller of the Currency shall be known as the Comptroller of the Currency. The Comptroller of the Currency shall perform the duties of the Comptroller of the Currency under the general direction of the Secretary of the Treasury. The Secretary of the Treasury may not delay or prevent the issuance of any rule or the promulgation of any regulation by the Comptroller of the Currency, and may not intervene in any matter or proceeding before the Comptroller of the Currency (including agency enforcement actions), unless otherwise specifically provided by law. . . .

§ 2. Comptroller of the Currency: Appointment; Term

The Comptroller of the Currency shall be appointed by the President, by and with the advice and consent of the Senate, and shall hold his office for the term of five years unless sooner removed by the President, upon reason to be communicated by him to the Senate. . . .

§ 21. Forming a National Bank

Associations for carrying on the business of banking under this Act may be formed by any number of natural persons, not less in any case than five. They shall enter into articles of association, which shall specify in general terms the object for which the association is formed, and may contain any other provisions, not inconsistent with law, which the association may see fit to adopt for the regulation of its business and the conduct of its affairs. These articles shall be signed by the persons uniting to form the association, and a copy of them shall be forwarded to the Comptroller of the Currency, to be filed and preserved in his office.

§ 22. Organization Certificate

The persons uniting to form such an association shall, under their hands, make an organization certificate, which shall specifically state:

First. The name assumed by such association; which name shall include the word "national."

Second. The place where its operations of discount and deposit are to be carried on, designating the State, Territory, or District, and the particular county and city, town, or village.

Third. The amount of capital stock and the number of shares into which the same is to be divided.

Fourth. The names and places of residence of the shareholders and the number of shares held by each of them.

Fifth. The fact that the certificate is made to enable such persons to avail themselves of the advantages of this Act.

§ 24. Corporate Powers of National Banks

Upon duly making and filing articles of association and an organization certificate a national banking association shall become, as from the date of the execution of its organization certificate, a body corporate, and as such, and in the name designated in the organization certificate, it shall have power—

First. To adopt and use a corporate seal.

Second. To have succession . . . from the date of its organization . . . until such time as it be dissolved by the act of its shareholders owning two-thirds of its stock, or until its franchise becomes forfeited by reason of violation of law, or until terminated by either a general or a special Act of Congress or until its affairs be placed in the hands of a receiver and finally wound up by him.

Third. To make contracts.

Fourth. To sue and be sued, complain and defend, in any court of law and equity, as fully as natural persons.

Fifth. To elect or appoint directors, and by its board of directors to appoint a president, vice president, cashier, and other officers, define their duties, require bonds of them and fix the penalty thereof, dismiss such officers or any of them at pleasure, and appoint others to fill their places.

Sixth. To prescribe, by its board of directors, bylaws not inconsistent with law, regulating the manner in which its stock shall be transferred, its directors elected or appointed, its officers appointed, its property transferred, its general business conducted, and the privileges granted to it by law exercised and enjoyed.

Seventh. To exercise by its board of directors or duly authorized officers or agents, subject to law, all such incidental powers as shall be necessary to carry on the business of banking; by discounting and negotiating promissory notes drafts, bills of exchange, and other evidences of debt; by receiving deposits; by buying and selling exchange, coin, and bullion, by loaning money on personal security, and by obtaining, issuing, and circulating notes. . . . The business of dealing in securities and stock by the association shall be limited to purchasing and selling such securities and stock without recourse, solely upon the order, and for the account of, customers, and in no case for its own account, and the association shall not underwrite any issue of securities or stock: *Provided* That the association may purchase for its own account investment securities under such limitations and restrictions as the Comptroller of the Currency may by regulation prescribe. In no event shall the total amount of the investment securities of any one obligor or maker, held by the association for its own account, exceed at any time 10 per centum of its capital stock actually paid in and unimpaired and 10 per centum of its unimpaired surplus fund. . . . As used in this section the term "investment securities" shall mean marketable obligations, evidencing indebtedness of any person, copartnership, association, or corporation in the form of bonds, notes and/or debentures commonly known as investment securities under such further definition of the term "investment securities" as may by regulation be prescribed by the Comptroller of the Currency. Except as herein after provided or otherwise permitted by law, nothing herein contained shall authorize the purchase by the association for its own account of any shares of stock of any corporation. The limitations and restrictions herein contained as to dealing in, underwriting and purchasing for its own account, investment securities shall not apply to obligations of the United States, or general obligations of any State or of any political subdivision thereof, or obligations of the Washington Metropolitan Area Transit Authority which are guaranteed by the Secretary of Transportation under section 9 of the National Capital Transportation Act of 1969, or obligations issued under authority of the Federal Farm Loan Act, as amended, or issued by the thirteen banks for the cooperatives of any of them or the Federal Home Loan Banks, or obligations which are insured by the Secretary of Housing and Urban Development under title XI of the National Housing Act or obligations which are insured by the Secretary of Housing and Urban Development (hereafter in this sentence referred to as the "Secretary") pursuant to section 207 of the National Housing Act, if the debentures to be issued in payment of such insured obligations are guaranteed as to principal and interest by the United States, or obligations, participations, or other instruments of or issued by the Federal National Mortgage Association or the Government National Mortgage Association, or mortgages, obligations, or other securities which are or ever have been sold by the Federal Home Loan Mortgage Corporation pursuant to section 305 or section 306 of the Federal Home Loan Mortgage Corporation Act, or obligations of the Federal Financing Bank or obligations of the Environmental Financing Authority, or obligations or other instruments or securities of the Student Loan Marketing Association, or such obligations of any local public agency (as defined in section 110(h) of the Housing Act of 1949) as are secured by an agreement between the local public agency and the Secretary in which the local public agency agrees to borrow from said Secretary, and said Secretary agrees to lend to said local public agency, monies in an aggregate amount which (together with any other monies irrevocably committed to the payment of interest or such obligations) will suffice to pay, when due, the interest on and all installments (including the final installment) of the principal of such obligations, which monies under the terms of said agreement are required to be used for such payments, or such obligations of a public housing agency (as defined in the United States Housing Act of 1937, as amended) as are secured (1) by an agreement between the public housing agency and the Secretary in which the public housing agency agrees to borrow from the Secretary, and the Secretary agrees to lend to the public housing agency, prior to the maturity of such obligations, monies in an amount which (together with any other monies irrevocably committed to the payment of interest on such obligations) will suffice to pay the principal of such obligations with interest to maturity thereon, which monies under the terms of said agreement are required to be used for the purpose of paying the principal of and the interest on such obligations at their maturity, (2) by a pledge of annual contributions under an annual contributions contract between such public housing agency and the Secretary if such contract shall contain the covenant by the Secretary which is authorized by subsection (g) of section 6 of the United States Housing Act of 1937, as amended, and if the maximum sum and the maximum period specified in such contract pursuant to said subsection 6(g) shall not be less than the annual amount and the period for payment which are requisite to provide for the payment when due of all installments of principal and interest on such obligations, or (3) by a pledge of both annual contributions under an annual contributions contract containing the covenant by the Secretary which is authorized by section 6(g) of the United States Housing Act of 1937, and a loan under an agreement between the local public housing agency and the Secretary in which the public housing agency agrees to borrow from the Secretary, and the Secretary agrees to lend to the public housing agency, prior to the maturity of the obligations involved, moneys in an amount which (together with any other moneys irrevocably committed under the annual contributions contract to the payment of principal and interest on such obligations) will suffice to provide for the payment when due of all installments of principal and interest on such obligations, which moneys under the terms of the agreement are required to be used for the purpose of paying the principal and interest on such obligations at their maturity: *Provided*, That in carrying on the business commonly known as the safe-deposit business the association shall not invest in the capital stock of a corporation organized under the law of any State to conduct a safe-deposit business in an amount in excess of 15 per centum of the capital stock of the association actually paid in and unimpaired and 15 per centum of its unimpaired surplus. The limitations and restrictions herein, contained as to dealing in and underwriting investment securities shall not apply to obligations issued by the International Bank for Reconstruction and Development, the European Bank for Reconstruction and Development, the Inter-American Development Bank, Bank for Economic Cooperation and Development in the Middle East and North Africa, the North American Development Bank, the Asian Development Bank, the African Development Bank, the Inter-American Investment Corporation, or the International Finance Corporation, or obligations issued by any State or political subdivision or any agency of a State or political subdivision for housing, university, or dormitory purposes, which are at the time eligible for purchase by a national bank for its own account, nor to bonds, notes and other obligations issued by the Tennessee Valley Authority or by the United States Postal Service: *Provided*, That no association shall hold obligations, issued by any of said organizations as a result of underwriting, dealing, or purchasing for its own account (and for this purpose obligations as to which it is under commitment shall be deemed to be held by it) in a total amount exceeding at any one time 10 per centum of its capital stock actually paid in and unimpaired and 10 per centum of its unimpaired surplus fund. Notwithstanding any other provision in this paragraph, the association may purchase for its own account shares of stock issued by a corporation authorized to be created pursuant to title IX of the Housing and Urban Development Act of 1968, and may make investments in a partnership, limited partnership, or joint venture formed pursuant to section 907(a) or 907(c) of that Act). Notwithstanding any other provision of this paragraph, the association may purchase for its own account shares of stock issued by any State housing corporation incorporated in the State in which the association is located and may make investments in loans and commitments for loans to any such corporation: *Provided*, That in no event shall the total amount of such stock held for its own account and such investments in loans and commitments made by the association exceed at any time 5 per centum of its capital stock actually paid in an unimpaired plus 5 per centum of its unimpaired surplus fund. Notwithstanding any other provision in this paragraph, the association may purchase for its own account shares of stock issued by a corporation organized solely for the purpose of making loans to farmers and ranchers for agricultural purposes, including the breeding, raising, fattening, or marketing of livestock. However, unless the association owns at least 80 per centum of the stock of such agricultural credit corporation the amount invested by the association at any one time in the stock of such corporation shall not exceed 20 per centum of the unimpaired capital and surplus of the association: *Provided further*, That, notwithstanding any other provision of this paragraph, the association may purchase for its own account shares of stock of a bank insured by the Federal Deposit Insurance Corporation or a holding company which owns or controls such an insured bank if the stock of such bank or company is owned exclusively . . . by depository institutions or depository institution holding companies (as defined in § 1813) and such bank or company and all subsidiaries thereof are engaged exclusively in providing services to or for other depository institutions, their holding companies, and the officers, directors, and employees of such institutions and companies, and in providing correspondent banking services at the request of other depository institutions or their holding companies (also referred to as a "banker's bank"), but in no event shall the total amount of such stock held by the association in any bank or holding company exceed at any time 10 per centum of the association's capital stock and paid in and unimpaired surplus and in no event shall the purchase of such stock result in an association's acquiring more than 5 per centum of any class of voting securities of such bank or company. The limitations and restrictions contained in this paragraph as to an association purchasing for its own account investment securities shall not apply to securities that (A) are offered and sold pursuant to § 77d(5) of title 15; (B) are small business related securities (as defined in § 78c(a)(53) of title 15; or (C) are mortgage related securities (as that term is defined in § 78c(a)(41) of title 15). The exception provided for the securities described in subparagraphs (A), (B), and (C) shall be subject to such regulations as the Comptroller of the Currency may prescribe, including regulations prescribing minimum size of the issue (at the time of initial distribution) or minimum aggregate sales prices, or both. In addition to the provisions in this paragraph for dealing in, underwriting, or purchasing securities, the limitations and restrictions contained in this paragraph as to dealing in, underwriting, and purchasing investment securities for the national bank's own account shall not apply to obligations (including limited obligation bonds, revenue bonds, and obligations that satisfy the requirements of § 142(b)(1) of title 26) issued by or on behalf of any State or political subdivision of a State, including any municipal corporate instrumentality of 1 or more States, or any public agency or authority of any State or political subdivision of a State, if the national bank is well capitalized (as defined in § 1831o).

Eighth. To contribute to community funds, or to charitable, philanthropic, or benevolent instrumentalities conductive to public welfare, such sums as its board of directors may deem expedient and in the interests of the association, if it is located in a State the laws of which do not expressly prohibit State banking institutions from contributing to such funds or instrumentalities.

Ninth. To issue and sell securities which are guaranteed [by Ginnie Mae].

Tenth. To invest in tangible personal property, including without limitation, vehicles, manufactured homes, machinery, equipment, or furniture, for lease financing transactions on a net lease basis, but such investment may not exceed 10 percent of the assets of the association.

Eleventh. To make investments directly or indirectly, each of which is designed primarily to promote the public welfare, including the welfare of low- and moderate-income communities or families (such as by providing housing, services, or jobs). An association shall not make any such investment if the investment would expose the association to unlimited liability. The Comptroller of the Currency shall limit an association's investments in any 1 project and an association's aggregate investments under this paragraph. An association's aggregate investments under this paragraph shall not exceed an amount equal to the sum of 5 percent of the association's capital stock actually paid in and unimpaired and 5 percent of the association's unimpaired surplus fund, unless the Comptroller determines by order that the higher amount will pose no significant risk to the affected deposit insurance fund, and the association is adequately capitalized. In no case shall an association's aggregate investments under this paragraph exceed an amount equal to the sum of 15 percent of the association's capital stock actually paid in and unimpaired and 15 percent of the association's unimpaired surplus fund. The foregoing standards and limitations apply to investments under this paragraph made by a national bank directly and by its subsidiaries.

§ 24a. Financial Subsidiaries of National Banks

(a) Authorization to Conduct in Subsidiaries Certain Activities That Are Financial in Nature.—
    (1) In general.—Subject to paragraph (2), a national bank may control a financial subsidiary, or hold an interest in a financial subsidiary.
    (2) Conditions and requirements.—A national bank may control a financial subsidiary, or hold an interest in a financial subsidiary, only if
        (A) the financial subsidiary engages only in—
            (i) activities that are financial in nature or incidental to a financial activity pursuant to subsection (b); and
            (ii) activities that are permitted for national banks to engage in directly (subject to the same terms and conditions that govern the conduct of the activities by a national bank);
        (B) the activities engaged in by the financial subsidiary as a principal do not include—
            (i) insuring, guaranteeing, or indemnifying against loss, harm, damage, illness, disability, or death (except to the extent permitted under § 6712 or § 6713(c) of title 15) or providing or issuing annuities the income of which is subject to tax treatment under § 72 of title 26;
            (ii) real estate development or real estate investment activities, unless otherwise expressly authorized by law; or
            (iii) any activity permitted in subparagraph (H) or (I) of § 1843(k)(4) of this title, except activities described in § 1843(k)(4)(H) . . . ;
        (C) the national bank and each depository institution affiliate of the national bank are well capitalized and well managed;
        (D) the aggregate consolidated total assets of all financial subsidiaries of the national bank do not exceed the lesser of—
            (i) 45 percent of the consolidated total assets of the parent bank; or
            (ii) $50,000,000,000;
        (E) except as provided in paragraph (4), the national bank meets any applicable rating or other requirement set forth in paragraph (3); and
        (F) the national bank has received the approval of the Comptroller of the Currency for the financial subsidiary to engage in such activities, which approval shall be based solely upon the factors set forth in this section.

(3) Rating or comparable requirement.—

(A) In general.—A national bank meets the requirements of this paragraph if—

(i) the bank is 1 of the 50 largest insured banks and has not fewer than 1 issue of outstanding eligible debt that is currently rated within the 3 highest investment grade rating categories by a nationally recognized statistical rating organization; or

(ii) the bank is 1 of the second 50 largest insured banks and meets the criteria set forth in clause (i) or such other criteria as the Secretary of the Treasury and the Board of Governors of the Federal Reserve System may jointly establish by regulation and determine to be comparable to and consistent with the purposes of the rating required in clause (i). . . .

(4) Financial agency subsidiary.—The requirement in paragraph (2)(E) shall not apply with respect to the ownership or control of a financial subsidiary that engages in activities described in subsection (b)(1) solely as agent and not directly or indirectly as principal. . . .

(6) Indexed asset limit.—The dollar amount contained in paragraph (2)(D) shall be adjusted according to an indexing mechanism jointly established by regulation by the Secretary of the Treasury and the Board of Governors of the Federal Reserve System.

(7) Coordination with § 1843(*l*)(2).—Section 1843(*l*)(2) applies to a national bank that controls a financial subsidiary in the manner provided in that section.

(b) Activities That Are Financial in Nature.—

(1) Financial activities.—

(A) In general.—An activity shall be financial in nature or incidental to such financial activity only if—

(i) such activity has been defined to be financial in nature or incidental to a financial activity for bank holding companies pursuant to § 1843(k)(4); or

(ii) the Secretary of the Treasury determines the activity is financial in nature or incidental to a financial activity in accordance with subparagraph (B).

(B) Coordination between the Board and the Secretary of the Treasury.—

(i) Proposals raised before the Secretary of the Treasury.—

(I) Consultation.—The Secretary of the Treasury shall notify the Board of, and consult with the Board concerning, any request, proposal, or application under this section for a determination of whether an activity is financial in nature or incidental to a financial activity.

(II) Board view.—The Secretary of the Treasury shall not determine that any activity is financial in nature or incidental to a financial activity under this section if the Board notifies the Secretary in writing, not later than 30 days after the date of receipt of the notice described in subclause (I) (or such longer period as the Secretary determines to be appropriate under the circumstances) that the Board believes that the activity is not financial in nature or incidental to a financial activity or is not otherwise permissible under this section.

(ii) Proposals raised by the Board.—

(I) Board recommendation.—The Board may, at any time, recommend in writing that the Secretary of the Treasury find an activity to be financial in nature or incidental to a financial activity for purposes of this section.

(II) Time period for secretarial action.—Not later than 30 days after the date of receipt of a written recommendation from the Board under subclause (I) (or such longer period as the Secretary of the Treasury and the Board determine to be appropriate under the circumstances), the Secretary shall determine whether to initiate a public rulemaking proposing that the subject recommended activity be found to be financial in nature or incidental to a financial activity under this section, and shall notify the Board in writing of the determination of the Secretary and, in the event that the Secretary determines not to seek public comment on the proposal, the reasons for that determination.

(2) Factors to be considered.—In determining whether an activity is financial in nature or incidental to a financial activity, the Secretary shall take into account—

(A) the purposes of this Act and the Gramm-Leach-Bliley Act;

(B) changes or reasonably expected changes in the marketplace in which banks compete;

(C) changes or reasonably expected changes in the technology for delivering financial services; and

(D) whether such activity is necessary or appropriate to allow a bank and the subsidiaries of a bank to—

(i) compete effectively with any company seeking to provide financial services in the United States;

(ii) efficiently deliver information and services that are financial in nature through the use of technological means, including any application necessary to protect the security or efficacy of systems for the transmission of data or financial transactions; and

(iii) offer customers any available or emerging technological means for using financial services or for the document imaging of data.

(3) Authorization of new financial activities.—The Secretary of the Treasury shall, by regulation or order and in accordance with paragraph

(1)(B), define, consistent with the purposes of this Act and the Gramm-Leach-Bliley Act, the following activities as, and the extent to which such activities are, financial in nature or incidental to a financial activity:

(A) Lending, exchanging, transferring, investing for others, or safeguarding financial assets other than money or securities.

(B) Providing any device or other instrumentality for transferring money or other financial assets.

(C) Arranging, effecting, or facilitating financial transactions for the account of third parties.

(c) Capital Deduction.—

(1) Capital deduction required.—In determining compliance with applicable capital standards—

(A) the aggregate amount of the outstanding equity investment, including retained earnings, of a national bank in all financial subsidiaries shall be deducted from the assets and tangible equity of the national bank; and

(B) the assets and liabilities of the financial subsidiaries shall not be consolidated with those of the national bank.

(2) Financial statement disclosure of capital deduction.—Any published financial statement of a national bank that controls a financial subsidiary shall, in addition to providing information prepared in accordance with generally accepted accounting principles, separately present financial information for the bank in the manner provided in paragraph (1).

(d) Safeguards for the Bank.—A national bank that establishes or maintains a financial subsidiary shall assure that—

(1) the procedures of the national bank for identifying and managing financial and operational risks within the national bank and the financial subsidiary adequately protect the national bank from such risks;

(2) the national bank has, for the protection of the bank, reasonable policies and procedures to preserve the separate corporate identity and limited liability of the national bank and the financial subsidiaries of the national bank; and

(3) the national bank is in compliance with this section. . . .

(g) Definitions.—For purposes of this section, the following definitions shall apply:

(1) Affiliate, company, control, and subsidiary.—The terms "affiliate," "company," "control," and "subsidiary" have the meanings given those terms in § 1841.

(2) Appropriate Federal banking agency, depository institution, insured bank, and insured depository institution.—The terms "appropriate Federal banking agency," "depository institution," "insured bank," and "insured depository institution" have the meanings given those terms in § 1813.

(3) **Financial subsidiary**.—The term "financial subsidiary" means any company that is controlled by 1 or more insured depository institutions other than a subsidiary that—

(A) engages solely in activities that national banks are permitted to engage in directly and are conducted subject to the same terms and conditions that govern the conduct of such activities by national banks; or

(B) a national bank is specifically authorized by the express terms of a Federal statute (other than this section), and not by implication or interpretation, to control, such as by § 601 [relating to international banking] or the Bank Service Company Act [12 U.S.C. §§ 1861-1867].

(4) **Eligible debt**.—The term "eligible debt" means unsecured long-term debt that

(A) is not supported by any form of credit enhancement, including a guarantee or standby letter of credit; and

(B) is not held in whole or in any significant part by any affiliate, officer, director, principal shareholder, or employee of the bank or any other person acting on behalf of or with funds from the bank or an affiliate of the bank.

(5) **Well capitalized**.—The term "well capitalized" has the meaning given the term in § 1831o.

(6) **Well managed**.—The term "well managed" means—

(A) in the case of a depository institution that has been examined, unless otherwise determined in writing by the appropriate Federal banking agency—

(i) the achievement of a composite rating of 1 or 2 under the Uniform Financial Institutions Rating System (or an equivalent rating under an equivalent rating system) in connection with the most recent examination or subsequent review of the depository institution; and

(ii) at least a rating of 2 for management, if such rating is given; or

(B) in the case of any depository institution that has not been examined, the existence and use of managerial resources that the appropriate Federal banking agency determines are satisfactory.

§ 25b. State Law Preemption Standards for National Banks and Subsidiaries Clarified

(a) **Definitions**.—For purposes of this section, the following definitions shall apply: . . .

(2) **State consumer financial laws**.—The term "State consumer financial law" means a State law that does not directly or indirectly discriminate against national banks and that directly and specifically regulates the manner, content, or terms and conditions of any financial transaction . . . , or any account related thereto, with respect to a consumer. . . .

(b) Preemption Standard.—

(1) In general.—State consumer financial laws are preempted, only if—

(A) application of a State consumer financial law would have a discriminatory effect on national banks, in comparison with the effect of the law on a bank chartered by that State;

(B) in accordance with the legal standard for preemption in the decision of the Supreme Court of the United States in Barnett Bank of Marion County, N.A. v. Nelson, Florida Insurance Commissioner, et al., 517 U.S. 25 (1996), the State consumer financial law prevents or significantly interferes with the exercise by the national bank of its powers; and any preemption determination under this subparagraph may be made by a court, or by regulation or order of the Comptroller of the Currency on a case-by-case basis, in accordance with applicable law; or

(C) the State consumer financial law is preempted by a provision of Federal law other than [the National Bank Act]. . . .

(2) Savings clause.—This Act and § 371 do not preempt, annul, or affect the applicability of any State law to any subsidiary or affiliate of a national bank (other than a subsidiary or affiliate that is chartered as a national bank).

(3) Case-by-case basis.—

(A) **Definition.**—As used in this section the term "case-by-case basis" refers to a determination pursuant to this section made by the Comptroller concerning the impact of a particular State consumer financial law on any national bank that is subject to that law, or the law of any other State with substantively equivalent terms.

(B) **Consultation.**—When making a determination on a case-by-case basis that a State consumer financial law of another State has substantively equivalent terms as one that the Comptroller is preempting, the Comptroller shall first consult with the Bureau of Consumer Financial Protection and shall take the views of the Bureau into account when making the determination.

(4) Rule of construction.—This [Act] does not occupy the field in any area of State law.

(5) Standards of review.—

(A) **Preemption.**—A court reviewing any determinations made by the Comptroller regarding preemption of a State law by this Act or § 371 shall assess the validity of such determinations, depending upon the thoroughness evident in the consideration of the agency, the validity of the reasoning of the agency, the consistency with other valid determinations made by the agency, and other factors which the court finds persuasive and relevant to its decision.

(B) **Savings clause.**—Except as provided in subparagraph (A), nothing in this section shall affect the deference that a court may afford to the

Comptroller in making determinations regarding the meaning or interpretation of title LXII of the Revised Statutes of the United States [relating to the organization and powers of national banks and including §§ 21-24a and 29] or other Federal laws.

(6) Comptroller determination not delegable.—Any regulation, order, or determination made by the Comptroller of the Currency under paragraph (1)(B) shall be made by the Comptroller, and shall not be delegable to another officer or employee of the Comptroller of the Currency.

(c) Substantial Evidence.—No regulation or order of the Comptroller of the Currency prescribed under subsection (b)(1)(B), shall be interpreted or applied so as to invalidate, or otherwise declare inapplicable to a national bank, the provision of the State consumer financial law, unless substantial evidence, made on the record of the proceeding, supports the specific finding regarding the preemption of such provision in accordance with the legal standard of the decision of the Supreme Court of the United States in Barnett Bank of Marion County, N.A. v. Nelson, Florida Insurance Commissioner, et al., 517 U.S. 25 (1996).

(d) Periodic Review of Preemption Determinations.— . . . The Comptroller of the Currency shall periodically conduct a review, through notice and public comment, of each determination that a provision of Federal law preempts a State consumer financial law. The agency shall conduct such review within the 5-year period after prescribing or otherwise issuing such determination, and at least once during each 5-year period thereafter. After conducting the review of, and inspecting the comments made on, the determination, the agency shall publish a notice in the Federal Register announcing the decision to continue or rescind the determination or a proposal to amend the determination. Any such notice of a proposal to amend a determination and the subsequent resolution of such proposal shall comply with the procedures set forth in § 43(a)-(b).

(e) Application of State Consumer Financial Law to Subsidiaries and Affiliates.—Notwithstanding any provision of this Act or § 371, a State consumer financial law shall apply to a subsidiary or affiliate of a national bank (other than a subsidiary or affiliate that is chartered as a national bank) to the same extent that the State consumer financial law applies to any person, corporation, or other entity subject to such State law.

(f) Preservation of Powers Related to Charging Interest.—No provision of this Act shall be construed as altering or otherwise affecting the authority conferred by § 85 for the charging of interest by a national bank at the rate allowed by the laws of the State . . . where the bank is located, including with respect to the meaning of "interest" under such provision.

(g) Transparency of OCC Preemption Determinations.—The Comptroller of the Currency shall publish and update no less frequently than quarterly, a list of preemption determinations by the Comptroller of the Currency then in effect that identifies the activities and practices covered by each determination and the requirements and constraints determined to be preempted.

(h) Clarification of Law Applicable to Nondepository Institution Subsidiaries and Affiliates of National Banks.— ... No provision of this Act or § 371 shall be construed as preempting, annulling, or affecting the applicability of State law to any subsidiary, affiliate, or agent of a national bank (other than a subsidiary, affiliate, or agent that is chartered as a national bank).

(i) Visitorial Powers.— ... In accordance with the decision of the Supreme Court of the United States in Cuomo v. Clearing House Assn., L.L.C., 129 S. Ct. 2710 (2009), no provision of this Act which relates to visitorial powers or otherwise limits or restricts the visitorial authority to which any national bank is subject shall be construed as limiting or restricting the authority of any attorney general (or other chief law enforcement officer) of any State to bring an action against a national bank in a court of appropriate jurisdiction to enforce an applicable law and to seek relief as authorized by such law. ...

(j) Enforcement Actions.—The ability of the Comptroller of the Currency to bring an enforcement action under this Act or § 45 does not preclude any private party from enforcing rights granted under Federal or State law in the courts.

§ 26. Commencing Business

Whenever a certificate is transmitted to the Comptroller of the Currency, as provided in this Act, and the association transmitting the same notifies the Comptroller that all of its capital stock has been duly paid in, and that such association has complied with all the provisions of this Act required to be complied with before an association shall be authorized to commence the business of banking, the Comptroller shall examine into the condition of such association, ascertain especially the amount of money paid in on account of its capital, the name and place of residence of each of its directors, and the amount of the capital stock of which each is the owner in good faith, and generally whether such association has complied with all the provisions of this Act required to entitle it to engage in the business of banking; and shall cause to be made and attested by the oaths of a majority of the directors, and by the president or cashier of the association, a statement of all the facts necessary to enable the Comptroller to determine whether the association is lawfully entitled to commence the business of banking.

§ 27. Granting Charter

(a) If, upon a careful examination of the facts so reported, and of any other facts which may come to the knowledge of the Comptroller, whether by means of a special commission appointed by him for the purpose of inquiring into the condition of such association, or otherwise, it appears that such association is lawfully entitled to commence the business of banking, the Comptroller shall give to such association a certificate, under his hand and official seal, that such association has complied with all the provisions required to be complied with before commencing the business of banking, and that such association is authorized to commence such business. But the Comptroller may withhold from an association his certificate authorizing the commencement of business, whenever he has reason to suppose that the shareholders have formed the same for any other than the legitimate objects contemplated by this Act. A National Bank Association, to which the Comptroller of the Currency has heretofore issued or hereafter issues such certificate, is not illegally constituted solely because its operations are or have been required by the Comptroller of the Currency to be limited to those of a trust company and activities related thereto. . . .

§ 29. Holding Real Property

A national banking association may purchase, hold, and convey real estate for the following purposes, and for no others:

First. Such as shall be necessary for its accommodation in the transaction of its business.

Second. Such as shall be mortgaged to it in good faith by way of security for debts previously contracted.

Third. Such as shall be conveyed to it in satisfaction of debts previously contracted in the course of its dealings.

Fourth. Such as it shall purchase at sales under judgments, decrees or mortgages held by the association, or shall purchase to secure debts due to it.

But no such association shall hold the possession of any real estate under mortgage, or the title and possession of any real estate purchased to secure any debts due to it, for a longer period than five years except as otherwise provided in this section. . . .

§ 30. Changing Name or Location

(a) Name Change.—Any national banking association, upon written notice to the Comptroller of the Currency, may change its name, except that such new name shall include the word "national."

(b) Location Change.—Any national banking association, upon written notice to the Comptroller of the Currency, may change the location of its main office to any authorized branch location within the limits of the city, town, or village in which it is situated, or, with a vote of shareholders owning two-thirds of the stock of such association for a relocation outside such limits and upon receipt of a certificate of approval from the Comptroller of the Currency, to any other location within or outside the limits of the city, town, or village in which it is located, but not more than thirty miles beyond such limits. . . .

§ 35. Converting State Bank into National Bank

Any [state bank with sufficient unimpaired capital] may, by the vote of the shareholders owning not less than fifty-one per centum of the capital stock of such bank . . . , with the approval of the Comptroller of the Currency be converted into a national banking association, with a name that contains the word "national": Provided, however, That said conversion shall not be in contravention of the State law. . . . The Comptroller of the Currency may not approve the conversion . . . during any period in which the State bank . . . is subject to a cease and desist order (or other formal enforcement order) issued by, or a memorandum of understanding entered into with, a State bank supervisor or the appropriate Federal banking agency with respect to a significant supervisory matter or a final enforcement action by a State Attorney General.

§ 36. Branching

The conditions upon which a national banking association may retain or establish and operate a branch or branches are the following:. . . .

(c) New Branches.—A national banking association may, with the approval of the Comptroller of the Currency, establish and operate new branches:

(1) Within the limits of the city, town or village in which said association is situated, if such establishment and operation are at the time expressly authorized to State banks by the law of the State in question; and

(2) at any point within the State in which said association is situated, if such establishment and operation are at the time authorized to State banks by the statute law of the State in question by language specifically granting such authority affirmatively and not merely by implication or recognition, and subject to the restrictions as to location imposed by the law of the State on State banks. . . .

(d) Branches Resulting from Interstate Merger Transactions.—A national bank resulting from an interstate merger transaction (as defined in § 1831u(f)(6)) may maintain and operate a branch in a State other than the home State (as defined in subsection (g)(3)(B) of this section) of such bank in accordance with § 1831u.

(e) Exclusive Authority for Additional Branches.—

(1) In general.—[A] national bank may not acquire, establish, or operate a branch in any State other than the bank's home State (as defined in subsection (g)(3)(B) of this section) or a State in which the bank already has a branch unless the acquisition, establishment, or operation of such branch in such State by such national bank is authorized under this section or § 1823(f), § 1823(k), or § 1831u. . . .

(f) Law Applicable to Interstate Branching Operations.—

(1) Law applicable to national bank branches.—

(A) In general.—The laws of the host State regarding community reinvestment, consumer protection, fair lending, and establishment of intrastate branches shall apply to any branch in the host State of an out-of-State national bank to the same extent as such State laws apply to a branch of a bank chartered by that State, except—

(i) when Federal law preempts the application of such State laws to a national bank; or

(ii) when the Comptroller of the Currency determines that the application of such State laws would have a discriminatory effect on the branch in comparison with the effect the application of such State laws would have with respect to branches of a bank chartered by the host State.

(B) Enforcement of applicable State laws.—The provisions of any State law to which a branch of a national bank is subject under this paragraph shall be enforced, with respect to such branch, by the Comptroller of the Currency.

(C) Review and report on actions by Comptroller.—The Comptroller of the Currency shall conduct an annual review of the actions it has taken with regard to the applicability of State law to national banks (or their branches) during the preceding year, and shall include in its annual report . . . the results of the review and the reasons for each such action. . . .

(2) Treatment of branch as bank.—All laws of a host State, other than the laws regarding community reinvestment, consumer protection, fair lending, establishment of intrastate branches, and the application or administration of any tax or method of taxation, shall apply to a branch (in such State) of an out-of-State national bank to the same extent as such laws would apply if the branch were a national bank the main office of which is in such State.

(3) Rule of construction.—No provision of this subsection may be construed as affecting the legal standards for preemption of the application of State law to national banks.

(g) . . . Interstate Branching Through De Novo Branches.—

(1) In general.—[T]he Comptroller of the Currency may approve an application by a national bank to establish and operate a de novo branch in a State (other than the bank's home State) in which the bank does not maintain a branch if—

(A) the law of the State in which the branch is located, or is to be located, would permit establishment of the branch, if the national bank were a State bank chartered by such State; and

(B) the conditions established in, or made applicable to this paragraph by, paragraph (2) are met.

(2) Conditions on establishment and operation of interstate branch.—

(A) **Establishment**.—An application by a national bank to establish and operate a de novo branch in a host State shall be subject to the same requirements and conditions to which an application for an interstate merger transaction is subject under paragraphs (1), (3), and (4) of § 1831u(b).

(B) **Operation**.—Subsections (c) and (d)(2) of § 1831u shall apply with respect to each branch of a national bank which is established and operated pursuant to an application approved under this subsection in the same manner and to the same extent such provisions of such § 1831u apply to a branch of a national bank which resulted from an interstate merger transaction approved pursuant to such § 1831u.

(3) Definitions.—The following definitions shall apply for purposes of this section:

(A) **De novo branch**.—The term "de novo branch" means a branch of a national bank which—

(i) is originally established by the national bank as a branch; and

(ii) does not become a branch of such bank as a result of—

(I) the acquisition by the bank of an insured depository institution or a branch of an insured depository institution; or

(II) the conversion, merger, or consolidation of any such institution or branch.

(B) **Home State**.—The term "home State" means the State in which the main office of a national bank is located.

(C) **Host State**.—The term "host State" means, with respect to a bank, a State, other than the home State of the bank, in which the bank maintains, or seeks to establish and maintain, a branch. . . .

(i) Prior Approval of Branch Locations.—No branch of any national banking association shall be established or moved from one location to another without first obtaining the consent and approval of the Comptroller of the Currency.

(j) Branch Defined.—The term "branch" as used in this section shall be held to include any branch bank, branch office, branch agency, additional office, or any branch place of business located in any State or Territory of the United States or in the District of Columbia at which deposits are received, or checks paid, or money lent. The term "branch," as used in this section, does not include an automated teller machine or a remote service unit. . . .

(I) "State Bank" and "Bank" Defined.—The words "State bank," "State banks," "bank," or "banks," as used in this section, shall be held to include trust companies, savings banks, or other such corporations or institutions carrying on the banking business under the authority of State laws.

§ 43. Interpretations Concerning Preemption of Certain State Laws

(a) Notice and Opportunity for Comment Required.—Before issuing any opinion letter or interpretive rule, in response to a request or upon the agency's own motion, that concludes that Federal law preempts the application to a national bank of any State law regarding community reinvestment, consumer protection, fair lending, or the establishment of intrastate branches, or before making a determination under § 36(f)(1)(A)(ii) the appropriate Federal banking agency (as defined in § 1813) shall—

(1) publish in the Federal Register notice of the preemption or discrimination issue that the agency is considering (including a description of each State law at issue);

(2) give interested parties not less than 30 days in which to submit written comments; and

(3) in developing the final opinion letter or interpretive rule issued by the agency, or making any determination under § 36(f)(1)(A)(ii), consider any comments received.

(b) Publication Required.—The appropriate Federal banking agency shall publish in the Federal Register—

(1) any final opinion letter or interpretive rule concluding that Federal law preempts the application of any State law regarding community reinvestment, consumer protection, fair lending, or establishment of intrastate branches to a national bank; and

(2) any determination under § 36(f)(1)(A)(ii). . . .

§ 71. Board of Directors

The affairs of each association shall be managed by not less than five directors, who shall be elected by the shareholders. . . .

§ 72. Directors' Qualifications

Every director must, during his whole term of service, be a citizen of the United States, and at least a majority of the directors must have resided in the

State, Territory, or District in which the association is located, or within one hundred miles of the location of the office of the association, for at least one year immediately preceding their election, and must be residents of such State or within a one-hundred-mile territory of the location of the association during their continuance in office, except that the Comptroller may, in the discretion of the Comptroller, waive the requirement of residency, and waive the requirement of citizenship in the case of not more than a minority of the total number of directors. Every director must own in his or her own right either shares of the capital stock of the association of which he or she is a director the aggregate par value of which is not less than $1,000, or an equivalent interest, as determined by the Comptroller of the Currency, in any company which has control over such association within the meaning of § 1841. . . . Any director who ceases to be the owner of the required number of shares of the stock, or who becomes in any other manner disqualified, shall thereby vacate his place.

§ 81. Place of Business

The general business of each national banking association shall be transacted in the place specified in its organization certificate and in the branch or branches, if any, established or maintained by it in accordance with the provisions of § 36.

§ 83. Loans by Bank on Its Own Stock

(a) General Prohibition.—No national bank shall make any loan or discount on the security of the shares of its own capital stock.

(b) Exclusion.—For purposes of this section, a national bank shall not be deemed to be making a loan or discount on the security of the shares of its own capital stock if it acquires the stock to prevent loss upon a debt previously contracted for in good faith.

§ 84. Lending Limits

(a) Total Loans and Extensions of Credit.—

(1) 15 percent limit.—The total loans and extensions of credit by a national banking association to a person outstanding at one time and not fully secured, as determined in a manner consistent with paragraph (2) of this subsection, by collateral having a market value at least equal to the amount of the loan or extension of credit shall not exceed 15 per centum of the unimpaired capital and unimpaired surplus of the association.

(2) Additional lending secured by readily marketable collateral.—The total loans and extensions of credit by a national banking association to a person outstanding at one time and fully secured by readily marketable collateral having a market value, as determined by reliable and continuously available price quotations, at least equal to the amount of the funds outstanding shall not exceed 10 per centum of the unimpaired capital and unimpaired surplus of the association. This limitation shall be separate from and in addition to the limitation contained in paragraph (1) of this subsection.

(b) Definitions.—For the purposes of this section—

(1) the term **"loans and extensions of credit"** shall include—

(A) all direct or indirect advances of funds to a person made on the basis of any obligation of that person to repay the funds or repayable from specific property pledged by or on behalf of the person;

(B) to the extent specified by the Comptroller of the Currency, any liability of a national banking association to advance funds to or on behalf of a person pursuant to a contractual commitment; and

(C) any credit exposure to a person arising from a derivative transaction, repurchase agreement, reverse repurchase agreement, securities lending transaction, or securities borrowing transaction between the national banking association and the person; and

(2) the term **"person"** shall include an individual, sole proprietorship, partnership, joint venture, association, trust, estate, business trust, corporation, sovereign government or agency, instrumentality, or political subdivision thereof, or any similar entity or organization; and

(3) the term **"derivative transaction"** includes any transaction that is a contract, agreement, swap, warrant, note, or option that is based, in whole or in part, on the value of, any interest in, or any quantitative measure or the occurrence of any event relating to, one or more commodities, securities, currencies, interest or other rates, indices, or other assets.

(c) Exceptions.—The limitations contained in subsection (a) of this section shall be subject to the following exceptions:

(1) Commercial paper.—Loans or extensions of credit arising from the discount of commercial or business paper evidencing an obligation to the person negotiating it with recourse shall not be subject to any limitation based on capital and surplus.

(2) Bankers' acceptances.—The purchase of bankers' acceptances ... issued by other banks [and meeting specified criteria] shall not be subject to any limitation based on capital and surplus.

(3) Marketable staples.—Loans and extensions of credit secured by bills of lading, warehouse receipts, or similar documents transferring or securing title to readily marketable staples shall be subject to a limitation of 35 per centum of capital and surplus in addition to the general limitations if the market value of the staples securing each additional loan or extension of credit at all times equals or exceeds 115 per centum of the outstanding amount of such loan or extension of credit. The staples shall be fully covered by insurance whenever it is customary to insure such staples.

(4) **Federal obligations**.—Loans or extensions of credit secured by bonds, notes, certificates of indebtedness, or Treasury bills of the United States or by other such obligations fully guaranteed as to principal and interest by the United States shall not be subject to any limitation based on capital and surplus.

(5) **Federal agencies and government corporations**.—Loans or extensions of credit to or secured by unconditional takeout commitments or guarantees of any department, agency, bureau, board, commission, or establishment of the United States or any corporation wholly owned directly or indirectly by the United States shall not be subject to any limitation based on capital and surplus.

(6) **Segregated deposit account**.—Loans or extensions of credit secured by a segregated deposit account in the lending bank shall not be subject to any limitation based on capital and surplus.

(7) **Financial institution**.—Loans or extensions of credit to any financial institution or to any receiver, conservator, superintendent of banks, or other agent in charge of the business and property of such financial institution, when such loans or extensions of credit are approved by the Comptroller of the Currency, shall not be subject to any limitation based on capital and surplus.

(8) **Installment consumer paper**.—

(A) **In general**.—Loans and extensions of credit arising from the discount of negotiable or nonnegotiable installment consumer paper which carries a full recourse endorsement or unconditional guarantee by the person transferring the paper shall be subject under this section to a maximum limitation equal to 25 per centum of such capital and surplus, notwithstanding the collateral requirements set forth in subsection (a)(2) of this section.

(B) **Relying on maker rather than transferor**.—If the bank's files or the knowledge of its officers of the financial condition of each maker of such consumer paper is reasonably adequate, and an officer of the bank designated for that purpose by the board of directors of the bank certifies in writing that the bank is relying primarily upon the responsibility of each maker for payment of such loans or extensions of credit and not upon any full or partial recourse endorsement or guarantee by the transferor, the limitations of this section as to the loans or extensions of credit of each such maker shall be the sole applicable loan limitations.

(9) **Livestock; dairy cattle**.—

(A) **Livestock**.—Loans and extensions of credit secured by shipping documents or instruments transferring or securing title covering livestock or giving a lien on livestock when the market value of the livestock securing the obligation is not at any time less than 115 per centum of the face amount of the note covered, shall be subject under this section, notwithstanding the collateral requirements set forth in subsection (a)(2) of this section, to a maximum limitation equal to 25 per centum of such capital and surplus.

(B) Dairy cattle.—Loans and extensions of credit which arise from the discount by dealers in dairy cattle of paper given in payment for dairy cattle, which paper carries a full recourse endorsement or unconditional guarantee of the seller, and which are secured by the cattle being sold, shall be subject under this section, notwithstanding the collateral requirements set forth in subsection (a)(2) of this section, to a limitation of 25 per centum of such capital and surplus. . . .

(d) Authority of Comptroller of the Currency.—

(1) Rulemaking.—The Comptroller of the Currency may prescribe rules and regulations to administer and carry out the purposes of this section including rules or regulations to define or further define terms used in this section and to establish limits or requirements other than those specified in this section for particular classes or categories of loans or extensions of credit.

(2) Attributing loans.—The Comptroller of the Currency also shall have authority to determine when a loan putatively made to a person shall for purposes of this section be attributed to another person.

§ 85. Interest Rate on Loans

Any association may take, receive, reserve, and charge on any loan or discount made, or upon any notes, bills of exchange, or other evidence of debt, interest at the rate allowed by the laws of the State, Territory, or District where the bank is located, or at a rate of 1 per centum in excess of the discount rate on ninety-day commercial paper in effect at the Federal reserve bank in the Federal reserve district where the bank is located, whichever may be the greater, and no more, except that where by the laws of any State a different rate is limited for banks organized under state laws, the rate so limited shall be allowed for associations organized or existing in any such State under this Act. When no rate is fixed by the laws of the State, or Territory, or District, the bank may take, receive, reserve, or charge a rate not exceeding 7 per centum, or 1 per centum in excess of the discount rate on ninety-day commercial paper in effect at the Federal reserve bank in the Federal reserve district where the bank is located, whichever may be the greater, and such interest may be taken in advance, reckoning the days for which the note, bill, or other evidence of debt has to run. . . .

§ 86. Usury

The taking, receiving, reserving, or charging a rate of interest greater than is allowed by § 85, when knowingly done, shall be deemed a forfeiture of the entire interest which the note, bill, or other evidence of debt carries with it, or which has been agreed to be paid thereon. In case the greater rate of interest has been paid, the person by whom it has been paid, or his legal representatives, may recover back, in an action in the nature of an action of debt, twice the amount of the interest thus paid from the association taking or receiving the same. . . .

§ 90. Depositaries of Public Moneys and Financial Agents of Government

All national banking associations, designated for that purpose by the Secretary of the Treasury, shall be depositaries of public money, under such regulations as may be prescribed by the Secretary; and they may also be employed as financial agents of the Government; and they shall perform all such reasonable duties, as depositaries of public money and financial agents of the Government, as may be required of them. The Secretary of the Treasury shall require the associations thus designated to give satisfactory security, by the deposit of United States bonds and otherwise, for the safekeeping and prompt payment of the public money deposited with them, and for the faithful performance of their duties as financial agents of the Government. . . .

§ 91. Fraudulent Transfers

All transfers of the notes, bonds, bills of exchange, or other evidences of debt owing to any national banking association, or of deposits to its credit; all assignments of mortgages, sureties on real estate, or of judgments or decrees in its favor; all deposits of money, bullion, or other valuable thing for its use, or for the use of any of its shareholders or creditors; and all payments of money to either, made after the commission of an act of insolvency, or in contemplation thereof, made with a view to prevent the application of its assets in the manner prescribed by this Act, or with a view to the preference of one creditor to another, . . . shall be utterly null and void; and no attachment, injunction, or execution, shall be issued against such association or its property before final judgment in any suit, action, or proceeding, in any State, county, or municipal court.

§ 92. Acting as Insurance Agent

In addition to the powers now vested by law in national banking associations organized under the laws of the United States any such association located and doing business in any place the population of which does not exceed five thousand inhabitants, as shown by the last preceding decennial census, may, under such rules and regulations as may be prescribed by the Comptroller of the Currency, act as the agent for any fire, life, or other insurance company authorized by the authorities of the State in which said bank is located to do business in said State, by soliciting and selling insurance and collecting premiums on policies issued by such company; and may receive for services so rendered such fees or commissions as may be agreed upon between the said association and the insurance company for which it may act as agent: *Provided, however*, That no such bank shall in any case assume or guarantee the payment of any case assume or guarantee the payment of any premium on insurance policies issued through its agency by its principal: *And provided further*, That the bank shall not guarantee the truth of any statement made by an assured in filing his application for insurance.

§ 92a. Trust Powers

(a) **Authority of Comptroller of the Currency**.—The Comptroller of the Currency shall be authorized and empowered to grant by special permit to national banks applying therefor, when not in contravention of State or local law, the right to act as trustee, executor, administrator, registrar of stocks and bonds, guardian of estates, assignee, receiver, committee of estates of lunatics, or in any other fiduciary capacity in which State banks, trust companies, or other corporations which come into competition with national banks are permitted to act under the laws of the State in which the national bank is located.

(b) **Grant and Exercise of Powers Deemed Not in Contravention of State or Local Law**.—Whenever the laws of such State authorize or permit the exercise of any or all of the foregoing powers by State banks, trust companies, or other corporations which compete with national banks, the granting to and the exercise of such powers by national banks shall not be deemed to be in contravention of State or local law within the meaning of this section.

(c) **Segregating Fiduciary Assets from General Assets**.—National banks exercising any or all of the powers enumerating in this section shall segregate all assets held in any fiduciary capacity from the general assets of the bank and shall keep a separate set of books and records showing in proper detail all transactions engaged in under authority of this section. The State banking authorities may have access to reports of examination made by the

Comptroller of the Currency insofar as such reports relate to the trust department of such bank, but nothing in this section shall be construed as authorizing the State banking authorities to examine the books, records, and assets of such bank.

(d) Prohibited Operations; Separate Investment Account; Collateral for Certain Funds Used in Conduct of Business.—No national bank shall receive in its trust department deposits of current funds subject to check or the deposit of checks, drafts, bills of exchange, or other items for collection or exchange purposes. Funds deposited or held in trust by the bank awaiting investment shall be carried in a separate account and shall not be used by the bank in the conduct of its business unless it shall first set aside in the trust department United States bonds or other securities approved by the Comptroller of the Currency.

(e) Lien and Claim upon Bank Failure.—In the event of the failure of such bank the owners of the funds held in trust for investment shall have a lien on the bonds or other securities so set apart in addition to their claim against the estate of the bank. . . .

§ 93. Penalty for Violating This Act

(a) Forfeiture of Franchise; Personal Liability of Directors.—If the directors of any national banking association shall knowingly violate, or knowingly permit any of the officers, agents, or servants of the association to violate any of the provisions of this Act, all the rights, privileges, and franchises of the association shall be thereby forfeited. Such violation shall, however, be determined and adjudged by a proper district . . . court of the United States in a suit brought for that purpose by the Comptroller of the Currency . . . before the association shall be declared dissolved. And in cases of such violation, every director who participated in or assented to the same shall be held liable in his personal and individual capacity for all damages which the association, its shareholders, or any other person, shall have sustained in consequence of such violation.

(b) Civil Money Penalty.— . . .

§ 93a. Authority to Prescribe Rules and Regulations

Except to the extent that authority to issue such rules and regulations has been expressly and exclusively granted to another regulatory agency, the Comptroller of the Currency is authorized to prescribe rules and regulations to carry out the responsibilities of the office, except that the authority conferred by this section does not apply to § 36 or to securities activities of National Banks under the Act commonly known as the "Glass-Steagall Act."

§ 191. Appointment of Receiver

(a) **In General**.—The Comptroller of the Currency may, without prior notice or hearings, appoint a receiver for any national bank (and such receiver shall be the Federal Deposit Insurance Corporation if the national bank is an insured bank (as defined in § 1813(h))) if the Comptroller determines, in the Comptroller's discretion, that—

    (1) 1 or more of the grounds specified in § 1821(c)(5) exist; or

    (2) the association's board of directors consists of fewer than 5 members.

(b) **Judicial Review**.—If the Comptroller of the Currency appoints a receiver under subsection (a), the national bank may, within 30 days thereafter, bring an action in the United States district court for the judicial district in which the home office of such bank is located, or in the United States District Court for the District of Columbia, for an order requiring the Comptroller of the Currency to remove the receiver, and the court shall, upon the merits, dismiss such action or direct the Comptroller of the Currency to remove the receiver.

§ 203. Appointment of Conservator

(a) **Appointment**.—The Comptroller of the Currency may, without prior notice or hearings, appoint a conservator (which may be the Federal Deposit Insurance Corporation) to the possession and control of a bank whenever the Comptroller of the Currency determines that 1 or more of the grounds specified in § 1821(c)(5) exist. . . .

§ 206. Conservator; Powers and Duties

(a) **General Powers**.—A conservator shall have all the powers of the shareholders, directors, and officers of the bank and may operate the bank in its own name unless the Comptroller in the order of appointment limits the conservator's authority.

(b) **Subject to Rules of Comptroller**.—The conservator shall be subject to such rules, regulations, and orders as the Comptroller from time to time deems appropriate; and . . . shall have the same rights and privileges and be subject to the same duties, restrictions, penalties, conditions, and limitations as apply to directors, officers, or employees of a national bank. . . .

§ 214a. Procedure for Conversion, Merger, or Consolidation

A national banking association may, by vote of the holders of at least two-thirds of each class of its capital stock, convert into, or merge or consolidate with, a State bank in the same State in which the national banking association is located, under a State charter, in the following manner:

(a) Approval Procedure.—The plan of conversion, merger, or consolidation must be approved by a majority of the entire board of directors of the national banking association. The bank shall publish notice of the time, place, and object of the shareholders' meeting to act upon the plan, in some newspaper with general circulation in the place where the principal office of the national banking association is located, at least once a week for four consecutive weeks. . . . The national banking association shall send such notice to each shareholder of record by registered mail or by certified mail at least ten days prior to the meeting, which notice may be waived specifically by any shareholder.

(b) Rights of Dissenting Stockholders.—A shareholder of a national banking association who votes against the conversion, merger, or consolidation, or who has given notice in writing to the bank at or prior to such meeting that he dissents from the plan, shall be entitled to receive in cash the value of the shares held by him . . . .

§ 214d. Prohibition on Conversion

A national banking association may not convert to a State bank or State savings association during any period in which the national banking association is subject to a cease and desist order (or other formal enforcement order) issued by, or a memorandum of understanding entered into with, the Comptroller of the Currency with respect to a significant supervisory matter.

NATIONAL BANK CONSOLIDATION AND MERGER ACT

§ 215. Consolidation of Banks Within the Same State

(a) In General.—Any national bank or any bank incorporated under the laws of any State may, with the approval of the Comptroller, be consolidated with one or more national banking associations located in the same State under the charter of a national banking association on such terms and conditions as may be lawfully agreed upon by a majority of the board of directors of each association or bank proposing to consolidate, and be ratified and confirmed by the affirmative vote of the shareholders of each such association or bank owning at least two-thirds of its capital stock outstanding, or by a greater proportion of such capital stock in the case of such State bank if the laws of the State where it is organized so require, at a meeting to be held on the call of the directors after publishing notice of the time, place, and object of the meeting . . . and after sending such notice to each shareholder of record by certified or registered mail at least ten days prior to the meeting. . . .

(b) Liability of Consolidated Association; Rights of Dissenting Shareholders.—The consolidated association shall be liable for all liabilities of the respective consolidating banks or associations. . . . *Provided*, That if such consolidation shall be voted for at such meetings by the necessary majorities of the shareholders of each association and State bank proposing to consolidate, and thereafter the consolidation shall be approved by the Comptroller, any shareholder of any of the associations or State banks so consolidated who has voted against such consolidation . . . or who has given notice in writing . . . that he dissents from the plan of consolidation, shall be entitled to receive the value of the shares so held by him . . . .

§ 215a. Merger of National Banks or State Banks into National Banks

(a) Approval Procedure.—One or more national banking associations or one or more State banks, with the approval of the Comptroller, under an agreement not inconsistent with this Act, may merge into a national banking association located within the same State, under the charter of the receiving association. The merger agreement shall—

(1) be agreed upon in writing by a majority of the board of directors of each association or State bank participating in the plan of merger;

(2) be ratified and confirmed by the affirmative vote of the shareholders of each such association or State bank owning at least two-thirds of its capital stock outstanding, or by a greater proportion of such capital stock in the case of a State bank if the laws of the State where it is organized so require, at a meeting to be held on the call of the directors, after publishing notice of the time, place, and object of the meeting . . . and after sending such notice to each shareholder of record by certified or registered mail at least ten days prior to the meeting . . ;

(3) specify the amount of the capital stock of the receiving association . . . , the amount of stock (if any) to be allocated, and cash (if any) to be paid, to the shareholders of the association or State bank being merged into the receiving association; and

(4) provide that the receiving association shall be liable for all liabilities of the association or State bank being merged into the receiving association.

(b) Rights of Dissenting Shareholders.—If a merger shall be voted for at the called meetings by the necessary majorities of the shareholders of each association or State bank participating in the plan of merger, and thereafter the merger shall be approved by the Comptroller, any shareholder of any association or State bank to be merged into the receiving association who has voted against such merger . . . or has given notice in writing . . . that he dissents from the plan of merger, shall be entitled to receive the value of the shares so held by him. . . .

§ 215a-1. Interstate Consolidations and Mergers

(a) In General.—A national bank may engage in a consolidation or merger under this Act with an out-of-State bank if the consolidation or merger is approved pursuant to § 1831u. . . .

§ 215a-3. Mergers and Consolidations with Subsidiaries and Nonbank Affiliates

(a) In General.—Upon the approval of the Comptroller, a national bank may merge with one or more of its nonbank subsidiaries or affiliates.
(b) Scope.—Nothing in this section shall be construed . . . to grant a national bank any power or authority that is not permissible for a national bank under other applicable provisions of law.

§ 215c. Mergers, Consolidations, and Other Acquisitions Authorized

(a) In General.—Subject to §§ 1815(d)(3) and 1828(c) and all other applicable laws, any national bank may acquire or be acquired by any insured depository institution. . . .

FEDERAL RESERVE ACT

§ 241. Federal Reserve Board

The Board of Governors of the Federal Reserve System . . . shall be composed of seven members, to be appointed by the President, by and with the advice and consent of the Senate . . . for terms of fourteen years except as hereinafter provided. . . . In selecting the members of the Board . . . , the President shall have due regard to a fair representation of the financial, agricultural, industrial, and commercial interests, and geographical divisions of the country. . . .

§ 250. Independence of Financial Regulatory Agencies

No officer or agency of the United States shall have any authority to require the Securities and Exchange Commission, the Board of Governors of the Federal Reserve System, the Federal Deposit Insurance Corporation, the Comptroller of the Currency, the Director of the Federal Housing Finance Agency, or the National Credit Union Administration to submit legislative recommendations, or testimony, or comments on legislation, to any officer or agency of the United States for approval, comments, or review, prior to the submission of such recommendations, testimony, or comments to the Congress if such recommendations, testimony, or comments to the Congress include a statement indicating that the views expressed therein are those of the agency submitting them and do not necessarily represent the views of the President.

§ 321. Application for Membership

Any bank ... organized under the ... laws of any State or of the United States ... , desiring to become a member of the Federal Reserve System, may make application to the Board of Governors of the Federal Reserve System, under such rules and regulations as it may prescribe, for the right to subscribe to the stock of the Federal Reserve bank organized within the district in which the applying bank is located. ... The Board of Governors of the Federal Reserve System, subject to the provisions of this title and to such conditions as it may prescribe pursuant thereto may permit the applying bank to become a stockholder of such Federal Reserve bank. ...

[N]othing herein contained shall prevent any State member bank from establishing and operating branches ... on the same terms and conditions and subject to the same limitations and restrictions as are applicable to the establishment of branches by national banks. ...

§ 335. Underwriting and Dealing in Securities

State member banks shall be subject to the same limitations and conditions with respect to the purchasing, selling, underwriting, and holding of investment securities and stock as are applicable in the case of national banks under paragraph "Seventh" of § 24. This paragraph shall not apply to any interest [in a financial subsidiary] held by a State member bank in accordance with § 24a and subject to the same conditions and limitations provided in such section.

§ 343. Emergency Lending Through Discount Window

(A) **Emergency lending**.—In unusual and exigent circumstances, the Federal Reserve Board, by the affirmative vote of not less than five members, may authorize any Federal reserve bank ... to discount for any participant in any program or facility with broad-based eligibility, notes, drafts, and bills of exchange when such notes, drafts, and bills of exchange are indorsed or otherwise secured to the satisfaction of the Federal reserve bank: *Provided*, That . . . the Federal reserve bank shall obtain evidence that such participant . . . is unable to secure adequate credit accommodations from other banking institutions. . . .

(B) Safeguards required.—

(i) In general.—[T]he Board shall establish, by regulation, in consultation with the Secretary of the Treasury, . . . policies and procedures . . . designed to ensure that any emergency lending program or facility is for the purpose of providing liquidity to the financial system, and not to aid a failing financial company, and that the security for emergency loans is sufficient to protect taxpayers from losses and that any such program is terminated in a timely and orderly fashion. . . .

(ii) Insolvent borrowers.—The Board shall establish procedures to prohibit borrowing from programs and facilities by borrowers that are insolvent. . . .

(iii) Single-firm rescue program precluded.—A program or facility that is structured to remove assets from the balance sheet of a single and specific company, or that is established for the purpose of assisting a single and specific company avoid bankruptcy [or other] insolvency proceeding, shall not be considered a program or facility with broad-based eligibility.

(iv) Treasury approval required.—The Board may not establish any program or facility under this paragraph without the prior approval of the Secretary of the Treasury. . . .

§ 347b. Ordinary Lending Through Discount Window

(a) In General.—Any Federal Reserve bank, under rules and regulation prescribed by the Board of Governors of the Federal Reserve System, may make advances to any member bank on its time or demand notes having maturities of not more than four months and which are secured to the satisfaction of such Federal Reserve bank. [A]ny Federal Reserve bank, under rules and regulations prescribed by the Board of Governors of the Federal Reserve System, may make advances to any member bank on its time notes having such maturities as the Board may prescribe and which are secured by mortgage loans covering a one-to-four family residence. . . .

(b) Limitations on Advances.—

(1) Limitation on extended periods.—[N]o advances to any undercapitalized depository institution by any Federal Reserve bank under this section may be outstanding for more than 60 days in any 120-day period [unless the institution meets certain viability criteria]. . . .

§ 371. Real Estate Loans

Any national banking association may make, arrange, purchase or sell loans or extensions of credit secured by liens on interests in real estate, subject to . . . such restrictions and requirements as the Comptroller of the Currency may prescribe by regulation or order. . . .

§ 371b-2. Interbank Liabilities

(a) **Purpose**.—The purpose of this section is to limit the risks that the failure of a large depository institution . . . would pose to insured depository institutions.

(b) **Aggregate Limits on Insured Depository Institutions' Exposure to Other Depository Institutions**.—The Board shall, by regulation or order, prescribe standards that have the effect of limiting the risks posed by an insured depository institution's exposure to any other depository institution.

(c) **"Exposure" Defined**.—

(1) **In general**.—For purposes of subsection (b), an insured depository institution's "exposure" to another depository institution means—

(A) all extensions of credit to the other depository institution, regardless of name or description, including—

(i) all deposits at the other depository institution;

(ii) all purchases of securities or other assets from the other depository institution subject to an agreement to repurchase; and

(iii) all guarantees, acceptances, or letters of credit (including endorsements or standby letters of credit) on behalf of the other depository institution;

(B) all purchases of or investments in securities issued by the other depository institution;

(C) all securities issued by the other depository institution accepted as collateral for an extension of credit to any person; and

(D) all similar transactions that the Board by regulation determines to be exposure for purposes of this section.

(2) **Exemptions**.—The Board may, at its discretion, by regulation or order, exempt transactions from the definition of "exposure" if it finds the exemptions to be in the public interest and consistent with the purpose of this section. . . .

§ 371c. Banking Affiliates

(a) **Restrictions on Transactions with Affiliates**.—

(1) **Quantitative limits**.—A member bank and its subsidiaries may engage in a covered transaction with an affiliate only if—

(A) in the case of any affiliate, the aggregate amount of covered transactions of the member bank and its subsidiaries will not exceed 10 per centum of the capital stock and surplus of the member bank; and

(B) in the case of all affiliates, the aggregate amount of covered transactions of the member bank and its subsidiaries will not exceed 20 per centum of the capital stock and surplus of the member bank.

(2) **Direct benefit rule**.—For the purpose of this section, any transaction by a member bank with any person shall be deemed to be a transaction with an affiliate to the extent that the proceeds of the transaction are used for the benefit of, or transferred to, that affiliate.

(3) **Low quality asset**.—A member bank and its subsidiaries may not purchase a low quality asset from an affiliate unless the bank or such subsidiary, pursuant to an independent credit evaluation, committed itself to purchase such asset prior to the time such asset was acquired by the affiliate.

(4) **Overarching safety and soundness requirement**.—Any covered transactions and any transactions exempt under subsection (d) of this section between a member bank and an affiliate shall be on terms and conditions that are consistent with safe and sound banking practices.

(b) **Definitions**.—For the purpose of this section—

(1) the term **"affiliate"** with respect to a member bank means—

(A) any company that controls the member bank and any other company that is controlled by the company that controls the member bank;

(B) a bank subsidiary of the member bank;

(C) any company—

(i) that is controlled directly or indirectly, by a trust or otherwise, by or for the benefit of shareholders who beneficially or otherwise control, directly or indirectly, by trust or otherwise, the member bank or any company that controls the member bank; or

(ii) in which a majority of its directors or trustees constitute a majority of the persons holding any such office with the member bank or any company that controls the member bank;

(D) any investment fund with respect to which a member bank or affiliate thereof is an investment adviser; and

(E) any company that the board determines by regulation or order to have a relationship with the member bank or any subsidiary or affiliate of the member bank, such that covered transactions by the member bank or its subsidiary with that company may be affected by the relationship to the detriment of the member bank or its subsidiary; and

(2) the following shall not be considered to be an affiliate:

(A) any company, other than a bank, that is a subsidiary of a member bank, unless a determination is made under paragraph (1)(E) not to exclude such subsidiary company from the definition of affiliate;

(B) any company engaged solely in holding the premises of the member bank;

(C) any company engaged solely in conducting a safe deposit business;

(D) any company engaged solely in holding obligations of the United States or its agencies or obligations fully guaranteed by the United States or its agencies as to principal and interest; and

(E) any company where control results from the exercise of rights arising out of a bona fide debt previously contracted, but only for the period of time specifically authorized under applicable State or Federal law or regulation or, in the absence of such law or regulation, for a period of two years from the date of the exercise of such rights or the effective date of this Act, whichever date is later, subject, upon application, to authorization by the Board for good cause shown of extensions of time for not more than one year at a time, but such extensions in the aggregate shall not exceed three years;

(3) (A) a company or shareholder shall be deemed to have **control** over another company if—

(i) such company or shareholder, directly or indirectly, or acting through one or more other persons owns, controls, or has power to vote 25 per centum or more of any class of voting securities of the other company;

(ii) such company or shareholder controls in any manner the election of a majority of the directors or trustees of the other company; or

(iii) the Board determines, after notice and opportunity for hearing, that such company or shareholder, directly or indirectly, exercises a controlling influence over the management or policies of the other company; and

(B) notwithstanding any other provision of this section, no company shall be deemed to own or control another company by virtue of its ownership or control of shares in a fiduciary capacity, except as provided in paragraph (1)(C) of this subsection or if the company owning or controlling such shares is a business trust;

(4) the term **"subsidiary"** with respect to a specified company means a company that is controlled by such specified company;

(5) the term **"bank"** includes a State bank, national bank, banking association, and trust company;

(6) the term **"company"** means a corporation, partnership, business trust, association, or similar organization and, unless specifically excluded, the term "company" includes a "member bank" and a "bank";

(7) the term **"covered transaction"** means with respect to an affiliate of a member bank—

(A) a loan or extension of credit to the affiliate, including a purchase of assets subject to an agreement to repurchase;

(B) a purchase of or an investment in securities issued by the affiliate;

(C) a purchase of assets except such purchase of real and personal property as may be specifically exempted by the Board by order or regulation;

(D) the acceptance of securities or other debt obligations issued by the affiliate as collateral security for a loan or extension of credit to any person or company;

(E) the issuance of a guarantee, acceptance, or letter of credit, including an endorsement or standby letter of credit, on behalf of an affiliate;

(F) a transaction with an affiliate that involves the borrowing or lending of securities, to the extent that the transaction causes a member bank or a subsidiary to have credit exposure to the affiliate; or

(G) a derivative transaction, as defined in § 84(b)(3), with an affiliate, to the extent that the transaction causes a member bank or a subsidiary to have credit exposure to the affiliate.

(8) the term **"aggregate amount of covered transactions"** means the amount of the covered transactions about to be engaged in added to the current amount of all outstanding covered transactions;

(9) the term **"securities"** means stocks, bonds, debentures, notes, or other similar obligations; and

(10) the term **"low-quality asset"** means an asset that falls in any one or more of the following categories:

(A) an asset classified as "substandard," "doubtful," or "loss" or treated as "other loans especially mentioned" in the most recent report of examination or inspection of an affiliate prepared by either a Federal or State supervisory agency;

(B) an asset in a nonaccrual status;

(C) an asset on which principal or interest payments are more than thirty days past due; or

(D) an asset whose terms have been renegotiated or compromised due to the deteriorating financial condition of the obligor.

(11) Rebuttable presumption of control of portfolio companies.—In addition to paragraph (3), a company or shareholder shall be presumed to control any other company if the company or shareholder, directly or indirectly, or acting through 1 or more other persons, owns or controls 15 percent or more of the equity capital of the other company pursuant to subparagraph (H) or (I) of § 1843(k)(4) . . . unless the company or shareholder provides information acceptable to the Board to rebut this presumption of control.

(c) Collateral for Certain Transactions with Affiliates.—

(1) Collateral requirement.—Each loan or extension of credit to, or guarantee, acceptance, or letter of credit issued on behalf of, an affiliate by a member bank or its subsidiary, and any credit exposure of a member bank or a subsidiary to an affiliate resulting from a securities borrowing or lending transaction, or a derivative transaction, shall be secured at all times by collateral having a market value equal to—

    (A) 100 per centum of the amount of such loan or extension of credit, guarantee, acceptance, letter of credit, or credit exposure, if the collateral is composed of—

        (i) obligations of the United States or its agencies;

        (ii) obligations fully guaranteed by the United States or its agencies as to principal and interest,

        (iii) notes, drafts, bills of exchange or bankers' acceptances that are eligible for rediscount or purchase by a Federal Reserve Bank; or

        (iv) a segregated, earmarked deposit account with the member bank;

    (B) 110 per centum of the amount of such loan or extension of credit, guarantee, acceptance, letter of credit, or credit exposure if the collateral is composed of obligations of any State or political subdivision of any State;

    (C) 120 per centum of the amount of such loan or extension of credit, guarantee, acceptance, letter of credit, or credit exposure if the collateral is composed of other debt instruments, including receivables; or

    (D) 130 per centum of the amount of such loan or extension of credit, guarantee, acceptance, letter of credit, or credit exposure if the collateral is composed of stock, leases, or other real or personal property.

(2) Low quality asset.—A low-quality asset shall not be acceptable as collateral for a loan or extension of credit to, or guarantee, acceptance, or letter of credit issued on behalf of, an affiliate, or credit exposure to an affiliate resulting from a securities borrowing or lending transaction, or derivative transaction.

(3) Securities issued by affiliate.—The securities or other debt obligations issued by an affiliate of the member bank shall not be acceptable as collateral for a loan or extension of credit to, guarantee, acceptance, or letter of credit issued on behalf of, or credit exposure from a securities borrowing or lending transaction, or derivative transaction to, that affiliate or any other affiliate of the member bank.

(4) Fully secured acceptance.—The collateral requirements of this paragraph shall not be applicable to an acceptance that is already fully secured either by attached documents or by other property having an ascertainable market value that is involved in the transaction.

(d) Exemptions.—The provisions of this section, except [subsection] (a)(4), shall not be applicable to—

    (1) any transaction, subject to the prohibition contained in subsection (a)(3) of this section, with a bank—

        (A) which controls 80 per centum or more of the voting shares of the member bank;

        (B) in which the member bank controls 80 per centum or more of the voting shares; or

(C) in which 80 per centum or more of the voting shares are controlled by the company that controls 80 per centum or more of the voting shares of the member bank;

(2) making deposits in an affiliated bank or affiliated foreign bank in the ordinary course of correspondent business, subject to any restrictions that the Board may prescribe by regulation or order;

(3) giving immediate credit to an affiliate for uncollected items received in the ordinary course of business;

(4) making a loan or extension of credit to, issuing a guarantee, acceptance, or letter of credit on behalf of, or having credit exposure resulting from a securities borrowing or lending transaction, or derivative transaction to, or issuing a guarantee, acceptance, or letter of credit on behalf of, an affiliate that is fully secured by—

(A) obligations of the United States or its agencies;

(B) obligations fully guaranteed by the United States or its agencies as to principal and interest; or

(C) a segregated, earmarked deposit account with the member bank;

(5) purchasing securities issued by any company of the kinds described in § 1843(c)(1);

(6) purchasing assets having a readily identifiable and publicly available market quotation and purchased at that market quotation or, subject to the prohibition contained in subsection (a)(3) of this section, purchasing loans on a nonrecourse basis from affiliated banks; and

(7) purchasing from an affiliate a loan or extension of credit that was originated by the member bank and sold to the affiliate subject to a repurchase agreement or with recourse.

(e) Rules Relating to Banks with Financial Subsidiaries.—

(1) Financial subsidiary defined.—For purposes of this section and § 371c-1, the term "financial subsidiary" means any company that is a subsidiary of a bank that would be a financial subsidiary of a national bank under § 24a.

(2) Financial subsidiary treated as an affiliate.—For purposes of applying this section and § 371c-1, and notwithstanding subsection (b)(2) of this section or § 371c-1(d)(1), a financial subsidiary of a bank—

(A) shall be deemed to be an affiliate of the bank; and

(B) shall not be deemed to be a subsidiary of the bank.

(3) Anti-evasion provision.—For purposes of this section and § 371c-1—

(A) any purchase of, or investment in, the securities of a financial subsidiary of a bank by an affiliate of the bank shall be considered to be a purchase of or investment in such securities by the bank; and

(B) any extension of credit by an affiliate of a bank to a financial subsidiary of the bank shall be considered to be an extension of credit by the bank to the financial subsidiary if the Board determines that such treatment is necessary or appropriate to prevent evasions of this Act and the Gramm-Leach-Bliley Act. . . .

(f) Rulemaking and Additional Exemptions.—

(1) Rulemaking.—The Board may issue such further regulations and orders, including definitions consistent with this section, as may be necessary to administer and carry out the purposes of this section and to prevent evasions thereof.

(2) Exemptions.—

(A) **In general.**—The Board may, at its discretion, by regulation or order exempt transactions or relationships from the requirements of this section if—

(i) the Board finds the exemption to be in the public interest and consistent with the purposes of this section, and notifies the Federal Deposit Insurance Corporation of such finding; and

(ii) before the end of the 60-day period beginning on the date on which the Federal Deposit Insurance Corporation receives notice of the finding under clause (i), the Federal Deposit Insurance Corporation does not object, in writing, to the finding, based on a determination that the exemption presents an unacceptable risk to the Deposit Insurance Fund.

(B) **Additional exemptions.—**

(i) **National banks.**—The Comptroller of the Currency may, by order, exempt a transaction of a national bank from the requirements of this section if—

(I) the Board and the Office of the Comptroller of the Currency jointly find the exemption to be in the public interest and consistent with the purposes of this section and notify the Federal Deposit Insurance Corporation of such finding; and

(II) before the end of the 60-day period beginning on the date on which the Federal Deposit Insurance Corporation receives notice of the finding under subclause (I), the Federal Deposit Insurance Corporation does not object, in writing, to the finding, based on a determination that the exemption presents an unacceptable risk to the Deposit Insurance Fund.

(ii) **State banks.**—The Federal Deposit Insurance Corporation may, by order, exempt a transaction of a State nonmember bank, and the Board may, by order, exempt a transaction of a State member bank, from the requirements of this section if—

(I) the Board and the Federal Deposit Insurance Corporation jointly find that the exemption is in the public interest and consistent with the purposes of this section; and

(II) the Federal Deposit Insurance Corporation finds that the exemption does not present an unacceptable risk to the Deposit Insurance Fund.

(3) Rulemaking required concerning derivative transactions and intraday credit.—

(A) **In general.**—[T]he Board shall adopt final rules under this section to address as covered transactions credit exposure arising out of derivative transactions between member banks and their affiliates and intraday extensions of credit by member banks to their affiliates. . . .

(4) Amounts of covered transactions.—The Board may issue such regulations or interpretations as the Board determines are necessary or appropriate with respect to the manner in which a netting agreement may be taken into account in determining the amount of a covered transaction between a member bank or a subsidiary and an affiliate, including the extent to which netting agreements between a member bank or a subsidiary and an affiliate may be taken into account in determining whether a covered transaction is fully secured for purposes of subsection (d)(4). An interpretation under this paragraph with respect to a specific member bank, subsidiary, or affiliate shall be issued jointly with the appropriate Federal banking agency for such member bank, subsidiary, or affiliate.

§ 371c-1. Restrictions on Transactions with Affiliates

(a) In General.—

(1) Terms.—A member bank and its subsidiaries may engage in any of the transactions described in paragraph (2) only—

(A) on terms and under circumstances, including credit standards, that are substantially the same, or at least as favorable to such bank or its subsidiary, as those prevailing at the time for comparable transactions with or involving other nonaffiliated companies, or

(B) in the absence of comparable transactions, on terms and under circumstances, including credit standards, that in good faith would be offered to, or would apply to, nonaffiliated companies.

(2) Transactions covered.—Paragraph (1) applies to the following:

(A) Any covered transaction with an affiliate.

(B) The sale of securities or other assets to an affiliate, including assets subject to an agreement to repurchase.

(C) The payment of money or the furnishing of services to an affiliate under contract, lease, or otherwise.

(D) Any transaction in which an affiliate acts as an agent or broker or receives a fee for its services to the bank or to any other person.

(E) Any transaction or series of transactions with a third party—

(i) if an affiliate has a financial interest in the third party, or

(ii) if an affiliate is a participant in such transaction or series of transactions.

(3) Transactions that benefit an affiliate.—For the purpose of this subsection, any transaction by a member bank or its subsidiary with any person shall be deemed to be a transaction with an affiliate of such bank if any of the proceeds of the transaction are used for the benefit of, or transferred to, such affiliate.

(b) Prohibited Transactions.—

   (1) In general.—A member bank or its subsidiary—

   (A) shall not purchase as fiduciary any securities or other assets from any affiliate unless such purchase is permitted—

   (i) under the instrument creating the fiduciary relationship,

   (ii) by court order, or

   (iii) by law of the jurisdiction governing the fiduciary relationship; and

   (B) whether acting as principal or fiduciary, shall not knowingly purchase or otherwise acquire, during the existence of any underwriting or selling syndicate, any security if a principal underwriter of that security is an affiliate of such bank.

   (2) Exception.—Subparagraph (B) of paragraph (1) shall not apply if the purchase or acquisition of such securities has been approved, before such securities are initially offered for sale to the public, by a majority of the directors of the bank based on a determination that the purchase is a sound investment for the bank irrespective of the fact that an affiliate of the bank is a principal underwriter of the securities.

   (3) Definitions.—For the purpose of this subsection—

   (A) the term **"security"** has the meaning given to such term in § 78c(a)(10) of title 15; and

   (B) the term **"principal underwriter"** means any underwriter who, in connection with a primary distribution of securities—

   (i) is in privity of contract with the issuer or an affiliated person of the issuer;

   (ii) acting alone or in concert with one or more other persons, initiates or directs the formation of an underwriting syndicate; or

   (iii) is allowed a rate of gross commission, spread, or other profit greater than the rate allowed another underwriter participating in the distribution.

(c) Advertising Restriction.—A member bank or any subsidiary or affiliate of a member bank shall not publish any advertisement or enter into any agreement stating or suggesting that the bank shall in any way be responsible for the obligations of its affiliates. . . .

(e) Regulations.—

   (1) In general.—The Board may prescribe regulations to administer and carry out the purposes of this section, including—

   (A) regulations to further define terms used in this section; and

   (B) subject to paragraph (2), if the Board finds that an exemption or exclusion is in the public interest and is consistent with the purposes of this section, and notifies the Federal Deposit Insurance Corporation of such finding, regulations to—

(i) exempt transactions or relationships from the requirements of this section; and

(ii) exclude any subsidiary of a bank holding company from the definition of affiliate for purposes of this section.

(2) Exception.—The Board may grant an exemption or exclusion under this subsection only if, during the 60-day period beginning on the date of receipt of notice of the finding from the Board under paragraph (1)(B), the Federal Deposit Insurance Corporation does not object, in writing, to such exemption or exclusion, based on a determination that the exemption presents an unacceptable risk to the Deposit Insurance Fund.

§ 375a. Loans to Executive Officers of Member Banks

(1) In general.—Except as authorized under this section, no member bank may extend credit in any manner to any of its own executive officers. No executive officer of any member bank may become indebted to that member bank except by means of an extension of credit which the bank is authorized to make under this section. Any extension of credit under this section shall be promptly reported to the board of directors of the bank, and may be made only if—

(A) the bank would be authorized to make it to borrowers other than its officers;

(B) it is on terms not more favorable than those afforded other borrowers;

(C) the officer has submitted a detailed current financial statement; and

(D) it is on condition that it shall become due and payable on demand of the bank at any time when the officer is indebted to any other bank or banks on account of extensions of credit of any one of the three categories respectively referred to in paragraphs (2), (3), and (4) in an aggregate amount greater than the amount of credit of the same category that could be extended to him by the bank of which he is an officer.

(2) Mortgage loans.—A member bank may make a loan to any executive officer of the bank if, at the time the loan is made—

(A) it is secured by a first lien on a dwelling which is expected, after the making of the loan, to be owned by the officer and used by him as his residence, and

(B) no other loan by the bank to the officer under authority of this paragraph is outstanding.

(3) Educational loans.—A member bank may make extensions of credit to any executive officer of the bank to finance the education of the children of the officer.

(4) Other credit.—A member bank may make extensions of credit not otherwise specifically authorized under this section to any executive officer of the bank, in an amount prescribed in a regulation of the member bank's appropriate Federal banking agency.

(5) Partnership loans.—Except to the extent permitted under paragraph (4), a member bank may not extend credit to a partnership in which one or more of its executive officers are partners having either individually or together a majority interest. For the purposes of paragraph (4), the full amount of any credit so extended shall be considered to have been extended to each officer of the bank who is a member of the partnership.

(6) Protecting bank.—This section does not prohibit any executive officer of a member bank from endorsing or guaranteeing for the protection of the bank any loan or other asset previously acquired by the bank in good faith or from incurring any indebtedness to the bank for the purpose of protecting the bank against loss or giving financial assistance to it. . . .

(8) Rules and regulations; definitions.—The Board of Governors of the Federal Reserve System may prescribe such rules and regulations, including definitions of terms, as it deems necessary to effectuate the purposes and to prevent evasions of this section.

§ 375b. Extensions of Credit to Executive Officers, Directors, and Principal Shareholders of Member Banks

(1) In general.—No member bank may extend credit to any of its executive officers, directors, or principal shareholders, or to any related interest of such a person, except to the extent permitted under paragraphs (2), (3), (4), (5), and (6).

(2) Preferential terms prohibited.—

(A) **In general**.—A member bank may extend credit to its executive officers, directors, or principal shareholders, or to any related interest of such a person, only if the extension of credit—

(i) is made on substantially the same terms, including interest rates and collateral, as those prevailing at the time for comparable transactions by the bank with persons who are not executive officers, directors, principal shareholders, or employees of the bank;

(ii) does not involve more than the normal risk of repayment or present other unfavorable features; and

(iii) the bank follows credit underwriting procedures that are not less stringent than those applicable to comparable transactions by the bank with persons who are not executive officers, directors, principal shareholders, or employees of the bank.

(B) Exception.—Nothing in this paragraph shall prohibit any extension of credit made pursuant to a benefit or compensation program—

(i) that is widely available to employees of the member bank; and

(ii) that does not give preference to any officer, director, or principal shareholder of the member bank, or to any related interest of such person, over other employees of the member bank.

(3) Prior approval required.—A member bank may extend credit to a person described in paragraph (1) in an amount that, when aggregated with the amount of all other outstanding extensions of credit by that bank to each such person and that person's related interests, would exceed an amount prescribed by regulation of the appropriate Federal banking agency (as defined in § 1813) only if—

(A) the extension of credit has been approved in advance by a majority vote of that bank's entire board of directors; and

(B) the interested party has abstained from participating, directly or indirectly, in the deliberations or voting on the extension of credit.

(4) Aggregate limit on extensions of credit to any executive officer, director, or principal shareholder.—A member bank may extend credit to any executive officer, director, or principal shareholder, or to any related interest of such a person, only if the extension of credit is in an amount that, when aggregated with the amount of all outstanding extensions of credit by that bank to that person and that person's related interests, would not exceed the limits on loans to a single borrower established by § 84. For purposes of this paragraph, § 84 shall be deemed to apply to a State member bank as if the State member bank were a national banking association.

(5) Aggregate limit on extensions of credit to all executive officers, directors, and principal shareholders.—

(A) In general.—A member bank may extend credit to any executive officer, director, or principal shareholder, or to any related interest of such a person, if the extension of credit is in an amount that, when aggregated with the amount of all outstanding extensions of credit by that bank to its executive officers, directors, principal shareholders, and those persons' related interests would not exceed the bank's unimpaired capital and unimpaired surplus.

(B) More stringent limit authorized.—The Board may, by regulation, prescribe a limit that is more stringent than that contained in subparagraph (A).

(C) Board may make exceptions for certain banks.—The Board may, by regulation, make exceptions to subparagraph (A) for member banks with less than $100,000,000 in deposits if the Board determines that the exceptions are important to avoid constricting the availability of credit in small communities or to attract directors to such banks. In no case may the aggregate amount of all outstanding extensions of credit to a bank's executive officers, directors, principal shareholders, and those persons' related interests be more than 2 times the bank's unimpaired capital and unimpaired surplus.

(6) Overdrafts by executive officers and directors prohibited.—

(A) In general.—If any executive officer or director has an account at the member bank, the bank may not pay on behalf of that person an amount exceeding the funds on deposit in the account.

(B) Exceptions.—Subparagraph (A) does not prohibit a member bank from paying funds in accordance with—

(i) a written preauthorized, interest-bearing extension of credit specifying a method of repayment; or

(ii) a written preauthorized transfer of funds from another account of the executive officer or director at that bank.

(7) Prohibition on knowingly receiving unauthorized extension of credit.—No executive officer, director, or principal shareholder shall knowingly receive (or knowingly permit any of that person's related interests to receive) from a member bank, directly or indirectly, any extension of credit not authorized under this section.

(8) Executive officer, director, or principal shareholder of certain affiliates treated as executive officer, director, or principal shareholder of member bank.—

(A) In general.—For purposes of this section, any executive officer, director, or principal shareholder (as the case may be) of any company of which the member bank is a subsidiary, or of any other subsidiary of that company, shall be deemed to be an executive officer, director, or principal shareholder (as the case may be) of the member bank.

(B) Exception.—The Board may, by regulation, make exceptions to subparagraph (A) for any executive officer or director of a subsidiary of a company that controls the member bank if—

(i) the executive officer or director does not have authority to participate, and does not participate, in major policymaking functions of the member bank; and

(ii) the assets of such subsidiary do not exceed 10 percent of the consolidated assets of a company that controls the member bank and such subsidiary (and is not controlled by any other company).

(9) Definitions.—For purposes of this section:

(A) Company.—

(i) **In general.**—Except as provided in clause (ii), the term "company" means any corporation, partnership, business or other trust, association, joint venture, pool syndicate, sole proprietorship, unincorporated organization, or other business entity.

(ii) **Exceptions.**—The term "company" does not include

(I) an insured depository institution (as defined in § 1813); or

(II) a corporation the majority of the shares of which are owned by the United States or by any State.

(B) Control.—A person controls a company or bank if that person, directly or indirectly, or acting through or in concert with 1 or more persons—

(i) owns, controls, or has the power to vote 25 percent or more of any class of the company's voting securities;

(ii) controls in any manner the election of a majority of the company's directors; or

(iii) has the power to exercise a controlling influence over the company's management or policies.

(C) Executive officer.—A person is an "executive officer" of a company or bank if that person participates or has authority to participate (other than as a director) in major policymaking functions of the company or bank.

(D) Extension of credit.—

(i) **In general**.—A member bank extends credit to a person by—

(I) making or renewing any loan, granting a line of credit, or entering into any similar transaction as a result of which the person becomes obligated (directly or indirectly, or by any means whatsoever) to pay money or its equivalent to the bank; or

(II) having credit exposure to the person arising from a derivative transaction (as defined in § 84(b)), repurchase agreement, reverse repurchase agreement, securities lending transaction, or securities borrowing transaction between the member bank and the person.

(E) Member bank.—The term "member bank" includes any subsidiary of a member bank.

(F) Principal shareholder.—The term "principal shareholder"—

(i) means any person that directly or indirectly, or acting through or in concert with one or more persons, owns, controls, or has the power to vote more than 10 percent of any class of voting securities of a member bank or company; and

(ii) does not include a company of which a member bank is a subsidiary.

(G) Related interest.—A "related interest" of a person is—

(i) any company controlled by that person; and

(ii) any political or campaign committee that is controlled by that person or the funds or services of which will benefit that person.

(H) Subsidiary.—The term "subsidiary" has the same meaning as in § 1841.

(10) Board's rulemaking authority.—The Board of Governors of the Federal Reserve System may prescribe such regulations, including definitions of terms, as it determines to be necessary to effectuate the purposes and prevent evasions of this section.

§ 378. Deposit-Taking by Securities Dealers and Unregulated Firms

(a) **In General.**—[I]t shall be unlawful—

(1) **Deposit-taking by securities underwriter prohibited.**—For any person, firm, corporation, association, business trust, or other similar organization, engaged in the business of issuing, underwriting, selling, or distributing, at wholesale or retail, or through syndicate participation, stocks, bonds, debentures, notes, or other securities, to engage at the same time to any extent whatever in the business of receiving deposits subject to check or to repayment upon presentation of a passbook, certificate of deposit, or other evidence of debt, or upon request of the depositor: *Provided*, That the provisions of this paragraph shall not prohibit national banks or State banks or trust companies (whether or not members of the Federal Reserve System) or other financial institutions or private bankers from dealing in, underwriting, purchasing, and selling investment securities, or issuing securities, to the extent permitted to national banking associations by the provisions of § 24: *Provided further*, That nothing in this paragraph shall be construed as affecting in any way such right as any bank, banking association, savings bank, trust company, or other banking institution, may otherwise possess to sell, without recourse or agreement to repurchase, obligations evidencing loans on real estate; or

(2) **Unregulated deposit-taking prohibited.**—For any person, firm, corporation, association, business trust, or other similar organization to engage, to any extent whatever with others than his or its officers, agents or employees, in the business of receiving deposits subject to check or to repayment upon presentation of a pass book, certificate of deposit, or other evidence of debt, or upon request of the depositor, unless such person, firm, corporation, association, business trust, or other similar organization (A) shall be incorporated under, and authorized to engage in such business by, the laws of the United States or of any State . . . and subjected, by the laws of the United States, or of the State . . . wherein located, to examination and regulation, or (B) shall be permitted by the United States, any State . . . to engage in such business and shall be subjected by the laws of the United States, or such State . . . , (C) shall submit to periodic examination by the banking authority of the State . . . where such business is carried on and shall make and publish periodic reports of its condition, exhibiting in detail its resources and liabilities . . . .

(b) **Penalty.**—Whoever shall willfully violate any of the provisions of this section shall upon conviction be fined not more than $5,000 or imprisoned not more than five years, or both, and any officer, director, employee, or agent of any person, firm, corporation, association, business trust, or other similar organization who knowingly participates in any such violation shall be punished by a like fine or imprisonment or both.

§ 484. Limit [on] Visitorial Powers

(A) In general.—No national bank shall be subject to any visitorial powers except as authorized by Federal law, vested in the courts of justice or such as shall be, or have been exercised or directed by Congress or by either House thereof or by any committee of Congress or of either House duly authorized.

(B) Unclaimed property laws.—Notwithstanding subparagraph (A), lawfully authorized State auditors and examiners may, at reasonable times and upon reasonable notice to a bank, review its records solely to ensure compliance with applicable State unclaimed property or escheat laws upon reasonable cause to believe that the bank has failed to comply with such laws.

§ 601. Foreign Banking

Any national banking association possessing a capital and surplus of $1,000,000 or more may file application with the Board of Governors of the Federal Reserve System for permission to exercise, upon such conditions and under such regulations as may be prescribed by the said board, the following powers:

First. To establish branches in foreign countries or dependencies or insular possessions of the United States for the furtherance of the foreign commerce of the United States, and to act if required to do so as fiscal agents of the United States.

Second. To invest an amount not exceeding in the aggregate 10 per centum of its paid—in capital stock and surplus in the stock of one or more banks or corporations chartered or incorporated under the laws of the United States or of any State thereof, and principally engaged in international or foreign banking, or banking in a dependency or insular possession of the United States either directly or through the agency, ownership, or control of local institutions in foreign countries, or in such dependencies or insular possessions.

Third. To acquire and hold, directly or indirectly, stock or other evidences of ownership in one or more banks organized under the law of a foreign country or a dependency or insular possession of the United States and not engaged, directly or indirectly, in any activity in the United States except as, in the judgment of the Board of Governors of the Federal Reserve System, shall be incidental to the international or foreign business of such foreign bank; and, notwithstanding the provisions of § 371c, to make loans or extensions of credit to or for the account of such bank in the manner and within the limits prescribed by the Board by general or specific regulation or ruling. . . .

§ 604. Separate Accounts for Foreign Branches

Every national banking association operating foreign branches shall conduct the accounts of each foreign branch independently of the accounts of other foreign branches established by it and of its home office, and shall at the end of each fiscal period transfer to its general ledger the profit or loss accrued at each branch as a separate item.

§ 604a. Foreign Branches May Have Usual Powers of Local Banks

Regulations issued by the Board of Governors of the Federal Reserve System under this Act, in addition to regulating powers which a foreign branch may exercise under other provisions of law, may authorize such a foreign branch, subject to such conditions and requirements as such regulations may prescribe, to exercise such further powers as may be usual in connection with the transaction of the business of banking in the places where such foreign branch shall transact business. Such regulations shall not authorize a foreign branch to engage in the general business of producing, distributing, buying or selling goods, wares, or merchandise; nor, except to such limited extent as the Board may deem to be necessary with respect to securities issued by any "foreign state" . . . , shall such regulations authorize a foreign branch to engage or participate, directly or indirectly, in the business of underwriting, selling, or distributing securities.

HOME OWNERS' LOAN ACT

§ 1462. Definitions

For purposes of this Act—
    (1) Corporation.—The term "Corporation" means the Federal Deposit Insurance Corporation.
    (2) Savings association.—The term "savings association" means a savings association, as defined in § 1813, the deposits of which are insured by the Corporation.
    (3) Federal savings association.—The term "Federal savings association" means a Federal savings association or a Federal savings bank chartered under § 1464. . . .
    (7) Affiliate.—The term "affiliate" means any person that controls, is controlled by, or is under common control with, a savings association, except as provided in § 1467a.

(8) Board.—The term "Board", other than in the context of the Board of Directors of the Corporation, means the Board of Governors of the Federal Reserve System. . . .

(11) Functionally regulated subsidiary.—The term "functionally regulated subsidiary" has the same meaning as in § 1844(c)(5).

§ 1463. Supervision of Savings Associations

(a) Savings Associations.—
  (1) Examination and safe and sound operation.—
    (A) Federal savings associations.—The Comptroller shall provide for the examination and safe and sound operation of Federal savings associations.
    (B) State savings associations.—The Corporation shall provide for the examination and safe and sound operation of State savings associations.
  (2) Regulations for savings associations.—The Comptroller may prescribe regulations with respect to savings associations, as the Comptroller determines to be appropriate to carry out the purposes of this Act.
  (3) Safe and sound housing credit to be encouraged.—The Comptroller and the Corporation shall exercise all powers granted to the Comptroller and the Corporation under this Act so as to encourage savings associations to provide credit for housing safely and soundly.
(b) Accounting and Disclosure.—
  (1) In general.—The Comptroller shall, by regulation, prescribe uniform accounting and disclosure standards for savings associations, to be used in determining savings associations' compliance with all applicable regulations.
  (2) Specific requirements for accounting standards.—[T]he uniform accounting standards prescribed under paragraph (1) shall . . . incorporate generally accepted accounting principles to the same degree that such principles are used to determine compliance with regulations prescribed by the Federal banking agencies. . . .
  (3) Authority to prescribe more stringent accounting standards.—The Comptroller may at any time prescribe accounting standards more stringent than required under paragraph (2) if the Comptroller determines that the more stringent standards are necessary to ensure the safe and sound operation of savings associations.
(c) Stringency of Standards.—The regulations of the Comptroller and the policies of the Comptroller and the Corporation governing the safe and sound operation of savings associations, including regulations and policies governing asset classification and appraisals, shall be no less stringent than those established by the Comptroller for national banks. . . .

§ 1464. Federal Savings Associations

(a) **In General**.—In order to provide thrift institutions for the deposit of funds and for the extension of credit for homes and other goods and services, the Comptroller of the Currency is authorized, under such regulations as the Comptroller of the Currency may prescribe—

(1) to provide for the organization, incorporation, examination, operation, and regulation of associations to be known as Federal savings associations (including Federal savings banks), and

(2) to issue charters therefor,

giving primary consideration of the best practices of thrift institutions in the United States. The lending and investment powers conferred by this section are intended to encourage such institutions to provide credit for housing safely and soundly.

(b) **Deposits and Related Powers**.—

(1) **Deposit accounts**.—

(A) Subject to the terms of its charter and regulations of the Comptroller of the Currency, a Federal savings association may—

(i) raise funds through such deposit, share, or other accounts, including demand deposit accounts (hereafter in this section referred to as "accounts"); and

(ii) issue passbooks, certificates, or other evidence of accounts.

(B) A Federal savings association may not permit any overdraft (including an intraday overdraft) on behalf of an affiliate. . . .

(2) **Other liabilities**.—To such extent as the Comptroller of the Currency may authorize in writing, a Federal savings association may borrow, may give security, may be surety . . . and may issue such notes, bonds, debentures, or other obligations, or other securities, including capital stock. . . .

(c) **Loans and Investments**.—To the extent specified in regulations of the Comptroller, a Federal savings association may invest in, sell, or otherwise deal in the following loans and other investments:

(1) **Loans or investments without percentage of assets limitation**.—Without limitation as a percentage of assets, the following are permitted:

(A) **Account loans**.—Loans on the security of its savings accounts and loans specifically related to transaction accounts.

(B) **Residential real property loans**.—Loans on the security of liens upon residential real property.

(C) **United States government securities**.—Investments in obligations of, or fully guaranteed as to principal and interest by, the United States.

(D) **Federal home loan bank and Federal National Mortgage Association Securities**.—Investments in the stock or bonds of a Federal home loan bank or in the stock of the Federal National Mortgage Association.

(E) Federal Home Loan Mortgage Corporation instruments.—Investments in mortgages, obligations, or other securities . . . sold by the Federal Home Loan Mortgage Corporation. . . .

(F) Other government securities.—Investments in obligations, participations, securities, or other instruments issued by, or fully guaranteed as to principal and interest by, the Federal National Mortgage Association, . . . the Government National Mortgage Association, or any agency of the United States. . . .

(G) Deposits.—Investments in accounts of any insured depository institution. . . .

(H) State securities.—Investments in obligations issued by any State or political subdivision thereof (including any agency, corporation, or instrumentality of a State or political subdivision). A Federal savings association may not invest more than 10 percent of its capital in obligations of any one issuer, exclusive of investments in general obligations of any issuer.

(I) Purchase of insured loans.—Purchase of loans secured by liens on improved real estate which are insured or guaranteed [by the Federal Housing Administration or the Department of Veterans Affairs].

(J) Home improvement and manufactured home loans.—Loans made to repair, equip, alter, or improve any residential real property, and loans made for manufactured home financing.

(K) Insured loans to finance the purchase of fee simple.—Loans insured [by the Federal Housing Administration] under § 1715z-5.

(L) Loans to financial institutions, brokers, and dealers.—Loans to—

    (i) financial institutions with respect to which the United States or an agency or instrumentality thereof has any function of examination or supervision, or

    (ii) any broker or dealer registered with the Securities and Exchange Commission,

which are secured by loans, obligations, or investments in which the Federal savings association has the statutory authority to invest directly.

(M) Liquidity investments.—Investments (other than equity investments), identified by the Comptroller, for liquidity purposes, including cash, funds on deposit at a Federal reserve bank or a Federal home loan bank, or bankers' acceptances. . . .

(O) Certain HUD insured or guaranteed investments.—Loans that are secured by mortgages . . . guaranteed . . . under § 1440 of title 42. . . .

(Q) **Investment companies.**—A Federal savings association may invest in, redeem, or hold shares or certificates issued by any open-end management investment company which—

(i) is registered with the Securities and Exchange Commission under the Investment Company Act of 1940, and

(ii) the portfolio of which is restricted by such management company's investment policy (changeable only if authorized by shareholder vote) solely to investments that a Federal savings association by law or regulation may, without limitation as to percentage of assets, invest in, sell, redeem, hold, or otherwise deal in.

(R) **Mortgage-backed securities.**—Investments in securities that—

(i) are offered and sold pursuant to 15 U.S.C. § 77d(5); or

(ii) are mortgage related securities (as defined in 15 U.S.C. § 78c(a)(41)),

subject to such regulations as the Comptroller may prescribe, including regulations prescribing minimum size of the issue (at the time of initial distribution) or minimum aggregate sales price, or both.

(S) **Small business related securities.**—Investments in small business related securities (as defined in 15 U.S.C. § 78c(a)(53)). . . .

(T) **Credit card loans.**—Loans made through credit cards or credit card accounts.

(U) **Educational loans.**—Loans made for the payment of educational expenses.

(2) **Loans or investments limited to a percentage of assets or capital.**—The following loans or investments are permitted, but only to the extent specified:

(A) **Commercial and other loans.**—Secured or unsecured loans for commercial, corporate, business, or agricultural purposes. The aggregate amount of loans made under this subparagraph may not exceed 20 percent of the total assets of the Federal savings association, and amounts in excess of 10 percent of such total assets may be used under this subparagraph only for small business loans, as that term is defined by the Comptroller.

(B) **Nonresidential real property loans.**—

(i) **In general.**—Loans on the security of liens upon nonresidential real property.—Except as provided in clause (ii), the aggregate amount of such loans shall not exceed 400 percent of the Federal savings association's capital. . . .

(ii) **Exception.**—The Comptroller may permit a savings association to exceed the limitation set forth in clause (i) if the Comptroller determines that the increased authority—

(I) poses no significant risk to the safe and sound operation of the association, and

(II) is consistent with prudent operating practices. . . .

(C) Investments in personal property.—Investments in tangible personal property including vehicles, manufactured homes, machinery, equipment, or furniture, for rental or sale. Investments under this subparagraph may not exceed 10 percent of the assets of the Federal savings association.

(D) Consumer loans and certain securities.—A Federal savings association may make loans for personal, family, or household purposes, including loans reasonably incident to providing such credit, and may invest in, sell, or hold commercial paper and corporate debt securities, as defined and approved by the Comptroller. Loans and other investments under this subparagraph may not exceed 35 percent of the assets of the Federal savings association, except that amounts in excess of 30 percent of the assets may be invested only in loans which are made by the association directly to the original obligor and with respect to which the association does not pay any finder, referral, or other fee, directly or indirectly, to any third party.

(3) Loans or investments limited to 5 percent of assets.—The following loans or investments are permitted, but not to exceed 5 percent of assets of a Federal savings association for each subparagraph:

(A) Community development investments.—Investments in real property and obligations secured by liens on real property located within a geographic area or neighborhood receiving concentrated development assistance by a local government under title I of the Housing and Community Development Act of 1974. No investment under this subparagraph in such real property may exceed an aggregate of 2 percent of the assets of the Federal savings association.

(B) Nonconforming loans.—Loans upon the security of or respecting real property or interests therein used for primarily residential or farm purposes that do not comply with the limitations of this subsection.

(C) Construction loans without security.—Loans—

(i) the principal purpose of which is to provide financing with respect to what is or is expected to become primarily residential real estate; and

(ii) with respect to which the association—

(I) relies substantially on the borrower's general credit standing and projected future income for repayment, without other security; or

(II) relies on other assurances for repayment, including a guarantee or similar obligation of a third party.

The aggregate amount of such investments shall not exceed the greater of the Federal savings association's capital or 5 percent of its assets.

(4) Other loans and investments.—The following additional loans and other investments to the extent authorized below: . . .

(B) **Service corporations**.—Investments in the capital stock, obligations, or other securities of any corporation organized under the laws of the State in which the Federal savings association's home office is located, if such corporation's entire capital stock is available for purchase only by savings associations of such State and by Federal associations having their home offices in such State. No Federal savings association may make any investment under this subparagraph if the association's aggregate outstanding investment under this subparagraph would exceed 3 percent of the association's assets. Not less than one-half of the investment permitted under this subparagraph which exceeds 1 percent of the association's assets shall be used primarily for community, inner-city, and community development purposes.

(E) **Bankers' banks**.—A Federal savings association may purchase for its own account shares of stock of a bankers' bank . . . on the same terms and conditions as a national bank may purchase such shares.

(F) **New Markets Venture Capital companies**.—A Federal savings association may invest in stock, obligations, or other securities of any New Markets Venture Capital company as defined in . . . the Small Business Investment Act of 1958, except that a Federal savings association may not make any investment under this subparagraph if its aggregate outstanding investment under this subparagraph would exceed 5 percent of the capital and surplus of such savings association. . . .

(6) **Definitions**.—For purposes of this subsection, the following definitions shall apply:

(A) **Residential property**.—The terms "residential real property" or "residential real estate" mean leaseholds, homes (including condominiums and cooperatives, except that in connection with loans on individual cooperative units, such loans shall be adequately secured as defined by the Comptroller) and, combinations of homes or dwelling units and business property, involving only minor or incidental business use, or property to be improved by construction of such structures.

(B) **Loans**.—The term "loans" includes obligations and extensions or advances of credit; and any reference to a loan or investment includes an interest in such a loan or investment. . . .

(e) **Character and Responsibility**.—A charter may be granted only—

(1) to persons of good character and responsibility,

(2) if in the judgment of the Comptroller a necessity exists for such an institution in the community to be served,

(3) if there is a reasonable probability of its usefulness and success, and

(4) if the association can be established without undue injury to properly conducted existing local thrift and home financing institutions. . . .

(n) **Trusts**.— . . . The Comptroller may grant by special permit to a Federal savings association applying therefor the right to act as trustee, executor, administrator, guardian, or in any other fiduciary capacity in which State banks, trust companies, or other corporations which compete with Federal savings associations are permitted to act under the laws of the State in which the Federal savings association is located. . . . .

(r) Out-of-State Branches.—

(1) In general.—No Federal savings association may establish, retain, or operate a branch outside the State in which the Federal savings association has its home office, unless the association qualifies as a domestic building and loan association under 26 U.S.C. § 7701(a)(19) or meets the asset composition test imposed by § 7701(a)(19)(C) on institutions seeking so to qualify, or qualifies as a qualified thrift lender, as determined under § 1467a(m). No out-of-State branch so established shall be retained or operated unless the total assets of the Federal savings association attributable to all branches of the Federal savings association in that State would qualify the branches as a whole, were they otherwise eligible, for treatment as a domestic building and loan association under 26 U.S.C. § 7701(a)(19) or as a qualified thrift lender . . . under § 1467a(m), as applicable.

(2) Exceptions.—The limitations of paragraph (1) shall not apply if— . . .

(C) the law of the State where the branch is located, or is to be located, would permit establishment of the branch if the association was a savings association or savings bank chartered by the State in which its home office is located; or

(D) the branch was operated lawfully as a branch under State law prior to the association's conversion to a Federal charter. . . .

§ 1467a. Regulation of Holding Companies

(a) Definitions.—

(1) In general.—As used in this section, unless the context otherwise requires—

(A) Savings association.—The term "savings association" includes a savings bank or cooperative bank which is deemed by the appropriate Federal banking agency to be a savings association under subsection (*l*).

(B) Uninsured institution.—The term "uninsured institution" means any depository institution the deposits of which are not insured by the Federal Deposit Insurance Corporation. . . .

(D) Savings and loan holding company.—

(i) In general.—Except as provided in clause (ii), the term "savings and loan holding company" means any company that directly or indirectly controls a savings association or that controls any other company that is a savings and loan holding company.

(ii) Exceptions.—The term "savings and loan holding company" does not include—

(I) a bank holding company that is registered under, and subject to, the Bank Holding Company Act of 1956, or to any company directly or indirectly controlled by such company (other than a savings association);

(II) a company that controls a savings association that functions solely in a trust or fiduciary capacity . . . ; or

(III) a company described in subsection (c)(9)(C) solely by virtue of such company's control of an intermediate holding company established pursuant to § 1467b.

(E) Multiple savings and loan holding company.—The term "multiple savings and loan holding company" means any savings and loan holding company which directly or indirectly controls 2 or more savings associations. . . .

(b) Registration and Examination.—

(1) In general.—Within 90 days after becoming a savings and loan holding company, each savings and loan holding company shall register with the Board on forms prescribed by the Board, which shall include such information . . . with respect to the financial condition, ownership, operations, management, and intercompany condition, ownership, operations, management, and intercompany relationships of such holding company and its subsidiaries, and related matters, as the Board may deem necessary or appropriate to carry out the purposes of this section. . . .

(4) Examinations.—

(A) In general.—[T]he Board may make examinations of a savings and loan holding company and each subsidiary of a savings and loan holding company system, in order to—

(i) inform the Board of—

(I) the nature of the operations and financial condition of the savings and loan holding company and the subsidiary;

(II) the financial, operational, and other risks within the savings and loan holding company system that may pose a threat to—

(aa) the safety and soundness of the savings and loan holding company or of any depository institution subsidiary of the savings and loan holding company; or

(bb) the stability of the financial system of the United States; and

(III) the systems of the savings and loan holding company for monitoring and controlling the risks described in subclause (II); and

(ii) monitor the compliance of the savings and loan holding company and the subsidiary with—

(I) this Act;

(II) Federal laws that the Board has specific jurisdiction to enforce against the company or subsidiary; and

(III) other than in the case of an insured depository institution or functionally regulated subsidiary, any other applicable provisions of Federal law. . . .

(C) Coordination with other regulators.—The Board shall—

(i) provide reasonable notice to, and consult with, the appropriate Federal banking agency, the Securities and Exchange Commission, the Commodity Futures Trading Commission, or State regulatory agency, as appropriate, for a subsidiary that is a depository institution or a functionally regulated subsidiary of a savings and loan holding company before commencing an examination of the subsidiary under this section; and

(ii) to the fullest extent possible, avoid duplication of examination activities, reporting requirements, and requests for information. . . .

(c) Holding Company Activities.—

(1) Prohibited activities.—Except as otherwise provided in this subsection, no savings and loan holding company and no subsidiary which is not a savings association shall—

(A) engage in any activity or render any service for or on behalf of a savings association subsidiary for the purpose or with the effect of evading any law or regulation applicable to such savings association;

(B) commence any business activity, other than the activities described in paragraph (2); or

(C) continue any business activity, other than the activities described in paragraph (2), after the end of the 2-year period beginning on the date on which such company received approval under subsection (e) of this section to become a savings and loan holding company subject to the limitations contained in this subparagraph.

(2) Exempt activities.—The prohibitions of subparagraphs (B) and (C) of paragraph (1) shall not apply to the following business activities of any savings and loan holding company or any subsidiary (of such company) which is not a savings association:

(A) Furnishing or performing management services for a savings association subsidiary of such company.

(B) Conducting an insurance agency or escrow business.

(C) Holding, managing, or liquidating assets owned or acquired from a savings association subsidiary of such company.

(D) Holding or managing properties used or occupied by a savings association subsidiary of such company.

(E) Acting as trustee under deed of trust.

(F) Any other activity—

(i) which the Board, by regulation, has determined to be permissible for bank holding companies § 1843(c), unless the Board, by regulation, prohibits or limits any such activity for savings and loan holding companies; or

(ii) in which multiple savings and loan holding companies were authorized (by regulation) to directly engage on March 5, 1987. . . .

(H) Any activity that is permissible for a financial holding company . . . to conduct under § 1843(k) if—

(i) the savings and loan holding company meets all of the criteria to qualify as a financial holding company, and complies with all of the requirements applicable to a financial holding company, under § 1843(*l*) and (m) and § 2903(c) as if the savings and loan holding company was a bank holding company; and

(ii) the savings and loan holding company conducts the activity in accordance with the same terms, conditions, and requirements that apply to the conduct of such activity by a bank holding company under the Bank Holding Company Act of 1956 and the Board's regulations and interpretations under such Act.

(3) Certain limitations on activities not applicable to certain holding companies.—[T]he limitations contained in subparagraphs (B) and (C) of paragraph (1) shall not apply to any savings and loan holding company (or any subsidiary of such company) which controls—

(A) only 1 savings association, if the savings association subsidiary of such company is a qualified thrift lender . . . ; or

(B) more than 1 savings association, if—

(i) all, or all but 1, of the savings association subsidiaries of such company were initially acquired by the company . . . pursuant to an acquisition [of a failed or failing insured depository institution; and]

(ii) all of the savings association subsidiaries of such company are qualified thrift lenders. . . .

(4) Prior approval of certain new activities required.—

(A) In general.—No savings and loan holding company and no subsidiary which is not a savings association shall commence, either de novo or by an acquisition (in whole or in part) of a going concern, any activity described in paragraph (2)(F)(i) of this subsection without the prior approval of the Board.

(B) Factors to be considered.—In considering any application under subparagraph (A) by any savings and loan holding company or any subsidiary of any such company which is not a savings association, the Board shall consider—

(i) whether the performance of the activity described in such application by the company or the subsidiary can reasonably be expected to produce benefits to the public (such as greater convenience, increased competition, or gains in efficiency) that outweigh possible adverse effects of such activity (such as undue concentration of resources, decreased or unfair competition, conflicts of interest, or unsound financial practices);

(ii) the managerial resources of the companies involved; and

(iii) the adequacy of the financial resources, including capital, of the companies involved. . . .

(5) Grace period to achieve compliance.—If any savings association referred to in paragraph (3) fails to maintain the status of such association as a qualified thrift lender, the Board may allow, for good cause shown, any company that controls such association (or any subsidiary of such company which is not a savings association) up to 3 years to comply with the limitations contained in paragraph (1)(C). . . .

(9) Prevention of new affiliations between S&L holding companies and commercial firms.—

(A) In general.—Notwithstanding paragraph (3), no company may directly or indirectly, including through any merger, consolidation, or other type of business combination, acquire control of a savings association after May 4, 1999, unless the company is engaged, directly or indirectly (including through a subsidiary other than a savings association), only in activities that are permitted—

(i) under paragraph (1)(C) or (2) of this subsection; or

(ii) for financial holding companies under § 1843(k).

(B) Prevention of new commercial affiliations.—Notwithstandsing paragraph (3), no savings and loan holding company may engage directly or indirectly (including through a subsidiary other than a savings association) in any activity other than as described in clauses (i) and (ii) of subparagraph (A).

(C) Preservation of authority of existing unitary S&L holding companies.—Subparagraphs (A) and (B) do not apply with respect to any company that was a savings and loan holding company on May 4, 1999, or that becomes a savings and loan holding company pursuant to an application pending before the Office on or before that date, and that—

(i) meets and continues to meet the requirements of paragraph (3); and

(ii) continues to control not fewer than 1 savings association that it controlled on May 4, 1999, or that it acquired pursuant to an application pending before the Office on or before that date, or the successor to such savings association.

(D) Corporate reorganizations permitted.—This paragraph does not prevent a transaction that—

(i) involves solely a company under common control with a savings and loan holding company from acquiring, directly or indirectly, control of the savings and loan holding company or any savings association that is already a subsidiary of the savings and loan holding company; or

(ii) involves solely a merger, consolidation, or other type of business combination as a result of which a company under common control with the savings and loan holding company acquires, directly or indirectly, control of the savings and loan holding company or any savings association that is already a subsidiary of the savings and loan holding company.

(E) Authority to prevent evasions.—The Board may issue interpretations, regulations, or orders that the Board determines necessary to administer and carry out the purpose and prevent evasions of this paragraph, including a determination ... that, notwithstanding the form of a transaction, the transaction would in substance result in a company acquiring control of a savings association. ...

(e) Acquisitions.—

(1) In general.—It shall be unlawful for—

(A) any savings and loan holding company directly or indirectly, or through one or more subsidiaries or through one or more transactions—

(i) to acquire, except with the prior written approval of the Board, the control of a savings association or a savings and loan holding company, or to retain the control of such an association or holding company acquired or retained in violation of this section as heretofore or hereafter in effect;

(ii) to acquire, except with the prior written approval of the Board, by the process of merger, consolidation, or purchase of assets, another savings association or a savings and loan holding company, or all or substantially all of the assets of any such association or holding company;

(iii) to acquire, by purchase or otherwise, or to retain, except with the prior written approval of the Board, more than 5 percent of the voting shares of a savings association not a subsidiary, or of a savings and loan holding company not a subsidiary, or in the case of a multiple savings and loan holding company ... , to acquire or retain, and the Board may not authorize acquisition or retention of, more than 5 percent of the voting shares of any company not a subsidiary which is engaged in any business activity other than the activities specified in subsection (c)(2). This clause shall not apply to shares of a savings association or of a savings and loan holding company—

(I) held as a bona fide fiduciary (whether with or without the sole discretion to vote such shares);

(II) held temporarily pursuant to an underwriting commitment in the normal course of an underwriting business;

(III) held in an account solely for trading purposes;

(IV) over which no control is held other than control of voting rights acquired in the normal course of a proxy solicitation;

(V) acquired in securing or collecting a debt previously contracted in good faith, during the 2-year period beginning on the date of such acquisition or for such additional time (not exceeding 3 years) as the Board may permit if the Board determines that such an extension will not be detrimental to the public interest;

(VI) acquired [in connection with the acquisition of a failed or failing insured depository institution; or]

(VII) held by any insurance company . . . , except as provided in paragraph (6); or

except that the aggregate amount of shares held under this clause (other than under subclauses (I), (II), (III), (IV), and (VI)) may not exceed 15 percent of all outstanding shares or of the voting power of a savings association or savings and loan holding company; or

(iv) to acquire [or retain] the control of an uninsured institution. . . . , ; and

(B) any other company, without the prior written approval of the Board, directly or indirectly, or through one or more subsidiaries or through one or more transactions, to acquire the control of one or more savings associations. . . . The Board shall approve an acquisition of a savings association under this subparagraph unless the Board finds the financial and managerial resources and future prospects of the company and association involved to be such that the acquisition would be detrimental to the association or the insurance risk of the Deposit Insurance Fund, and shall render a decision within 90 days after submission to the Board of the complete record on the application.

Consideration of the managerial resources of a company or savings association under subparagraph (B) shall include consideration of the competence, experience, and integrity of the officers, directors, and principal shareholders of the company or association.

(2) Factors to be considered.—The Board shall not approve any acquisition under subparagraph (A)(i) or (A)(ii), or of more than one savings association under subparagraph (B) of paragraph (1) of this subsection, . . . or any transaction under section § 1823(k), except in accordance with this paragraph. In every case, the Board shall take into consideration the financial and managerial resources and future prospects of the company and association involved, the effect of the acquisition on the association, the insurance risk to the Deposit Insurance Fund, and the convenience and needs of the community to be served, and shall render a decision within 90 days after submission to the Board of the complete record on the application. Consideration of the managerial resources of a company or savings association shall include consideration of the competence, experience, and integrity of the officers, directors, and principal shareholders of the company or association. . . . The Board shall not approve any proposed acquisition—

(A) which would result in a monopoly, or which would be in furtherance of any combination or conspiracy to monopolize or to attempt to monopolize the savings and loan business in any part of the United States,

(B) the effect of which in any section of the country may be substantially to lessen competition, or tend to create a monopoly, or which in any other manner would be in restraint of trade, unless it finds that the anticompetitive effects of the proposed acquisition are clearly outweighed in the public interest by the probable effect of the acquisition in meeting the convenience and needs of the community to be served,

(C) if the company fails to provide adequate assurances to the Board that the company will make available to the Board such information on the operations or activities of the company, and any affiliate of the company, as the Board determines to be appropriate to determine and enforce compliance with this Act,

(D) in the case of an application involving a foreign bank, if the foreign bank is not subject to comprehensive supervision or regulation on a consolidated basis by the appropriate authorities in the bank's home country, or

(E) in the case of an application by a savings and loan holding company to acquire an insured depository institution, if—

(i) the home State of the insured depository institution is a State other than the home State of the savings and loan holding company;

(ii) the applicant (including all insured depository institutions which are affiliates of the applicant) controls, or upon consummation of the transaction would control, more than 10 percent of the total amount of deposits of insured depository institutions in the United States; and

(iii) the acquisition does not involve [a failed or failing insured depository institution]. . . .

(6) Shares held by insurance affiliates.—Shares described in clause (iii)(VII) of paragraph (1)(A) shall not be excluded for purposes of clause (iii) of such paragraph if—

(A) all shares held under such clause (iii)(VII) by all insurance company affiliates of such savings association or savings and loan holding company in the aggregate exceed 5 percent of all outstanding shares or of the voting power of the savings association or savings and loan holding company; or

(B) such shares are acquired or retained with a view to acquiring, exercising, or transferring control of the savings association or savings and loan holding company. . . .

(g) Administration and Enforcement.—

(1) In general.—The Board is authorized to issue such regulations and orders, including regulations and orders relating to capital requirements for savings and loan holding companies, as the Board deems necessary or appropriate to enable the Board to administer and carry out the purposes of this section, and to require compliance therewith and prevent evasions thereof. In establishing capital regulations pursuant to this subsection, the appropriate Federal banking agency shall seek to make such requirements countercyclical so that the amount of capital required to be maintained by a company increases in times of economic expansion and decreases in times of economic contraction, consistent with the safety and soundness of the company. . . .

(m) Qualified Thrift Lender Test.—

(1) In general.—[A]ny savings association is a qualified thrift lender if—

(A) the savings association qualifies as a domestic building and loan association, as such term is defined in 26 U.S.C. § 7701(a)(19); or

(B)

(i) the savings association's qualified thrift investments equal or exceed 65 percent of the savings association's portfolio assets; and

(ii) the savings association's qualified thrift investments continue to equal or exceed 65 percent of the savings association's portfolio assets on a monthly average basis in 9 out of every 12 months.

(2) Exceptions granted by appropriate Federal banking agency.—Notwithstanding paragraph (1), the appropriate Federal banking agency may grant such temporary and limited exceptions from the minimum actual thrift investment percentage requirement contained in such paragraph as the appropriate Federal banking agency deems necessary if—

(A) the appropriate Federal banking agency determines that extraordinary circumstances exist, such as when the effects of high interest rates reduce mortgage demand to such a degree that an insufficient opportunity exists for a savings association to meet such investment requirements. . . .

(3) Failure to become and remain a qualified thrift lender.—

(A) In general.—A savings association that fails to become or remain a qualified thrift lender shall immediately be subject to the restrictions under subparagraph (B).

(B) Restrictions applicable to savings associations that are not qualified thrift lenders.—

(i) **Restrictions effective immediately.**—The following restrictions shall apply to a savings association beginning on the date on which the savings association should have become or ceases to be a qualified thrift lender:

   (I) **Activities**.—The savings association shall not make any new investment (including an investment in a subsidiary) or engage, directly or indirectly, in any other new activity unless that investment or activity would be permissible for the savings association if it were a national bank, and is also permissible for the savings association as a savings association. . . .

   (III) **Dividends**.—The savings association may not pay dividends, except for dividends that—

      (aa) would be permissible for a national bank;

      (bb) are necessary to meet obligations of a company that controls such savings association; and

      (cc) are specifically approved by the Comptroller of the Currency and the Board after a written request submitted to the Comptroller of the Currency and the Board by the savings association not later than 30 days before the date of the proposed payment. . . .

   (ii) **Additional restrictions effective after 3 years**.—Beginning 3 years after the date on which a savings association should have become a qualified thrift lender, or the date on which the savings association ceases to be a qualified thrift lender, as applicable, the savings association shall not retain any investment (including an investment in any subsidiary) or engage, directly or indirectly, in any activity, unless that investment or activity—

      (I) would be permissible for the savings association if it were a national bank; and

      (II) is permissible for the savings association as a savings association.

   (C) **Holding company regulation**.—Any company that controls a savings association that is subject to any provision of subparagraph (B) shall, within one year after the date on which the savings association should have become or ceases to be a qualified thrift lender, register as and be deemed to be a bank holding company subject to all of the provisions of the Bank Holding Company Act of 1956 . . . and other statutes applicable to bank holding companies, in the same manner and to the same extent as if the company were a bank holding company and the savings association were a bank. . . .

   (D) **Requalification**.—A savings association that should have become or ceases to be a qualified thrift lender shall not be subject to subparagraph (B) or (C) if the savings association becomes a qualified thrift lender by meeting the qualified thrift lender requirement in paragraph (1) on a monthly average basis in 9 out of the preceding 12 months and remains a qualified thrift lender. If the savings association (or any savings association that acquired all or substantially all of its assets from that savings association) at any time thereafter ceases to be a qualified thrift lender, it shall immediately be subject to all provisions of subparagraphs (B) and (C) as if all the periods described in subparagraphs (B)(ii) and (C) had expired. . . .

(4) Definitions.—For purposes of this subsection, the following definitions shall apply:

(A) Actual thrift investment percentage.—The term "actual thrift investment percentage" means the percentage determined by dividing—

(i) the amount of a savings association's qualified thrift investments, by

(ii) the amount of the savings association's portfolio assets.

(B) Portfolio assets.—The term "portfolio assets" means, with respect to any savings association, the total assets of the savings association, minus the sum of—

(i) goodwill and other intangible assets;

(ii) the value of property used by the savings association to conduct its business; and

(iii) liquid assets of the type required to be maintained under section 6 of the Home Owners' Loan Act, as in effect on the day before the date of the enactment of the Financial Regulatory Relief and Economic Efficiency Act of 2000 [enacted Dec. 27, 2000], in an amount not exceeding the amount equal to 20 percent of the savings association's total assets.

(C) Qualified thrift investments.—

(i) In general.—The term "qualified thrift investments" means, with respect to any savings association, the assets of the savings association that are described in clauses (ii) and (iii).

(ii) Assets includible without limit.—The following assets are described in this clause for purposes of clause (i):

(I) The aggregate amount of loans held by the savings association that were made to purchase, refinance, construct, improve, or repair domestic residential housing or manufactured housing.

(II) Home-equity loans.

(III) Securities backed by or representing an interest in mortgages on domestic residential housing or manufactured housing. . . .

(VI) Shares of stock issued by any Federal home loan bank.

(VII) Loans for educational purposes, loans to small businesses, and loans made through credit cards or credit card accounts.

(iii) Assets includible subject to percentage restriction.—The following assets are described in this clause for purposes of clause (i):

(I) 50 percent of the dollar amount of the residential mortgage loans originated by such savings association and sold within 90 days of origination.

(II) Investments in the capital stock or obligations of, and any other security issued by, any service corporation if such service corporation derives at least 80 percent of its annual gross revenues from activities directly related to purchasing, refinancing, constructing, improving, or repairing domestic residential real estate or manufactured housing.

(III) 200 percent of the dollar amount of loans and investments made to acquire, develop, and construct 1- to 4-family residences the purchase price of which is or is guaranteed to be not greater than 60 percent of the median value of comparable newly constructed 1- to 4-family residences within the local community in which such real estate is located, except that not more than 25 percent of the amount included under this subclause may consist of commercial properties related to the development if those properties are directly related to providing services to residents of the development.

(IV) 200 percent of the dollar amount of loans for the acquisition or improvement of residential real property, churches, schools, and nursing homes located within, and loans for any other purpose to any small businesses located within any area which has been identified by the appropriate Federal banking agency, in connection with any review or examination of community reinvestment practices, as a geographic area or neighborhood in which the credit needs of the low- and moderate-income residents of such area or neighborhood are not being adequately met.

(V) Loans for the purchase or construction of churches, schools, nursing homes, and hospitals . . . and loans for the improvement and upkeep of such properties.

(VI) Loans for personal, family, or household purposes. . . .

(VII) Shares of stock issued by the Federal Home Loan Mortgage Corporation or the Federal National Mortgage Association.

(iv) Percentage restriction applicable to certain assets.—The aggregate amount of the assets described in clause (iii) which may be taken into account in determining the amount of the qualified thrift investments of any savings association shall not exceed the amount which is equal to 20 percent of a savings association's portfolio assets. . . .

(p) Holding Company Activities Constituting Serious Risk to Subsidiary Savings Association.—

(1) Determination and imposition of restrictions.—If the Board or the appropriate Federal banking agency for the savings association determines that there is reasonable cause to believe that the continuation by a savings and loan holding company of any activity constitutes a serious risk to the financial safety, soundness, or stability of a savings and loan holding company's subsidiary savings association, the Board may impose such restrictions as the Board, in consultation with the appropriate Federal banking agency for the savings association determines to be necessary to address such risk. Such restrictions shall be issued in the form of a directive to the holding company and any of its subsidiaries, limiting—

(A) the payment of dividends by the savings association;

(B) transactions between the savings association, the holding company, and the subsidiaries or affiliates of either; and

(C) any activities of the savings association that might create a serious risk that the liabilities of the holding company and its other affiliates may be imposed on the savings association. . . .

(t) Exemption for Bank Holding Companies.—This section shall not apply to a bank holding company that is subject to the Bank Holding Company Act of 1956, or any company controlled by such bank holding company.

§ 1467b. Intermediate Holding Companies

(a) Definition.—For purposes of this section:

(1) Financial activities.—The term "financial activities" means activities described in clauses (i) and (ii) of § 1467a(c)(9)(A).

(2) Grandfathered unitary savings and loan holding company.—The term "grandfathered unitary savings and loan holding company" means a company described in § 1467a(c)(9)(C).

(3) Internal financial activities.—The term "internal financial activities" includes—

(A) internal financial activities conducted by a grandfathered savings and loan holding company or any affiliate; and

(B) internal treasury, investment, and employee benefit functions.

(b) Requirement.—

(1) In general.—

(A) **Activities other than financial activities.**—If a grandfathered unitary savings and loan holding company conducts activities other than financial activities, the Board may require such company to establish and conduct all or a portion of such financial activities in or through an intermediate holding company, which shall be a savings and loan holding company, established pursuant to regulations of the Board, not later than 90 days (or such longer period as the Board may deem appropriate) after the transfer date.

(B) Other activities.—Notwithstanding subparagraph (A), the Board shall require a grandfathered unitary savings and loan holding company to establish an intermediate holding company if the Board makes a determination that the establishment of such intermediate holding company is necessary—

(i) to appropriately supervise activities that are determined to be financial activities; or

(ii) to ensure that supervision by the Board does not extend to the activities of such company that are not financial activities.

(2) Internal financial activities.—

(A) Treatment of internal financial activities.—For purposes of this subsection, the internal financial activities of a grandfathered unitary savings and loan holding company shall not be required to be placed in an intermediate holding company.

(B) Grandfathered activities.—A grandfathered unitary savings and loan holding company may continue to engage in an internal financial activity, subject to review by the Board to determine whether engaging in such activity presents undue risk to the grandfathered unitary savings and loan holding company or to the financial stability of the United States, if—

(i) the grandfathered unitary savings and loan holding company engaged in the activity during the year before the date of enactment of this section; and

(ii) at least 2/3 of the assets or 2/3 of the revenues generated from the activity are from or attributable to the grandfathered unitary savings and loan holding company.

(3) Source of strength.—A grandfathered unitary savings and loan holding company that directly or indirectly controls an intermediate holding company established under this section shall serve as a source of strength to its subsidiary intermediate holding company. . . .

(c) Regulations.—The Board—

(1) shall promulgate regulations to establish the criteria for determining whether to require a grandfathered unitary savings and loan holding company to establish an intermediate holding company under subsection (b); and

(2) may promulgate regulations to establish any restrictions or limitations on transactions between an intermediate holding company or a parent of such company and its affiliates, as necessary to prevent unsafe and unsound practices in connection with transactions between the

intermediate holding company, or any subsidiary thereof, and its parent company or affiliates that are not subsidiaries of the intermediate holding company, except that such regulations shall not restrict or limit any transaction in connection with the bona fide acquisition or lease by an unaffiliated person of assets, goods, or services.

(d) Rules of Construction.—

(1) **Activities.**—Nothing in this section shall be construed to require a grandfathered unitary savings and loan holding company to conform its activities to permissible activities.

(2) **Permissible corporate reorganization.**—The formation of an intermediate holding company as required in subsection (b) shall be presumed to be a permissible corporate reorganization as described in § 1467a(c)(9)(D).

FEDERAL DEPOSIT INSURANCE ACT

§ 1811. Federal Deposit Insurance Corporation

(a) **Establishment of Corporation.**—There is hereby established a Federal Deposit Insurance Corporation (hereinafter referred to as the "Corporation") which shall insure, as hereinafter provided, the deposits of all banks and savings associations which are entitled to the benefits of insurance under this Act, and which shall have the powers hereinafter granted. . . .

§ 1812. Management

(a) **Board of Directors.—**

(1) **In general.**—The management of the Corporation shall be vested in a Board of Directors consisting of 5 members—

(A) 1 of whom shall be the Comptroller of the Currency;

(B) 1 of whom shall be the Director of the Consumer Financial Protection Bureau; and

(C) 3 of whom shall be appointed by the President, by and with the advice and consent of the Senate, from among individuals who are citizens of the United States, 1 of whom shall have State bank supervisory experience.

(2) **Political affiliation.**—[N]ot more than 3 of the members of the Board of Directors may be members of the same political parry.

(b) **Chairperson and Vice Chairperson.—**

(1) **Chairperson.**—1 of the appointed members shall be designated by the President, by and with the advice and consent of the Senate, to serve as Chairperson of the Board of Directors for a term of 5 years.

(2) Vice chairperson.—1 of the appointed members shall be designated by the President, by and with the advice and consent of the Senate, to serve as Vice Chairperson of the Board of Directors.

(3) Acting chairperson.—In the event of a vacancy in the position of Chairperson of the Board of Directors or during the absence or disability of the Chairperson, the Vice Chairperson shall act as Chairperson.

(c) Terms.—

(1) Appointed members.—Each appointed member shall be appointed for a term of 6 years.

(2) Interim appointments.—Any member appointed to fill a vacancy occurring before the expiration of the term for which such member's predecessor was appointed shall be appointed only for the remainder of such term. . . .

§ 1813. Definitions

As used in this Act—. . . .

(c) Definitions Relating to Depository Institutions.—

(1) Depository institution.—The term "depository institution" means any bank or savings association.

(2) Insured depository institution.—The term "insured depository institution" means any bank or savings association the deposits of which are insured by the Corporation pursuant to this Act. . . .

(k) Board of Directors.—The term "Board of Directors" means the Board of Directors of the Corporation.

(*l*) Deposit.—The term "deposit" means—

(1) the unpaid balance of money or its equivalent received or held by a bank or savings association in the usual course of business and for which it has given or is obligated to give credit, either conditionally or unconditionally, to a commercial, checking, savings, time, or thrift account, or which is evidenced by its certificate of deposit, thrift certificate, investment certificate, certificate of indebtedness, or other similar name, or a check or draft drawn against a deposit account and certified by the bank or savings association, or a letter of credit or a traveler's check on which the bank or savings association is primarily liable: *Provided*, That, without limiting the generality of the term "money or its equivalent," any such account or instrument must be regarded as evidencing the receipt of the equivalent of money when credited or issued in exchange for checks or drafts or for a promissory note upon which the person obtaining any such credit or instrument is primarily or secondarily liable, or for a charge against a deposit account, or in settlement of checks, drafts, or other instruments forwarded to such bank or savings association for collection,

(2) trust funds as defined in this Act received or held by such bank or savings association, whether held in the trust department or held or deposited in any other department of such bank or savings association,

(3) money received or held by a bank or savings association, or the credit given for money or its equivalent received or held by a bank or savings association, in the usual course of business for a special or specific purpose, regardless of the legal relationship thereby established, including without being limited to, escrow funds, funds held as security for an obligation due to the bank or savings association or others (including funds held as dealers reserves) or for securities loaned by the bank or savings association, funds deposited by a debtor to meet maturing obligations, funds deposited as advance payment on subscriptions to United States Government securities, funds held for distribution or purchase of securities, funds held to meet its acceptances or letters of credit, and withheld taxes: *Provided*, That there shall not be included funds which are received by the bank or savings association for immediate application to the reduction of an indebtedness to the receiving bank or savings association, or under condition that the receipt thereof immediately reduces or extinguishes such an indebtedness,

(4) outstanding draft (including advice or authorization to charge a bank's or a savings association's balance in another bank or savings association), cashier's check, money order, or other officer's check issued in the usual course of business for any purpose, including without being limited to those issued in payment for services, dividends, or purchases, and

(5) such other obligations of a bank or savings association as the Board of Directors . . . shall find and prescribe by regulation to be deposit liabilities by general usage, except that the following shall not be a deposit for any of the purposes of this Act or be included as part of the total deposits or of an insured deposit:

(A) any obligation of a depository institution which is carried on the books and records of an office of such bank or savings association located outside of any State, unless—

(i) such obligation would be a deposit if it were carried on the books and records of the depository institution, and would be payable at, an office located in any State; and

(ii) the contract evidencing the obligation provides by express terms, and not by implication, for payment at an office of the depository institution located in any State;

(B) any international banking facility deposit . . . ; and

(C) any liability of an insured depository institution that arises under an annuity contract, the income of which is tax deferred under § 72 of title 26.

(m) Insured Deposit.—

(1) In general.—Subject to paragraph (2), the term "insured deposit" means the net amount due to any depositor for deposits in an insured depository institution as determined under §§ 1817(i) [relating to insurance of trust funds] and 1821(a) of this title.

(2) U.S. deposits of foreign banks.—In the case of any deposit in a branch of a foreign bank, the term "insured deposit" means an insured deposit as defined in paragraph (1) of this subsection which—

(A) is payable in the United States to—

(i) an individual who is a citizen or resident of the United States,

(ii) a partnership, corporation, trust, or other legally cognizable entity created under the laws of the United States or any State and having its principal place of business within the United States or any State, or

(iii) an individual, partnership, corporation, trust, or other legally cognizable entity which is determined by the Board of Directors in accordance with its regulations to have such business or financial relationships in the United States as to make the insurance of such deposit consistent with the purposes of this Act; and

(B) meets any other criteria prescribed by the Board of Directors by regulation as necessary or appropriate in its judgment to carry out the purposes of this Act or to facilitate the administration thereof.

(3) Uninsured deposits.—The term "uninsured deposit" means the amount of any deposit of any depositor at any insured depository institution in excess of the amount of the insured deposits of such depositor (if any) at such depository institution. . . .

(q) Appropriate Federal Banking Agency.—The term "appropriate Federal banking agency" means—

(1) the Office of the Comptroller of the Currency, in the case of—

(A) any national banking association;

(B) any Federal branch or agency of a foreign bank; and

(C) any Federal savings association;

(2) the Federal Deposit Insurance Corporation, in the case of—

(A) any State nonmember insured bank;

(B) any foreign bank having an insured branch; and

(C) any State savings association;

(3) the Board of Governors of the Federal Reserve System, in the case of—

(A) any State member bank;

(B) any branch or agency of a foreign bank with respect to any provision of the Federal Reserve Act which is made applicable under the International Banking Act of 1978;

(C) any foreign bank which does not operate an insured branch;

(D) any agency or commercial lending company other than a Federal agency;

(E) supervisory or regulatory proceedings arising from the authority given to the Board of Governors under . . . the International Banking Act of 1978 . . . ;

(F) any bank holding company and any subsidiary (other than a depository institution) of a bank holding company; and

(G) any savings and loan holding company and any subsidiary (other than a depository institution) of a savings and loan holding company.

(u) Institution-Affiliated Party.—The term "institution-affiliated party" means—

(1) any director, officer, employee, or controlling stockholder (other than a bank holding company) of, or agent for, an insured depository institution;

(2) any other person who has filed or is required to file a change-in-control notice with the appropriate Federal banking agency under § 1817(j);

(3) any shareholder (other than a bank holding company), consultant, joint venture partner, and any other person as determined by the appropriate Federal banking agency (by regulation or case-by-case) who participates in the conduct of the affairs of an insured depository institution; and

(4) any independent contractor (including any attorney, appraiser, or accountant) who knowingly or recklessly participates in—

(A) any violation of any law or regulation;

(B) any breach of fiduciary duty; or

(C) any unsafe or unsound practice, which caused or is likely to cause more than a minimal financial loss to, or a significant adverse effect on, the insured depository institution. . . .

(w) Definitions relating to affiliates of depository institutions.— . . .

(4) Subsidiary.—The term "subsidiary"—

(A) means any company which is owned or controlled directly or indirectly by another company; and

(B) includes any service corporation owned in whole or in part by an insured depository institution or any subsidiary of such a service corporation.

(5) Control.—The term "control" has the meaning given to such term in § 1841.

(6) Affiliate.—The term "affiliate" has the meaning given to such term in § 1841(k).

(7) Company. The term "company" has the same meaning as in § 1841(b).

(x) Definitions Relating to Default.—

(1) Default.—The term "default" means, with respect to an insured depository institution, any adjudication or other official determination by any court of competent jurisdiction, the appropriate Federal banking agency, or other public authority pursuant to which a conservator, receiver, or other legal custodian is appointed for an insured depository institution or, in the case of a foreign bank having an insured branch, for such branch.

(2) In danger of default.—The term "in danger of default" means an insured depository institution with respect to which (or in the case of a foreign bank having an insured branch, with respect to such insured branch) the appropriate Federal banking agency or State chartering authority has advised the Corporation (or, if the appropriate Federal banking agency is the Corporation, the Corporation has determined) that—

(A) in the opinion of such agency or authority—

(i) the depository institution or insured branch is not likely to be able to meet the demands of the institution's or branch's depositors or pay the institution's or branch's obligations in the normal course of business; and

(ii) there is no reasonable prospect that the depository institution or insured branch will be able to meet such demands or pay such obligations without Federal assistance; or

(B) in the opinion of such agency or authority—

(i) the depository institution or insured branch has incurred or is likely to incur losses that will deplete all or substantially all of its capital; and

(ii) there is no reasonable prospect that the capital of the depository institution or insured branch will be replenished without Federal assistance.

(y) Definitions Relating to Deposit Insurance Fund.—

(1) Deposit Insurance Fund.—The term "Deposit Insurance Fund" means the Deposit Insurance Fund established under § 1821(a)(4). . . .

(3) Reserve ratio.—The term "reserve ratio," when used with regard to the Deposit Insurance Fund other than in connection with a reference to the designated reserve ratio, means the ratio of the net worth of the Deposit Insurance Fund to the value of the aggregate estimated insured deposits.

(z) Federal Banking Agency.—The term "Federal banking agency" means the Comptroller of the Currency, the Board of Governors of the Federal Reserve System, or the Federal Deposit Insurance Corporation.

§ 1815. Deposit Insurance

(a) Application to Corporation Required.—

(1) In general.—Except as provided in paragraphs (2) and (3), any depository institution which is engaged in the business of receiving deposits other than trust funds (as defined in § 1813(p)), upon application to and examination by the Corporation and approval by the Board of Directors, may become an insured depository institution. . . .

(e) Liability of Commonly Controlled Depository Institutions.—
(1) In general.—
(A) **Liability established.**—Any insured depository institution shall be liable for any loss incurred by the Corporation, or any loss which the Corporation reasonably anticipates incurring, . . . in connection with—

(i) the default of a commonly controlled insured depository institution; or

(ii) any assistance provided by the Corporation to any commonly controlled insured depository institution in danger of default. . . .

(8) Commonly controlled defined.—For purposes of this subsection, depository institutions are commonly controlled if—

(A) such institutions are controlled by the same company; or

(B) 1 depository institution is controlled by another depository institution.

§ 1816. Factors to Be Considered [in Granting Insurance]

The factors that are required, under § 1814, to be considered in connection with, and enumerated in, any certificate issued pursuant to § 1814 and that are required, under § 1815, to be considered by the Board of Directors in connection with any determination by such Board pursuant to § 1815 are the following:

(1) The financial history and condition of the depository institution.

(2) The adequacy of the depository institution's capital structure.

(3) The future earnings prospects of the depository institution.

(4) The general character and fitness of the management of the depository institution.

(5) The risk presented by such depository institution to the Deposit Insurance Fund.

(6) The convenience and needs of the community to be served by such depository institution.

(7) Whether the depository institution's corporate powers are consistent with the purposes of this Act. . . .

§ 1817. Assessments

. . . **(b) Assessments.—**
(1) Risk-based assessment system.—
(A) **Risk-based assessment system required.**—The Board of Directors shall, by regulation, establish a risk-based assessment system for insured depository institutions. . . .

(C) Risk-based assessment system defined.—For purposes of this paragraph, the term "risk-based assessment system" means a system for calculating a depository institution's assessment based on—

(i) the probability that the Deposit Insurance Fund will incur a loss with respect to the institution, taking into consideration the risks attributable to—

(I) different categories and concentrations of assets;

(II) different categories and concentrations of liabilities, both insured and uninsured, contingent and noncontingent; and

(III) any other factors the Corporation determines are relevant to assessing such probability;

(ii) the likely amount of any such loss; and

(iii) the revenue needs of the Deposit Insurance Fund.

(D) Separate assessment systems.—The Board of Directors may establish separate risk-based assessment systems for large and small members of the Deposit Insurance Fund. . . .

(F) Modifications to the risk-based assessment system allowed only after notice and comment.—In revising or modifying the risk-based assessment system . . . , the Board of Directors may implement such revisions or modification in final form only after notice and opportunity for comment.

(2) Setting assessments.—

(A) In general.—The Board of Directors shall set assessments for insured depository institutions in such amounts as the Board of Directors may determine to be necessary or appropriate, subject to subparagraph (D).

(B) Factors to be considered.—In setting assessments under subparagraph (A), the Board of Directors shall consider the following factors:

(i) The estimated operating expenses of the Deposit Insurance Fund.

(ii) The estimated case resolution expenses and income of the Deposit Insurance Fund.

(iii) The projected effects of the payment of assessments on the capital and earnings of insured depository institutions.

(iv) The risk factors and other factors taken into account pursuant to paragraph (1) under the risk-based assessment system, including the requirement under such paragraph to maintain a risk-based system.

(v) Any other factors the Board of Directors may determine to be appropriate. . . .

(D) No discrimination based on size.—No insured depository institution shall be barred from the lowest-risk category solely because of size. . . .

(3) Designated reserve ratio.—
(A) Establishment.—
(i) **In general**.—Before the beginning of each calendar year, the Board of Directors shall designate the reserve ratio applicable with respect to the Deposit Insurance Fund and publish the reserve ratio so designated.

(ii) **Rulemaking requirement**.—Any change to the designated reserve ratio shall be made by the Board of Directors by regulation after notice and opportunity for comment.

(B) Range.—The reserve ratio designated by the Board of Directors for any year—

(i) may not exceed 1.5 percent of estimated insured deposits; and

(ii) may not be less than 1.15 percent of estimated insured deposits.

(C) Factors.—In designating a reserve ratio for any year, the Board of Directors shall—

(i) take into account the risk of losses to the Deposit Insurance Fund in such year and future years, including historic experience and potential and estimated losses from insured depository institutions;

(ii) take into account economic conditions generally affecting insured depository institutions so as to allow the designated reserve ratio to increase during more favorable economic conditions and to decrease during less favorable economic conditions, notwithstanding the increased risks of loss that may exist during such less favorable conditions, as determined to be appropriate by the Board of Directors;

(iii) seek to prevent sharp swings in the assessment rates for insured depository institutions; and

(iv) take into account such other factors as the Board of Directors may determine to be appropriate, consistent with the requirements of this subparagraph. . . .

(j) Change in Control of Insured Depository Institutions.—

(1) Prior written notice required.—No person, acting directly or indirectly or through or in concert with one or more other persons, shall acquire control of any insured depository institution through a purchase, assignment, transfer, pledge, or other disposition of voting stock of such insured depository institution unless the appropriate Federal banking agency has been given sixty days' prior written notice of such proposed acquisition and within that time period the agency has not issued a notice disapproving the proposed acquisition or, in the discretion of the agency, extending for an additional 30 days the period during which such a disapproval may issue. The period for disapproval under the preceding sentence may be extended not to exceed 2 additional times for not more than 45 days each time if—

(A) the agency determines that any acquiring party has not furnished all the information required under paragraph (6);

(B) in the agency's judgment, any material information submitted is substantially inaccurate;

(C) the agency has been unable to complete the investigation of an acquiring party under paragraph (2)(B) because of any delay caused by, or the inadequate cooperation of, such acquiring party; or

(D) the agency determines that additional time is needed—

(i) to investigate and determine that no acquiring party has a record of failing to comply with the requirements of subchapter II of chapter 53 of title 31 [relating to monetary transactions and money laundering]; or

(ii) to analyze the safety and soundness of any plans or proposals described in paragraph (6)(E) or the future prospects of the institution.

An acquisition may be made prior to expiration of the disapproval period if the agency issues written notice of its intent not to disapprove the action.

(2) Procedure.— . . .

(B) Investigation of principals required.—Upon receiving any notice under this subsection, the appropriate Federal banking agency shall—

(i) conduct an investigation of the competence, experience, integrity, and financial ability of each person named in a notice of a proposed acquisition as a person by whom or for whom such acquisition is to be made; and

(ii) make an independent determination of the accuracy and completeness of any information described in paragraph (6) with respect to such person.

(C) Report.—The appropriate Federal banking agency shall prepare a written report of any investigation under subparagraph (B) which shall contain, at a minimum, a summary of the results of such investigation. The agency shall retain such written report as a record of the agency.

(D) Public comment.—Upon receiving notice of a proposed acquisition, the appropriate Federal banking agency shall, unless such agency determines that an emergency exists, within a reasonable period of time—

(i) publish the name of the insured depository institution proposed to be acquired and the name of each person identified in such notice as a person by whom or for whom such acquisition is to be made; and

(ii) solicit public comment on such proposed acquisition, particularly from persons in the geographic area where the [depository institution] proposed to be acquired is located, before final consideration of such notice by the agency,

unless the agency determines in writing that such disclosure or solicitation would seriously threaten the safety or soundness of such [depository institution].

(3) Disapproval.—Within three days after its decision to disapprove any proposed acquisition, the appropriate Federal banking agency shall notify the acquiring party in writing of the disapproval. Such notice shall provide a statement of the basis for the disapproval.

(4) Hearing.—Within ten days of receipt of such notice of disapproval, the acquiring party may request an agency hearing on the proposed acquisition. In such hearing all issues shall be determined on the record pursuant to § 554 of title 5, United States Code. . . . At the conclusion thereof, the appropriate Federal banking agency shall by order approve or disapprove the proposed acquisition on the basis of the record made at such hearing.

(5) Judicial review.—Any person whose proposed acquisition is disapproved after agency hearings under this subsection may obtain review by the United States court of appeals for the circuit in which the home office of the [depository institution] to be acquired is located, or the United States Court of Appeals for the District of Columbia Circuit. . . . The findings of the appropriate Federal banking agency shall be set aside if found to be arbitrary or capricious or if found to violate procedures established by this subsection.

(6) Content of notice.—Except as otherwise provided by regulation of the appropriate Federal banking agency, a notice filed pursuant to this subsection shall contain the following information:

(A) The identity, personal history, business background and experience of each person by whom or on whose behalf the acquisition is to be made, including his material business activities and affiliations during the past five years, and a description of any material pending legal or administrative proceedings in which he is a party and any criminal indictment or conviction of such person by a State or Federal court.

(B) A statement of the assets and liabilities of each person by whom or on whose behalf the acquisition is to be made, as of the end of the fiscal year for each of the five fiscal years immediately preceding the date of the notice, together with related statements of income and source and application of funds for each of the fiscal years then concluded, all prepared in accordance with generally accepted accounting principles consistently applied, and an interim statement of the assets and liabilities for each such person, together with related statements of income and source and application of funds, as of a date not more than ninety days prior to the date of the filing of the notice.

(C) The terms and conditions of the proposed acquisition and the manner in which the acquisition is to be made.

(D) The identity, source and amount of the funds or other consideration used or to be used in making the acquisition, and if any part of these funds or other consideration has been or is to be borrowed or otherwise obtained for the purpose of making the acquisition, a description of the transaction, the names of the parties, and any arrangements, agreements, or understandings with such persons.

(E) Any plans or proposals which any acquiring party making the acquisition may have to liquidate the [depository institution], to sell its assets or merge it with any company or to make any other major change in its business or corporate structure or management.

(F) The identification of any person employed, retained, or to be compensated by the acquiring party, or by any person on his behalf, to make solicitations or recommendations to stockholders for the purpose of assisting in the acquisition, and a brief description of the terms of such employment, retainer, or arrangement for compensation.

(G) Copies of all invitations or tenders or advertisements making a tender offer to stockholders for purchase of their stock to be used in connection with the proposed acquisition.

(H) Any additional relevant information in such form as the appropriate Federal banking agency may require by regulation or by specific request in connection with any particular notice.

(7) Grounds for disapproval.—The appropriate Federal banking agency may disapprove any proposed acquisition if—

(A) the proposed acquisition of control would result in a monopoly or would be in furtherance of any combination or conspiracy to monopolize or to attempt to monopolize the business of banking in any part of the United States;

(B) the effect of the proposed acquisition of control in any section of the country may be substantially to lessen competition or to tend to create a monopoly or the proposed acquisition of control would in any other manner be in restraint of trade, and the anticompetitive effects of the proposed acquisition of control are not clearly outweighed in the public interest by the probable effect of the transaction in meeting the convenience and needs of the community to be served;

(C) either the financial condition of any acquiring person or the future prospects of the institution is such as might jeopardize the financial stability of the [depository institution] or prejudice the interests of the depositors of the [depository institution];

(D) the competence, experience, or integrity of any acquiring person or of any of the proposed management personnel indicates that it would not be in the interest of the depositors of the bank, or in the interest of the public to permit such person to control the [depository institution];

(E) any acquiring person neglects, fails, or refuses to furnish the appropriate Federal banking agency all the information required by the appropriate Federal banking agency; or

(F) the appropriate Federal banking agency determines that the proposed transaction would result in an adverse effect on the Deposit Insurance Fund.

(8) **Definitions**.—For the purposes of this subsection, the term—

(A) **"person"** means an individual or a corporation, partnership, trust, association, joint venture, pool, syndicate, sole proprietorship, unincorporated organization, or any other form of entity not specifically listed herein; and

(B) **"control"** means the power, directly or indirectly, to direct the management or policies of an insured bank or to vote 25 per centum or more of any class of voting securities of an insured depository institution.

(9) **Reporting of stock loans[by foreign banks**.—

(A) **Report required**.—Any foreign bank, or any affiliate thereof, that has credit outstanding to any person or group of persons which is secured, directly or indirectly, by shares of an insured depository institution shall file a consolidated report with the appropriate Federal banking agency for such insured depository institution if the extensions of credit by the foreign bank or any affiliate thereof, in the aggregate, are secured, directly or indirectly, by 25 percent or more of any class of shares of the same insured depository institution. . . .

(C) **Inclusion of shares held by the financial institution**.—Any shares of the insured depository institution held by the foreign bank or any affiliate thereof as principal shall be included in the calculation of the number of shares in which the foreign bank or any affiliate thereof has a security interest for purposes of subparagraph (A). . . .

(12) **Change in CEO or directors**.—Whenever such a change in control occurs, each insured shall report promptly to the appropriate Federal banking agency any changes or replacement of its chief executive officer or of any director occurring in the next twelve-month period, including in its report a statement of the past and current business and professional affiliations of the new chief executive officer or directors.

(13) **Rulemaking**.—The appropriate Federal banking agencies are authorized to issue rules and regulations to carry out this subsection. . . .

(15) **Investigative and enforcement authority**.— . . .

(16) **Civil money penalty**.— . . .

(17) **Exceptions**.—This subsection shall not apply with respect to a transaction which is subject to—

(A) § 1842 [relating to bank holding companies];

(B) § 1828(c) [relating to bank mergers]; or

(C) § 1467a [relating to savings and loan holding companies].

(18) **Applicability of change in control provisions to other institutions**.—For purposes of this subsection, the term "insured depository institution" includes—

(A) any depository institution holding company; and

(B) any other company which controls an insured depository institution and is not a depository institution holding company.

§ 1818. Enforcement

(a) **Termination of Insurance**.— . . .

(2) **Involuntary termination**.—

(A) **Notice to primary regulator**.—If the Board of Directors determines that—

(i) an insured depository institution or the directors or trustees of an insured depository institution have engaged or are engaging in unsafe or unsound practices in conducting the business of the depository institution;

(ii) an insured depository institution is in an unsafe or unsound condition to continue operations as an insured institution; or

(iii) an insured depository institution or the directors or trustees of the insured institution have violated any applicable law, regulation, order, condition imposed in writing by the Corporation in connection with the approval of any application or other request by the insured depository institution, or written agreement entered into between the insured depository institution and the Corporation,

the Board of Directors shall notify the appropriate Federal banking agency with respect to such institution (if other than the Corporation) or the State banking supervisor of such institution (if the Corporation is the appropriate Federal banking agency) of the Board's determination and the facts and circumstances on which such determination is based for the purpose of securing the correction of such practice, condition, or violation. Such notice shall be given to the appropriate Federal banking agency not less than 30 days before the notice required by subparagraph (B), except that this period for notice to the appropriate Federal banking agency may be reduced or eliminated with the agreement of such agency.

(B) **Notice of intention to terminate insurance**.—If, after giving the notice required under subparagraph (A) with respect to an insured depository institution, the Board of Directors determines that any unsafe or unsound practice or condition or any violation specified in such notice requires the termination of the insured status of the insured depository institution, the Board shall—

(i) serve written notice to the insured depository institution of the Board's intention to terminate the insured status of the institution;

(ii) provide the insured depository institution with a statement of the charges on the basis of which the determination to terminate such institution's insured status was made (or a copy of the notice under subparagraph (A)); and

(iii) notify the insured depository institution of the date (not less than 30 days after notice under this subparagraph) and place for a hearing before the Board of Directors (or any person designated by the Board) with respect to the termination of the institution's insured status.

(3) Hearing; termination.—If, on the basis of the evidence presented at a hearing before the Board of Directors (or any person designated by the Board for such purpose), in which all issues shall be determined on the record pursuant to § 554 of title 5 and the written findings of the Board of Directors (or such person) with respect to such evidence (which shall be conclusive), the Board of Directors finds that any unsafe or unsound practice or condition or any violation specified in the notice to an insured depository institution under paragraph (2)(B) . . . of this section has been established, the Board of Directors may issue an order terminating the insured status of such depository institution effective as of a date subsequent to such finding.

(4) Appearance; consent to termination.—Unless the depository institution shall appear at the hearing by a duly authorized representative, it shall be deemed to have consented to the termination of its status as an insured depository institution and termination of such status thereupon may be ordered.

(5) Judicial review.—Any insured depository institution whose insured status has been terminated by order of the Board of Directors under this subsection shall have the right of judicial review of such order only to the same extent as provided for the review of orders under subsection (h) of this section. . . .

(b) Cease-and-Desist Order.—

(1) In general.—If, in the opinion of the appropriate Federal banking agency, any insured depository institution, depository institution which has insured deposits, or any institution-affiliated party is engaging or has engaged, or the agency has reasonable cause to believe that the depository institution or any institution-affiliated party is about to engage, in an unsafe or unsound practice in conducting the business of such depository institution, or is violating or has violated, or the agency has reasonable cause to believe that the depository institution or any institution-affiliated party is about to violate, a law, rule, or regulation, or any condition imposed in writing by a Federal banking agency in connection with any action on any application, notice, or other request by the credit union or institution-affiliated party, or any written agreement entered into with the agency, the appropriate Federal banking agency for the depository institution may issue and serve upon the depository institution or such party a notice of charges in respect thereof. The notice shall contain a statement of the facts constituting the alleged violation or violations or the unsafe or unsound practice or practices, and shall fix a time and place at which a hearing will be held to determine whether an order to cease and desist therefrom should issue against the depository institution or the institution-affiliated party. Such hearing shall be fixed for a date not earlier than thirty days nor later than sixty days after service of such notice unless an earlier or a later date is set by the agency at the request of any party so served. Unless the party or parties so served shall appear at the hearing personally or by a duly authorized representative, they shall be deemed to have consented to the issuance of the cease-and-desist order. In the event of such consent, or if upon the record made at any such hearing, the agency shall find that any violation or unsafe or unsound practice specified in the notice of charges has been established, the agency may issue and serve upon the depository institution or the institution-affiliated party an order to cease and desist from any such violation or practice. Such order may, by provisions which may be mandatory or otherwise, require the depository institution or its institution-affiliated parties to cease and desist from the same, and, further, to take affirmative action to correct the conditions resulting from any such violation or practice.

(2) Effective date of order.—A cease-and-desist order shall become effective at the expiration of thirty days after the service of such order upon the depository institution or other person concerned (except in the case of a cease-and-desist order issued upon consent, which shall become effective at the time specified therein), and shall remain effective and enforceable as provided therein, except to such extent as it is stayed, modified, terminated, or set aside by action of the agency or a reviewing court.

(3) Bank holding company.—This subsection, subsections (c) through (s) and subsection (u) of this section, and § 1831aa shall apply to any bank holding company, and to any subsidiary (other than a bank) of a bank holding company, [and] any savings and loan holding company and any subsidiary (other than a depository institution) of a savings and loan holding company, in the same manner as they apply to a State member insured bank. Nothing in this subsection or in subsection (c) of this section shall authorize any Federal banking agency, other than the Board of Governors of the Federal Reserve System, to issue a notice of charges or cease-and-desist order against a bank holding company or any subsidiary thereof (other than a bank or subsidiary of that bank) or against a savings and loan holding company or any subsidiary thereof (other than a depository institution or a subsidiary of such depository institution).

(4) Foreign bank.—This subsection, subsections (c) through (s) and subsection (u) of this section, and § 1831aa of this title shall apply to any foreign bank or company to which § 3106(a) applies and to any subsidiary (other than a bank) of any such foreign bank or company in the same manner as they apply to a bank holding company and any subsidiary thereof (other than a bank) under paragraph (3) of this subsection. For the purposes of this paragraph, the term "subsidiary" shall have the meaning assigned it in § 1841. . . .

(6) Affirmative action to correct conditions resulting from violations or practices.—The authority to issue an order under this subsection and subsection (c) of this section which requires an insured depository institution or any institution-affiliated party to take affirmative action to correct or remedy any conditions resulting from any violation or practice with respect to which such order is issued includes the authority to require such depository institution or such party to—

(A) make restitution or provide reimbursement, indemnification, or guarantee against loss if—

(i) such depository institution or such party was unjustly enriched in connection with such violation or practice; or

(ii) the violation or practice involved a reckless disregard for the law or any applicable regulations or prior order of the appropriate Federal banking agency;

(B) restrict the growth of the institution;

(C) dispose of any loan or asset involved;

(D) rescind agreements or contracts; and

(E) employ qualified officers or employees (who may be subject to approval by the appropriate Federal banking agency at the direction of such agency); and

(F) take such other action as the banking agency determines to be appropriate.

(7) Authority to limit activities.—The authority to issue an order under this subsection or subsection (c) of this section includes the authority to place limitations on the activities or functions of an insured depository institution or any institution-affiliated party.

(8) Unsatisfactory asset quality, management, earnings, or liquidity as unsafe or unsound practice.—If an insured depository institution receives, in its most recent report of examination, a less-than-satisfactory rating for asset quality, management, earnings, or liquidity, the appropriate Federal banking agency may (if the deficiency is not corrected) deem the institution to be engaging in an unsafe or unsound practice for purposes of this subsection. . . .

(10) Standard for certain orders.—No authority under this subsection or subsection (c) of this section to prohibit any institution-affiliated party from withdrawing, transferring, removing, dissipating, or disposing of any funds, assets, or other property may be exercised unless the appropriate Federal banking agency meets the standards of Rule 65 of the Federal Rules of Civil Procedure, without regard to the requirement of such rule that the applicant show that the injury, loss, or damage is irreparable and immediate.

(c) Temporary Cease-and-Desist Orders.—

(1) In general.—Whenever the appropriate Federal banking agency shall determine that the violation or threatened violation or the unsafe or unsound practice or practices, specified in the notice of charges served upon the depository institution or any institution-affiliated party pursuant to paragraph (1) of subsection (b) of this section, or the continuation thereof, is likely to cause insolvency or significant dissipation of assets or earnings of the depository institution, or is likely to weaken the condition of the depository institution or otherwise prejudice the interests of its depositors prior to the completion of the proceedings conducted pursuant to paragraph (1) of subsection (b) of this section, the agency may issue a temporary order requiring the depository institution or such party to cease and desist from any such violation or practice and to take affirmative action to prevent or remedy such insolvency, dissipation, condition, or prejudice pending completion of such proceedings. . . .

(d) Enforcing Temporary Cease-and-Desist Orders.—In the case of violation or threatened violation of, or failure to obey, a temporary cease-and-desist order issued pursuant to paragraph (1) of subsection (c) of this section, the appropriate Federal banking agency may apply to the United States district court, or the United States court of any territory, within the jurisdiction of which the home office of the depository institution is located, for an injunction to enforce such order, and, if the court shall determine that there has been such violation or threatened violation or failure to obey, it shall be the duty of the court to issue such injunction.

(e) Removal and Prohibition Authority.—

(1) Authority to issue order.—Whenever the appropriate Federal banking agency determines that—

(A) any institution-affiliated parry has, directly or indirectly—

(i) violated—

(I) any law or regulation;

(II) any cease-and-desist order which has become final;

(III) in writing by a Federal banking agency in connection with any action on any application, notice, or request by such credit union or institution-affiliated party; or

(IV) any written agreement between such depository institution and such agency;

(ii) engaged or participated in any unsafe or unsound practice in connection with any insured depository institution or business institution; or

(iii) committed or engaged in any act, omission, or practice which constitutes a breach of such party's fiduciary duty;

(B) by reason of the violation, practice, or breach described in any clause of subparagraph (A)—

(i) such insured depository institution or business institution has suffered or will probably suffer financial loss or other damage;

(ii) the interests of the insured depository institution's depositors have been or could be prejudiced; or

(iii) such party has received financial gain or other benefit by reason of such violation, practice, or breach; and

(C) such violation, practice, or breach—

(i) involves personal dishonesty on the part of such party; or

(ii) demonstrates willful or continuing disregard by such party for the safety or soundness of such insured depository institution or business institution,

the appropriate Federal banking for the depository institution agency may serve upon such party a written notice of the agency's intention to remove such party from office or to prohibit any further participation by such party, in any manner, in the conduct of the affairs of any insured depository institution.

(2) Specific violations.—

(A) In general.—Whenever the appropriate Federal banking agency determines that—

(i) an institution-affiliated party has committed a violation of any provision of subchapter II of chapter 53 of title 31 [part of the Bank Secrecy Act] and such violation was not inadvertent or unintentional;

(ii) an officer or director of an insured depository institution has knowledge that an institution-affiliated party of the insured depository institution has violated any such provision or any provision of law referred to in subsection (g)(1)(A)(ii) of this section;

(iii) an officer or director of an insured depository institution has committed any violation of the Depository Institution Management Interlocks Act; or

(iv) an institution-affiliated party of a subsidiary (other than a bank) of a bank holding company or of a subsidiary (other than a savings association) of a savings and loan holding company has been convicted of any criminal offense involving dishonesty or a breach of trust or a criminal offense under § 1956 [relating to money laundering], § 1957 [monetary transactions in criminally derived property], or § 1960 [unlicensed money transmitting] of title 18, United States Code, or has agreed to enter into a pretrial diversion or similar program in connection with a prosecution for such an offense,

the agency may serve upon such party, officer, or director a written notice of the agency's intention to remove such party from office.

(B) Factors to be considered.—In determining whether an officer or director should be removed as a result of the application of subparagraph (A)(ii), the agency shall consider whether the officer or director took appropriate action to stop, or to prevent the recurrence of, a violation described in such subparagraph.

(3) Suspension order.—

(A) Suspension or prohibition authorized.—If the appropriate Federal banking agency serves written notice under paragraph (1) or (2) to any institution-affiliated party of such agency's intention to issue an order under such paragraph, the appropriate Federal banking agency may suspend such party from office or prohibit such party from further participation in any manner in the conduct of the affairs of the depository institution, if the agency—

(i) determines that such action is necessary for the protection of the depository institution or the interests of the depository institution's depositors; and

(ii) serves such party with written notice of the suspension order.

(B) Effective period.—Any suspension order issued under subparagraph (A)—

(i) shall become effective upon service; and

(ii) unless a court issues a stay of such order under subsection (f) of this section, shall remain in effect and enforceable until—

(I) the date the appropriate Federal banking agency dismisses the charges contained in the notice served under paragraph (1) or (2) with respect to such party; or

(II) the effective date of an order issued by the agency to such party under paragraph (1) or (2).

(C) Copy of order.—If an appropriate Federal banking agency issues a suspension order under subparagraph (A) to any institution-affiliated party, the agency shall serve a copy of such order on any insured depository institution with which such party is associated at the time such order is issued.

(4) Procedure.—A notice of intention to remove an institution-affiliated party from office or to prohibit such party from participating in the conduct of the affairs of an insured depository institution, shall contain a statement of the facts constituting grounds therefor, and shall fix a time and place at which a hearing will be held thereon. Such hearing shall be fixed for a date not earlier than thirty days nor later than sixty days after the date of service of such notice, unless an earlier or a later date is set by the agency at the request of (A) such party, and for good cause shown, or (B) the Attorney General of the United States. Unless such party shall appear at the hearing in person or by a duly authorized representative, such party shall be deemed to have consented to the issuance of an order of such removal or prohibition. In the event of such consent, or if upon the record made at any such hearing the agency shall find that any of the grounds specified in such notice have been established, the agency may issue such orders of suspension or removal from office, or prohibition from participation in the conduct of the affairs of the depository institution, as it may deem appropriate. Any such order shall become effective at the expiration of thirty days after service upon such depository institution and such party (except in the case of an order issued upon consent, which shall become effective at the time specified therein). Such order shall remain effective and enforceable except to such extent as it is stayed, modified, terminated, or set aside by action of the agency or a reviewing court.

(6) Prohibition of certain specific activities.—Any person subject to an order issued under this subsection shall not—

(A) participate in any manner in the conduct of the affairs of any institution or agency specified in paragraph (7)(A);

(B) solicit, procure, transfer, attempt to transfer, vote, or attempt to vote any proxy, consent, or authorization with respect to any voting rights in any institution described in subparagraph (A);

(C) violate any voting agreement previously approved by the appropriate Federal banking agency; or

(D) vote for a director, or serve or act as an institution-affiliated party.

(7) Industrywide prohibition.—

(A) In general.—Except as provided in subparagraph (B), any person who, pursuant to an order issued under this subsection or subsection (g) of this section, has been removed or suspended from office in an insured depository institution or prohibited from participating in the conduct of the affairs of an insured depository institution may not, while such order is in effect, continue or commence to hold any office in, or participate in any manner in the conduct of the affairs of—

(i) any insured depository institution;

(ii) any institution treated as an insured bank under subsection (b)(3) or (b)(4) of this section, or as a savings association under subsection (b)(9) of this section;

(iii) any insured credit union under the Federal Credit Union Act;

(iv) any institution chartered under the Farm Credit Act of 1971;

(v) any appropriate Federal depository institution regulatory agency; and

(vi) the Federal Housing Finance Agency and any Federal home loan bank.

(B) Exception if agency provides written consent.—If, on or after the date an order is issued under this subsection which removes or suspends from office any institution-affiliated party or prohibits such party from participating in the conduct of the affairs of an insured depository institution, such party receives the written consent of—

(i) the agency that issued such order; and

(ii) the appropriate Federal financial institutions regulatory agency of the institution described in any clause of subparagraph (A) with respect to which such party proposes to become an institution-affiliated party, subparagraph (A) shall, to the extent of such consent, cease to apply to such party with respect to the institution described in each written consent. Any agency that grants such a written consent shall report such action to the Corporation and publicly disclose such consent. . . .

(f) Judicial Review of Suspension or Prohibition.—Within ten days after any institution-affiliated party has been suspended from office and/or prohibited from participation in the conduct of the affairs of an insured depository institution under subsection (e)(3) of this section, such party may apply to the United States district court for the judicial district in which the home office of the depository institution is located, or the United States District Court for the District of Columbia, for a stay of such suspension and/or prohibition pending the completion of the administrative proceedings pursuant to the notice served upon such party under subsection (e)(1) or (e)(2) of this section, and such court shall have jurisdiction to stay such suspension and/or prohibition.

(g) Suspension or Prohibition of Individual Charged with Felony.—

(1) Suspension or prohibition.—

(A) **In general.**—Whenever any institution-affiliated party is the subject of any information, indictment, or complaint, involving the commission of or participation in—

(i) a crime involving dishonesty or breach of trust which is punishable by imprisonment for a term exceeding one year under State or Federal law, or

(ii) a criminal violation of § 1956, § 1957, or § 1960 of title 18 [relating to money laundering and unlicensed money transmitting] or § 5322 or § 5324 of title 31 [relating to money laundering],

the appropriate Federal banking agency may, if continued service or participation by such party posed, poses, or may pose a threat to the interests of the depositors of, or threatened, threatens, or may threaten to impair public confidence in, any relevant depository institution . . . , by written notice served upon such party, suspend such party from office or prohibit such party from further participation in any manner in the conduct of the affairs of the depository institution. . . .

(h) Hearing and Judicial Review.—

(1) Hearing.—Any hearing provided for in this section (other than the hearing provided for in subsection (g)(3) of this section) shall be held in the Federal judicial district or in the territory in which the home office of the depository institution is located unless the party afforded the hearing consents to another place, and shall be conducted in accordance with the provisions of chapter 5 of title 5. After such hearing, and within ninety days after the appropriate Federal banking agency or Board of Governors of the Federal Reserve System has notified the parties that the case has been submitted to it for final decision, it shall render its decision (which shall include findings of fact upon which its decision is predicated) and shall issue and serve upon each party to the proceeding an order or orders consistent with the provisions of this section. Judicial review of any such order shall be exclusively as provided in this subsection (h) of this section. Unless a petition for review is timely filed in a court of appeals of the United States, as hereinafter provided in paragraph (2) of this subsection, and thereafter until the record in the proceeding has been filed as so provided, the issuing agency may at any time, upon such notice and in such manner as it shall deem proper, modify, terminate, or set aside any

Federal Deposit Insurance Act   **12 U.S.C. § 1818**

such order. Upon such filing of the record, the agency may modify, terminate, or set aside any such order with permission of the court.

(2) Judicial review.—Any party to any proceeding under paragraph (1) may obtain a review of any order served pursuant to paragraph (1) of this subsection (other than an order issued with the consent of the depository institution or the institution-affiliated party concerned, or an order issued under paragraph (1) of subsection (g) of this section) by the filing in the court of appeals of the United States for the circuit in which the home office of the depository institution is located, or in the United States Court of Appeals for the District of Columbia Circuit, within thirty days after the date of service of such order, a written petition praying that the order of the agency be modified, terminated, or set aside. A copy of such petition shall be forthwith transmitted by the clerk of the court to the agency, and thereupon the agency shall file in the court the record in the proceeding, as provided in § 2112 of title 28. Upon the filing of such petition, such court shall have jurisdiction, which upon the filing of the record shall except as provided in the last sentence of said paragraph (1) be exclusive, to affirm, modify, terminate, or set aside, in whole or in part, the order of the agency. Review of such proceedings shall be had as provided in chapter 7 of title 5. The judgment and decree of the court shall be final, except that the same shall be subject to review by the Supreme Court upon certiorari, as provided in § 1254 of title 28.

(3) Petition for judicial review does not stay order.—The commencement of proceedings for judicial review under paragraph (2) of this subsection shall not, unless specifically ordered by the court, operate as a stay of any order issued by the agency.

(i) Enforcement; Civil Money Penalty.—

(1) Jurisdiction and enforcement.—The appropriate Federal banking agency may in its discretion apply to the United States district court, or the United States court of any territory, within the jurisdiction of which the home office of the depository institution is located, for the enforcement of any effective and outstanding notice or order issued under this section or under § 1831o . . . , and such courts shall have jurisdiction and power to order and require compliance herewith; but except as otherwise provided in this section or under § 1831o . . . , no court shall have jurisdiction to affect by injunction or otherwise the issuance or enforcement of any notice or order under any such section, or to review, modify, suspend, terminate, or set aside any such notice or order.

(2) Civil money penalty.—

(A) **First tier**.—Any insured depository institution which, and any institution-affiliated party who—

(i) violates any law or regulation;

(ii) violates any final order or temporary order issued pursuant to subsection (b), (c), (e), (g), or (s) of this section or any final order under § 1831o . . . ;

(iii) violates any condition imposed in writing by a Federal banking agency in connection with any action on any application, notice, or other request by the credit union or institution-affiliated party; or

(iv) violates any written agreement between such depository institution and such agency,

shall forfeit and pay a civil penalty of not more than $5,000 for each day during which such violation continues.

(B) Second tier.—Notwithstanding subparagraph (A), any insured depository institution which, and any institution-affiliated party who—

(i) (I) commits any violation described in any clause of subparagraph (A);

(II) recklessly engages in an unsafe or unsound practice in conducting the affairs of such insured depository institution; or

(III) breaches any fiduciary duty;

(ii) which violation, practice, or breach—

(I) is part of a pattern of misconduct;

(II) causes or is likely to cause more than a minimal loss to such depository institution; or

(III) results in pecuniary gain or other benefit to such party,

shall forfeit and pay a civil penalty of not more than $25,000 for each day during which such violation, practice, or breach continues.

(C) Third tier.—Notwithstanding subparagraphs (A) and (B), any insured depository institution which, and any institution-affiliated party who—

(i) knowingly—

(I) commits any violation described in any clause of subparagraph (A);

(II) engages in any unsafe or unsound practice in conducting the affairs of such depository institution; or

(III) breaches any fiduciary duty; and

(ii) knowingly or recklessly causes a substantial loss to such depository institution or a substantial pecuniary gain or other benefit to such party by reason of such violation, practice, or breach,

shall forfeit and pay a civil penalty in an amount not to exceed the applicable maximum amount determined under subparagraph (D) for each day during which such violation, practice, or breach continues.

(D) Maximum amounts of penalties for any violation described in subparagraph (C).—The maximum daily amount of any civil penalty which may be assessed pursuant to subparagraph (C) for any violation, practice, or breach described in such subparagraph is—

(i) in the case of any person other than an insured depository institution, an amount to not exceed $1,000,000; and

(ii) in the case of any insured depository institution, an amount not to exceed the lesser of—

(I) $1,000,000; or

(II) 1 percent of the total assets of such institution.

(E) Assessment.—

(i) Written notice.—Any penalty imposed under subparagraph (A), (B), or (C) may be assessed and collected by the appropriate Federal banking agency by written notice.

(ii) Finality of assessment.—If, with respect to any assessment under clause (i), a hearing is not requested pursuant to subparagraph (H) within the period of time allowed under such subparagraph, the assessment shall constitute a final and unappealable order. . . .

(G) Mitigating factors.—In determining the amount of any penalty imposed under subparagraph (A), (B), or (C), the appropriate agency shall take into account the appropriateness of the penalty with respect to—

(i) the size of financial resources and good faith of the insured depository institution or other person charged;

(ii) the gravity of the violation;

(iii) the history of previous violations; and

(iv) such other matters as justice may require.

(H) Hearing.—The insured depository institution or other person against whom any penalty is assessed under this paragraph shall be afforded an agency hearing if such institution or person submits a request for such hearing within 20 days after the issuance of the notice of assessment.

(I) Collection.—

(i) Referral.—If any insured depository institution or other person fails to pay an assessment after any penalty assessed under this paragraph has become final, the agency that imposed the penalty shall recover the amount assessed by action in the appropriate United States district court.

(ii) Appropriateness of penalty not reviewable.—In any civil action under clause (i), the validity and appropriateness of the penalty shall not be subject to review.

(J) Disbursement.—All penalties collected under authority of this paragraph shall be deposited into the Treasury.

(K) Regulations.—Each appropriate Federal banking agency shall prescribe regulations establishing such procedures as may be necessary to carry out this paragraph.

(3) Notice under this section after separation from service.—The resignation, termination of employment or participation, or separation of an institution-affiliated party (including a separation caused by the closing of an insured depository institution) shall not affect the jurisdiction and authority of the appropriate Federal banking agency to issue any notice or order and proceed under this section against any such party, if such notice or order is served before the end of the 6-year period beginning on the date such party ceased to be such a party with respect to such depository institution. . . .

(4) Prejudgment attachment.—

(A) In general.—In any action brought by an appropriate Federal banking agency (excluding the Corporation when acting in a manner described in § 1821(d)(18)) pursuant to this section, or in actions brought in aid of, or to enforce an order in, any administrative or other civil action for money damages, restitution, or civil money penalties brought by such agency, the court may, upon application of the agency, issue a restraining order that—

(i) prohibits any person subject to the proceeding from withdrawing, transferring, removing, dissipating, or disposing of any funds, assets or other property; and

(ii) appoints a temporary receiver to administer the restraining order.

(B) Standard.—

(i) Showing.—Rule 65 of the Federal Rules of Civil Procedure shall apply with respect to any proceeding under subparagraph (A) without regard to the requirement of such rule that the applicant show that the injury, loss, or damage is irreparable and immediate.

(ii) State proceeding.—If, in the case of any proceeding in a State court, the court determines that rules of civil procedure available under the laws of such State provide substantially similar protections to a party's right to due process as Rule 65 (as modified with respect to such proceeding by clause (i)), the relief sought under subparagraph (A) may be requested under the laws of such State.

(j) Criminal Penalty.—Whoever, being subject to an order in effect under subsection (e) or (g) of this section, without the prior written approval of the appropriate Federal financial institutions regulatory agency, knowingly participates, directly or indirectly, in any manner (including by engaging in an activity specifically prohibited in such an order or in subsection (e)(6) of this section) in the conduct of the affairs of—

(1) any insured depository institution;

(2) any institution treated as an insured bank under subsection (b)(3) or (b)(4) of this section, or as a savings association under subsection (b)(9) of this section;

(3) any [federally] insured credit union . . . ; or

(4) any institution chartered under the Farm Credit Act . . . , shall be fined not more than $1,000,000, imprisoned for not more than 5 years, or both.

(s) Compliance with Monetary Transaction Recordkeeping and Report Requirements.—

(1) Compliance procedures required.—Each appropriate Federal banking agency shall prescribe regulations requiring insured depository institutions to establish and maintain procedures reasonably designed to assure and monitor the compliance of such depository institutions with the requirements of subchapter 11 of chapter 53 of title 31 [part of the Bank Secrecy Act].

(2) Examinations of bank to include review of compliance procedures.—

(A) In general.—Each examination of an insured depository institution by the appropriate Federal banking agency shall include a review of the procedures required to be established and maintained under paragraph (1).

(B) Exam report requirement.—The report of examination shall describe any problem with the procedures maintained by the insured depository institution.

(3) Order to comply with requirements.—If the appropriate Federal banking agency determines that an insured depository institution—

(A) has failed to establish and maintain the procedures described in paragraph (1); or

(B) has failed to correct any problem with the procedures maintained by such depository institution which was previously reported to the depository institution by such agency,

the agency shall issue an order in the manner prescribed in subsection (b) or (c) of this section requiring such depository institution to cease and desist from its violation of this subsection or regulations prescribed under this subsection.

(t) Authority of FDIC to Take Enforcement Action Against Insured Depository Institutions and Institution-Affiliated Parties.—

(1) Recommending action by appropriate Federal banking agency.—The Corporation, based on an examination of an insured depository institution by the Corporation or by the appropriate Federal banking agency or on other information, may recommend in writing to the appropriate Federal banking agency that the agency take any enforcement action authorized under § 1817(j), this section, or § 1828(j) with respect to any insured depository institution or any institution-affiliated parry. The recommendation shall be accompanied by a written explanation of the concerns giving rise to the recommendation.

(2) FDIC's authority to act if appropriate Federal banking agency fails to follow recommendation.—If the appropriate Federal banking agency does not, before the end of the 60-day period beginning on the date on which the agency receives the recommendation under paragraph (1), take the enforcement action recommended by the Corporation or provide a plan acceptable to the Corporation for responding to the Corporation's concerns, the Corporation may take the recommended enforcement action if the Board of Directors determines, upon a vote of its members, that—

(A) the insured depository institution is in an unsafe or unsound condition;

(B) the institution or institution-affiliated party is engaging in unsafe or unsound practices, and the recommended enforcement action will prevent the institution or institution-affiliated party from continuing such practices; or

(C) the conduct or threatened conduct (including any acts or omissions) poses a risk to the Deposit Insurance Fund, or may prejudice the interests of the institution's depositors.

(3) Effect of exigent circumstances.—

(A) Authority to act.—The Corporation may, upon a vote of the Board of Directors, and after notice to the appropriate Federal banking agency, exercise its authority under paragraph (2) in exigent circumstances without regard to the time period set forth in paragraph (2).

(B) Agreement on exigent circumstances.—The Corporation shall, by agreement with the appropriate Federal banking agency, set forth those exigent circumstances in which the Corporation may act under subparagraph (A).

(4) Corporation's powers; institution's duties.—For purposes of this subsection—

(A) The Corporation shall have the same powers with respect to any insured depository institution and its affiliates as the appropriate Federal banking agency has with respect to the institution and its affiliates; and

(B) the institution and its affiliates shall have the same duties and obligations with respect to the Corporation as the institution and its affiliates have with respect to the appropriate Federal banking agency.

(5) Requests for formal actions and investigations.—

(A) Submission of requests.—A regional office of an appropriate Federal banking agency (including a Federal Reserve bank) that requests a formal investigation of or civil enforcement action against an insured depository institution or institution-affiliated party shall submit the request concurrently to the chief officer of the appropriate Federal banking agency and to the Corporation.

(B) Agencies required to report on requests.—Each appropriate Federal banking agency shall report semiannually to the Corporation on the status or disposition of all requests under subparagraph (A), including the reasons for any decision by the agency to approve or deny such requests.

(6) Referral to Bureau of Consumer Financial Protection.—[E]ach appropriate Federal banking agency shall make a referral to the Bureau of Consumer Financial Protection when the Federal banking agency has a reasonable belief that a violation of an enumerated consumer law, as defined in the Consumer Financial Protection Act of 2010, has been committed by any insured depository institution or institution-affiliated party within the jurisdiction of that appropriate Federal banking agency.

(u) Public Disclosures of Final Orders and Agreements.—

(1) **In general.**—The appropriate Federal banking agency shall publish and make available to the public on a monthly basis—

(A) any written agreement or other written statement for which a violation may be enforced by the appropriate Federal banking agency, unless the appropriate Federal banking agency, in its discretion, determines that publication would be contrary to the public interest;

(B) any final order issued with respect to any administrative enforcement proceeding initiated by such agency under this section or any other law; and

(C) any modification to or termination of any order or agreement made public pursuant to this paragraph.

(2) **Hearings.**—All hearings on the record with respect to any notice of charges issued by a Federal banking agency shall be open to the public, unless the agency, in its discretion, determines that holding an open hearing would be contrary to the public interest.

(3) **Transcript of hearing.**—A transcript that includes all testimony and other documentary evidence shall be prepared for all hearings commenced pursuant to subsection (i) of this section. A transcript of public hearings shall be made available to the public pursuant to § 552 of title 5 [i.e., the Freedom of Information Act].

(4) **Delay of publication under exceptional circumstances.**—If the appropriate Federal banking agency makes a determination in writing that the publication of a final order pursuant to paragraph (1)(B) would seriously threaten the safety and soundness of an insured depository institution, the agency may delay the publication of the document for a reasonable time.

(5) **Documents filed under seal in public enforcement hearings.**—The appropriate Federal banking agency may file any document or part of a document under seal in any administrative enforcement hearing commenced by the agency if disclosure of the document would be contrary to the public interest. A written report shall be made part of any determination to withhold any part of a document from the transcript of the hearing required by paragraph (2).

(6) **Retention of documents.**—Each Federal banking agency shall keep and maintain a record, for a period of at least 6 years, of all documents described in paragraph (1) and all informal enforcement agreements and other supervisory actions and supporting documents issued with respect to or in connection with any administrative enforcement proceeding initiated by such agency under this section or any other laws.

(7) **Disclosures to Congress.**—No provision of this subsection may be construed to authorize the withholding, or to prohibit the disclosure, of any information to the Congress or any committee or subcommittee of the Congress. . . .

§ 1819. Corporate Powers

(a) In General.—[T]he Corporation [is] a body corporate and as such shall have power—

First. To adopt and use a corporate seal.

Second. To have succession until dissolved by an Act of Congress.

Third. To make contracts.

Fourth. To sue and be sued, and complain and defend, by and through its own attorneys, in any court of law or equity, State or Federal.

Fifth. To appoint by its Board of Directors such officers and employees as are not otherwise provided for in this Act, to define their duties, fix their compensation, require bonds of them and fix the penalty thereof, and to dismiss at pleasure such officers or employees. Nothing in this Act or any other Act shall be construed to prevent the appointment and compensation as an officer or employee of the Corporation of any officer or employee of the United States in any board, commission, independent establishment, or executive department thereof.

Sixth. To prescribe, by its Board of Directors, bylaws not inconsistent with law, regulating the manner in which its general business may be conducted, and the privileges granted to it by law may be exercised and enjoyed.

Seventh. To exercise by its Board of Directors, or duly authorized officers or agents, all powers specifically granted by the provisions of this Act, and such incidental powers as shall be necessary to carry out the powers so granted.

Eighth. To make examinations of and to require information and reports from depository institutions, as provided in this Act.

Ninth. To act as receiver.

Tenth. To prescribe by its Board of Directors such rules and regulations as it may deem necessary to carry out the provisions of this Act or of any other law which it has the responsibility of administering or enforcing (except to the extent that authority to issue such rules and regulations has been expressly and exclusively granted to any other regulatory agency). . . .

§ 1820. Administering Corporation

. . . **(b) Examinations.**—

(1) Appointment of examiners and claims agents.—The Board of Directors shall appoint examiners and claims agents.

(2) Regular examinations.—Any examiner appointed under paragraph (1) shall have power, on behalf of the Corporation, to examine—

(A) any insured State nonmember bank or insured State branch of any foreign bank;

(B) any depository institution which files an application with the Corporation to become an insured depository institution; and

(C) any insured depository institution in default,

whenever the Board of Directors determines an examination of any such depository institution is necessary.

(3) Special examination of any insured depository institution.—In addition to the examinations authorized under paragraph (2), any examiner appointed under paragraph (1) shall have power, on behalf of the Corporation, to make any special examination of any insured depository institution whenever the Board of Directors determines a special examination of any such depository institution is necessary to determine the condition of such depository institution for insurance purposes.

(4) Examination of affiliates.—

(A) **In general.**—In making any examination under paragraph (2) or (3), any examiner appointed under paragraph (1) shall have power, on behalf of the Corporation, to make such examinations of the affairs of any affiliate of any depository institution as may be necessary to disclose fully—

(i) the relationship between such depository institution and any such affiliate; and

(ii) the effect of such relationship on the depository institution.

(B) Commitment by foreign banks to allow examinations of affiliates.—No branch or depository institution subsidiary of a foreign bank may become an insured depository institution unless such foreign bank submits a written binding commitment to the Board of Directors to permit any examination of any affiliate of such branch or depository institution subsidiary pursuant to subparagraph (A) to the extent determined by the Board of Directors to be necessary to carry out the purposes of this Act.

(5) Examination of insured State branches.—The Board of Directors shall—

(A) coordinate examinations of insured State branches of foreign banks with examinations conducted by the Board of Governors of the Federal Reserve System under § 3105(c)(1); and

(B) to the extent possible, participate in any simultaneous examination of the United States operations of a foreign bank requested by the Board under such section.

(6) Power and duty of examiners.—Each examiner appointed under paragraph (1) shall—

(A) have power to make a thorough examination of any insured depository institution or affiliate under paragraph (2), (3), (4), or (5); and

(B) shall make a full and detailed report of condition of any insured depository institution or affiliate examined to the Corporation. . . .

(d) Annual On-Site Examinations of All Insured Depository Institutions Required.—

(1) In general.—The appropriate Federal banking agency shall, not less than once during each 12-month period, conduct a full-scope, on-site examination of each insured depository institution.

(2) Examinations by Corporation.—Paragraph (1) shall not apply during any 12-month period in which the Corporation has conducted a full-scope, on-site examination of the insured depository institution.

(3) State examinations acceptable.—The examinations required by paragraph (1) may be conducted in alternate 12-month periods, as appropriate, if the appropriate Federal banking agency determines that an examination of the insured depository institution conducted by the State during the intervening 12-month period carries out the purpose of this subsection.

(4) 18-month rule for certain small institutions.—Paragraphs (1), (2), and (3) shall apply with "18-month" substituted for "12-month" if—

(A) the insured depository institution has total assets of less than $500,000,000;

(B) the institution is well capitalized, as defined in § 1831o;

(C) when the institution was most recently examined, it was found to be well managed, and its composite condition—

(i) was found to be outstanding; or

(ii) was found to be outstanding or good, in the case of an insured depository institution that has total assets of not more than $100,000,000;

(D) the insured institution is not currently subject to a formal enforcement proceeding or order by the Corporation or the appropriate Federal banking agency; and

(E) no person acquired control of the institution during the 12-month period in which a full-scope, on-site examination would be required but for this paragraph. . . .

(6) Coordinated examinations.—To minimize the disruptive effects of examinations on the operations of insured depository institutions—

(A) each appropriate Federal banking agency shall, to the extent practicable and consistent with principles of safety and soundness and the public interest—

(i) coordinate examinations to be conducted by that agency at an insured depository institution and its affiliates;

(ii) coordinate with the other appropriate Federal banking agencies in the conduct of such examinations;

(iii) work to coordinate with the appropriate State bank supervisor—

(I) the conduct of all examinations made pursuant to this subsection; and

(II) the number, types, and frequency of reports required to be submitted to such agencies and supervisors by insured depository institutions, and the type and amount of information required to be included in such reports; and

(iv) use copies of reports of examinations of insured depository institutions made by any other Federal banking agency or appropriate State bank supervisor to eliminate duplicative requests for information. . . .

(h) Coordination of Examination Authority.—

(1) State bank supervisors of home and host States.—

(A) Home state of bank.—The appropriate State bank supervisor of the home State of an insured State bank has authority to examine and supervise the bank.

(B) Host state branches.—The State bank supervisor of the home State of an insured State bank and any State bank supervisor of an appropriate host State shall exercise its respective authority to supervise and examine the branches of the bank in a host State in accordance with the terms of any applicable cooperative agreement between the home State bank supervisor and the State bank supervisor of the relevant host State.

(C) Supervisory fees.—Except as expressly provided in a cooperative agreement between the State bank supervisors of the home State and any host State of an insured State bank, only the State bank supervisor of the home State of an insured State bank may levy or charge State supervisory fees on the bank.

(2) Host state examination.—

(A) In general.—With respect to a branch operated in a host State by an out-of-State insured State bank that resulted from an interstate merger transaction approved under § 1831u, or that was established in such State pursuant to § 36, . . . § 321 or § 1828(d)(4), the appropriate State bank supervisor of such host State may—

(i) with written notice to the State bank supervisor of the bank's home State and subject to the terms of any applicable cooperative agreement with the State bank supervisor of such home State, examine such branch for the purpose of determining compliance with host State laws that are applicable pursuant to § 1831a(j), including those that govern community reinvestment, fair lending, and consumer protection; and

(ii) if expressly permitted under and subject to the terms of a cooperative agreement with the State bank supervisor of the bank's home State or if such out-of-State insured State bank has been determined to be in a troubled condition by either the State bank supervisor of the bank's home State or the bank's appropriate Federal banking agency, participate in the examination of the bank by the State bank supervisor of the bank's home State to ascertain that the activities of the branch in such host State are not conducted in an unsafe or unsound manner.

(B) Notice of determination.—

(i) In general.—The State bank supervisor of the home State of an insured State bank shall notify the State bank supervisor of each host State of the bank if there has been a final determination that the bank is in a troubled condition.

(ii) Timing of notice.—The State bank supervisor of the home State of an insured State bank shall provide notice under clause (i) as soon as is reasonably possible, but in all cases not later than 15 business days after the date on which the State bank supervisor has made such final determination or has received written notification of such final determination.

(3) Host State enforcement.—If the State bank supervisor of a host State determines that a branch of an out-of-State insured State bank is violating any law of the host State that is applicable to such branch pursuant to §§ 1831a(j), including a law that governs community reinvestment, fair lending, or consumer protection, the State bank supervisor of the host State or, to the extent authorized by the law of the host State, a host State law enforcement officer may, with written notice to the State bank supervisor of the bank's home State and subject to the terms of any applicable cooperative agreement with the State bank supervisor of the bank's home State, undertake such enforcement actions and proceedings as would be permitted under the law of the host State as if the branch were a bank chartered by that host State.

(4) Cooperative agreement.—

(A) In general.—The State bank supervisors from 2 or more States may enter into cooperative agreements to facilitate State regulatory supervision of State banks, including cooperative agreements relating to the coordination of examinations and joint participation in examinations.

(B) Definition.—For purposes of this subsection, the term "cooperative agreement" means a written agreement that is signed by the home State bank supervisor and the host State bank supervisor to facilitate State regulatory supervision of State banks, and includes nationwide or multi-State cooperative agreements and cooperative agreements solely between the home State and host State.

(C) Rule of construction.—Except for State bank supervisors, no provision of this subsection relating to such cooperative agreements shall be construed as limiting in any way the authority of home State and host State law enforcement officers, regulatory supervisors, or other officials that have not signed such cooperative agreements to enforce host State laws that are applicable to a branch of an out-of-State insured State bank located in the host State pursuant to § 1831a(j). . . .

(7) Definitions.—For purpose of this section, the following definitions shall apply:

(A) **Host State, home State, out-of-State bank**.—The terms "host State," "home State," and "out-of-State bank" have the same meanings as in § 1831u(g). . . .

(C) **Troubled condition**.—Solely for purposes of paragraph (2)(B), an insured State bank has been determined to be in "troubled condition" if the bank—

(i) has a composite rating, as determined in its most recent report of examination, of 4 or 5 under the Uniform Financial Institutions Ratings System;

(ii) is subject to a proceeding initiated by the Corporation for termination or suspension of deposit insurance; or

(iii) is subject to a proceeding initiated by the State bank supervisor of the bank's home State to vacate, revoke, or terminate the charter of the bank, or to liquidate the bank, or to appoint a receiver for the bank.

(D) **Final determination**.—For purposes of paragraph (2)(B), the term "final determination" means the transmittal of a report of examination to the bank or transmittal of official notice of proceedings to the bank.

§ 1820a. Examination of Investment Companies

(a) **Exclusive Securities and Exchange Commission Authority**.—Except as provided in subsection (c), a Federal banking agency may not inspect or examine any registered investment company that is not a bank holding company or a savings and loan holding company.

(b) **Examination Results and Other Information**.—The [Securities and Exchange] Commission shall provide to any Federal banking agency, upon request, the results of any examination, reports, records, or other information with respect to any registered investment company to the extent necessary for the agency to carry out its statutory responsibilities.

(c) **Certain Examinations Authorized**.—Nothing in this section shall prevent the Corporation, if the Corporation finds it necessary to determine the condition of an insured depository institution for insurance purposes, from examining an affiliate of any insured depository institution, pursuant to its authority under § 1820(b)(4), as may be necessary to disclose fully the relationship between the insured depository institution and the affiliate, and the effect of such relationship on the insured depository institution. . . .

§ 1821. Insurance; Receivership

(a) **Deposit Insurance**.—

(1) **Insured amounts payable**.—

(A) **In general**.—The Corporation shall insure the deposits of all insured depository institutions as provided in this Act.

(B) Net amount of insured deposit.—

(i) In general.—Subject to clause (ii), the net amount due to any depositor at an insured depository institution shall not exceed the standard maximum deposit insurance amount as determined in accordance with subparagraphs (C), (D), (E) and (F) and paragraph (3).

(ii) Insurance for noninterest-bearing transaction accounts.—Notwithstanding clause (i), the Corporation shall fully insure the net amount that any depositor at an insured depository institution maintains in a noninterest-bearing transaction account. Such amount shall not be taken into account when computing the net amount due to such depositor under clause (i).

(iii) Noninterest-bearing transaction account defined.—For purposes of this subparagraph, the term "noninterest-bearing transaction account" means—

(I) a deposit or account maintained at an insured depository institution—

(aa) with respect to which interest is neither accrued nor paid;

(bb) on which the depositor or account holder is permitted to make withdrawals by negotiable or transferable instrument, payment orders of withdrawal, telephone or other electronic media transfers, or other similar items for the purpose of making payments or transfers to third parties or others; and

(cc) on which the insured depository institution does not reserve the right to require advance notice of an intended withdrawal; and

(II) a trust account established by an attorney or law firm on behalf of a client, commonly known as an "Interest on Lawyers Trust Account", or a functionally equivalent account, as determined by the Corporation.

(C) Aggregation of deposits.—For the purpose of determining the net amount due to any depositor under subparagraph (B)(i), the Corporation shall aggregate the amounts of all deposits in the insured depository institution which are maintained by a depositor in the same capacity and the same right for the benefit of the depositor either in the name of the depositor or in the name of any other person, other than [money in trust funds].

(D) Coverage for certain employee benefit plan deposits.—

(i) Pass-through insurance.—The Corporation shall provide pass-through deposit insurance for the deposits of any employee benefit plan.

(ii) Prohibition on acceptance of benefit plan deposits.—An insured depository institution that is not well capitalized or adequately capitalized may not accept employee benefit plan deposits.

(iii) Definitions.—For purposes of this subparagraph, the following definitions shall apply: ...

(III) Pass-through deposit insurance.—The term "pass-through deposit insurance" means, with respect to an employee benefit plan, deposit insurance coverage based on the interest of each participant, in accordance with regulations issued by the Corporation.

(E) Standard maximum deposit insurance amount defined.—For purposes of this Act , the term "standard maximum deposit insurance amount" means $250,000, adjusted as provided under subparagraph (F) after March 31, 2010. . . .

(F) Inflation adjustment.—

(i) In general.—By April 1 of 2010, and the 1st day of each subsequent 5-year period, the Board of Directors and the National Credit Union Administration Board shall jointly consider the factors set forth under clause (v), and, upon determining that an inflation adjustment is appropriate, shall jointly prescribe the amount by which the standard maximum deposit insurance amount . . . applicable to any depositor at an insured depository institution shall be increased by calculating the product of—

(I) $100,000; and

(II) the ratio of the published annual value of the Personal Consumption Expenditures Chain-Type Price Index (or any successor index thereto), published by the Department of Commerce, for the calendar year [2005.]

(ii) Rounding.—If the amount determined under clause (ii) for any period is not a multiple of $10,000, the amount so determined shall be rounded down to the nearest $10,000 . . .

(v) Inflation adjustment consideration.—In making any determination under clause (i) to increase the standard maximum deposit insurance amount . . . , the Board of Directors and the National Credit Union Administration Board shall jointly consider—

(I) the overall state of the Deposit Insurance Fund and the economic conditions affecting insured depository institutions;

(II) potential problems affecting insured depository institutions; or

(III) whether the increase will cause the reserve ratio of the fund to fall below 1.15 percent of estimated insured deposits.

(2) Government depositors.—

(A) In general.—Notwithstanding any limitation in this Act or in any other provision of law relating to the amount of deposit insurance available to any 1 depositor—

(i) a government depositor shall, for the purpose of determining the amount of insured deposits under this subsection, be deemed to be a depositor separate and distinct from any other officer, employee, or agent of the United States or any public unit referred to in subparagraph (B); and

(ii) except as provided in subparagraph (C), the deposits of a government depositor shall be insured in an amount equal to the standard maximum deposit insurance amount. . . .

(B) Government depositor.—In this paragraph, the term "government depositor" means a depositor that is—

(i) an officer, employee, or agent of the United States having official custody of public funds and lawfully investing or depositing the same in time and savings deposits in an insured depository institution; [or]

(ii) an officer, employee, or agent of any State of the United States, or of any county, municipality, or political subdivision thereof having official custody of public funds and lawfully investing or depositing the same in time and savings deposits in an insured depository institution in such State. . . .

(C) Authority to limit deposits.—The Corporation may limit the aggregate amount of funds that may be invested or deposited in deposits in any insured depository institution by any government depositor [based on the depository institution's asset size]: *Provided, however,* such limitation may be exceeded by the pledging of acceptable securities to the government depositor when and where required.

(3) Certain retirement accounts.—

(A) In general.—Notwithstanding any limitation in this Act relating to the amount of deposit insurance available for the account of any 1 depositor, deposits in an insured depository institution made in connection with—

(i) any individual retirement account described in 26 U.S.C. § 408(a);

(ii) . . . any eligible deferred compensation plan described in 26 U.S.C. § 457; and

(iii) any individual account plan defined in 29 U.S.C. § 1002(34), and any plan described in 26 U.S.C. § 401(d), to the extent that participants and beneficiaries under such plan have the right to direct the investment of assets held in individual accounts maintained on their behalf by the plan,

shall be aggregated and insured in an amount not to exceed $250,000 (which amount shall be subject to inflation adjustments as provided in paragraph (1)(F), except that $250,000 shall be substituted for $100,000 wherever such term appears in such paragraph) per participant per insured depository institution.

(B) Amounts taken into account.—For purposes of subparagraph (A), the amount aggregated for insurance coverage under this paragraph shall consist of the present vested and ascertainable interest of each participant under the plan, excluding any remainder interest created by, or as a result of, the plan.

(4) Deposit Insurance Fund.—

(A) **Establishment**.—There is established the Deposit Insurance Fund, which the Corporation shall—

(i) maintain and administer;

(ii) use to carry out its insurance purposes, in the manner provided by this subsection; and

(iii) invest in accordance with § 1823(a).

(B) **Uses**.—The Deposit Insurance Fund shall be available to the Corporation for use with respect to insured depository institutions the deposits of which are insured by the Deposit Insurance Fund.

(C) **Limitation on use**.—Notwithstanding any provision of law other than § 1823(c)(4)(G) [i.e., systemic-risk exception to least-cost resolution requirement], the Deposit Insurance Fund shall not be used in any manner to benefit any shareholder or affiliate (other than an insured depository institution that receives assistance in accordance with the provisions of this Act) of—

(i) any insured depository institution for which the Corporation has been appointed conservator or receiver, in connection with any type of resolution by the Corporation;

(ii) any other insured depository institution in default or in danger of default, in connection with any type of resolution by the Corporation; or

(iii) any insured depository institution, in connection with the provision of assistance under this section or § 1823 with respect to such institution, except that this clause shall not prohibit any assistance to any insured depository institution that is not in default, or that is not in danger of default, that is acquiring . . . another insured depository institution.

(D) **Deposits**.—All amounts assessed against insured depository institutions by the Corporation shall be deposited into the Deposit Insurance Fund. . . .

(b) Liquidation as Closing of Depository Institution.—For the purposes of this Act an insured depository institution shall be deemed to have been closed on account or inability to meet the demands of its depositors in any case in which it has been closed for the purpose of liquidation without adequate provision being made for payment of its depositors.

(c) Appointment of Corporation as Conservator or Receiver.—

(1) In general.—Notwithstanding any other provision of Federal law, the law of any State, or the constitution of any State, the Corporation may accept appointment and act as conservator or receiver for any insured depository institution upon appointment in the manner provided in paragraph (2) or (3).

(2) Federal depository institutions.—

(A) Appointment.—

(i) Conservator.—The Corporation may, at the discretion of the supervisory authority, be appointed conservator of any insured Federal depository institution and the Corporation may accept such appointment.

(ii) Receiver.—The Corporation shall be appointed receiver, and shall accept such appointment, whenever a receiver is appointed for the purpose of liquidation or winding up the affairs of an insured Federal depository institution by the appropriate Federal banking agency, notwithstanding any other provision of Federal law. . . .

(3) Insured State depository institutions.—

(A) Appointment by appropriate State supervisor.—Whenever the authority having supervision of any insured State depository institution appoints a conservator or receiver for such institution and tenders appointment to the Corporation, the Corporation may accept such appointment. . . .

(4) Appointment of Corporation by the Corporation.—Notwithstanding any other provision of Federal law, the law of any State, or the constitution of any State, the Corporation may appoint itself as sole conservator or receiver of any insured State depository institution if—

(A) the Corporation determines—

(i) that—

(I) a conservator, receiver, or other legal custodian has been appointed for such institution;

(II) such institution has been subject to the appointment of any such conservator, receiver, or custodian for a period of at least 15 consecutive days; and

(III) 1 or more of the depositors in such institution is unable to withdraw any amount of any insured deposit; or

(ii) that such institution has been closed by or under the laws of any State; and

(B) the Corporation determines that 1 or more of the grounds specified in paragraph (5)—

(i) existed with respect to such institution at the time—

(I) the conservator, receiver, or other legal custodian was appointed; or

(II) such institution was closed; or

(ii) exist at any time—

(I) during the appointment of the conservator, receiver, or other legal custodian; or

(II) while such institution is closed.

(5) Grounds for appointing conservator or receiver.—The grounds for appointing a conservator or receiver (which may be the Corporation) for any insured depository institution are as follows:

(A) Assets insufficient for obligations.—The institution's assets are less than the institution's obligations to its creditors and others, including members of the institution.

(B) Substantial dissipation.—Substantial dissipation of assets or earnings due to—

(i) any violation of any statute or regulation; or

(ii) any unsafe or unsound practice.

(C) Unsafe or unsound condition.—An unsafe or unsound condition to transact business.

(D) Cease and desist orders.—Any willful violation of a cease-and-desist order which has become final.

(E) Concealment.—Any concealment of the institution's books, papers, records, or assets, or any refusal to submit the institution's books, papers, records, or affairs for inspection to any examiner or to any lawful agent of the appropriate Federal banking agency or State bank or savings association supervisor.

(F) Inability to meet obligations.—The institution is likely to be unable to pay its obligations or meet its depositors' demands in the normal course of business.

(G) Losses.—The institution has incurred or is likely to incur losses that will deplete all or substantially all of its capital, and there is no reasonable prospect for the institution to become adequately capitalized. . . .

(H) Violations of law.—Any violation of any law or regulation, or any unsafe or unsound practice or condition that is likely to—

(i) cause insolvency or substantial dissipation of assets or earnings;

(ii) weaken the institution's condition; or

(iii) otherwise seriously prejudice the interests of the institution's depositors or the Deposit Insurance Fund.

(I) Consent.—The institution, by resolution of its board of directors or its shareholders or members, consents to the appointment.

(J) Cessation of insured status.—The institution ceases to be an insured institution.

(K) Undercapitalization.—The institution is undercapitalized (as defined in § 1831o(b)), and—

(i) has no reasonable prospect of becoming adequately capitalized . . . ;

(ii) fails to become adequately capitalized when required to do so under § 1831o(f)(2)(A);

(iii) fails to submit a capital restoration plan acceptable to that agency within the time prescribed under section § 1831o(e)(2)(D); or

(iv) materially fails to implement a capital restoration plan submitted and accepted under § 1831o(e)(2).

(L) Critically inadequate capital.—The institution—
 (i) is critically undercapitalized, as defined in § 1831o(b); or
 (ii) otherwise has substantially insufficient capital.

(M) Money laundering offense.—The Attorney General notifies the appropriate Federal banking agency or the Corporation in writing that the insured depository institution has been found guilty of a criminal offense under § 1956 or § 1957 of title 18 [relating to relating to money laundering and unlicensed money transmitting] or § 5322 or § 5324 of title 31 [relating to money laundering].

(6) Appointment by Comptroller of the Currency.—

(A) Conservator.—The Corporation may, at the discretion of the Comptroller of the Currency, be appointed conservator and the Corporation may accept any such appointment.

(B) Receiver.—The Corporation may, at the discretion of the Comptroller of the Currency, be appointed receiver and the Corporation may accept any such appointment.

(7) Judicial review.—If the Corporation is appointed (including the appointment of the Corporation as receiver by the Board of Directors) as conservator or receiver of a depository institution under paragraph (4), (9), or (10), the depository institution may, not later than 30 days thereafter, bring an action in the United States district court for the judicial district in which the home office of such depository institution is located, or in the United States District Court for the District of Columbia, for an order requiring the Corporation to be removed as the conservator or receiver (regardless of how such appointment was made), and the court shall, upon the merits, dismiss such action or direct the Corporation to be removed as the conservator or receiver.

(8) Replacement of conservator of State depository institution.—

(A) In general.—In the case of any insured State depository institution for which the Corporation appointed itself as conservator pursuant to paragraph (4), the Corporation may, without any requirement of notice, hearing, or other action, replace itself as conservator with itself as receiver of such institution.

(B) Replacement treated as removal of incumbent.—The replacement of a conservator with a receiver under subparagraph (A) shall be treated as the removal of the Corporation as conservator.

(C) Right of review of original appointment not affected.—The replacement of a conservator with a receiver under subparagraph (A) shall not affect any right of the insured State depository institution to obtain review, pursuant to paragraph (7), of the original appointment of the conservator.

(9) Appropriate Federal banking agency may appoint Corporation as conservator or receiver for insured state depository institution to carry out § 1831o.—

(A) **In general**.—The appropriate Federal banking agency may appoint the Corporation as sole receiver (or, subject to paragraph (11), sole conservator) of any insured State depository institution, after consultation with the appropriate State supervisor, if the appropriate Federal banking agency determines that—

(i) 1 or more of the grounds specified in subparagraphs (K) and (L) of paragraph (5) exist with respect to that institution; and

(ii) the appointment is necessary to carry out the purpose of § 1831o. . . .

(10) Corporation may appoint itself as conservator or receiver for insured depository institution to prevent loss to Deposit Insurance Fund.—The Board of Directors may appoint the Corporation as sole conservator or receiver of an insured depository institution, after consultation with the appropriate Federal banking agency and the appropriate State supervisor (if any), if the Board of Directors determines that—

(A) 1 or more of the grounds specified in any subparagraph of paragraph (5) exist with respect to the institution; and

(B) the appointment is necessary to reduce—

(i) the risk that the Deposit Insurance Fund would incur a loss with respect to the insured depository institution, or

(ii) any loss that the Deposit Insurance Fund is expected to incur with respect to that institution.

(11) Appropriate federal banking agency shall not appoint conservator under certain provisions without giving Corporation opportunity to appoint receiver.—The appropriate Federal banking agency shall not appoint a conservator for an insured depository institution under subparagraph (K) or (L) of paragraph (5) without the Corporation's consent unless the agency has given the Corporation 48 hours notice of the agency's intention to appoint the conservator and the grounds for the appointment. . . .

(d) Powers and Duties of Corporation as Conservator or Receiver.—

(1) **Rulemaking authority of Corporation**.—The Corporation may prescribe such regulations as the Corporation determines to be appropriate regarding the conduct of conservatorships or receiverships.

(2) **General powers.**—

(A) **Successor to institution**.—The Corporation shall, as conservator or receiver, and by operation of law, succeed to—

(i) all rights, titles, powers, and privileges of the insured depository institution, and of any stockholder, member, accountholder, depositor, officer, or director of such institution with respect to the institution and the assets of the institution; and

(ii) title to the books, records, and assets of any previous conservator or other legal custodian of such institution.

(B) Operate the institution.—The Corporation may . . . , as conservator or receiver—

(i) take over the assets of and operate the insured depository institution with all the powers of the members or shareholders, the directors, and the officers of the institution and conduct all business of the institution;

(ii) collect all obligations and money due the institution;

(iii) perform all functions of the institution in the name of the institution which are consistent with the appointment as conservator or receiver; and

(iv) preserve and conserve the assets and property of such institution.

(C) Functions of institution's officers, directors, and shareholders.—The Corporation may, by regulation or order, provide for the exercise of any function by any member or stockholder, director, or officer of any insured depository institution for which the Corporation has been appointed conservator or receiver.

(D) Powers as conservator.—The Corporation may, as conservator, take such action as may be—

(i) necessary to put the insured depository institution in a sound and solvent condition; and

(ii) appropriate to carry on the business of the institution and preserve and conserve the assets and property of the institution.

(E) Additional powers as receiver.—The Corporation may . . . , as receiver, place the insured depository institution in liquidation and proceed to realize upon the assets of the institution, having due regard to the conditions of credit in the locality.

(F) Organization of new institutions.—The Corporation may, as receiver, with respect to any insured depository institution, organize a new depository institution under subsection (m) or a bridge depository institution under subsection (n).

(G) Merger; transfer of assets and liabilities.—

(i) **In general**.—The Corporation may, as conservator or receiver—

(I) merge the insured depository institution with another insured depository institution; or

(II) subject to clause (ii), transfer any asset or liability of the institution in default (including assets and liabilities associated with any trust business) without any approval, assignment, or consent with respect to such transfer.

(ii) **Approval by appropriate Federal banking agency**.—No transfer described in clause (i)(II) may be made to another depository institution (other than a new depository institution or a bridge depository institution established pursuant to subsection (m) or (n)) without the approval of the appropriate Federal banking agency for such institution.

(H) Payment of valid obligations.—The Corporation, as conservator or receiver, shall pay all valid obligations of the insured depository institution in accordance with the prescriptions and limitations of this Act. . . .

(J) Incidental powers.—The Corporation may, as conservator or receiver—

(i) exercise all powers and authorities specifically granted to conservators or receivers, respectively, under this Act and such incidental powers as shall be necessary to carry out such powers; and

(ii) take any action authorized by this Act, which the Corporation determines is in the best interests of the depository institution, its depositors, or the Corporation. . . .

(3) Authority of receiver to determine claims.—

(A) In general.—The Corporation may, as receiver, determine claims in accordance with the requirements of this subsection and regulations prescribed under paragraph (4).

(B) Notice requirements.—The receiver, in any case involving the liquidation or winding up of the affairs of a closed depository institution, shall—

(i) promptly publish a notice to the depository institution's creditors to present their claims, together with proof, to the receiver by a date specified in the notice which shall be not less than 90 days after the publication of such notice; and

(ii) republish such notice approximately 1 month and 2 months, respectively, after the publication under clause (i).

(C) Mailing required.—The receiver shall mail a notice similar to the notice published under subparagraph (B)(i) at the time of such publication to any creditor shown on the institution's books—

(i) at the creditor's last address appearing in such books; or

(ii) upon discovery of the name and address of a claimant not appearing on the institution's books within 30 days after the discovery of such name and address. . . .

(5) Procedures for determination of claims.—

(A) Determination period.—

(i) In general.—Before the end of the 180-day period beginning on the date any claim against a depository institution is filed with the Corporation as receiver, the Corporation shall determine whether to allow or disallow the claim and shall notify the claimant of any determination with respect to such claim.

(ii) Extension of time.—The period described in clause (i) may be extended by a written agreement between the claimant and the Corporation.

(iii) Mailing of notice sufficient.—The requirements of clause (i) shall be deemed to be satisfied if the notice of any determination with respect to any claim is mailed to the last address of the claimant which appears—

  (I) on the depository institution's books;
  (II) in the claim filed by the claimant; or
  (III) in documents submitted in proof of the claim.

(iv) Contents of notice of disallowance.—If any claim filed under clause (i) is disallowed, the notice to the claimant shall contain—

  (I) a statement of each reason for the disallowance; and
  (II) the procedures available for obtaining agency review of the determination to disallow the claim or judicial determination of the claim.

(B) Allowance of proven claims.—The receiver shall allow any claim received on or before the date specified in the notice published under paragraph (3)(B)(i) by the receiver from any claimant which is proved to the satisfaction of the receiver.

(C) Disallowance of claims filed after end of filing period.—

(i) In general.—Except as provided in clause (ii), claims filed after the date specified in the notice published under paragraph (3)(B)(i) shall be disallowed and such disallowance shall be final.

(ii) Certain exceptions.—Clause (i) shall not apply with respect to any claim filed by any claimant after the date specified in the notice published under paragraph (3)(B)(i) and such claim may be considered by the receiver if—

  (I) the claimant did not receive notice of the appointment of the receiver in time to file such claim before such date; and
  (II) such claim is filed in time to permit payment of such claim.

(D) Authority to disallow claims.—

(i) In general.—The receiver may disallow any portion of any claim by a creditor or claim of security, preference, or priority which is not proved to the satisfaction of the receiver.

(ii) Payments to less than fully secured creditors.—In the case of a claim of a creditor against an insured depository institution which is secured by any property or other asset of such institution, any receiver appointed for any insured depository institution—

  (I) may treat the portion of such claim which exceeds an amount equal to the fair market value of such property or other asset as an unsecured claim against the institution; and
  (II) may not make any payment with respect to such unsecured portion of the claim other than in connection with the disposition of all claims of unsecured creditors of the institution.

(iii) Exceptions.—No provision of this paragraph shall apply with respect to—

(I) any extension of credit from any Federal home loan bank or Federal Reserve bank to any insured depository institution; or

(II) any security interest in the assets of the institution securing any such extension of credit.

(E) No judicial review of determination pursuant to subparagraph (D).—No court may review the Corporation's determination pursuant to subparagraph (D) to disallow a claim.

(F) Legal effect of filing.—

(i) **Statute of limitation tolled**.—For purposes of any applicable statute of limitations, the filing of a claim with the receiver shall constitute a commencement of an action.

(ii) **No prejudice to other actions**.—Subject to paragraph (12), the filing of a claim with the receiver shall not prejudice any right of the claimant to continue any action which was filed before the appointment of the receiver.

(6) Provision for agency review or judicial determination of claims.—

(A) In general.—Before the end of the 60-day period beginning on the earlier of—

(i) the end of the period described in paragraph (5)(A)(i) with respect to any claim against a depository institution for which the Corporation is receiver; or

(ii) the date of any notice of disallowance of such claim pursuant to paragraph (5)(A)(i),

the claimant may request administrative review of the claim in accordance with subparagraph (A) or (B) of paragraph (7) or file suit on such claim (or continue an action commenced before the appointment of the receiver) in the district ... court of the United States for the district within which the depository institution's principal place of business is located or the United States District Court for the District of Columbia (and such court shall have jurisdiction to hear such claim).

(B) Statute of limitations.—If any claimant fails to—

(i) request administrative review of any claim in accordance with subparagraph (A) or (B) of paragraph (7); or

(ii) file suit on such claim (or continue an action commenced before the appointment of the receiver),

before the end of the 60-day period described in subparagraph (A), the claim shall be deemed to be disallowed (other than any portion of such claim which was allowed by the receiver) as of the end of such period, such disallowance shall be final, and the claimant shall have no further rights or remedies with respect to such claim.

(7) Review of claims.—

(A) Administrative hearing.—If any claimant requests review under this subparagraph in lieu of filing or continuing any action under paragraph (6) and the Corporation agrees to such request, the Corporation shall consider the claim after opportunity for a hearing on the record. The final determination of the Corporation with respect to such claim shall be subject to judicial review under 5 U.S.C. §§ 701-706.

(B) Other review procedures.—

(i) In general.—The Corporation shall also establish such alternative dispute resolution processes as may be appropriate for the resolution of claims filed under paragraph (5)(A)(i).

(ii) Criteria.—In establishing alternative dispute resolution processes, the Corporation shall strive for procedures which are expeditious, fair, independent, and low cost.

(iii) Voluntary binding or nonbinding procedures.—The Corporation may establish both binding and nonbinding processes, which may be conducted by any government or private party, but all parties, including the claimant and the Corporation, must agree to the use of the process in a particular case.

(iv) Consideration of incentives.—The Corporation shall seek to develop incentives for claimants to participate in the alternative dispute resolution process.

(8) Expedited determination of claims.—

(A) Establishment required.—The Corporation shall establish a procedure for expedited relief outside of the routine claims process established under paragraph (5) for claimants who—

(i) allege the existence of legally valid and enforceable or perfected security interests in assets of any depository institution for which the Corporation has been appointed receiver; and

(ii) allege that irreparable injury will occur if the routine claims procedure is followed.

(B) Determination period.—Before the end of the 90-day period beginning on the date any claim is filed in accordance with the procedures established pursuant to subparagraph (A), the Corporation shall—

(i) determine—

(I) whether to allow or disallow such claim; or

(II) whether such claim should be determined pursuant to the procedures established pursuant to paragraph (5); and

(ii) notify the claimant of the determination, and if the claim is disallowed, provide a statement of each reason for the disallowance and the procedure for obtaining agency review or judicial determination.

(C) Period for filing or renewing suit.—Any claimant who files a request for expedited relief shall be permitted to file a suit, or to continue a suit filed before the appointment of the receiver, seeking a determination of the claimant's rights with respect to such security interest after the earlier of—

    (i) the end of the 90-day period beginning on the date of the filing of a request for expedited relief; or

    (ii) the date the Corporation denies the claim.

(D) Statute of limitations.—If an action described in subparagraph (C) is not filed, or the motion to renew a previously filed suit is not made, before the end of the 30-day period beginning on the date on which such action or motion may be filed in accordance with subparagraph (B), the claim shall be deemed to be disallowed as of the end of such period (other than any portion of such claim which was allowed by the receiver), such disallowance shall be final, and the claimant shall have no further rights or remedies with respect to such claim.

(E) Legal effect of filing.—

    (i) Statute of limitation tolled.—For purposes of any applicable statute of limitations, the filing of a claim with the receiver shall constitute a commencement of an action.

    (ii) No prejudice to other actions.—Subject to paragraph (12), the filing of a claim with the receiver shall not prejudice any right of the claimant to continue any action which was filed before the appointment of the receiver.

(9) Agreement as basis of claim.—[A]ny agreement which does not meet the requirements set forth in § 1823(e) shall not form the basis of, or substantially comprise, a claim against the receiver or the Corporation. . . .

(10) Payment of claims.—

(A) In general.—The receiver may, in the receiver's discretion and to the extent funds are available, pay creditor claims which are allowed by the receiver, approved by the Corporation pursuant to a final determination pursuant to paragraph (7) or (8), or determined by the final judgment of any court of competent jurisdiction in such manner and amounts as are authorized under this Act.

(B) Payment of dividends on claims.—The receiver may, in the receiver's sole discretion, pay dividends on proved claims at any time, and no liability shall attach to the Corporation (in such Corporation's corporate capacity or as receiver), by reason of any such payment, for failure to pay dividends to a claimant whose claim is not proved at the time of any such payment.

(C) Rulemaking authority of Corporation.—The Corporation may prescribe such rules, including definitions of terms, as it deems appropriate to establish a single uniform interest rate for or to make payments of post insolvency interest to creditors holding proven claims against the receivership estates of insured Federal or State depository institutions following satisfaction by the receiver of the principal amount of all creditor claims.

(11) Depositor preference.—

(A) **In general.**—Subject to § 1815(e)(2)(C), amounts realized from the liquidation or other resolution of any insured depository institution by any receiver appointed for such institution shall be distributed to pay claims (other than secured claims to the extent of any such security) in the following order of priority:

(i) Administrative expenses of the receiver.

(ii) Any deposit liability of the institution.

(iii) Any other general or senior liability of the institution (which is not a liability described in clause (iv) or (v)).

(iv) Any obligation subordinated to depositors or general creditors (which is not an obligation described in clause (v)).

(v) Any obligation to shareholders or members arising as a result of their status as shareholders or members (including any depository institution holding company or any shareholder or creditor of such company).

(B) **Effect on State law.—**

(i) **In general.**—The provisions of subparagraph (A) shall not supersede the law of any State except to the extent such law is inconsistent with the provisions of such subparagraph, and then only to the extent of the inconsistency. . . .

(12) Suspension of legal actions.—

(A) **In general.**—After the appointment of a conservator or receiver for an insured depository institution, the conservator or receiver may request a stay for a period not to exceed—

(i) 45 days, in the case of any conservator; and

(ii) 90 days, in the case of any receiver,

in any judicial action or proceeding to which such institution is or becomes a party.

(B) **Grant of stay by all courts required.**—Upon receipt of a request by any conservator or receiver pursuant to subparagraph (A) for a stay of any judicial action or proceeding in any court with jurisdiction of such action or proceeding, the court shall grant such stay as to all parties.

(13) Additional rights and duties.—

(A) **Prior final adjudication.**—The Corporation shall abide by any final unappealable judgment of any court of competent jurisdiction which was rendered before the appointment of the Corporation as conservator or receiver.

(B) **Rights and remedies of conservator or receiver.**—In the event of any appealable judgment, the Corporation as conservator or receiver shall—

(i) have all the rights and remedies available to the insured depository institution (before the appointment of such conservator or receiver) and the Corporation in its corporate capacity, including removal to Federal court and all appellate rights; and

(ii) not be required to post any bond in order to pursue such remedies.

(C) No attachment or execution.—No attachment or execution may issue by any court upon assets in the possession of the receiver.

(D) Limitation on judicial review.—Except as otherwise provided in this subsection, no court shall have jurisdiction over—

(i) any claim or action for payment from, or any action seeking a determination of rights with respect to, the assets of any depository institution for which the Corporation has been appointed receiver, including assets which the Corporation may acquire from itself as such receiver; or

(ii) any claim relating to any act or omission of such institution or the Corporation as receiver.

(E) Disposition of assets.—In exercising any right, power, privilege, or authority as conservator or receiver in connection with any sale or disposition of assets of any insured depository institution for which the Corporation has been appointed conservator or receiver, including any sale or disposition of assets acquired by the Corporation under § 1823(d)(1), the Corporation shall conduct its operations in a manner which—

(i) maximizes the net present value return from the sale or disposition of such assets;

(ii) minimizes the amount of any loss realized in the resolution of cases;

(iii) ensures adequate competition and fair and consistent treatment of offerors;

(iv) prohibits discrimination on the basis of race, sex, or ethnic groups in the solicitation and consideration of offers; and

(v) maximizes the preservation of the availability and affordability of residential real property for low- and moderate-income individuals.

(14) Statute of limitations for actions brought by conservator or receiver.—. . . .

(17) Fraudulent transfers.—

(A) In general.—The Corporation, as conservator or receiver for any insured depository institution, and any conservator appointed by the Comptroller of the Currency may avoid a transfer of any interest of an institution-affiliated party, or any person who the Corporation or conservator determines is a debtor of the institution, in property, or any obligation incurred by such party or person, that was made within 5 years of the date on which the Corporation or conservator was appointed conservator or receiver if such party or person voluntarily or involuntarily made such transfer or incurred such liability with the intent to hinder, delay, or defraud the insured depository institution, the Corporation or other conservator, or any other appropriate Federal banking agency.

(B) Right of recovery.—To the extent a transfer is avoided under subparagraph (A), the Corporation or any conservator described in such subparagraph may recover, for the benefit of the insured depository institution, the property transferred, or, if a court so orders, the value of such property (at the time of such transfer) from—

(i) the initial transferee of such transfer or the institution-affiliated party or person for whose benefit such transfer was made; or

(ii) any immediate or mediate transferee of any such initial transferee.

(C) Rights of transferee or obligee.—The Corporation or any conservator described in subparagraph (A) may not recover under subparagraph (B) from—

(i) any transferee that takes for value, including satisfaction or securing of a present or antecedent debt, in good faith; or

(ii) any immediate or mediate good faith transferee of such transferee.

(D) Rights under this paragraph.—The rights under this paragraph of the Corporation and any conservator described in subparagraph (A) shall be superior to any rights of a trustee or any other party (other than any party which is a Federal agency) under title 11, United States Code.

(18) Attachment of assets and other injunctive relief.—Subject to paragraph (19), any court of competent jurisdiction may, at the request of —

(A) the Corporation (in the Corporation's capacity as conservator or receiver for any insured depository institution or in the Corporation's corporate capacity with respect to any asset acquired or liability assumed by the Corporation under § 1821, § 1822, or § 1823); or

(B) any conservator appointed by the Comptroller of the Currency,

issue an order in accordance with Rule 65 of the Federal Rules of Civil Procedure, including an order placing the assets of any person designated by the Corporation or such conservator under the control of the court and appointing a trustee to hold such assets.

(19) Standards.—

(A) Showing.—Rule 65 of the Federal Rules of Civil Procedure shall apply with respect to any proceeding under paragraph (18) without regard to the requirement of such rule that the applicant show that the injury, loss, or damage is irreparable and immediate. . . .

(20) Treatment of claims arising from breach of contracts executed by the receiver or conservator.—Notwithstanding any other provision of this subsection, any final and unappealable judgment for monetary damages entered against a receiver or conservator for an insured depository institution for the breach of an agreement executed or approved by such receiver or conservator after the date of its appointment shall be paid as an administrative expense of the receiver or conservator. Nothing in this paragraph shall be construed to limit the power of a receiver or conservator to exercise any rights under contract or law, including to terminate, breach, cancel, or otherwise discontinue such agreement.

(e) Provisions Relating to Contracts Entered into Before Appointment of Conservator or Receiver.—

(1) Authority to repudiate contracts.—In addition to any other rights a conservator or receiver may have, the conservator or receiver for any insured depository institution may disaffirm or repudiate any contract or lease—

(A) to which such institution is a party;

(B) the performance of which the conservator or receiver, in the conservator's or receiver's discretion, determines to be burdensome; and

(C) the disaffirmance or repudiation of which the conservator or receiver determines, in the conservator's or receiver's discretion, will promote the orderly administration of the institution's affairs.

(2) Timing of repudiation.—The conservator or receiver appointed for any insured depository institution in accordance with subsection (c) shall determine whether or not to exercise the rights of repudiation under this subsection within a reasonable period following such appointment.

(3) Claims for damages for repudiation.—

(A) In general.—Except as otherwise provided in subparagraph (C) and paragraphs (4), (5), and (6), the liability of the conservator or receiver for the disaffirmance or repudiation of any contract pursuant to paragraph (1) shall be—

(i) limited to actual direct compensatory damages; and

(ii) determined as of—

(I) the date of the appointment of the conservator or receiver; or

(II) in the case of any contract or agreement referred to in paragraph (8), the date of the disaffirmance or repudiation of such contract or agreement.

(B) No liability for other damages.—For purposes of subparagraph (A), the term "actual direct compensatory damages" does not include—

(i) punitive or exemplary damages;

(ii) damages for lost profits or opportunity; or

(iii) damages for pain and suffering.

(C) Measure of damages for repudiation of financial contracts.—In the case of any qualified financial contract or agreement to which paragraph (8) applies, compensatory damages shall be—

(i) deemed to include normal and reasonable costs of cover or other reasonable measures of damages utilized in the industries for such contract and agreement claims; and

(ii) paid in accordance with this subsection and subsection (i) except as otherwise specifically provided in this section.

(4) Leases under which the institution is the lessee.—

(A) In general.—If the conservator or receiver disaffirms or repudiates a lease under which the insured depository institution was the lessee, the conservator or receiver shall not be liable for any damages (other than damages determined pursuant to subparagraph (B)) for the disaffirmance or repudiation of such lease.

(B) Payments of rent.—Notwithstanding subparagraph (A), the lessor under a lease to which such subparagraph applies shall—

(i) be entitled to the contractual rent accruing before the later of the date—

(I) the notice of disaffirmance or repudiation is mailed; or

(II) the disaffirmance or repudiation becomes effective, unless the lessor is in default or breach of the terms of the lease;

(ii) have no claim for damages under any acceleration clause or other penalty provision in the lease; and

(iii) have a claim for any unpaid rent, subject to all appropriate offsets and defenses, due as of the date of the appointment which shall be paid in accordance with this subsection and subsection (i).

(5) Leases under which the institution is the lessor.—

(A) In general.—If the conservator or receiver repudiates an unexpired written lease of real property of the insured depository institution under which the institution is the lessor and the lessee is not, as of the date of such repudiation, in default, the lessee under such lease may either—

(i) treat the lease as terminated by such repudiation; or

(ii) remain in possession of the leasehold interest for the balance of the term of the lease unless the lessee defaults under the terms of the lease after the date of such repudiation.

(B) Provisions applicable to lessee remaining in possession.—If any lessee under a lease described in subparagraph (A) remains in possession of a leasehold interest pursuant to clause (ii) of such subparagraph—

(i) the lessee—

(I) shall continue to pay the contractual rent pursuant to the terms of the lease after the date of the repudiation of such lease;

(II) may offset against any rent payment which accrues after the date of the repudiation of the lease, any damages which accrue after such date due to the nonperformance of any obligation of the insured depository institution under the lease after such date; and

Federal Deposit Insurance Act 12 U.S.C. § 1821

(ii) the conservator or receiver shall not be liable to the lessee for any damages arising after such date as a result of the repudiation other than the amount of any offset allowed under clause (i)(II).

(6) Contracts for the sale of real property.—

(A) In general.—If the conservator or receiver repudiates any contract (which meets the requirements of each paragraph of § 1823(e)) for the sale of real property and the purchaser of such real property under such contract is in possession and is not, as of the date of such repudiation, in default, such purchaser may either—

(i) treat the contract as terminated by such repudiation; or

(ii) remain in possession of such real property.

(B) Provisions applicable to purchaser remaining in possession.—If any purchaser of real property under any contract described in subparagraph (A) remains in possession of such property pursuant to clause (ii) of such subparagraph—

(i) the purchaser—

(I) shall continue to make all payments due under the contract after the date of the repudiation of the contract; and

(II) may offset against any such payments any damages which accrue after such date due to the nonperformance (after such date) of any obligation of the depository institution under the contract; and

(ii) the conservator or receiver shall—

(I) not be liable to the purchaser for any damages arising after such date as a result of the repudiation other than the amount of any offset allowed under clause (i)(II);

(II) deliver title to the purchaser in accordance with the provisions of the contract; and

(III) have no obligation under the contract other than the performance required under subclause (II).

(C) Assignment and sale allowed.—

(i) In general.—No provision of this paragraph shall be construed as limiting the right of the conservator or receiver to assign the contract described in subparagraph (A) and sell the property subject to the contract and the provisions of this paragraph.

(ii) No liability after assignment and sale.—If an assignment and sale described in clause (i) is consummated, the conservator or receiver shall have no further liability under the contract described in subparagraph (A) or with respect to the real property which was the subject of such contract.

(7) Provisions applicable to service contracts.—

(A) Services performed before appointment.—In the case of any contract for services between any person and any insured depository institution for which the Corporation has been appointed conservator or receiver, any claim of such person for services performed before the appointment of the conservator or the receiver shall be—

(i) a claim to be paid in accordance with subsections (d) and (i); and

(ii) deemed to have arisen as of the date the conservator or receiver was appointed.

(B) Services performed after appointment and prior to repudiation.—If, in the case of any contract for services described in subparagraph (A), the conservator or receiver accepts performance by the other person before the conservator or receiver makes any determination to exercise the right of repudiation of such contract under this section—

(i) the other party shall be paid under the terms of the contract for the services performed; and

(ii) the amount of such payment shall be treated as an administrative expense of the conservatorship or receivership.

(C) Acceptance of performance no bar to subsequent repudiation.—The acceptance by any conservator or receiver of services referred to in subparagraph (B) in connection with a contract described in such subparagraph shall not affect the right of the conservator or receiver to repudiate such contract under this section at any time after such performance.

(8) Certain qualified financial contracts.—

(A) Rights of parties to contracts.—Subject to paragraphs (9) and (10) of this subsection and notwithstanding any other provision of this Act (other than subsection (d)(9) of this section and § 1823(e)), any other Federal law, or the law of any State, no person shall be stayed or prohibited from exercising—

(i) any right such person has to cause the termination, liquidation, or acceleration of any qualified financial contract with an insured depository institution which arises upon the appointment of the Corporation as receiver for such institution at any time after such appointment;

(ii) any right under any security agreement or arrangement or other credit enhancement related to one or more qualified financial contracts described in clause (i); [or]

(iii) any right to offset or net out any termination value, payment amount, or other transfer obligation arising under or in connection with 1 or more contracts and agreements described in clause (i), including any master agreement for such contracts or agreements.

(B) Applicability of other provisions.—Subsection (d)(12) shall apply in the case of any judicial action or proceeding brought against any receiver referred to in subparagraph (A), or the insured depository institution for which such receiver was appointed, by any party to a contract or agreement described in subparagraph (A)(i) with such institution.

(C) Certain transfers not avoidable.—

(i) In general.—Notwithstanding . . . any . . . Federal or State law relating to the avoidance of preferential or fraudulent transfers, the Corporation, whether acting as such or as conservator or receiver of an insured depository institution, may not avoid any transfer of money or other property in connection with any qualified financial contract with an insured depository institution.

(ii) Exception for certain transfers.—Clause (i) shall not apply to any transfer of money or other property in connection with any qualified financial contract with an insured depository institution if the Corporation determines that the transferee had actual intent to hinder, delay, or defraud such institution, the creditors of such institution, or any conservator or receiver appointed for such institution.

(D) Certain contracts and agreements defined.—For purposes of this subsection, the following definitions shall apply:

(i) Qualified financial contract.—The term "qualified financial contract" means any securities contract, commodity contract, forward contract, repurchase agreement, swap agreement, and any similar agreement that the Corporation determines by regulation, resolution or order to be a qualified financial contract for purposes of this paragraph.

(ii) Securities contract.—The term "securities contract"—

(I) means a contract for the purchase, sale, or loan of a security, a certificate of deposit, a mortgage loan, any interest in a mortgage loan, a group or index of securities, certificates of deposit, or mortgage loans or interests therein (including any interest therein or based on the value thereof) or any option on any of the foregoing, including any option to purchase or sell any such security, certificate of deposit, mortgage loan, interest, group or index, or option, and including any repurchase or reverse repurchase transaction on any such security, certificate of deposit, mortgage loan, interest, group or index, or option (whether or not such repurchase or reverse repurchase transaction is a "repurchase agreement", as defined in clause (v));

(II) does not include any purchase, sale, or repurchase obligation under a participation in a commercial mortgage loan unless the Corporation determines by regulation, resolution, or order to include any such agreement within the meaning of such term;

(III) means any option entered into on a national securities exchange relating to foreign currencies;

(IV) means the guarantee (including by novation) by or to any securities clearing agency of any settlement of cash, securities, certificates of deposit, mortgage loans or interests therein, group or index of securities, certificates of deposit, or mortgage loans or interests therein (including any interest therein or based on the value thereof) or option on any of the foregoing, including any option to purchase or sell any such security, certificate of deposit, mortgage loan, interest, group or index, or option (whether or not such settlement is in connection with any agreement or transaction referred to in subclauses (I) through (XII) (other than subclause (II));

(V) means any margin loan;

(VI) means any extension of credit for the clearance or settlement of securities transactions;

(VII) means any loan transaction coupled with a securities collar transaction, any prepaid securities forward transaction, or any total return swap transaction coupled with a securities sale transaction;

(VIII) means any other agreement or transaction that is similar to any agreement or transaction referred to in this clause;

(IX) means any combination of the agreements or transactions referred to in this clause;

(X) means any option to enter into any agreement or transaction referred to in this clause;

(XI) means a master agreement that provides for an agreement or transaction referred to in subclause (I), (III), (IV), (V), (VI), (VII), (VIII), (IX), or (X), together with all supplements to any such master agreement, without regard to whether the master agreement provides for an agreement or transaction that is not a securities contract under this clause, except that the master agreement shall be considered to be a securities contract under this clause only with respect to each agreement or transaction under the master agreement that is referred to in subclause (I), (III), (IV), (V), (VI), (VII), (VIII), (IX), or (X); and

(XII) means any security agreement or arrangement or other credit enhancement related to any agreement or transaction referred to in this clause, including any guarantee or reimbursement obligation in connection with any agreement or transaction referred to in this clause.

(iii) **Commodity contract**.—The term ''commodity contract'' means—

(I) with respect to a futures commission merchant, a contract for the purchase or sale of a commodity for future delivery on, or subject to the rules of, a contract market or board of trade;

(II) with respect to a foreign futures commission merchant, a foreign future;

(III) with respect to a leverage transaction merchant, a leverage transaction;

(IV) with respect to a clearing organization, a contract for the purchase or sale of a commodity for future delivery on, or subject to the rules of, a contract market or board of trade that is cleared by such clearing organization, or commodity option traded on, or subject to the rules of, a contract market or board of trade that is cleared by such clearing organization;

(V) with respect to a commodity options dealer, a commodity option;

(VI) any other agreement or transaction that is similar to any agreement or transaction referred to in this clause;

(VII) any combination of the agreements or transactions referred to in this clause;

(VIII) any option to enter into any agreement or transaction referred to in this clause;

(IX) a master agreement that provides for an agreement or transaction referred to in subclause (I), (II), (III), (IV), (V), (VI), (VII), or (VIII), together with all supplements to any such master agreement, without regard to whether the master agreement provides for an agreement or transaction that is not a commodity contract under this clause, except that the master agreement shall be considered to be a commodity contract under this clause only with respect to each agreement or transaction under the master agreement that is referred to in subclause (I), (II), (III), (IV), (V), (VI), (VII), or (VIII); or

(X) any security agreement or arrangement or other credit enhancement related to any agreement or transaction referred to in this clause, including any guarantee or reimbursement obligation in connection with any agreement or transaction referred to in this clause.

(iv) Forward contract.—The term "forward contract" means—

(I) a contract (other than a commodity contract) for the purchase, sale, or transfer of a commodity or any similar good, article, service, right, or interest which is presently or in the future becomes the subject of dealing in the forward contract trade, or product or byproduct thereof, with a maturity date more than 2 days after the date the contract is entered into, including a repurchase or reverse repurchase transaction (whether or not such repurchase or reverse repurchase transaction is a "repurchase agreement", as defined in clause (v)), consignment, lease, swap, hedge transaction, deposit, loan, option, allocated transaction, unallocated transaction, or any other similar agreement;

(II) any combination of agreements or transactions referred to in subclauses (I) and (III);

(III) any option to enter into any agreement or transaction referred to in subclause (I) or (II);

(IV) a master agreement that provides for an agreement or transaction referred to in subclauses (I), (II), or (III), together with all supplements to any such master agreement, without regard to whether the master agreement provides for an agreement or transaction that is not a forward contract under this clause, except that the master agreement shall be considered to be a forward contract under this clause only with respect to each agreement or transaction under the master agreement that is referred to in subclause (I), (II), or (III); or

(V) any security agreement or arrangement or other credit enhancement related to any agreement or transaction referred to in subclause (I), (II), (III), or (IV), including any guarantee or reimbursement obligation in connection with any agreement or transaction referred to in any such subclause.

(v) Repurchase agreement.—The term "repurchase agreement" (which definition also applies to a reverse repurchase agreement)—

(I) means an agreement, including related terms, which provides for the transfer of one or more certificates of deposit, mortgage-related securities (as such term is defined in the Securities Exchange Act of 1934), mortgage loans, interests in mortgage-related securities or mortgage loans, eligible bankers' acceptances, qualified foreign government securities or securities that are direct obligations of, or that are fully guaranteed by, the United States or any agency of the United States against the transfer of funds by the transferee of such certificates of deposit, eligible bankers' acceptances, securities, mortgage loans, or interests with a simultaneous agreement by such transferee to transfer to the transferor thereof certificates of deposit, eligible bankers' acceptances, securities, mortgage loans, or interests as described above, at a date certain not later than 1 year after such transfers or on demand, against the transfer of funds, or any other similar agreement;

(II) does not include any repurchase obligation under a participation in a commercial mortgage loan unless the Corporation determines by regulation, resolution, or order to include any such participation within the meaning of such term;

(III) means any combination of agreements or transactions referred to in subclauses (I) and (IV);

(IV) means any option to enter into any agreement or transaction referred to in subclause (I) or (III);

(V) means a master agreement that provides for an agreement or transaction referred to in subclause (I), (III), or (IV), together with all supplements to any such master agreement, without regard to whether the master agreement provides for an agreement or transaction that is not a repurchase agreement under this clause, except that the master agreement shall be considered to be a repurchase agreement under this subclause only with respect to each agreement or transaction under the master agreement that is referred to in subclause (I), (III), or (IV); and

(VI) means any security agreement or arrangement or other credit enhancement related to any agreement or transaction referred to in subclause (I), (III), (IV), or (V), including any guarantee or reimbursement obligation in connection with any agreement or transaction referred to in any such subclause.

For purposes of this clause, the term "qualified foreign government security" means a security that is a direct obligation of, or that is fully guaranteed by, the central government of a member of the Organization for Economic Cooperation and Development (as determined by regulation or order adopted by the appropriate Federal banking authority).

(vi) Swap agreement.—The term "swap agreement" means—

(I) any agreement, including the terms and conditions incorporated by reference in any such agreement, which is an interest rate swap, option, future, or forward agreement, including a rate floor, rate cap, rate collar, cross-currency rate swap, and basis swap; a spot, same day-tomorrow, tomorrow-next, forward, or other foreign exchange, precious metals, or other commodity agreement; a currency swap, option, future, or forward agreement; an equity index or equity swap, option, future, or forward agreement; a debt index or debt swap, option, future, or forward agreement; a total return, credit spread or credit swap, option, future, or forward agreement; a commodity index or commodity swap, option, future, or forward agreement; weather swap, option, future, or forward agreement; an emissions swap, option, future, or forward agreement; or an inflation swap, option, future, or forward agreement;

(II) any agreement or transaction that is similar to any other agreement or transaction referred to in this clause and that is of a type that has been, is presently, or in the future becomes, the subject of recurrent dealings in the swap or other derivatives markets (including terms and conditions incorporated by reference in such agreement) and that is a forward, swap, future, option, or spot transaction on one or more rates, currencies, commodities, equity securities or other equity instruments, debt securities or other debt instruments, quantitative measures associated with an occurrence, extent of an occurrence, or contingency associated with a financial, commercial, or economic consequence, or economic or financial indices or measures of economic or financial risk or value;

(III) any combination of agreements or transactions referred to in this clause;

(IV) any option to enter into any agreement or transaction referred to in this clause;

(V) a master agreement that provides for an agreement or transaction referred to in subclause (I), (II), (III), or (IV), together with all supplements to any such master agreement, without regard to whether the master agreement contains an agreement or transaction that is not a swap agreement under this clause, except that the master agreement shall be considered to be a swap agreement under this clause only with respect to each agreement or transaction under the master agreement that is referred to in subclause (I), (II), (III), or (IV); and

(VI) any security agreement or arrangement or other credit enhancement related to any agreements or transactions referred to in subclause (I), (II), (III), (IV), or (V), including any guarantee or reimbursement obligation in connection with any agreement or transaction referred to in any such subclause. . . .

(vii) Treatment of master agreement as one agreement.—Any master agreement for any contract or agreement described in any preceding clause of this subparagraph (or any master agreement for such master agreement or agreements), together with all supplements to such master agreement, shall be treated as a single agreement and a single qualified financial contract.—If a master agreement contains provisions relating to agreements or transactions that are not themselves qualified financial contracts, the master agreement shall be deemed to be a qualified financial contract only with respect to those transactions that are themselves qualified financial contracts.

(viii) Transfer.—The term "transfer" means every mode, direct or indirect, absolute or conditional, voluntary or involuntary, of disposing of or parting with property or with an interest in property, including retention of title as a security interest and foreclosure of the depository institution's equity of redemption. . . .

(E) Certain protections in event of appointment of conservator.—Notwithstanding any other provision of this Act (other than subsections (d)(9) and (e)(10) of this section, and § 1323(e)), any other Federal law, or the law of any State, no person shall be stayed or prohibited from exercising—

(i) any right such person has to cause the termination, liquidation, or acceleration of any qualified financial contract with a depository institution in a conservatorship based upon a default under such financial contract which is enforceable under applicable noninsolvency law;

(ii) any right under any security agreement or arrangement or other credit enhancement related to one or more qualified financial contracts described in clause (i); [or]

(iii) any right to offset or net out any termination values, payment amounts, or other transfer obligations arising under or in connection with such qualified financial contracts.

(F) **Clarification**.—No provision of law shall be construed as limiting the right or power of the Corporation, or authorizing any court or agency to limit or delay, in any manner, the right or power of the Corporation to transfer any qualified financial contract in accordance with paragraphs (9) and (10) of this subsection or to disaffirm or repudiate any such contract in accordance with subsection (e)(1) of this section.

(G) **Walkaway clauses not effective**.—

(i) **In general**.—[N]o walkaway clause shall be enforceable in a qualified financial contract of an insured depository institution in default.

(ii) **Limited suspension of certain obligations**.—In the case of a qualified financial contract referred to in clause (i), any payment or delivery obligations otherwise due from a party pursuant to the qualified financial contract shall be suspended from the time the receiver is appointed until the earlier of—

(I) the time such party receives notice that such contract has been transferred pursuant to subparagraph (A); or

(II) 5:00 p.m. (eastern time) on the business day following the date of the appointment of the receiver.

(iii) **Walkaway clause defined**.—For purposes of this subparagraph, the term "walkaway clause" means any provision in a qualified financial contract that suspends, conditions, or extinguishes a payment obligation of a party, in whole or in part, or does not create a payment obligation of a party that would otherwise exist, solely because of such party's status as a nondefaulting party in connection with the insolvency of an insured depository institution that is a party to the contract or the appointment of or the exercise of rights or powers by a conservator or receiver of such depository institution, and not as a result of a party's exercise of any right to offset, setoff, or net obligations that exist under the contract, any other contract between those parties, or applicable law. . . .

(9) **Transfer of qualified financial contracts**.—

(A) **In general**.—In making any transfer of assets or liabilities of a depository institution in default which includes any qualified financial contract, the conservator or receiver for such depository institution shall either—

(i) transfer to one financial institution, other than a financial institution for which a conservator, receiver, trustee in bankruptcy, or other legal custodian has been appointed or which is otherwise the subject of a bankruptcy or insolvency proceeding—

(I) all qualified financial contracts between any person or any affiliate of such person and the depository institution in default;

(II) all claims of such person or any affiliate of such person against such depository institution under any such contract (other than any claim which, under the terms of any such contract, is subordinated to the claims of general unsecured creditors of such institution);

(III) all claims of such depository institution against such person or any affiliate of such person under any such contract; and

(IV) all property securing or any other credit enhancement for any contract described in subclause (I) or any claim described in subclause (II) or (III) under any such contract; or

(ii) transfer none of the qualified financial contracts, claims, property or other credit enhancement referred to in clause (i) (with respect to such person and any affiliate of such person). . . .

(C) Transfer of contracts subject to the rules of a clearing organization.—In the event that a conservator or receiver transfers any qualified financial contract and related claims, property, and credit enhancements pursuant to subparagraph (A)(i) and such contract is cleared by or subject to the rules of a clearing organization, the clearing organization shall not be required to accept the transferee as a member by virtue of the transfer.

(D) Definitions.—For purposes of this paragraph, the term "financial institution" means a broker or dealer, a depository institution, a futures commission merchant, or any other institution, as determined by the Corporation by regulation to be a financial institution, and the term "clearing organization" has the same meaning as in § 4402.

(10) Notification of transfer.—

(A) In general.—If—

(i) the conservator or receiver for an insured depository institution in default makes any transfer of the assets and liabilities of such institution; and

(ii) the transfer includes any qualified financial contract,

the conservator or receiver shall notify any person who is a party to any such contract of such transfer by 5:00 p.m. (eastern time) on the business day following the date of the appointment of the receiver in the case of a receivership, or the business day following such transfer in the case of a conservatorship.

(B) Certain rights not enforceable.—

(i) Receivership.—A person who is a party to a qualified financial contract with an insured depository institution may not exercise any right that such person has to terminate, liquidate, or net such contract under paragraph (8)(A) of this subsection or § 4403 or § 4404, solely by reason of or incidental to the appointment of a receiver for the depository institution (or the insolvency or financial condition of the depository institution for which the receiver has been appointed)—

(I) until 5:00 p.m. (eastern time) on the business day following the date of the appointment of the receiver; or

(II) after the person has received notice that the contract has been transferred pursuant to paragraph (9)(A).

(ii) Conservatorship.—A person who is a party to a qualified financial contract with an insured depository institution may not exercise any right that such person has to terminate, liquidate, or net such contract under paragraph (8)(E) of this subsection or § 4403 or § 4404, solely by reason of or incidental to the appointment of a conservator for the depository institution (or the insolvency or financial condition of the depository institution for which the conservator has been appointed). . . .

(C) Treatment of bridge depository institutions.—The following institutions shall not be considered to be a financial institution for which a conservator, receiver, trustee in bankruptcy, or other legal custodian has been appointed or which is otherwise the subject of a bankruptcy or insolvency proceeding for purposes of paragraph (9):

(i) A bridge depository institution.

(ii) A depository institution organized by the Corporation, for which a conservator is appointed either—

(I) immediately upon the organization of the institution; or

(II) at the time of a purchase and assumption transaction between the depository institution and the Corporation as receiver for a depository institution in default. . . .

(11) Disaffirmance or repudiation of qualified financial contracts.—In exercising the rights of disaffirmance or repudiation of a conservator or receiver with respect to any qualified financial contract to which an insured depository institution is a party, the conservator or receiver for such institution shall either—

(A) disaffirm or repudiate all qualified financial contracts between—

(i) any person or any affiliate of such person; and

(ii) the depository institution in default; or

(B) disaffirm or repudiate none of the qualified financial contracts referred to in subparagraph (A) (with respect to such person or any affiliate of such person).

(12) Certain security interests not avoidable.—No provision of this subsection shall be construed as permitting the avoidance of any legally enforceable or perfected security interest in any of the assets of any depository institution except where such an interest is taken in contemplation of the institution's insolvency or with the intent to hinder, delay, or defraud the institution or the creditors of such institution.

(13) Authority to enforce contracts.—

(A) In general.—The conservator or receiver may enforce any contract, other than a director's or officer's liability insurance contract or a depository institution bond, entered into by the depository institution notwithstanding any provision of the contract providing for termination, default, acceleration, or exercise of rights upon, or solely by reason of, insolvency or the appointment of or the exercise of rights or powers by a conservator or receiver.

(B) Certain rights not affected.—No provision of this paragraph may be construed as impairing or affecting any right of the conservator or receiver to enforce or recover under a director's or officer's liability insurance contract or depository institution bond under other applicable law.

(C) Consent requirement.—

(i) In general.—Except as otherwise provided by this section . . . , no person may exercise any right or power to terminate, accelerate, or declare a default under any contract to which the depository institution is a party, or to obtain possession of or exercise control over any property of the institution or affect any contractual rights of the institution, without the consent of the conservator or receiver, as appropriate, during the 45-day period beginning on the date of the appointment of the conservator, or during the 90-day period beginning on the date of the appointment of the receiver, as applicable.

(ii) Certain exceptions.—No provision of this subparagraph shall apply to a director or officer liability insurance contract or a depository institution bond, to the rights of parties to certain qualified financial contracts pursuant to paragraph (8), or to the rights of parties to netting contracts pursuant to §§ 4401-4407, or shall be construed as permitting the conservator or receiver to fail to comply with otherwise enforceable provisions of such contract.

(iii) Rule of construction.—Nothing in this subparagraph shall be construed to limit or otherwise affect the applicability of title 11, United States Code.

(14) Exception for Federal Reserve and Federal home loan banks.—No provision of this subsection shall apply with respect to—

(A) any extension of credit from any Federal home loan bank or Federal Reserve bank to any insured depository institution; or

(B) any security interest in the assets of the institution securing any such extension of credit.

(15) Selling credit card accounts receivable.—

(A) Notification required.—An undercapitalized insured depository institution . . . shall notify the Corporation in writing before entering into an agreement to sell credit card accounts receivable.

(B) Waiver by Corporation.—The Corporation may at any time, in its sole discretion and upon such terms as it may prescribe, waive its right to repudiate an agreement to sell credit card accounts receivable if the Corporation—

(i) determines that the waiver is in the best interests of the Deposit Insurance Fund; and

(ii) provides a written waiver to the selling institution.

(C) Effect of waiver on successors.—

(i) In general.—If, under subparagraph (B), the Corporation has waived its right to repudiate an agreement to sell credit card accounts receivable—

(I) any provision of the agreement that restricts solicitation of a credit card customer of the selling institution, or the use of a credit card customer list of the institution, shall bind any receiver or conservator of the institution; and

(II) the Corporation shall require any acquirer of the selling institution, or of substantially all of the selling institution's assets or liabilities, to agree to be bound by a provision described in subclause (I) as if the acquirer were the selling institution.

(ii) Exception.—Clause (i)(II) does not—

(I) restrict the acquirer's authority to offer any product or service to any person identified without using a list of the selling institution's customers in violation of the agreement;

(II) require the acquirer to restrict any preexisting relationship between the acquirer and a customer; or

(III) apply to any transaction in which the acquirer acquires only insured deposits.

(D) Waiver not actionable.—The Corporation shall not, in any capacity, be liable to any person for damages resulting from the waiver of or failure to waive the Corporation's right under this section to repudiate any contract or lease, including an agreement to sell credit card accounts receivable. No court shall issue any order affecting any such waiver or failure to waive. . . .

(f) Payment of Insured Deposits.—

(1) In general.—In case of the liquidation of, or other closing or winding up of the affairs of, any insured depository institution, payment of the insured deposits in such institution shall be made by the Corporation as soon as possible, subject to the provisions of subsection (g), either by cash or by making available to each depositor a transferred deposit in a new insured depository institution in the same community or in another insured depository institution in an amount equal to the insured deposit of such depositor.

(2) Proof of claims.—The Corporation, in its discretion, may require proof of claims to be filed and may approve or reject such claims for insured deposits.

(3) Resolution of disputes.—A determination by the Corporation regarding any claim for insurance coverage shall be treated as a final determination for purposes of this section. In its discretion, the Corporation may promulgate regulations prescribing procedures for resolving any disputed claim relating to any insured deposit or any determination of insurance coverage with respect to any deposit.

(4) Review of Corporation determination.—A final determination made by the Corporation regarding any claim for insurance coverage shall be a final agency action reviewable in accordance with 5 U.S.C. §§ 701-706 by the United States district court for the Federal judicial district where the principal place of business of the depository institution is located.

(5) Statute of limitations.—Any request for review of a final determination by the Corporation regarding any claim for insurance coverage shall be filed with the appropriate United States district court not later than 60 days after the date on which such determination is issued.

(g) Subrogation of Corporation.—

(1) In general.—Notwithstanding any other provision of Federal law, the law of any State, or the constitution of any State, the Corporation, upon the payment to any depositor as provided in subsection (f) in connection with any insured depository institution or insured branch described in such subsection or the assumption of any deposit in such institution or branch by another insured depository institution pursuant to this section or § 1823, shall be subrogated to all rights of the depositor against such institution or branch to the extent of such payment or assumption.

(2) Dividends on subrogated amounts.—The subrogation of the Corporation under paragraph (1) with respect to any insured depository institution shall include the right on the part of the Corporation to receive the same dividends from the proceeds of the assets of such institution and recoveries on account of stockholders' liability as would have been payable to the depositor on a claim for the insured deposit, but such depositor shall retain such claim for any uninsured or unassumed portion of the deposit. . . .

(4) Applicability of State law.—Subject to subsection (d)(11), if the Corporation is appointed pursuant to subsection (c)(3), or determines not to invoke the authority conferred in subsection (c)(4), the rights of depositors and other creditors of any State depository institution shall be determined in accordance with the applicable provisions of State law.

(h) Conditions Applicable to Resolution Proceedings.—

(1) Consideration of local economic impact required.—The Corporation shall fully consider the adverse economic impact on local communities, including businesses and farms, of actions to be taken by it during the administration and liquidation of loans of a depository institution in default. . . .

(i) Valuation of Claims in Default.—

(1) In general.—Notwithstanding any other provision of Federal law or the law of any State and regardless of the method which the Corporation determines to utilize with respect to an insured depository institution in default or in danger of default, including transactions authorized under subsection (n) and § 1823(c), this subsection shall govern the rights of the creditors (other than insured depositors) of such institution.

(2) Maximum liability.—The maximum liability of the Corporation, acting as receiver or in any other capacity, to any person having a claim against the receiver or the insured depository institution for which such receiver is appointed shall equal the amount such claimant would have received if the Corporation had liquidated the assets and liabilities of such institution without exercising the Corporation's authority under subsection (n) of this section or § 1823.

(3) Additional payments authorized.—

(A) In general.—The Corporation may, in its discretion and in the interests of minimizing its losses, use its own resources to make additional payments or credit additional amounts to or with respect to or for the account of any claimant or category of claimants.—Notwithstanding any other provision of Federal or State law, or the constitution of any State, the Corporation shall not be obligated, as a result of having made any such payment or credited any such amount to or with respect to or for the account of any claimant or category of claimants, to make payments to any other claimant or category of claimants.

(B) Manner of payment.—The Corporation may make the payments or credit the amounts specified in subparagraph (A) directly to the claimants or may make such payments or credit such amounts to an open insured depository institution to induce such institution to accept liability for such claims.

(j) Limitation on Court Action.—Except as provided in this section, no court may take any action, except at the request of the Board of Directors by regulation or order, to restrain or affect the exercise of powers or functions of the Corporation as a conservator or a receiver.

(k) Liability of Directors and Officers.—A director or officer of an insured depository institution may be held personally liable for monetary damages in any civil action by, on behalf of, or at the request or direction of the Corporation, which action is prosecuted wholly or partially for the benefit of the Corporation—

(1) acting as conservator or receiver of such institution,

(2) acting based upon a suit, claim, or cause of action purchased from, assigned by, or otherwise conveyed by such receiver or conservator, or

(3) acting based upon a suit, claim, or cause of action purchased from, assigned by, or otherwise conveyed in whole or in part by an insured depository institution or its affiliate in connection with assistance provided under § 1823,

for gross negligence, including any similar conduct or conduct that demonstrates a greater disregard of a duty of care (than gross negligence) including intentional tortious conduct, as such terms are defined and determined under applicable State law.—Nothing in this paragraph shall impair or affect any right of the Corporation under other applicable law.

(*l*) **Damages.**—In any proceeding related to any claim against an insured depository institution's director, officer, employee, agent, attorney, accountant, appraiser, or any other party employed by or providing services to an insured depository institution, recoverable damages determined to result from the improvident or otherwise improper use or investment of any insured depository institution's assets shall include principal losses and appropriate interest.

(m) New Depository Institutions.—

(1) **Organization authorized.**—As soon as possible after the default of an insured depository institution, the Corporation, if it finds that it is advisable and in the interest of the depositors of the insured depository institution in default or the public shall organize a new national bank or Federal savings association in the same community as the insured depository institution in default to assume the insured deposits of such depository institution in default and otherwise to perform temporarily the functions hereinafter provided for. . . .

(n) Bridge Depository Institutions.—

(1) **Organization.—**

(A) **Purpose.**—When 1 or more insured depository institutions are in default, or when the Corporation anticipates that 1 or more insured depository institutions may become in default, the Corporation may, in its discretion, organize, and the Office of the Comptroller of the Currency, with respect to 1 or more insured banks or 1 or more insured savings associations, shall charter, 1 or more national banks or Federal savings associations, as appropriate, with respect thereto with the powers and attributes of national banking associations or Federal savings associations, as applicable, subject to the provisions of this subsection, to be referred to as "bridge depository institutions".

(B) **Authorities.**—Upon the granting of a charter to a bridge depository institution, the bridge depository institution may—

(i) assume such deposits of such insured depository institution or institutions that is or are in default or in danger of default as the Corporation may, in its discretion, determine to be appropriate;

(ii) assume such other liabilities . . . of such insured depository institution or institutions . . . as the Corporation may, in its discretion, determine to be appropriate;

(iii) purchase such assets . . . of such insured depository institution or institutions . . . as the Corporation may, in its discretion, determine to be appropriate; and

(iv) perform any other temporary function which the Corporation may, in its discretion, prescribe in accordance with this Act. . . .

(E) National bank or Federal savings association.—A bridge depository institution shall be organized as a national bank, in the case of 1 or more insured banks, and as a Federal savings association, in the case of 1 or more insured savings associations.

(2) Chartering.—

(A) Conditions.—A national bank or Federal savings association may be chartered by the Comptroller of the Currency as a bridge depository institution only if the Board of Directors determines that—

(i) the amount which is reasonably necessary to operate such bridge depository institution will not exceed the amount which is reasonably necessary to save the cost of liquidating, including paying the insured accounts of, 1 or more insured depository institutions in default or in danger of default with respect to which the bridge depository institution is chartered;

(ii) the continued operation of such insured depository institution or institutions in default or in danger of default with respect to which the bridge depository institution is chartered is essential to provide adequate banking services in the community where each such depository institution in default or in danger of default is located; or

(iii) the continued operation of such insured depository institution or institutions in default or in danger of default with respect to which the bridge depository institution is chartered is in the best interest of the depositors of such depository institution or institutions in default or in danger of default or the public.

(B) Insured national bank or Federal savings association.—A bridge depository institution shall be an insured depository institution from the time it is chartered as a national bank or Federal savings association.

(C) Bridge bank treated as being in default for certain purposes.—A bridge depository institution shall be treated as an insured depository institution in default at such times and for such purposes as the Corporation may, in its discretion, determine.

(D) Management.—A bridge depository institution, upon the granting of its charter, shall be under the management of a board of directors consisting of not fewer than 5 nor more than 10 members appointed by the Corporation.

(E) Bylaws.—The board of directors of a bridge depository institution shall adopt such bylaws as may be approved by the Corporation.

(3) Transfer of assets and liabilities.—

(A) In general.—

(i) Transfer upon grant of charter.—Upon the granting of a charter to a bridge depository institution pursuant to this subsection, the Corporation, as receiver, or any other receiver appointed with respect to any insured depository institution in default with respect to which the bridge depository institution is chartered may transfer any assets and liabilities of such depository institution in default to the bridge depository institution in accordance with paragraph (1).

(ii) Subsequent transfers.—At any time after a charter is granted to a bridge depository institution, the Corporation, as receiver, or any other receiver appointed with respect to an insured depository institution in default may transfer any assets and liabilities of such insured depository institution in default as the Corporation may, in its discretion, determine to be appropriate in accordance with paragraph (1).

(iii) Treatment of trust business.—For purposes of this paragraph, the trust business, including fiduciary appointments, of any insured depository institution in default is included among its assets and liabilities.

(iv) Effective without approval.—The transfer of any assets or liabilities, including those associated with any trust business, of an insured depository institution in default transferred to a bridge depository institution shall be effective without any further approval under Federal or State law, assignment, or consent with respect thereto.

(B) Intent of Congress regarding continuing operations.—It is the intent of the Congress that, in order to prevent unnecessary hardship or losses to the customers of any insured depository institution in default with respect to which a bridge depository institution is chartered, especially creditworthy farmers, small businesses, and households, the Corporation should—

(i) continue to honor commitments made by the depository institution in default to creditworthy customers, and

(ii) not interrupt or terminate adequately secured loans which are transferred under subparagraph (A) and are being repaid by the debtor in accordance with the terms of the loan instrument.

(4) Powers of bridge depository institutions.—Each bridge depository institution chartered under this subsection shall have all corporate powers of, and be subject to the same provisions of law as, a national bank or Federal savings association. . . .

Federal Deposit Insurance Act   **12 U.S.C. § 1821**

(5) **Capital**.—

(A) **No capital required**.—The Corporation shall not be required to—

(i) issue any capital stock on behalf of a bridge depository institution chartered under this subsection; or

(ii) purchase any capital stock of a bridge depository institution, except that notwithstanding any other provision of Federal or State law, the Corporation may purchase and retain capital stock of a bridge depository institution in such amounts and on such terms as the Corporation, in its discretion, determines to be appropriate. . . .

(C) **Authority to issue capital stock**.—Whenever the Board of Directors determines it is advisable to do so, the Corporation shall cause capital stock of a bridge depository institution to be issued and offered for sale in such amounts and on such terms and conditions as the Corporation may, in its discretion, determine. . . .

(6) **No Federal status**.—

(A) **Agency status**.—A bridge depository institution is not an agency, establishment, or instrumentality of the United States.

(B) **Employee status**.—Representatives for purposes of paragraph (1)(B), interim directors, directors, officers, employees, or agents of a bridge depository institution are not, solely by virtue of service in any such capacity, officers or employees of the United States.—Any employee of the Corporation or of any Federal instrumentality who serves at the request of the Corporation as a representative for purposes of paragraph (1)(B), interim director, director, officer, employee, or agent of a bridge depository institution shall not—

(i) solely by virtue of service in any such capacity lose any existing status as an officer or employee of the United States for purposes of title 5, United States Code, or any other provision of law, or

(ii) receive any salary or benefits for service in any such capacity with respect to a bridge depository institution in addition to such salary or benefits as are obtained through employment with the Corporation or such Federal instrumentality.

(7) **Assistance authorized**.—The Corporation may, in its discretion, provide assistance under § 1823(c) to facilitate any transaction described in clause (i), (ii), or (iii) of paragraph (10)(A) with respect to any bridge depository institution in the same manner and to the same extent as such assistance may be provided under such section with respect to an insured depository institution in default, or to facilitate a bridge depository institution's acquisition of any assets or the assumption of any liabilities of an insured depository institution in default.

(8) **Acquisition**.—

(A) **In general**.—The responsible agency shall notify the Attorney General of any transaction involving the merger or sale of a bridge depository institution requiring approval under § 1828(c) and if a report on competitive factors is requested within 10 days, such transaction may not be consummated before the 5th calendar day after the date of approval by the responsible agency with respect thereto. If the responsible agency has found that it must act immediately to prevent the probable failure of 1 of the depository institutions involved, the preceding sentence does not apply and the transaction may be consummated immediately upon approval by the agency. . . .

(9) Duration of bridge depository institution.—[T]he status of a bridge depository institution as such shall terminate at the end of the 2-year period following the date it was granted a charter.—The Board of Directors may, in its discretion, extend the status of the bridge depository institution as such for 3 additional 1-year periods.

(10) Termination of bridge depository institution status.—The status of any bridge depository institution as such shall terminate upon the earliest of—

(A) the merger or consolidation of the bridge depository institution with a depository institution that is not a bridge depository institution;

(B) at the election of the Corporation, the sale of a majority of the capital stock of the bridge depository institution to an entity other than the Corporation and other than another bridge depository institution;

(C) the sale of 80 percent, or more, of the capital stock of the bridge depository institution to an entity other than the Corporation and other than another bridge depository institution;

(D) at the election of the Corporation, either the assumption of all or substantially all of the deposits and other liabilities of the bridge depository institution by a depository institution holding company or a depository institution that is not a bridge depository institution, or the acquisition of all or substantially all of the assets of the bridge depository institution by a depository institution holding company, a depository institution that is not a bridge depository institution, or other entity as permitted under applicable law; and

(E) the expiration of the period provided in paragraph (9), or the earlier dissolution of the bridge depository institution as provided in paragraph (12).

(11) Effect of termination events.—

(A) **Merger or consolidation.**—A bridge depository institution that participates in a merger or consolidation as provided in paragraph (10)(A) shall be for all purposes a national bank or a Federal savings association, as the case may be, with all the rights, powers, and privileges thereof, and such merger or consolidation shall be conducted in accordance with, and shall have the effect provided in, the provisions of applicable law . . . .

(13) Multiple bridge depository institutions.—Subject to paragraph (1)(B)(i), the Corporation may, in the Corporation's discretion, organize 2 or more bridge depository institutions under this subsection to assume any deposits of, assume any other liabilities of, and purchase any assets of a single depository institution in default. . . .

(s) Prohibition on Entering Secrecy Agreements and Protective Orders.—The Corporation may not enter into any agreement or approve any protective order which prohibits the Corporation from disclosing the terms of any settlement of an administrative or other action for damages or restitution brought by the Corporation in its capacity as conservator or receiver for an insured depository institution. . . .

§ 1822. Corporation as Receiver . . .

(b) Payment of Insured Deposit as Discharge from Liability.—Payment of an insured deposit to any person by the Corporation shall discharge the Corporation, and payment of a transferred deposit to any person by the new bank or by an insured depository institution in which a transferred deposit has been made available shall discharge the Corporation and such new bank or other insured depository institution, to the same extent that payment to such person by the depository institution in default would have discharged it from liability for the insured deposit.

(c) Recognition of Claimant Not on Bank Records.—Except as otherwise prescribed by the Board of Directors, neither the Corporation nor such new bank or other insured depository institution shall be required to recognize as the owner of any portion of a deposit appearing on the records of the depository institution in default under a name other than that of the claimant, any person whose name or interest as such owner is not disclosed on the records of such depository institution in default as part owner of said deposit, if such recognition would increase the aggregate amount of the insured deposits in such depository institution in default.

(d) Withholding Payments to Meet Liability to Depository Institution.—The Corporation may withhold payment of such portion of the insured deposit of any depositor in a depository institution in default as may be required to provide for the payment of any liability of such depositor to the depository institution in default or its receiver, which is not offset against a claim due from such depository institution, pending the determination and payment of such liability by such depositor or any other person liable therefor. . . .

§ 1823. Investment of Corporation's Funds

(a) Investment of Corporation's Funds.—

(1) Authority.—Funds held in the Deposit Insurance Fund or the FSLIC Resolution Fund, that are not otherwise employed shall be invested in obligations of the United States or in obligations guaranteed as to principal and interest by the United States. . . .

(c) Assistance to Insured Depository Institutions.—

(1) Open-bank assistance.—The Corporation is authorized, in its sole discretion and upon such terms and conditions as the Board of Directors may prescribe, to make loans to, to make deposits in, to purchase the assets or securities of, to assume the liabilities of, or to make contributions to, any insured depository institution—

    (A) if such action is taken to prevent the default of such insured depository institution;

    (B) if, with respect to an insured bank in default, such action is taken to restore such insured bank to normal operation; or

    (C) if, when severe financial conditions exist which threaten the stability of a significant number of insured depository institutions or of insured depository institutions possessing significant financial resources, such action is taken in order to lessen the risk to the Corporation posed by such insured depository institution under such threat of instability.

(2) Assisting acquisition.—

    (A) Types of assistance authorized.—In order to facilitate a merger or consolidation of an insured depository institution described in subparagraph (B) with another insured depository institution or the sale of any or all of the assets of such insured depository institution or the assumption of any or all of such insured depository institution's liabilities by another insured depository institution, or the acquisition of the stock of such insured depository institution, the Corporation is authorized, in its sole discretion and upon such terms and conditions as the Board of Directors may prescribe—

        (i) to purchase any such assets or assume any such liabilities;

        (ii) to make loans or contributions to, or deposits in, or purchase the securities of, such other insured depository institution or the company which controls or will acquire control of such other insured depository institution;

        (iii) to guarantee such other insured depository institution or the company which controls or will acquire control of such other insured depository institution against loss by reason of such insured institution's merging or consolidating with or assuming the liabilities and purchasing the assets of such insured depository institution or by reason of such company acquiring control of such insured depository institution; or

(iv) to take any combination of the actions referred to in subparagraphs (i) through (iii).

(B) Eligibility.—For the purpose of subparagraph (A), the insured depository institution must be an insured depository institution—

(i) which is in default;

(ii) which, in the judgment of the Board of Directors, is danger of default; or

(iii) which, when severe financial conditions exist which threaten the stability of a significant number of insured depository institutions or of insured depository institutions possessing significant financial resources, is determined by the Corporation, in its sole discretion, to require assistance under subparagraph (A) in order to lessen the risk to the Corporation posed by such insured depository institution under such threat of instability.

(C) Stay of litigation.—Any action to which the Corporation is or becomes a party by acquiring any asset or exercising any other authority set forth in this section shall be stayed for a period of 60 days at the request of the Corporation.

(3) Nonbank acquirer.—The Corporation may provide any person acquiring control of, merging with, consolidating with or acquiring the assets of an insured depository institution under subsection (f) or (k) of this section with such financial assistance as it could provide an insured institution under this subsection.

(4) Least-cost resolution required.—

(A) In general.—Notwithstanding any other provision of this Act, the Corporation may not exercise any authority under this subsection or subsection (d), (f), (h), (i), or (k) of this section with respect to any insured depository institution unless—

(i) the Corporation determines that the exercise of such authority is necessary to meet the obligation of the Corporation to provide insurance coverage for the insured deposits in such institution; and

(ii) the total amount of the expenditures by the Corporation and obligations incurred by the Corporation (including any immediate and long-term obligation of the Corporation and any direct or contingent liability for future payment by the Corporation) in connection with the exercise of any such authority with respect to such institution is the least costly to the Deposit Insurance Fund of all possible methods for meeting the Corporation's obligation under this section.

(B) Determining least costly approach.—In determining how to satisfy the Corporation's obligations to an institution's insured depositors at the least possible cost to the Deposit Insurance Fund, the Corporation shall comply with the following provisions:

(i) Present-value analysis; documentation required.—The corporation shall—

(I) evaluate alternatives on a present-value basis, using a realistic discount rate;

(II) document that evaluation and the assumptions on which the evaluation is based, including any assumptions with regard to interest rates, asset recovery rates, asset holding costs, and payment of contingent liabilities; and

(III) retain the documentation for not less than 5 years.

(ii) Foregone tax revenues.—Federal tax revenues that the Government would forego as the result of a proposed transaction, to the extent reasonably ascertainable, shall be treated as if they were revenues foregone by the Deposit Insurance Fund.

(C) Time of determination.—

(i) General rule.—For purposes of this subsection, the determination of the costs of providing any assistance under paragraph (1) or (2) or any other provision of this section with respect to any depository institution shall be made as of the date on which the Corporation makes the determination to provide such assistance to the institution under this section.

(ii) Rule for liquidations.—For purposes of this subsection, the determination of the costs of liquidation of any depository institution shall be made as of the earliest of—

(I) the date on which a conservator is appointed for such institution;

(II) the date on which a receiver is appointed for such institution, or

(III) the date on which the Corporation makes any determination to provide any assistance under this section with respect to such institution.

(D) Liquidation costs.—In determining the cost of liquidating any depository institution for the purpose of comparing the costs under subparagraph (A) (with respect to such institution), the amount of such cost may not exceed the amount which is equal to the sum of the insured deposits of such institution as of the earliest of the dates described in subparagraph (C), minus the present value of the total net amount the Corporation reasonably expects to receive from the disposition of the assets of such institution in connection with such liquidation.

(E) Deposit Insurance Fund available for intended purpose only.—

(i) In general.—After December 31, 1994, . . . the Corporation may not take any action, directly or indirectly, with respect to any insured depository institution that would have the effect of increasing losses to the Deposit Insurance Fund by protecting—

(I) depositors for more than the insured portion of deposits (determined without regard to whether such institution is liquidated); or

(II) creditors other than depositors. . . .

(iii) Purchase and assumption transactions.—No provision of this subparagraph shall be construed as prohibiting the Corporation from allowing any person who acquires any assets or assumes any liabilities of any insured depository institution for which the Corporation has been appointed conservator or receiver to acquire uninsured deposit liabilities of such institution so long as the Deposit Insurance Fund does not incur any loss with respect to such deposit liabilities in an amount greater than the loss which would have been incurred with respect to such liabilities if the institution had been liquidated.

(F) Discretionary determinations.—Any determination which the Corporation may make under this paragraph shall be made in the sole discretion of the Corporation.

(G) Systemic risk.—

(i) Emergency determination by Secretary of the Treasury.—Notwithstanding subparagraphs (A) and (E), if, upon the written recommendation of the Board of Directors (upon a vote of not less than two-thirds of the members of the Board of Directors) and the Board of Governors of the Federal Reserve System (upon a vote of not less than two-thirds of the members of such Board), the Secretary of the Treasury (in consultation with the President) determines that—

(I) the Corporation's compliance with subparagraphs (A) and (E) with respect to an insured depository institution would have serious adverse effects on economic conditions or financial stability, and

(II) any action or assistance under this subparagraph would avoid or mitigate such adverse effects,

the Corporation may take other action or provide assistance under this section as necessary to avoid or mitigate such effects.

(ii) Repayment of loss.—The Corporation shall recover the loss to the Deposit Insurance Fund arising from any action taken or assistance provided with respect to an insured depository institution under clause (i) expeditiously from 1 or more emergency special assessments on insured depository institutions equal to the product of

(I) an assessment rate established by the Corporation; and

(II) the amount of each depository institution's average total assets during the assessment period, minus the sum of the amount of the institution's average total tangible equity and the amount of the institution's average total subordinated debt.

(iii) **Documentation required**.—The Secretary of the Treasury shall
(I) document any determination under clause (i); and
(II) retain the documentation for review under clause (iv).

(iv) **GAO review**.—The Comptroller General of the United States shall review and report to the Congress on any determination under clause (i), including—
(I) the basis for the determination;
(II) the purpose for which any action was taken pursuant to such clause; and
(III) the likely effect of the determination and such action on the incentives and conduct of insured depository institutions and uninsured depositors.

(v) **Notice**.—
(I) **In general**.—The Secretary of the Treasury shall provide written notice of any determination under clause (i) to the Committee on Banking, Housing, and Urban Affairs of the Senate and the Committee on Banking, Finance and Urban Affairs of the House of Representatives.

(II) **Description of basis of determination**.—The notice under subclause (I) shall include a description of the basis for any determination under clause (i).

(H) **Rule of construction**.—No provision of law shall be construed as permitting the Corporation to take any action prohibited by paragraph (4) unless such provision expressly provides, by direct reference to this paragraph, that this paragraph shall not apply with respect to such action.

(5) **FDIC may not acquire voting shares**.—The Corporation may not use its authority under this subsection to purchase the voting or common stock of an insured depository institution. Nothing in the preceding sentence shall be construed to limit the ability of the Corporation to enter into and enforce covenants and agreements that it determines to be necessary to protect its financial interest.

(6) **State and local taxes**.—

(A) **Deferral**.—During any period in which an insured depository institution has received assistance under this subsection and such assistance is still outstanding, such insured depository institution may defer the payment of any State or local tax which is determined on the basis of the deposits held by such insured depository institution or of the interest or dividends paid on such deposits.

(B) **Payment**.—When such insured depository institution no longer has any outstanding assistance, such insured depository institution shall pay all taxes which were deferred under subparagraph (A). Such payments shall be made in accordance with a payment plan established by the Corporation, after consultation with the applicable State and local taxing authorities.

(7) Trust business.—The transfer of any assets or liabilities associated with any trust business of an insured depository institution in default under subparagraph (2)(A) shall be effective without any State or Federal approval, assignment, or consent with respect thereto.

(8) Assistance before appointment of conservator or receiver.—

(A) In general.—Subject to the least-cost provisions of paragraph (4), the Corporation shall consider providing direct financial assistance under this section for depository institutions before the appointment of a conservator or receiver for such institution only under the following circumstances:

(i) Troubled condition criteria.—The corporation determines

(I) grounds for the appointment of a conservator or receiver exist or likely will exist in the future unless the depository institution's capital levels are increased; and

(II) it is unlikely that the institution can meet all currently applicable capital standards without assistance.

(ii) Other criteria.—The depository institution meets the following criteria:

(I) The appropriate Federal banking agency and the Corporation have determined that, during such period of time preceding the date of such determination as the agency or the Corporation considers to be relevant, the institution's management has been competent and has complied with applicable laws, rules, and supervisory directives and orders.

(II) The institution's management did not engage in any insider dealing, speculative practice, or other abusive activity.

(B) Public disclosure.—Any determination under this paragraph to provide assistance under this section shall be made in writing and published in the Federal Register. . . .

(d) Sale of Assets to Corporation.—

(1) In general.—Any conservator, receiver, or liquidator appointed for any insured depository institution in default, including the Corporation acting in such capacity, shall be entitled to offer the assets of such depository institutions for sale to the Corporation or as security for loans from the Corporation.

(2) Proceeds.—The proceeds of every sale or loan of assets to the Corporation shall be utilized for the same purposes and in the same manner as other funds realized from the liquidation of the assets of such depository institutions.

(3) Rights and powers of Corporation.—

(A) In general.—With respect to any asset acquired or liability assumed pursuant to this section, the Corporation shall have all of the rights, powers, privileges, and authorities of the Corporation as receiver under §§ 1821 and 1825(b).

(B) **Rule of construction**.—Such rights, powers, privileges, and authorities shall be in addition to and not in derogation of any rights, powers, privileges, and authorities otherwise applicable to the Corporation.

(C) **Fiduciary responsibility**.—In exercising any right, power, privilege, or authority describe in subparagraph (A), the Corporation shall continue to be subject to the fiduciary duties and obligations of the Corporation as receiver to claimants against the insured depository institution in receivership.

(D) **Disposition of assets**.—In exercising any right, power, privilege, or authority described in subparagraph (A) regarding the sale or disposition of assets sold to the Corporation pursuant to paragraph (1), the Corporation shall conduct its operations in a manner which

(i) maximizes the net present value return from the sale or disposition of such assets;

(ii) minimizes the amount of any loss realized in the resolution of cases;

(iii) ensures adequate competition and fair and consistent treatment of offerors;

(iv) prohibits discrimination on the basis of race, sex, or ethnic groups in the solicitation and consideration of offers; and

(v) maximizes the preservation of the availability and affordability of residential real property for low- and moderate-income individuals.

(4) **Loans**.—The Corporation, in its discretion, may make loans on the security of or may purchase and liquidate or sell any part of the assets of an insured depository institution which is now or may hereafter be in default.

(e) **Agreements Against Interests of Corporation**.—

(1) **In general**.—No agreement which tends to diminish or defeat the interest of the Corporation in any asset acquired by it under this section or § 1821, either as security for a loan or by purchase or as receiver of any insured depository institution, shall be valid against the Corporation unless such agreement—

(A) is in writing,

(B) was executed by the depository institution and any person claiming an adverse interest thereunder, including the obligor, contemporaneously with the acquisition of the asset by the depository institution,

(C) was approved by the board of directors of the depository institution or its loan committee, which approval shall be reflected in the minutes of said board or committee, and

(D) has been, continuously, from the time of its execution, an official record of the depository institution. . . .

§ 1828. Regulations Governing Insured Depository Institutions

(a) Insurance Logo.—

(1) **Insured depository institutions.—**

(A) **In general.**—Each insured depository institution shall display at each place of business maintained by that institution a sign or signs relating to the insurance of the deposits of the institution, in accordance with regulations to be prescribed by the Corporation.

(B) **Statement to be included.**—Each sign required under subparagraph (A) shall include a statement that insured deposits are backed by the full faith and credit of the United States Government.

(2) **Regulations.**—The Corporation shall prescribe regulations to carry out this subsection, including regulations governing the substance of signs required by paragraph (1) and the manner of display or use of such signs.

(b) Payment of Dividends by Defaulting Depository Institutions.—No insured depository institution shall pay any dividends on its capital stock or interest on its capital notes or debentures (if such interest is required to be paid only out of net profits) or distribute any of its capital assets while it remains in default in the payment of any assessment due to the Corporation. . . .

(c) Bank Merger Transactions.—

(1) **FDIC approval required for certain transactions.**—Except with the prior written approval of the responsible agency, which shall in every case referred to in this paragraph be the Corporation, no insured depository institution shall—

(A) merge or consolidate with any noninsured bank or institution;

(B) assume liability to pay any deposits (including liabilities which would be "deposits" except for the proviso in § 1813(1)(5)) made in, or similar liabilities of, any noninsured bank or institution; or

(C) transfer assets to any noninsured bank or institution in consideration of the assumption of liabilities for any portion of the deposits made in such insured depository institution.

(2) **Approval by primary federal regulator required.**—No insured depository institution shall merge or consolidate with any other insured depository institution or, either directly or indirectly, acquire the assets of, or assume liability to pay any deposits made in, any other insured depository institution except with the prior written approval of the responsible agency, which shall be—

(A) the Comptroller of the Currency if the acquiring, assuming, or resulting bank is to be a national bank;

(B) the Board of Governors of the Federal Reserve System if the acquiring, assuming, or resulting bank is to be a State member bank;

(C) the Corporation if the acquiring, assuming, or resulting bank is to be a State nonmember insured bank (except a savings bank supervised by the Director of the Office of Thrift Supervision); and

(D) the Director of the Office of Thrift Supervision if the acquiring, assuming, or resulting institution is to be a savings association.

(3) Publication required.—Notice of any proposed transaction for which approval is required under paragraph (1) or (2) (referred to hereafter in this subsection as a "merger transaction") shall, unless the responsible agency finds that it must act immediately in order to prevent the probable default of one of the banks or savings associations involved, be published—

(A) prior to the granting of approval of such transaction,

(B) in a form approved by the responsible agency,

(C) at appropriate intervals during a period at least as long as the period allowed for furnishing reports under paragraph (4) of this subsection, and

(D) in a newspaper of general circulation in the community or communities where the main offices of the banks or savings associations involved are located, or, if there is no such newspaper in any such community, then in the newspaper of general circulation published nearest thereto.

(4) Reports on competitive factors.—

(A) Request for report.—In the interests of uniform standards and subject to subparagraph (B), before acting on any application for approval of a merger transaction, the responsible agency shall—

(i) request a report on the competitive factors involved from the Attorney General of the United States; and

(ii) provide a copy of the request to the Corporation (when the Corporation is not the responsible agency).

(B) Furnishing of report.—The report requested under subparagraph (A) shall be furnished by the Attorney General to the responsible agency—

(i) not later than 30 calendar days after the date on which the Attorney General received the request; or

(ii) not later than 10 calendar days after such date, if the requesting agency advises the Attorney General that an emergency exists requiring expeditious action.

(C) Exceptions.—A responsible agency may not be required to request a report under subparagraph (A) if—

(i) the responsible agency finds that it must act immediately in order to prevent the probable failure of 1 of the insured depository institutions involved in the merger transaction; or

(ii) the merger transaction involves solely an insured depository institution and 1 or more of the affiliates of such depository institution.

(5) Preserving competition.—The responsible agency shall not approve—

(A) any proposed merger transaction which would result in a monopoly, or which would be in furtherance of any combination or conspiracy to monopolize or to attempt to monopolize the business of banking in any part of the United States, or

(B) any other proposed merger transaction whose effect in any section of the country may be substantially to lessen competition, or to tend to create a monopoly, or which in any other manner would be in restraint of trade, unless it finds that the anticompetitive effects of the proposed transaction are clearly outweighed in the public interest by the probable effect of the transaction in meeting the convenience and needs of the community to be served.

In every case, the responsible agency shall take into consideration the financial and managerial resources and future prospects of the existing and proposed institutions, and the convenience and needs of the community to be served.

(6) Notice and stay.—The responsible agency shall immediately notify the Attorney General of any approval by it pursuant to this subsection of a proposed merger transaction. If the agency has found that it must act immediately to prevent the probable failure of one of the insured depository institutions involved, or if the proposed merger transaction is solely between an insured depository institution and 1 or more of its affiliates, and the report on the competitive factors has been dispensed with, the transaction may be consummated immediately upon approval by the agency. If the agency has advised the Attorney General under paragraph (4)(B)(ii) of the existence of an emergency requiring expeditious action and has requested a report on the competitive factors within 10 days, the transaction may not be consummated before the fifth calendar day after the date of approval by the agency. In all other cases, the transaction may not be consummated before the thirtieth calendar day after the date of approval by the agency or, if the agency has not received any adverse comment from the Attorney General of the United States relating to competitive factors, such shorter period of time as may be prescribed by the agency with the concurrence of the Attorney General, but in no event less than 15 calendar days after the date of approval.

(7) Antitrust litigation.—

(A) Limitation period.—Any action brought under the antitrust laws arising out of a merger transaction shall be commenced prior to the earliest time under paragraph (6) at which a merger transaction approved under paragraph (5) might be consummated. The commencement of such an action shall stay the effectiveness of the agency's approval unless the court shall otherwise specifically order. In any such action, the court shall review de novo the issues presented.

(B) Substantive standards.—In any judicial proceeding attacking a merger transaction approved under paragraph (5) on the ground that the merger transaction alone and of itself constituted a violation of any antitrust laws other than § 2 of title 15, the standards applied by the court shall be identical with those that the banking agencies are directed to apply under paragraph (5).

(C) **No subsequent antitrust attack**.—Upon the consummation of a merger transaction in compliance with this subsection and after the termination of any antitrust litigation commenced within the period prescribed in this paragraph, or upon the termination of such period if no such litigation is commenced therein, the transaction may not thereafter be attacked in any judicial proceeding on the ground that it alone and of itself constituted a violation of any antitrust laws other than § 2 of title 15, but nothing in this subsection shall exempt any bank or savings association resulting from a merger transaction from complying with the antitrust laws after the consummation of such transaction.

(D) **Agencies as parties to action**.—In any action brought under the antitrust laws arising out of a merger transaction approved by a Federal supervisory agency pursuant to this subsection, such agency, and any State banking supervisory agency having jurisdiction within the State involved, may appear as a party of its own motion and as of right, and be represented by its counsel.

(8) **Antitrust laws defined**.—For the purposes of this subsection, the term "antitrust laws" means the Act of July 2, 1890 (the Sherman Antitrust Act), the Act of October 15, 1914 (the Clayton Act), and any other Acts in pari materia. . . .

(12) **Foreign bank**.—The provisions of this subsection do not apply to any merger transaction involving a foreign bank if no party to the transaction is principally engaged in business in the United States.

(13) **Deposit concentration limit**.—

(A) **In general**.—Except as provided in subparagraph (B), the responsible agency may not approve an application for an interstate merger transaction if the resulting insured depository institution (including all insured depository institutions which are affiliates of the resulting insured depository institution), upon consummation of the transaction, would control more than 10 percent of the total amount of deposits of insured depository institutions in the United States.

(B) **Exception for failed bank**.—Subparagraph (A) shall not apply to an interstate merger transaction that involves 1 or more insured depository institutions in default or in danger of default, or with respect to which the Corporation provides assistance under § 1823.

(C) **Definitions**.—In this paragraph—

(i) the term **"interstate merger transaction"** means a merger transaction involving 2 or more insured depository institutions that have different home States and that are not affiliates; and

(ii) the term **"home State"** means—

(I) with respect to a national bank, the State in which the main office of the bank is located;

(II) with respect to a State bank or State savings association, the State by which the State bank or State savings association is chartered; and

(III) with respect to a Federal savings association, the State in which the home office ... of the Federal savings association is located.

(d) Branching by State Nonmember Bank.—

(1) Prior approval required.—No State nonmember insured bank shall establish and operate any new domestic branch unless it shall have the prior written consent of the Corporation, and no State nonmember insured bank shall move its main office or any such branch from one location to another without such consent. No foreign bank may move any insured branch from one location to another without such consent. The factors to be considered in granting or withholding the consent of the Corporation under this subsection shall be those enumerated in § 1816.

(2) Foreign branch.—No State nonmember insured bank shall establish or operate any foreign branch, except with the prior written consent of the Corporation and upon such conditions and pursuant to such regulations as the Corporation may prescribe from time to time.

(3) Exclusive authority for additional branches.—

(A) In general.—[A] State nonmember bank may not acquire, establish, or operate a branch in any State other than the bank's home State (as defined in § 1831u(f)(4)) or a State in which the bank already has a branch unless the acquisition, establishment, or operation of a branch in such State by a State nonmember bank is authorized under this subsection or § 1823(f), § 1823(k), or § 1831u.

(B) Retention of branches.—In the case of a State nonmember bank which relocates the main office of such bank from 1 State to another State after May 31, 1997, the bank may retain and operate branches within the State which was the bank's home State (as defined in § 1831u(f)(4)) before the relocation of such office only to the extent the bank would be authorized, under this section or any other provision of law referred to in subparagraph (A), to acquire, establish, or commence to operate a branch in such State if—

(i) the bank had no branches in such State; or

(ii) the branch resulted from—

(I) an interstate merger transaction approved pursuant to § 1831u; or

(II) a transaction after May 31, 1997, pursuant to which the bank received assistance from the Corporation under § 1823(c).

(4) [I]nterstate branching through de novo branches.—

(A) In general.—Subject to subparagraph (B), the Corporation may approve an application by an insured State nonmember bank to establish and operate a de novo branch in a State (other than the bank's home State) in which the bank does not maintain a branch if—

(i) the law of the State in which the branch is located, or is to be located, would permit establishment of the branch, if the bank were a State bank chartered by such State; and

(ii) the conditions established in, or made applicable to this paragraph by, subparagraph (B) are met.

(B) Conditions on establishment and operation of interstate branch.—

(i) Establishment.—An application by an insured State nonmember bank to establish and operate a de novo branch in a host State shall be subject to the same requirements and conditions to which an application for a merger transaction is subject under paragraphs (1), (3), and (4) of § 183lu(b).

(ii) Operation.—Subsections (c) and (d)(2) of § 183lu shall apply with respect to each branch of an insured State nonmember bank which is established and operated pursuant to an application approved under this paragraph in the same manner and to the same extent such provisions of such section apply to a branch of a State bank which resulted from a merger transaction under such § 1831u.

(C) De novo branch defined.—For purposes of this paragraph, the term "de novo branch" means a branch of a State bank which—

(i) is originally established by the State bank as a branch, and

(ii) does not become a branch of such bank as a result of

(I) the acquisition by the bank of an insured depository institution or a branch of an insured depository institution; or

(II) the conversion, merger, or consolidation of any such institution or branch.

(D) Home State defined.—The term "home State" means the State by which a State bank is chartered.

(E) Host State defined.—The term "host State" means, with respect to a bank, a State, other than the home State of the bank, in which the bank maintains, or seeks to establish and maintain, a branch. . . .

(j) Restrictions on Transactions with Affiliates and Insiders.—

(1) Transactions with affiliates.—

(A) In general.—Sections 371c and 371c-1 shall apply with respect to every nonmember insured bank in the same manner and to the same extent as if the nonmember insured bank were a member bank.

(B) Affiliate defined.—For the purpose of subparagraph (A), any company that would be an affiliate (as defined in §§ 371c and 371c-1) of a nonmember insured bank if the nonmember insured bank were a member bank shall be deemed to be an affiliate of that nonmember insured bank.

(2) Extensions of credit to officers, directors, and principal shareholders.—Sections 375a and 375b shall apply with respect to every nonmember insured bank in the same manner and to the same extent as if the nonmember insured bank were a member bank.

(3) Avoiding extraterritorial application to foreign banks.—

(A) Transactions with affiliates.—Paragraph (1) shall not apply with respect to a foreign bank solely because the foreign bank has an insured branch.

(B) Extensions of credit to officers, directors, and principal shareholders.—Paragraph (2) shall not apply with respect to a foreign bank solely because the foreign bank has an insured branch, but shall apply with respect to the insured branch.

(C) Foreign bank defined.—For purposes of this paragraph, the term "foreign bank" has the same meaning as in § 3101(7).

(k) Authority to Regulate or Prohibit Certain Forms of Benefits to Institution-Affiliated Parties . . .

(*l*) Acquisition of Foreign Banks or Entities.—When authorized by State law, a State nonmember insured bank may, but only with the prior written consent of the Corporation and upon such conditions and under such regulations as the Corporation may prescribe from time to time, acquire and hold, directly or indirectly, stock or other evidences of ownership in one or more banks or other entities organized under the law of a foreign country or a dependency or insular possession of the United States and not engaged, directly or indirectly, in any activity in the United States except as, in the judgment of the Board of Directors, shall be incidental to the international or foreign business of such foreign bank or entity; and, notwithstanding the provisions of subsection (j) of this section, such State nonmember insured bank may, as to such foreign bank or entity, engage in transactions that would otherwise be covered thereby, but only in the manner and within the limit prescribed by the Corporation by general or specific regulation or ruling.

(m) Activities of Savings Associations and Their Subsidiaries.—

(1) Procedures.—When an insured savings association establishes or acquires a subsidiary or when an insured savings association elects to conduct any new activity through a subsidiary that the insured savings association controls, the insured savings association—

(A) shall notify the Corporation and the Director of the Office of Thrift Supervision not less than 30 days prior to the establishment, or acquisition, of any such subsidiary, and not less than 30 days prior to the commencement of any such activity, and in either case shall provide at that time such information as each such agency may, by regulation, require; and

(B) shall conduct the activities of the subsidiary in accordance with regulations and orders of the Director of the Office of Thrift Supervision.

(2) Enforcement powers.—With respect to any subsidiary of an insured savings association:

(A) the Corporation and the Director of the Office of Thrift Supervision shall each have, with respect to such subsidiary, the respective powers that each has with respect to the insured savings association pursuant to this section or § 1818; and

(B) the Director of the Office of Thrift Supervision may determine, after notice and opportunity for hearing, that the continuation by the insured savings association of its ownership or control of, or its relationship to, the subsidiary—

(i) constitutes a serious risk to the safety, soundness, or stability of the insured savings association, or

(ii) is inconsistent with sound banking principles or with the purposes of this Act.

Upon making any such determination, the Corporation or the Director of the Office of Thrift Supervision shall have authority to order the insured savings association to divest itself of control of the subsidiary. The Director of the Office of Thrift Supervision may take any other corrective measures with respect to the subsidiary, including the authority to require the subsidiary to terminate the activities or operations posing such risks, as the Director may deem appropriate.

(3) Activities incompatible with deposit insurance.—

(A) **In general.**—The Corporation may determine by regulation or order that any specific activity poses a serious threat to the Deposit Insurance Fund. Prior to adopting any such regulation, the Corporation shall consult with the Director of the Office of Thrift Supervision and shall provide appropriate State supervisors the opportunity to comment thereon, and the Corporation shall specifically take such comments into consideration. Any such regulation shall be issued in accordance with § 553 of title 5. If the Board of Directors makes such a determination with respect to an activity, the Corporation shall have authority to order that no savings association may engage in the activity directly.

(B) **Authority of Director.**—This section does not limit the authority of the Office of Thrift Supervision to issue regulations to promote safety and soundness or to enforce compliance with other applicable laws.

(C) **Additional authority of FDIC to prevent serious risks to insurance fund.**—Notwithstanding subparagraph (A), the Corporation may prescribe and enforce such regulations and issue such orders as the Corporation determines to be necessary to prevent actions or practices of savings associations that pose a serious threat to the Deposit Insurance Fund. . . .

(p) Periodic Review of Capital Standards.—Each appropriate Federal banking agency shall, in consultation with the other Federal banking agencies, biennially review its capital standards for insured depository institutions to determine whether those standards require sufficient capital to facilitate prompt corrective action to prevent or minimize loss to the Deposit Insurance Fund, consistent with § 1831o. . . .

(r) Subsidiary Depository Institutions as Agents for Certain Affiliates.—

(1) In general.—Any bank subsidiary of a bank holding company may receive deposits, renew time deposits, close loans, service loans, and receive payments on loans and other obligations as an agent for a depository institution affiliate.

(2) Bank acting as agent is not a branch.—Notwithstanding any other provision of law, a bank acting as an agent in accordance with paragraph (1) for a depository institution affiliate shall not be considered to be a branch of the affiliate. . . .

(x) Privileges Not Affected by Disclosure to Banking Agency or Supervisor.—

(1) In general.—The submission by any person of any information to any Federal banking agency, State bank supervisor, or foreign banking authority for any purpose in the course of any supervisory or regulatory process of such agency, supervisor, or authority shall not be construed as waiving, destroying, or otherwise affecting any privilege such person may claim with respect to such information under Federal or State law as to any person or entity other than such agency, supervisor, or authority. . . .

(y) State Lending Limit Treatment of Derivatives Transactions.—An insured State bank may engage in a derivative transaction, as defined in § 84(b)(3), only if the law with respect to lending limits of the State in which the insured State bank is chartered takes into consideration credit exposure to derivative transactions.

(z) General Prohibition on Sale of Assets.—

(1) In general.—An insured depository institution may not purchase an asset from, or sell an asset to, an executive officer, director, or principal shareholder of the insured depository institution, or any related interest of such person (as such terms are defined in § 375b(h)), unless—

(A) the transaction is on market terms; and

(B) if the transaction represents more than 10 percent of the capital stock and surplus of the insured depository institution, the transaction has been approved in advance by a majority of the members of the board of directors of the insured depository institution who do not have an interest in the transaction. . . .

§ 1828a. Prudential Safeguards

(a) Comptroller of the Currency.—

(1) In general.—The Comptroller of the Currency may, by regulation or order, impose restrictions or requirements on relationships or transactions between a national bank and a subsidiary of the national bank that the Comptroller finds are—

(A) consistent with the purposes of this Act, the National Bank Act, and other Federal law applicable to national banks; and

(B) appropriate to avoid any significant risk to the safety and soundness of insured depository institutions or the Deposit Insurance Fund or other adverse effects, such as undue concentration of resources, decreased or unfair competition, conflicts of interests, or unsound banking practices.

(2) Review.—The Comptroller of the Currency shall regularly—

(A) review all restrictions or requirements established pursuant to paragraph (1) to determine whether there is a continuing need for any such restriction or requirement to carry out the purposes of the Act, including the avoidance of any adverse effect referred to in paragraph (1)(B); and

(B) modify or eliminate any such restriction or requirement the Comptroller finds is no longer required for such purposes.

(b) Board of Governors of the Federal Reserve System.—

(1) In general.—The Board of Governors of the Federal Reserve System may, by regulation or order, impose restrictions or requirements on relationships or transactions—

(A) between a depository institution subsidiary of a bank holding company and any affiliate of such depository institution (other than a subsidiary of such institution); or

(B) between a State member bank and a subsidiary of such bank; if the Board makes a finding described in paragraph (2) with respect to such restriction or requirement.

(2) Finding.—The Board of Governors of the Federal Reserve System may exercise authority under paragraph (1) if the Board finds that the exercise of such authority is—

(A) consistent with the purposes of this Act, the Bank Holding Company Act of 1956, the Federal Reserve Act, and other Federal law applicable to depository institution subsidiaries of bank holding companies or State member banks, as the case may be; and

(B) appropriate to prevent an evasion of any provision of law referred to in subparagraph (A) or to avoid any significant risk to the safety and soundness of depository institutions or the Deposit Insurance Fund or other adverse effects, such as undue concentration of resources, decreased or unfair competition, conflicts of interests, or unsound banking practices.

(3) Review.— . . .

(4) Foreign banks.—The Board may, by regulation or order, impose restrictions or requirements on relationships or transactions between a branch, agency, or commercial lending company of a foreign bank in the United States and any affiliate in the United States of such foreign bank that the Board finds are—

    (A) consistent with the purposes of this Act, the Bank Holding Company Act of 1956, the Federal Reserve Act, and other Federal law applicable to foreign banks and their affiliates in the United States; and

    (B) appropriate to prevent an evasion of any provision of law referred to in subparagraph (A) or to avoid any significant risk to the safety and soundness of depository institutions or the Deposit Insurance Fund or other adverse effects, such as undue concentration of resources, decreased or unfair competition, conflicts of interests, or unsound banking practices.

(c) Federal Deposit Insurance Corporation.— . . .

§ 1830. Nondiscrimination

It is not the purpose of this Act to discriminate in any manner against State nonmember banks or State savings associations and in favor of national or member banks or Federal savings associations, respectively. It is the purpose of this Act to provide all banks and savings associations with the same opportunity to obtain and enjoy the benefits of this Act.

§ 1831a. Activities of Insured State Banks

(a) Permissible Activities.—

(1) In general.—[A]n insured State bank may not engage as principal in any type of activity that is not permissible for a national bank unless—

    (A) the Corporation has determined that the activity would pose no significant risk to the Deposit Insurance Fund; and

    (B) the State bank is, and continues to be, in compliance with applicable capital standards prescribed by the appropriate Federal banking agency.

(2) Processing period.—

    (A) In general.—The Corporation shall make a determination under paragraph (1)(A) not later than 60 days after receipt of a completed application that may be required under this subsection.

    (B) Extension of time period.—The Corporation may extend the 60-day period referred to in subparagraph (A) for not more than 30 additional days, and shall notify the applicant of any such extension.

(b) Insurance Underwriting.—

(1) In general.—Notwithstanding subsection (a) of this section, an insured State bank may not engage in insurance underwriting except to the extent that activity is permissible for national banks.

(2) Exception for certain federally reinsured crop insurance.—Notwithstanding any other provision of law, an insured State bank or any of its subsidiaries that provided insurance on or before September 30, 1991, which was reinsured in whole or in part by the Federal Crop Insurance Corporation may continue to provide such insurance.

(c) Equity Investments by Insured State Banks.—

(1) In general.—An insured State bank may not, directly or indirectly, acquire or retain any equity investment of a type that is not permissible for a national bank.

(2) Exception for certain subsidiaries.—Paragraph (1) shall not prohibit an insured State bank from acquiring or retaining an equity investment in a subsidiary of which the insured State bank is a majority owner.

(3) Exception for qualified housing projects.—

(A) Exception.—Notwithstanding any other provision of this subsection, an insured State bank may invest as a limited partner in a partnership, the sole purpose of which is direct or indirect investment in the acquisition, rehabilitation, or new construction of a qualified housing project.

(B) Limitation.—The aggregate of the investments of any insured State bank pursuant to this paragraph shall not exceed 2 percent of the total assets of the bank.

(C) Qualified housing project defined.—As used in this paragraph—

(i) Qualified housing project.—The term "qualified housing project" means residential real estate that is intended to primarily benefit lower income people throughout the period of the investment.

(ii) Lower income.—The term "lower income" means income that is less than or equal to the median income based on statistics from State *or* Federal sources. . . .

(d) Subsidiaries of Insured State Banks.—

(1) In general.—[A] subsidiary of an insured State bank may not engage as principal in any type of activity that is not permissible for a subsidiary of a national bank unless—

(A) the Corporation has determined that the activity poses no significant risk to the Deposit Insurance Fund; and

(B) the bank is, and continues to be, in compliance with applicable capital standards prescribed by the appropriate Federal banking agency.

(2) Insurance underwriting prohibited.—

(A) Prohibition.—Notwithstanding paragraph (1), no subsidiary of an insured State bank may engage in insurance underwriting except to the extent such activities are permissible for national banks.

(B) Continuation of existing activities.—Notwithstanding subparagraph (A), a well-capitalized insured State bank or any of its subsidiaries that was lawfully providing insurance as principal in a State on

November 21, 1991, may continue to provide, as principal, insurance of the same type to residents of the State (including companies or partnerships incorporated in, organized under the laws of, licensed to do business in, or having an office in the State, but only on behalf of their employees resident in or property located in the State), individuals employed in the State, and any other person to whom the bank or subsidiary has provided insurance as principal, without interruption, since such person resided in or was employed in such State.

(C) **Exception**.—Subparagraph (A) does not apply to a subsidiary of an insured State bank if

(i) the insured State bank was required, before June 1, 1991, to provide title insurance as a condition of the bank's initial chartering under State law; and

(ii) control of the insured State bank has not changed since that date.

(3) **Processing period**.—

(A) **In general**.—The Corporation shall make a determination under paragraph (1)(A) not later than 60 days after receipt of a completed application that may be required under this subsection.

(B) **Extension of time period**.—The Corporation may extend the 60-day period referred to in subparagraph (A) for not more than 30 additional days, and shall notify the applicant of any such extension. . . .

(f) **Common and Preferred Stock Investment**.—

(1) **In general**.—An insured State bank shall not acquire or retain, directly or indirectly, any equity investment of a type or in an amount that is not permissible for a national bank or is not otherwise permitted under this section.

(2) **Exception for banks in certain states**.—Notwithstanding paragraph (1), an insured State bank may, to the extent permitted by the Corporation, acquire and retain ownership of securities described in paragraph (1) to the extent the aggregate amount of such investment does not exceed an amount equal to 100 percent of the bank's capital if such bank—

(A) is located in a State that permitted, as of September 30, 1991, investment in common or preferred stock listed on a national securities exchange or shares of an investment company registered under the Investment Company Act of 1940; and

(B) made or maintained an investment in such securities during the period beginning on September 30, 1990, and ending on November 26, 1991.

(3) **Exception for certain types of institutions**.—Notwithstanding paragraph (1), an insured State bank may—

(A) acquire not more than 10 percent of a corporation that only—

(i) provides directors', trustees', and officers' liability insurance coverage or bankers' blanket bond group insurance coverage for insured depository institutions; or

(ii) reinsures such policies; and

(B) acquire or retain shares of a depository institution if—

(i) the institution engages only in activities permissible for national banks;

(ii) the institution is subject to examination and regulation by a State bank supervisor;

(iii) 20 or more depository institutions own shares of the institution and none of those institutions owns more than 15 percent of the institution's shares; and

(iv) the institution's shares . . . are owned only by the institution. . . .

(h) "Activity" Defined.—For purposes of this section, the term "activity" includes acquiring or retaining any investment.

(i) Other Authority Not Affected.—This section shall not be construed as limiting the authority of any appropriate Federal banking agency or any State supervisory authority to impose more stringent restrictions.

(j) Activities of Branches of Out-of-State Banks.—

(1) Application of host state law.—The laws of a host State, including laws regarding community reinvestment, consumer protection, fair lending, and establishment of intrastate branches, shall apply to any branch in the host State of an out-of-State State bank to the same extent as such State laws apply to a branch in the host State of an out-of-State national bank. To the extent host State law is inapplicable to a branch of an out-of-State State bank in such host State pursuant to the preceding sentence, home State law shall apply to such branch.

(2) Activities of branches.—An insured State bank that establishes a branch in a host State may conduct any activity at such branch that is permissible under the laws of the home State of such bank, to the extent such activity is permissible either for a bank chartered by the host State (subject to the restrictions in this section) or for a branch in the host State of an out-of-State national bank.

(3) Savings provision.—No provision of this subsection shall be construed as affecting the applicability of—

(A) any State law of any home State under subsection (b), (c), or (d) of § 1831u; or

(B) Federal law to State banks and State bank branches in the home State or the host State. . . .

§ 1831c. Assuring Consistent Oversight of Subsidiaries of Holding Companies

(a) Definitions.—For purposes of this section:

(1) Board.—The term "Board" means the Board of Governors of the Federal Reserve System.

(2) Functionally regulated subsidiary.—The term "functionally regulated subsidiary" has the same meaning as in § 1844(c)(5).

(3) Lead insured depository institution.—The term "lead insured depository institution" has the same meaning as in § 1841(o)(8).

(b) Examination Requirements.—[T]he Board shall examine the activities of a nondepository institution subsidiary (other than a functionally regulated subsidiary or a subsidiary of a depository institution) of a depository institution holding company that are permissible for the insured depository institution subsidiaries of the depository institution holding company in the same manner, subject to the same standards, and with the same frequency as would be required if such activities were conducted in the lead insured depository institution of the depository institution holding company. . . .

(d) Appropriate Federal Banking Agency Backup Examination Authority.—

(1) In general.—In the event that the Board does not conduct examinations required under subsection (b) in the same manner, subject to the same standards, and with the same frequency as would be required if such activities were conducted by the lead insured depository institution subsidiary of the depository institution holding company, the appropriate Federal banking agency for the lead insured depository institution may recommend in writing (which shall include a written explanation of the concerns giving rise to the recommendation) that the Board perform the examination required under subsection (b).

(2) Examination by an appropriate federal banking agency.—If the Board does not, before the end of the 60-day period beginning on the date on which the Board receives a recommendation under paragraph (1), begin an examination as required under subsection (b) or provide a written explanation or plan to the appropriate Federal banking agency making such recommendation responding to the concerns raised by the appropriate Federal banking agency for the lead insured depository institution, the appropriate Federal banking agency for the lead insured depository institution may . . . examine the activities that are permissible for a depository institution subsidiary conducted by such nondepository institution subsidiary (other than a functionally regulated subsidiary or a subsidiary of a depository institution) of the depository institution holding company as if the nondepository institution subsidiary were an insured depository institution for which the appropriate Federal banking agency of the lead insured depository institution was the appropriate Federal banking agency, to determine whether the activities—

(A) pose a material threat to the safety and soundness of any insured depository institution subsidiary of the depository institution holding company;

(B) are conducted in accordance with applicable Federal law; and

(C) are subject to appropriate systems for monitoring and controlling the financial, operating, and other material risks of the activities that may pose a material threat to the safety and soundness of the insured depository institution subsidiaries of the holding company. . . .

(e) Referrals for Enforcement by Appropriate Federal Banking Agency.—

(1) Recommendation of enforcement action.—The appropriate Federal banking agency for the lead insured depository institution, based upon its examination of a nondepository institution subsidiary conducted pursuant to subsection (d), or other relevant information, may submit to the Board, in writing, a recommendation that the Board take enforcement action against such nondepository institution subsidiary, together with an explanation of the concerns giving rise to the recommendation, if the appropriate Federal banking agency determines (by a vote of its members, if applicable) that the activities of the nondepository institution subsidiary pose a material threat to the safety and soundness of any insured depository institution subsidiary of the depository institution holding company.

(2) Back-up authority of the appropriate federal banking agency.—If, within the 60-day period beginning on the date on which the Board receives a recommendation under paragraph (1), the Board does not take enforcement action against the nondepository institution subsidiary or provide a plan for supervisory or enforcement action that is acceptable to the appropriate Federal banking agency that made the recommendation pursuant to paragraph (1), such agency may take the recommended enforcement action against the nondepository institution subsidiary, in the same manner as if the nondepository institution subsidiary were an insured depository institution for which the agency was the appropriate Federal banking agency. . . .

§ 1831d. Interest Rate State Banks May Charge

(a) Certain State Limits Preempted.—In order to prevent discrimination against State-chartered insured depository institutions . . . with respect to interest rates, if the applicable rate prescribed in this subsection exceeds the rate such State bank . . . would be permitted to charge in the absence of this subsection, such State bank . . . may, notwithstanding any State constitution or statute which is hereby preempted for the purposes of this section, take, receive, reserve, and charge on any loan or discount made, or upon any note, bill of exchange, or other evidence of debt, interest at a rate of not more than 1 per centum in excess of the discount rate on ninety-day commercial paper in effect at the Federal Reserve bank in the Federal Reserve district where such State bank . . . is located or at the rate allowed by the laws of the State, territory, or district where the bank is located, whichever may be greater. . . .

§ 1831f. Brokered Deposits

(a) In General.—An insured depository institution that is not well capitalized may not accept funds obtained, directly or indirectly, by or through any deposit broker for deposit into 1 or more deposit accounts.

(b) Renewals and Rollovers Treated as Acceptance of Funds.—Any renewal of an account in any troubled institution and any rollover of any amount on deposit in any such account shall be treated as an acceptance of funds by such troubled institution for purposes of subsection (a) of this section.

(c) Waiver Authority.—The Corporation may, on a case-by-case basis and upon application by an insured depository institution which is adequately capitalized (but not well capitalized), waive the applicability of subsection (a) of this section upon a finding that the acceptance of such deposits does not constitute an unsafe or unsound practice with respect to such institution. . . .

(e) Restriction on Interest Rate Paid.—Any insured depository institution which, under subsection (c) or (d) of this section, accepts funds obtained, directly or indirectly, by or through a deposit broker, may not pay a rate of interest on such funds which, at the time that such funds are accepted, significantly exceeds—

(1) the rate paid on deposits of similar maturity in such institution's normal market area for deposits accepted in the institution's normal market area; or

(2) the national rate paid on deposits of comparable maturity, as established by the Corporation, for deposits accepted outside the institution's normal market area.

(f) Additional Restrictions.—The Corporation may impose, by regulation or order, such additional restrictions on the acceptance of brokered deposits by any institution as the Corporation may determine to be appropriate.

(g) Definitions Relating to Deposit Broker.—

(1) **Deposit broker.**—The term "deposit broker" means—

(A) any person engaged in the business of placing deposits, or facilitating the placement of deposits, of third parties with insured depository institutions or the business of placing deposits with insured depository institutions for the purpose of selling interests in those deposits to third parties; and

(B) an agent or trustee who establishes a deposit account to facilitate a business arrangement with an insured depository institution to use the proceeds of the account to fund a prearranged loan.

(2) **Exclusions.**—The term "deposit broker" does not include—

(A) an insured depository institution, with respect to funds placed with that depository institution;

(B) an employee of an insured depository institution, with respect to funds placed with the employing depository institution;

(C) a trust department of an insured depository institution, if the trust in question has not been established for the primary purpose of placing funds with insured depository institutions;

(D) the trustee of a pension or other employee benefit plan, with respect to funds of the plan;

(E) a person acting as a plan administrator or an investment adviser in connection with a pension plan or other employee benefit plan provided that that person is performing managerial functions with respect to the plan;

(F) the trustee of a testamentary account;

(G) the trustee of an irrevocable trust (other than one described in paragraph (1)(B)), as long as the trust in question has not been established for the primary purpose of placing funds with insured depository institutions;

(H) a trustee or custodian of a pension or profit sharing plan qualified under § 401(d) or § 403(a) of title 26; or

(I) an agent or nominee whose primary purpose is not the placement of funds with depository institutions.

(3) Inclusion of depository institutions engaging in certain activities.—Notwithstanding paragraph (2), the term "deposit broker" includes any insured depository institution that is not well capitalized (as defined in § 1831o of this title), and any employee of such institution, which engages, directly or indirectly, in the solicitation of deposits by offering rates of interest which are significantly higher than the prevailing rates of interest on deposits offered by other insured depository institutions in such depository institution's normal market area.

(4) Employee.—For purposes of this subsection, the term "employee" means any employee—

(A) who is employed exclusively by the insured depository institution;

(B) whose compensation is primarily in the form of a salary,

(C) who does not share such employee's compensation with a deposit broker; and

(D) whose office space or place of business is used exclusively for the benefit of the insured depository institution which employs such individual.

(h) Deposit Solicitation Restricted.—An insured depository institution that is undercapitalized, as defined in § 1831o, shall not solicit deposits by offering rates of interest that are significantly higher than the prevailing rates of interest on insured deposits—

(1) in such institution's normal market areas; or

(2) in the market area in which such deposits would otherwise be accepted.

§ 1831i. Agency Disapproval of Directors and Senior Executive Officers of Insured Depository Institutions or Depository Institution Holding Companies

(a) Prior Notice Required.—An insured depository institution or depository institution holding company shall notify the appropriate Federal banking agency of the proposed addition of any individual to the board of directors or the employment of any individual as a senior executive officer of such institution or holding company at least 30 days (or such other period, as determined by the appropriate Federal banking agency) before such addition or employment becomes effective, if—

(1) the insured depository institution or depository institution holding company is not in compliance with the minimum capital requirement applicable to such institution or is otherwise in a troubled condition, as determined by such agency on the basis of such institution's or holding company's most recent report of condition or report of examination or inspection; or

(2) the agency determines, in connection with the review by the agency of the plan required under § 1831o or otherwise, that such prior notice is appropriate.

(b) Disapproval by Agency.—An insured depository institution or depository institution holding company may not add any individual to the board of directors or employ any individual as a senior executive officer if the appropriate Federal banking agency issues a notice of disapproval of such addition or employment before the end of the notice period, not to exceed 90 days, beginning on the date the agency receives notice of the proposed action pursuant to subsection (a) of this section.

(c) Exception in Extraordinary Circumstances.—

(1) In general.—Each appropriate Federal banking agency may prescribe by regulation conditions under which the prior notice requirement of subsection (a) of this section may be waived in the event of extraordinary circumstances.

(2) No effect on disapproval authority of agency.—Such waivers shall not affect the authority of each agency to issue notices of disapproval of such additions or employment of such individuals within 30 days after each such waiver.

(d) Additional Information.—Any notice submitted to an appropriate Federal banking agency with respect to an individual by any insured depository institution or depository institution holding company pursuant to subsection (a) of this section shall include—

(1) the information described in § 1817(j)(6)(A) about the individual; and

(2) such other information as the agency may prescribe by regulation

(e) Standard for Disapproval.—The appropriate Federal banking agency shall issue a notice of disapproval with respect to a notice submitted pursuant to subsection (a) of this section if the competence, experience, character, or integrity of the individual with respect to whom such notice is submitted indicates that it would not be in the best interests of the depositors of the depository institution or in the best interests of the public to permit the individual to be employed by, or associated with, the depository institution or depository institution holding company.

(f) Definition Regulations.—Each appropriate Federal banking agency shall prescribe by regulation a definition for the terms "troubled condition" and "senior executive officer" for purposes of subsection (a) of this section.

§ 1831o. Prompt Corrective Action

(a) Resolving Problems to Protect Deposit Insurance Fund.—

(1) **Purpose.**—The purpose of this section is to resolve the problems of insured depository institutions at the least possible long-term loss to the Deposit Insurance Fund.

(2) **Prompt corrective action required.**—Each appropriate Federal banking agency and the Corporation (acting in the Corporation's capacity as the insurer of depository institutions under this Act) shall carry out the purpose of this section by taking prompt corrective action to resolve the problems of insured depository institutions.

(b) Definitions.—For purposes of this section:

(1) **Capital categories.**—

(A) **Well capitalized.** An insured depository institution is "well capitalized" if it significantly exceeds the required minimum level for each relevant capital measure.

(B) **Adequately capitalized.**—An insured depository institution is "adequately capitalized" if it meets the required minimum level for each relevant capital measure.

(C) **Undercapitalized.**—An insured depository institution is "undercapitalized" if it fails to meet the required minimum level for any relevant capital measure.

(D) **Significantly undercapitalized.**—An insured depository institution is "significantly undercapitalized" if it is significantly below the required minimum level for any relevant capital measure.

(E) **Critically undercapitalized.**—An insured depository institution is "critically undercapitalized" if it fails to meet any level specified under subsection (c)(3)(A) of this section.

(2) **Other definitions.** . . .

(B) **Capital distribution.**—The term "capital distribution" means—

Federal Deposit Insurance Act 12 U.S.C. § 1831o

(i) a distribution of cash or other property by any insured depository institution or company to its owners made on account of that ownership, but not including—

(I) any dividend consisting only of shares of the institution or company or rights to purchase such shares. . . .

(ii) a payment by an insured depository institution or company to repurchase, redeem, retire, or otherwise acquire any of its shares or other ownership interests, including any extension of credit to finance an affiliated company's acquisition of those shares or interests; or

(iii) a transaction that the appropriate Federal banking agency or the Corporation determines, by order or regulation, to be in substance a distribution of capital to the owners of the insured depository institution or company.

(C) Capital restoration plan.—The term "capital restoration plan" means a plan submitted under subsection (e)(2) of this section.

(D) Company.—The term "company" has the same meaning as in § 1841. . . .

(F) Relevant capital measure.—The term "relevant capital measure" means the measures described in subsection (c) of this section.

(G) Required minimum level.—The term "required minimum level" means, with respect to each relevant capital measure, the minimum acceptable capital level specified by the appropriate Federal banking agency by regulation.

(H) Senior executive officer.—The term "senior executive officer" has the same meaning as the term "executive officer" in § 375b.

(I) Subordinated debt.—The term "subordinated debt" means debt subordinated to the claims of general creditors.

(c) Capital Standards.—

(1) Relevant capital measures.—

(A) In general.—Except as provided in subparagraph (B)(f), the capital standards prescribed by each appropriate Federal banking agency shall include—

(i) a leverage limit; and

(ii) a risk-based capital requirement.

(B) Other capital measures.—An appropriate Federal banking agency may, by regulation—

(i) establish any additional relevant capital measures to carry out the purpose of this section; or

(ii) rescind any relevant capital measure required under subparagraph (A) upon determining (with the concurrence of the other Federal banking agencies) that the measure is no longer an appropriate means for carrying out the purpose of this section.

(2) Capital categories generally.—Each appropriate Federal banking agency shall, by regulation, specify for each relevant capital measure the levels at which an insured depository institution is well capitalized, adequately capitalized, undercapitalized, and significantly undercapitalized.

(3) Critical capital.—

(A) Agency to specify level.—

(i) Leverage limit.—Each appropriate Federal banking agency shall, by regulation, in consultation with the Corporation, specify the ratio of tangible equity to total assets at which an insured depository institution is critically undercapitalized.

(ii) Other relevant capital measures.—The agency may, by regulation, specify for 1 or more other relevant capital measures, the level at which an insured depository institution is critically undercapitalized.

(B) Leverage limit range.—The level specified under subparagraph (A)(i) shall require tangible equity in an amount—

(i) not less than 2 percent of total assets; and

(ii) except as provided in clause (i), not more than 65 percent of the required minimum level of capital under the leverage limit.

(C) FDIC's concurrence required.—The appropriate Federal banking agency shall not, without the concurrence of the Corporation, specify a level under subparagraph (A)(i) lower than that specified by the Corporation for State nonmember insured banks.

(d) Provisions Applicable to All Institutions.—

(1) Capital distributions restricted.—

(A) In general.—An insured depository institution shall make no capital distribution if, after making the distribution, the institution would be undercapitalized. . . .

(2) Management fees restricted.—An insured depository institution shall pay no management fee to any person having control of that institution if, after making the payment, the institution would be undercapitalized.

(e) Provisions Applicable to Undercapitalized Institutions.—

(1) Monitoring required.—Each, appropriate Federal banking agency shall—

(A) closely monitor the condition of any undercapitalized insured depository institution;

(B) closely monitor compliance with capital restoration plans, restrictions, and requirements imposed under this section; and

(C) periodically review the plan, restrictions, and requirements applicable to any undercapitalized insured depository institution to determine whether the plan, restrictions, and requirements are achieving the purpose of this section.

Federal Deposit Insurance Act   12 U.S.C. § 1831o

(2) Capital restoration plan required.—

(A) In general.—Any undercapitalized insured depository institution shall submit an acceptable capital restoration plan to the appropriate Federal banking agency within the time allowed by the agency under subparagraph (D).

(B) Contents of plan.—The capital restoration plan shall—

(i) specify—

(I) the steps the insured depository institution will take to become adequately capitalized;

(II) the levels of capital to be attained during each year which the plan will be in effect;

(III) how the institution will comply with the restrictions or requirements then in effect under this section; and

(IV) the types and levels of activities in which the institution will engage; and

(ii) contain such other information as the appropriate Federal banking agency may require.

(C) Criteria for accepting plan.—The appropriate Federal banking agency shall not accept a capital restoration plan unless the agency determines that—

(i) the plan—

(I) complies with subparagraph (B);

(II) is based on realistic assumptions, and is likely to succeed in restoring the institution's capital; and

(III) would not appreciably increase the risk (including credit risk, interest-rate risk, and other types of risk) to which the institution is exposed; and

(ii) if the insured depository institution is undercapitalized, each company having control of the institution has—

(I) guaranteed that the institution will comply with the plan until the institution has been adequately capitalized on average during each of 4 consecutive calendar quarters; and

(II) provided appropriate assurances of performance.

(D) Deadlines for submission and review of plans.—The appropriate Federal banking agency shall by regulation establish deadlines that—

(i) provide insured depository institutions with reasonable time to submit capital restoration plans, and generally require an institution to submit a plan not later than 45 days after the institution becomes undercapitalized;

(ii) require the agency to act on capital restoration plans expeditiously, and generally not later than 60 days after the plan is submitted; and

(iii) require the agency to submit a copy of any plan approved by the agency to the Corporation before the end of the 45-day period beginning on the date such approval is granted.

(E) Guarantee liability limited.—

(i) In general.—The aggregate liability under subparagraph (C)(ii) of all companies having control of an insured depository institution shall be the lesser of—

(I) an amount equal to 5 percent of the institution's total assets at the time the institution became undercapitalized; or

(II) the amount which is necessary (or would have been necessary) to bring the institution into compliance with all capital standards applicable with respect to such institution as of the time the institution fails to comply with a plan under this subsection.

(ii) Certain affiliates not affected.—This paragraph may not be construed as—

(I) requiring any company not having control of an undercapitalized insured depository institution to guarantee, or otherwise be liable on, a capital restoration plan;

(II) requiring any person other than an insured depository institution to submit a capital restoration plan; or

(III) affecting compliance by brokers, dealers, government securities brokers, and government securities dealers with the financial responsibility requirements of the Securities Exchange Act of 1934 and regulations and orders thereunder.

(3) Asset growth restricted. An undercapitalized insured depository institution shall not permit its average total assets during any calendar quarter to exceed its average total assets during the preceding calendar quarter unless—

(A) the appropriate Federal banking agency has accepted the institution's capital restoration plan;

(B) any increase in total assets is consistent with the plan; and

(C) the institution's ratio of tangible equity to assets increases during the calendar quarter at a rate sufficient to enable the institution to become adequately capitalized within a reasonable time.

(4) Prior approval required for acquisitions, branching, and new lines of business.—An undercapitalized insured depository institution shall not, directly or indirectly, acquire any interest in any company or insured depository institution, establish or acquire any additional branch office, or engage in any new line of business unless—

(A) the appropriate Federal banking agency has accepted the insured depository institution's capital restoration plan, the institution is implementing the plan, and the agency determines that the proposed action is consistent with and will further the achievement of the plan; or

(B) the Board of Directors determines that the proposed action will further the purpose of this section.

(5) Discretionary safeguards.—The appropriate Federal banking agency may, with respect to any undercapitalized insured depository institution, take actions described in any subparagraph of subsection (f)(2) of this section if the agency determines that those actions are necessary to carry out the purpose of this section.

(f) Provisions Applicable to Significantly Undercapitalized Institutions and Undercapitalized Institutions that Fail to Submit and Implement Capital Restoration Plans.—

(1) **In general**. This subsection shall apply with respect to any insured depository institution that—

(A) is significantly undercapitalized; or

(B) is undercapitalized and—

(i) fails to submit an acceptable capital restoration plan within the time allowed by the appropriate Federal banking agency under subsection (e)(2)(D) of this section; or

(ii) fails in any material respect to implement a plan accepted by the agency.

(2) **Specific actions authorized**.—The appropriate Federal banking agency shall carry out this section by taking 1 or more of the following actions:

(A) **Requiring recapitalization**.—Doing 1 or more of the following:

(i) Requiring the institution to sell enough shares or obligations of the institution so that the institution will be adequately capitalized after the sale.

(ii) Further requiring that instruments sold under clause (i) be voting shares.

(iii) Requiring the institution to be acquired by a depository institution holding company, or to combine with another insured depository institution, if 1 or more grounds exist for appointing a conservator or receiver for the institution.

(B) **Restricting transactions with affiliates.**—

(i) Requiring the institution to comply with § 371c as if subsection (d)(1) of that section (exempting transactions with certain affiliated institutions) did not apply.

(ii) Further restricting the institution's transactions with affiliates.

(C) **Restricting interest rates paid**.—

(i) **In general**.—Restricting the interest rates that the institution pays on deposits to the prevailing rates of interest on deposits of comparable amounts and maturities in the region where the institution is located, as determined by the agency.

(ii) **Retroactive restrictions prohibited**.—This subparagraph does not authorize the agency to restrict interest rates paid on time deposits made before (and not renewed or renegotiated after) the agency acted under this subparagraph.

(D) **Restricting asset growth**.—Restricting the institution's asset growth more stringently than subsection (e)(3) of this section, or requiring the institution to reduce its total assets.

(E) **Restricting activities.**—Requiring the institution or any of its subsidiaries to alter, reduce, or terminate any activity that the agency determines poses excessive risk to the institution.

(F) **Improving management.**—Doing 1 or more of the following:

(i) **New election of directors.**—Ordering a new election for the institution's board of directors.

(ii) **Dismissing directors or senior executive officers.**—Requiring the institution to dismiss from office any director or senior executive officer who had held office for more than 180 days immediately before the institution became undercapitalized. Dismissal under this clause shall not be construed to be a removal under § 1818.

(iii) **Employing qualified senior executive officers.**—Requiring the institution to employ qualified senior executive officers (who, if the agency so specifies, shall be subject to approval by the agency).

(G) **Prohibiting deposits from correspondent banks.**—Prohibiting the acceptance by the institution of deposits from correspondent depository institutions, including renewals and rollovers of prior deposits.

(H) **Requiring prior approval for capital distributions by bank holding company.**—Prohibiting any bank holding company having control of the insured depository institution from making any capital distribution without the prior approval of the Board of Governors of the Federal Reserve System.

(I) **Requiring divestiture.**—Doing one or more of the following:

(i) **Divestiture by the institution.**—Requiring the institution to divest itself of or liquidate any subsidiary if the agency determines that the subsidiary is in danger of becoming insolvent and poses a significant risk to the institution, or is likely to cause a significant dissipation of the institution's assets or earnings.

(ii) **Divestiture by parent company of nondepository affiliate.**—Requiring any company having control of the institution to divest itself of or liquidate any affiliate other than an insured depository institution if the appropriate Federal banking agency for that company determines that the affiliate is in danger of becoming insolvent and poses a significant risk to the institution, or is likely to cause a significant dissipation of the institution's assets or earnings.

(iii) **Divestiture of institution.**—Requiring any company having control of the institution to divest itself of the institution if the appropriate Federal banking agency for that company determines that divestiture would improve the institution's financial condition and future prospects.

(J) **Requiring other action.**—Requiring the institution to take any other action that the agency determines will better carry out the purpose of this section than any of the actions described in this paragraph.

(3) Presumption in favor of certain actions.—In complying with paragraph (2), the agency shall take the following actions, unless the agency determines that the actions would not further the purpose of this section:

(A) The action described in clause (i) or (iii) of paragraph (2)(A) (relating to requiring the sale of shares or obligations, or requiring the institution to be acquired by or combine with another institution).

(B) The action described in paragraph (2)(B)(i) (relating to restricting transactions with affiliates).

(C) The action described in paragraph (2)(C) (relating to restricting interest rates).

(4) Senior executive officers' compensation restricted.—

(A) In general.—The insured depository institution shall not do any of the following without the prior written approval of the appropriate Federal banking agency:

(i) Pay any bonus to any senior executive officer.

(ii) Provide compensation to any senior executive officer at a rate exceeding that officer's average rate of compensation (excluding bonuses, stock options, and profit-sharing) during the 12 calendar months preceding the calendar month in which the institution became undercapitalized.

(B) Failing to submit plan.—The appropriate Federal banking agency shall not grant any approval under subparagraph (A) with respect to an institution that has failed to submit an acceptable capital restoration plan.

(5) Discretion to impose certain additional restrictions.—The agency may impose 1 or more of the restrictions prescribed by regulation under subsection (i) of this section if the agency determines that those restrictions are necessary to carry out the purpose of this section.

(6) Consultation with other regulators.—Before the agency or Corporation makes a determination under paragraph (2)(I) with respect to an affiliate that is a broker, dealer, government securities broker, government securities dealer, investment company, or investment adviser, the agency or Corporation shall consult with the Securities and Exchange Commission and, in the case of any other affiliate which is subject to any financial responsibility or capital requirement, any other appropriate regulator of such affiliate with respect to the proposed determination of the agency or the corporation and actions pursuant to such determination.

(g) More Stringent Treatment Based on Other Supervisory Criteria.—

(1) In general.—If the appropriate Federal banking agency determines (after notice and an opportunity for hearing) that an insured depository institution is in an unsafe or unsound condition or, pursuant to § 1818(b)(8), deems the institution to be engaging in an unsafe or unsound practice, the agency may—

(A) if the institution is well capitalized, reclassify the institution as adequately capitalized;

(B) if the institution is adequately capitalized (but not well capitalized), require the institution to comply with 1 or more provisions of subsections (d) and (e) of this section, as if the institution were undercapitalized; or

(C) if the institution is undercapitalized, take any 1 or more actions authorized under subsection (f)(2) of this section as if the institution were significantly undercapitalized.

(2) Contents of plan.—Any plan required under paragraph (1) shall specify the steps that the insured depository institution will take to correct the unsafe or unsound condition or practice. Capital restoration plans shall not be required under paragraph (1)(B).

(h) Provisions Applicable to Critically Undercapitalized Institutions.—

(1) Activities restricted.—Any critically undercapitalized insured depository institution shall comply with restrictions prescribed by the Corporation under subsection (i) of this section.

(2) Payments on subordinated debt prohibited.—

(A) In general.—A critically undercapitalized insured depository institution shall not, beginning 60 days after becoming critically undercapitalized, make any payment of principal or interest on the institution's subordinated debt.

(B) Exceptions.—The Corporation may make exceptions to subparagraph (A) if—

(i) the appropriate Federal banking agency has taken action with respect to the insured depository institution under paragraph (3)(A)(ii); and

(ii) the Corporation determines that the exception would further the purpose of this section. . . .

(3) Conservatorship, receivership, or other action required.—

(A) In general.—The appropriate Federal banking agency shall, not later than 90 days after an insured depository institution becomes critically undercapitalized—

(i) appoint a receiver (or, with the concurrence of the Corporation, a conservator) for the institution; or

(ii) take such other action as the agency determines, with the concurrence of the Corporation, would better achieve the purpose of this section, after documenting why the action would better achieve that purpose.

(B) Periodic redeterminations required.—Any determination by an appropriate Federal banking agency under subparagraph (A)(ii) to take any action with respect to an insured depository institution in lieu of appointing a conservator or receiver shall cease to be effective not later than the end of the 90-day period beginning on the date that the determination is made and a conservator or receiver shall be appointed for that institution under subparagraph (A)(i) unless the agency makes a new determination under subparagraph (A)(ii) at the end of the effective period of the prior determination.

(C) Appointment of receiver required if other action fails to restore capital.—

(i) In general.—Notwithstanding subparagraphs (A) and (B), the appropriate Federal banking agency shall appoint a receiver for the insured depository institution if the institution is critically undercapitalized on average during the calendar quarter beginning 270 days after the date on which the institution became critically undercapitalized.

(ii) Exception.—Notwithstanding clause (i), the appropriate Federal banking agency may continue to take such other action as the agency determines to be appropriate in lieu of such appointment if—

(I) the agency determines, with the concurrence of the Corporation, that (aa) the insured depository institution has positive net worth, (bb) the insured depository institution has been in substantial compliance with an approved capital restoration plan which requires consistent improvement in the institution's capital since the date of the approval of the plan, (cc) the insured depository institution is profitable or has an upward trend in earnings the agency projects as sustainable, and (dd) the insured depository institution is reducing the ratio of nonperforming loans to total loans; and

(II) the head of the appropriate Federal banking agency and the Chairperson of the Board of Directors both certify that the institution is viable and not expected to fail.

(i) Restricting Activities of Critically Undercapitalized Institutions.—To carry out the purpose of this section, the Corporation shall, by regulation or order—

(1) restrict the activities of any critically undercapitalized insured depository institution; and

(2) at a minimum, prohibit any such institution from doing any of the following without the Corporation's prior written approval:

(A) Entering into any material transaction other than in the usual course of business, including any investment, expansion, acquisition, sale of assets, or other similar action with respect to which the depository institution is required to provide notice to the appropriate Federal banking agency.

(B) Extending credit for any highly leveraged transaction.

(C) Amending the institution's charter or bylaws, except to the extent necessary to carry out any other requirement of any law, regulation, or order.

(D) Making any material change in accounting methods.

(E) Engaging in any covered transaction (as defined in § 371c(b)).

(F) Paying excessive compensation or bonuses.

(G) Paying interest on new or renewed liabilities at a rate that would increase the institution's weighted average cost of funds to a level significantly exceeding the prevailing rates of interest on insured deposits in the institution's normal market arm. . . .

(k) Reviews Required When Deposit Insurance Fund Incurs Loss.—

(1) In general.—If the Deposit Insurance Fund incurs a material loss with respect to an insured depository institution . . . , the inspector general of the appropriate Federal banking agency shall—

(A) make a written report to that agency reviewing the agency's supervision of the institution (including the agency's implementation of this section), which shall—

(i) ascertain why the institution's problems resulted in a material loss to the Deposit Insurance Fund; and

(ii) make recommendations for preventing any such loss in the future. . . .

(n) Administrative Review of Dismissal Orders.—

(1) Timely petition required.—A director or senior executive officer dismissed pursuant to an order under subsection (f)(2)(F)(ii) may obtain review of that order by filing a written petition for reinstatement with the appropriate Federal banking agency not later than 10 days after receiving notice of the dismissal.

(2) Procedure.—

(A) **Hearing required.**—The agency shall give the petitioner an opportunity to—

(i) submit written materials in support of the petition; and

(ii) appear, personally or through counsel, before 1 or more members of the agency or designated employees of the agency. . . .

(3) Standard for review of dismissal orders.—The petitioner shall bear the burden of proving that the petitioner's continued employment would materially strengthen the insured depository institution's ability—

(A) to become adequately capitalized, to the extent that the order is based on the institution's capital level or failure to submit or implement a capital restoration plan; and

(B) to correct the unsafe or unsound condition or unsafe or unsound practice, to the extent that the order is based on subsection (g)(1).

§ 1831o-1. Source of Strength

(a) Holding Companies.—The appropriate Federal banking agency for a bank holding company or savings and loan holding company shall require the bank holding company or savings and loan holding company to serve as a source of financial strength for any subsidiary of the bank holding company or savings and loan holding company that is a depository institution.

Federal Deposit Insurance Act   12 U.S.C. § 1831t

(b) **Other Companies**.—If an insured depository institution is not the subsidiary of a bank holding company or savings and loan holding company, the appropriate Federal banking agency for the insured depository institution shall require any company that directly or indirectly controls the insured depository institution to serve as a source of financial strength for such institution.

(e) **Definition**.—[T]he term "source of financial strength" means the ability of a company that directly or indirectly owns or controls an insured depository institution to provide financial assistance to such insured depository institution in the event of the financial distress of the insured depository institution.

§ 1831r. Payments on Foreign Deposits Prohibited

(a) **In General**.—Notwithstanding any other provision of law, the Corporation, the Board of Governors of the Federal Reserve System, . . . any other agency, department, and instrumentality of the United States, and any corporation owned or controlled by the United States may not, directly or indirectly, make any payment or provide any assistance, guarantee, or transfer under this Act or any other provision of law in connection with any insured depository institution which would have the direct or indirect effect of satisfying, in whole or in part, any claim against the institution for obligations of the institution which would constitute deposits as defined in § 1813(*l*) but for subparagraphs (A) and (B) of § 1813(*l*)(5) [i.e., deposits booked at overseas branches or in international banking facilities].

(b) **Exception**.—Subsection (a) shall not apply to any payment, assistance, guarantee, or transfer made or provided by the Corporation if the Board of Directors determines in writing that such action is not inconsistent with any requirement of § 1823(c). . . .

§ 1831t. Depository Institutions Lacking Federal Deposit Insurance

(a) **Annual Independent Audit of Private Deposit Insurers**.—

(1) **Audit required**.—Any private deposit insurer shall obtain an annual audit from an independent auditor using generally accepted auditing standards. The audit shall include a determination of whether the private deposit insurer follows generally accepted accounting principles and has set aside sufficient reserves for losses. . . .

(b) **Disclosure Required**.—Any depository institution lacking Federal deposit insurance shall, within the United States, do the following:

(1) **Periodic statements; account records**.—Include conspicuously in all periodic statements of account, on each signature card, and on each

passbook, certificate of deposit, or share certificate. a notice that the institution is not federally insured, and that if the institution fails, the Federal Government does not guarantee that depositors will get back their money.

(2) Advertising; premises.—

(A) In general.—Include clearly and conspicuously in all advertising, . . . and at each station or window where deposits are normally received, its principal place of business and all its branches where it accepts deposits or opens accounts . . . and on its main Internet page, a notice that the institution is not federally insured. . . .

(c) Manner and Content of Disclosure.—To ensure that current and prospective customers understand the risks involved in foregoing Federal deposit insurance, the Bureau [of Consumer Financial Protection], by regulation or order, shall prescribe the manner and content of disclosure required under this section, which shall be presented in such format and in such type size and manner as to be simple and easy to understand. . . .

§ 1831u. Interstate Bank Mergers

(a) Approval of Interstate Merger Transactions Authorized.—

(1) In general.—[T]he responsible agency may approve a merger transaction under § 1828(c) between insured banks with different home States, without regard to whether such transaction is prohibited under the law of any State.

(2) State election to prohibit interstate merger transactions.—

(A) In general.—Notwithstanding paragraph (1), a merger transaction may not be approved pursuant to paragraph (1) if the transaction involves a bank the home State of which has enacted a law after September 29, 1994, and before June 1, 1997, that—

(i) applies equally to all out-of-State banks; and

(ii) expressly prohibits merger transactions involving out-of-State banks. . . .

(4) Interstate merger transactions involving acquisitions of branches.—

(A) In general.—An interstate merger transaction may involve the acquisition of a branch of an insured bank without the acquisition of the bank only if the law of the State in which the branch is located permits out-of-State banks to acquire a branch of a bank in such State without acquiring the bank.

(B) Treatment of branch for purposes of this section.—In the case of an interstate merger transaction which involves the acquisition of a branch of an insured bank without the acquisition of the bank, the branch shall be treated, for purposes of this section, as an insured bank the home State of which is the State in which the branch is located.

(5) Preservation of State age laws.—

(A) In general.—The responsible agency may not approve an application pursuant to paragraph (1) that would have the effect of permitting an out-of-State bank or out-of-State bank holding company to acquire a bank in a host State that has not been in existence for the minimum period of time, if any, specified in the statutory law of the host State.

(B) Special rule for State age laws specifying a period of more than 5 years.—Notwithstanding subparagraph (A), the responsible agency may approve a merger transaction pursuant to paragraph (1) involving the acquisition of a bank that has been in existence at least 5 years without regard to any longer minimum period of time specified in a statutory law of the host State.

(6) Shell banks.—For purposes of this subsection, a bank that has been chartered solely for the purpose of, and does not open for business prior to, acquiring control of, or acquiring all or substantially all of the assets of, an existing bank or branch shall be deemed to have been in existence for the same period of time as the bank or branch to be acquired.

(b) Provisions Relating to Application and Approval Process.—

(1) Compliance with State filing requirements.—

(A) In general.—Any bank which files an application for an interstate merger transaction shall—

(i) comply with the filing requirements of any host State of the bank which will result from such transaction to the extent that the requirement—

(I) does not have the effect of discriminating against out-of-State banks or out-of-State bank holding companies or subsidiaries of such banks or bank holding companies; and

(II) is similar in effect to any requirement imposed by the host State on a nonbanking corporation incorporated in another State that engages in business in the host State; and

(ii) submit a copy of the application to the State bank supervisor of the host State.

(B) Penalty for failure to comply.—The responsible agency may not approve an application for an interstate merger transaction if the applicant materially fails to comply with subparagraph (A).

(2) Concentration limits.—

(A) Nationwide concentration limits.—The responsible agency may not approve an application for an interstate merger transaction if the resulting bank (including all insured depository institutions which are affiliates of the resulting bank), upon consummation of the transaction, would control more than 10 percent of the total amount of deposits of insured depository institutions in the United States.

(B) Statewide concentration limits other than with respect to initial entries.—The responsible agency may not approve an application for an interstate merger transaction if—

(i) any bank involved in the transaction (including all insured depository institutions which are affiliates of any such bank) has a branch in any State in which any other bank involved in the transaction has a branch; and

(ii) the resulting bank (including all insured depository institutions which would be affiliates of the resulting bank), upon consummation of the transaction, would control 30 percent or more of the total amount of deposits of insured depository institutions in any such State.

(C) Effectiveness of State deposit caps.—No provision of this subsection shall be construed as affecting the authority of any State to limit, by statute, regulation, or order, the percentage of the total amount of deposits of insured depository institutions in the State which may be held or controlled by any bank or bank holding company (including all insured depository institutions which are affiliates of the bank or bank holding company) to the extent the application of such limitation does not discriminate against out-of-State banks, out-of-State bank holding companies, or subsidiaries of such banks or holding companies.

(D) Exceptions to subparagraph (B).—The responsible agency may approve an application for an interstate merger transaction pursuant to subsection (a) without regard to the applicability of subparagraph (B) with respect to any State if—

(i) there is a limitation described in subparagraph (C) in a State statute, regulation, or order which has the effect of permitting a bank or bank holding company (including all insured depository institutions which are affiliates of the bank or bank holding company) to control a greater percentage of total deposits of all insured depository institutions in the State than the percentage permitted under subparagraph (B); or

(ii) the transaction is approved by the appropriate State bank supervisor of such State and the standard on which such approval is based does not have the effect of discriminating against out-of-State banks, out-of-State bank holding companies, or subsidiaries of such banks or holding companies.

(E) Exception for certain banks.—This paragraph shall not apply with respect to any interstate merger transaction involving only affiliated banks.

(3) Community reinvestment compliance.—In determining whether to approve an application for an interstate merger transaction in which the resulting bank would have a branch or bank affiliate immediately following the transaction in any State in which the bank submitting the application (as the acquiring bank) had no branch or bank affiliate immediately before the transaction, the responsible agency shall—

(A) comply with the responsibilities of the agency regarding such application under § 2903;

(B) take into account the most recent written evaluation under § 2903 of any bank which would be an affiliate of the resulting bank; and

(C) take into account the record of compliance of any applicant bank with applicable State community reinvestment laws.

(4) Adequacy of capital and management skills.—The responsible agency may approve an application for an interstate merger transaction pursuant to subsection (a) of this section only if—

(A) each bank involved in the transaction is adequately capitalized as of the date the application is filed; and

(B) the responsible agency determines that the resulting bank will be well capitalized and well managed upon the consummation of the transaction.

(5) Surrender of charter after merger transaction.—The charters of all banks involved in an interstate merger transaction, other than the charter of the resulting bank, shall be surrendered, upon request, to the Federal banking agency or State bank supervisor which issued the charter.

(c) Applicability of Certain Laws to Interstate Banking Operations.—

(1) State taxation authority not affected.—

(A) **In general.**—No provision of this section shall be construed as affecting the authority of any State or political subdivision of any State to adopt, apply, or administer any tax or method of taxation to any bank, bank holding company, or foreign bank, or any affiliate of any bank, bank holding company, or foreign bank, to the extent such tax or tax method is otherwise permissible by or under the Constitution of the United States or other Federal law.

(B) **Imposition of shares tax by host States.**—In the case of a branch of an out-of-State bank which results from an interstate merger transaction, a proportionate amount of the value of the shares of the out-of-State bank may be subject to any bank shares tax levied or imposed by the host State, or any political subdivision of such host State that imposes such tax based upon a method adopted by the host State, which may include allocation and apportionment.

(2) Applicability of antitrust laws.—No provision of this section shall be construed as affecting—

(A) the applicability of the antitrust laws; or

(B) the applicability, if any, of any State law which is similar to the antitrust laws.

(3) Reservation of certain rights to States.—No provision of this section shall be construed as limiting in any way the right of a State to—

(A) determine the authority of State banks chartered by that State to establish and maintain branches; or

(B) supervise, regulate, and examine State banks chartered by that State.

(4) State-imposed notice requirements.—A host State may impose any notification or reporting requirement on a branch of an out-of-State bank if the requirement—

(A) does not discriminate against out-of-State banks or bank holding companies; and

(B) is not preempted by any Federal law regarding the same subject.

(d) Operations of the Resulting Bank.—

(1) Continued operations.—A resulting bank may, subject to the approval of the appropriate Federal banking agency, retain and operate, as a main office or a branch, any office that any bank involved in an interstate merger transaction was operating as a main office or a branch immediately before the merger transaction.

(2) Additional branches.—Following the consummation of any interstate merger transaction, the resulting bank may establish, acquire, or operate additional branches at any location where any bank involved in the transaction could have established, acquired, or operated a branch under applicable Federal or State law if such bank had not been a party to the merger transaction. . . .

(f) Applicable Rate and Other Charge Limitations.—

(1) In general.—In the case of any State that has a constitutional provision that sets a maximum lawful annual percentage rate of interest on any contract at not more than 5 percent above the discount rate for 90-day commercial paper in effect at the Federal reserve bank for the Federal reserve district in which such State is located, except as provided in paragraph (2), upon the establishment in such State of a branch of any out-of-State insured depository institution in such State under this section, the maximum interest rate or amount of interest, discount points, finance charges, or other similar charges that may be charged, taken, received, or reserved from time to time in any loan or discount made or upon any note, bill of exchange, financing transaction, or other evidence of debt by any insured depository institution whose home State is such State shall be equal to not more than the greater of—

(A) the maximum interest rate or amount of interest, discount points, finance charges, or other similar charges that may be charged, taken, received, or reserved in a similar transaction under the constitution or any statute or other law of the home State of the out-of-State insured depository institution establishing any such branch, without reference to this section, as such maximum interest rate or amount of interest may change from time to time; or

(B) the maximum rate or amount of interest, discount points, finance charges, or other similar charges that may be charged, taken, received, or reserved in a similar transaction by a State insured depository institution chartered under the laws of such State or a national bank or Federal savings association whose main office is located in such State without reference to this section.

(2) Rule of construction.—No provision of this subsection shall be construed as superseding or affecting—

(A) the authority of any insured depository institution to take, receive, reserve, and charge interest on any loan made in any State other than the State referred to in paragraph (1); or

(B) the applicability of § 1735f-7a, § 85, or § 1831d. . . .

§ 1831v. Authority of State Insurance Regulator and Securities and Exchange Commission

(a) In General.—Notwithstanding any other provision of law, the provisions of—

(1) § 1844(c) that limit the authority of the Board of Governors of the Federal Reserve System to require reports from, to make examinations of, or to impose capital requirements on holding companies and their functionally regulated subsidiaries or that require deference to other regulators;

(2) § 1844(8) that limit the authority of the Board to require a functionally regulated subsidiary of a holding company to provide capital or other funds or assets to a depository institution subsidiary of the holding company and to take certain actions including requiring divestiture of the depository institution; and

(3) § 1848a that limit whatever authority the Board might otherwise have to take direct or indirect action with respect to holding companies and their functionally regulated subsidiaries;

shall also limit whatever authority that a Federal banking agency might otherwise have under any statute or regulation to require reports, make examinations, impose capital requirements, or take any other direct or indirect action with respect to any functionally regulated affiliate of a depository institution, subject to the same standards and requirements as are applicable to the Board under those provisions

(b) Certain Exemption Authorized.—No provision of this section shall be construed as preventing the Corporation, if the Corporation finds it necessary to determine the condition of a depository institution for insurance purposes, from examining an affiliate of any depository institution, pursuant to § 1820(b)(4), as may be necessary to disclose fully the relationship between the depository institution and the affiliate, and the effect of such relationship on the depository institution.

(c) Definitions.—For purposes of this section, the following definitions shall apply:

(1) Functionally regulated subsidiary.—The term "functionally regulated subsidiary" has the meaning given the term in § 1844(c)(5).

(2) Functionally regulated affiliate.—The term "functionally regulated affiliate" means, with respect to any depository institution, any affiliate of such depository institution that is—

(A) not a depository institution holding company; and

(B) a company described in any clause of § 1844(c)(5)(B).

§ 1831w. Safety and Soundness Firewalls Applicable to Financial Subsidiaries of Banks

(a) In General.—An insured State bank may control or hold an interest in a subsidiary that engages in activities as principal that would only be permissible for a national bank to conduct through a financial subsidiary if—

(1) the State bank and each insured depository institution affiliate of the State bank are well capitalized (after the capital deduction required by paragraph (2));

(2) the State bank complies with the capital deduction and financial statement disclosure requirements in § 24a(c);

(3) the State bank complies with the financial and operational safeguards required by § 24a(d); and

(4) the State bank complies with the amendments to §§ 371c and 371c-1 made by section 121(b) of the Gramm-Leach-Bliley Act. . . .

§ 1831x. Insurance Customer Protections

(a) Regulations Required.—

(1) In general.—The Federal banking agencies shall prescribe . . . customer protection regulations (which the agencies jointly determine to be appropriate) that—

(A) apply to retail sales practices, solicitations, advertising, or offers of any insurance product by any depository institution or any person that is engaged in such activities at an office of the institution or on behalf of the institution; and

(B) are consistent with the requirements of this Act and provide such additional protections for customers to whom such sales, solicitations, advertising, or offers are directed

(2) Applicability to subsidiaries.—The regulations prescribed pursuant to paragraph (1) shall extend such protections to any subsidiary of a depository institution, as deemed appropriate by the regulators referred to in paragraph (3), where such extension is determined to be necessary to ensure the consumer protections provided by this section.

(3) **Consultation and joint regulations**.—The Federal banking agencies shall consult with each other and prescribe joint regulations pursuant to paragraph (1), after consultation with the State insurance regulators, as appropriate.

(b) Sales Practices.—The regulations prescribed pursuant to subsection (a) shall include antitying and anticoercion rules applicable to the sale of insurance products that prohibit a depository institution from engaging in any practice that would lead a customer to believe an extension of credit, in violation of § 1972, is conditional upon—

(1) the purchase of an insurance product from the institution or any of its affiliates; or

(2) an agreement by the consumer not to obtain, or a prohibition on the consumer from obtaining, an insurance product from an unaffiliated entity.

(c) Disclosures and Advertising.—The regulations prescribed pursuant to subsection (a) shall include the following provisions relating to disclosures and advertising in connection with the initial purchase of an insurance product:

(1) **Disclosures**.—

(A) **In general**.—Requirements that the following disclosures be made orally and in writing before the completion of the initial sale and, in the case of clause (iii), at the time of application for an extension of credit:

(i) **Uninsured status**.—As appropriate, the product is not insured by the Federal Deposit Insurance Corporation, the United States Government, or the depository institution.

(ii) **Investment risk**.—In the case of a variable annuity or other insurance product which involves an investment risk, that there is an investment risk associated with the product, including possible loss of value.

(iii) **Coercion**.—The approval of an extension of credit may not be conditioned on—

(I) the purchase of an insurance product from the institution in which the application for credit is pending or of any affiliate of the institution; or

(II) an agreement by the consumer not to obtain, or a prohibition on the consumer from obtaining, an insurance product from an unaffiliated entity.

(B) **Making disclosure readily understandable**.—Regulations prescribed under subparagraph (A) shall encourage the use of disclosure that is conspicuous, simple, direct, and readily understandable, such as the following:

(i) "NOT FDIC-INSURED".

(ii) "NOT GUARANTEED BY THE BANK".

(iii) "MAY GO DOWN IN VALUE".

(iv) "NOT INSURED BY ANY GOVERNMENT AGENCY".

(C) Limitation. Nothing in this paragraph requires the inclusion of the foregoing disclosures in advertisements of a general nature describing or listing the services or products offered by an institution.

(D) Meaningful disclosures.—Disclosures shall not be considered to be meaningfully provided under this paragraph if the institution or its representative states that disclosures required by this subsection were available to the customer in printed material available for distribution, where such printed material is not provided and such information is not orally disclosed to the customer.

(E) Adjustments for alternative methods of purchase.—In prescribing the requirements under subparagraphs (A) and (F), necessary adjustments shall be made for purchase in person, by telephone, or by electronic media to provide for the most appropriate and complete form of disclosure and acknowledgments.

(F) Consumer acknowledgment.—A requirement that a depository institution shall require any person selling an insurance product at any office of, or on behalf of, the institution to obtain, at the time a consumer receives the disclosures required under this paragraph or at the time of the initial purchase by the consumer of such product, an acknowledgment by such consumer of the receipt of the disclosure required under this subsection with respect to such product.

(2) Prohibition on misrepresentations.—A prohibition on any practice, or any advertising, at any office of, or on behalf of the depository institution, or any subsidiary, as appropriate, that could mislead any person or otherwise cause a reasonable person to reach an erroneous belief with respect to—

(A) the uninsured nature of any insurance product sold, or offered for sale, by the institution or any subsidiary of the institution;

(B) in the case of a variable annuity or insurance product that involves an investment risk, the investment risk associated with any such product; or

(C) in the case of an institution or subsidiary at which insurance products are sold or offered for sale, the fact that—

(i) the approval of an extension of credit to a customer by the institution or subsidiary may not be conditioned on the purchase of an insurance product by such customer from the institution or subsidiary; and

(ii) the customer is free to purchase the insurance product from another source.

(d) Separation of Banking and Nonbanking Activities.—

(1) Regulations required.—The regulations prescribed pursuant to subsection (a) shall include such provisions as the Federal banking agencies consider appropriate to ensure that the routine acceptance of deposits is kept, to the extent practicable, physically segregated from insurance product activity.

(2) **Requirements**.—Regulations prescribed pursuant to paragraph (1) shall include the following requirements:

(A) **Separate setting**—A clear delineation of the setting in which, and the circumstances under which, transactions involving insurance products should be conducted in a location physically segregated from an area where retail deposits are routinely accepted.

(B) **Referrals**.—Standards that permit any person accepting deposits from the public in an area where such transactions are routinely conducted in a depository institution to refer a customer who seeks to purchase any insurance product to a qualified person who sells such product, only if the person making the referral receives no more than a one-time nominal fee of a fixed dollar amount for each referral that does not depend on whether the referral results in a transaction.

(C) **Qualification and licensing requirements**.—Standards prohibiting any depository institution from permitting any person to sell or offer for sale any insurance product in any part of any office of the institution, or on behalf of the institution, unless such person is appropriately qualified and licensed. . . .

(g) **Effect on Other Authority**.—

(1) **In general**.—No provision of this section shall be construed as granting, limiting, or otherwise affecting—

(A) any authority of the Securities and Exchange Commission, any self-regulatory organization, the Municipal Securities Rulemaking Board, or the Secretary of the Treasury under any Federal securities law; or

(B) except as provided in paragraph (2), any authority of any State insurance commission (or any agency or office performing like functions), or of any State securities commission (or any agency or office performing like functions), or other State authority under any State law.

(2) **Coordination with State law**.—

(A) **In general**.—Except as provided in subparagraph (B), insurance customer protection regulations prescribed by a Federal banking agency under this section shall not apply to retail sales, solicitations, advertising, or offers of any insurance product by any depository institution or to any person who is engaged in such activities at an office of such institution or on behalf of the institution, in a State where the State has in effect statutes, regulations, orders, or interpretations, that are inconsistent with or contrary to the regulations prescribed by the Federal banking agencies.

(B) **Preemption**.—

(i) **In general**.—If, with respect to any provision of the regulations prescribed under this section, the Board of Governors of the Federal

Reserve System, the Comptroller of the Currency, and the Board of Directors of the Corporation determine jointly that the protection afforded by such provision for customers is greater than the protection provided by a comparable provision of the statutes, regulations, orders, or interpretations referred to in subparagraph (A) of any State, the appropriate State regulatory authority shall be notified of such determination in writing.

(ii) **Considerations.**—Before making a final determination under clause (i), the Federal agencies referred to in clause (i) shall give appropriate consideration to comments submitted by the appropriate State regulatory authorities relating to the level of protection afforded to consumers under State law.

(iii) **Federal preemption and ability of States to override Federal preemption.**—If the Federal agencies referred to in clause (i) jointly determine that any provision of the regulations prescribed under this section affords greater protections than a comparable State law, rule, regulation, order, or interpretation, those agencies shall send a written preemption notice to the appropriate State regulatory authority to notify the State that the Federal provision will preempt the State provision and will become applicable unless, not later than 3 years after the date of such notice, the State adopts legislation to override such preemption.

(h) **Non-Discrimination Against Non-Affiliated Agents.**—The Federal banking agencies shall ensure that the regulations prescribed pursuant to subsection (a) shall not have the effect of discriminating, either intentionally or unintentionally, against any person engaged in insurance sales or solicitations that is not affiliated with a depository institution.

§ 1831y. CRA Sunshine Requirements

(a) **Public Disclosure of Agreements.**—Any agreement (as defined in subsection (e)) entered into . . . by an insured depository institution or affiliate with a nongovernmental entity or person made pursuant to or in connection with the Community Reinvestment Act of 1977 involving funds or other resources of such insured depository institution or affiliate—

(1) shall be in its entirety fully disclosed, and the full text thereof made available to the appropriate Federal banking agency with supervisory responsibility over the insured depository institution and to the public by each party to the agreement; and

(2) shall obligate each party to comply with this section.

(b) **Annual Report of Activity by Insured Depository Institution.**—Each insured depository institution or affiliate that is a party to an agreement described in subsection (a) shall report to the appropriate Federal banking agency with supervisory responsibility over the insured depository institution, not less frequently than once each year, such information as the Federal banking agency may by rule require relating to the following actions taken by the party pursuant to the agreement during the preceding 12-month period:

(1) Payments, fees, or loans made to any party to the agreement or received from any party to the agreement and the terms and conditions of the same.

(2) Aggregate data on loans, investments, and services provided by each party in its community or communities pursuant to the agreement.

(3) Such other pertinent matters as determined by regulation by the appropriate Federal banking agency with supervisory responsibility over the insured depository institution.

(c) Annual Report of Activity by Nongovernmental Entities.—

(1) In general.—Each nongovernmental entity or person that is not an affiliate of an insured depository institution and that is a party to an agreement described in subsection (a) shall report to the appropriate Federal banking agency with supervisory responsibility over the insured depository institution that is a party to such agreement, not less frequently than once each year, an accounting of the use of funds received pursuant to each such agreement during the preceding 12 month period.

(2) Submission to insured depository institution.—A nongovernmental entity or person referred to in paragraph (1) may comply with the reporting requirement in such paragraph by transmitting the report to the insured depository institution that is a party to the agreement, and such insured depository institution shall promptly transmit such report to the appropriate Federal banking agency with supervisory authority over the insured depository institution.

(3) Information to be included.—The accounting referred to in paragraph (1) shall include a detailed, itemized list of the uses to which such funds have been made, including compensation, administrative expenses, travel, entertainment, consulting and professional fees paid, and such other categories, as determined by regulation by the appropriate Federal banking agency with supervisory responsibility over the insured depository institution. . . .

(e) Definitions.—

(1) Agreement.—For purposes of this section, the term "agreement"—
  (A) means—
    (i) any written contract, written arrangement, or other written understanding that provides for cash payments, grants, or other consideration with a value in excess of $10,000, or for loans the aggregate amount of principal of which exceeds $50,000, annually (or the sum of all such agreements during a 12-month period with an aggregate value of cash payments, grants, or other consideration in excess of $10,000, or with an aggregate amount of loan principal in excess of $50,000); or

(ii) a group of substantively related contracts with an aggregate value of cash payments, grants, or other consideration in excess of $10,000, or with an aggregate amount of loan principal in excess of $50,000, annually;

made pursuant to, or in connection with, the fulfillment of the Community Reinvestment Act of 1977 at least 1 party to which is an insured depository institution or affiliate thereof, whether organized on a profit or not-for-profit basis; and

(B) does not include—

(i) any individual mortgage loan;

(ii) any specific contract or commitment for a loan or extension of credit to individuals, businesses, farms, or other entities, if the funds are loaned at rates not substantially below market rates and if the purpose of the loan or extension of credit does not include any re-lending of the borrowed funds to other parties; or

(iii) any agreement entered into by an insured depository institution or affiliate with a nongovernmental entity or person who has not commented on, testified about, or discussed with the institution, or otherwise contacted the institution, concerning the Community Reinvestment Act of 1977.

(2) Fulfillment of CRA.—For purposes of subparagraph (A), the term "fulfillment" means a list of factors that the appropriate Federal banking agency determines have a material impact on the agency's decision—

(A) to approve or disapprove an application for a deposit facility (as defined in § 2902); or

(B) to assign a rating to an insured depository institution under § 2906.

(f) Violations.—

(1) Violations by persons other than insured depository institutions or their affiliates.—

(A) Material failure to comply.—If the party to an agreement described in subsection (a) that is not an insured depository institution or affiliate willfully fails to comply with this section in a material way, as determined by the appropriate Federal banking agency, the agreement shall be unenforceable after the offending party has been given notice and a reasonable period of time to perform or comply.

(B) Diversion of funds or resources.—If funds or resources received under an agreement described in subsection (a) have been diverted contrary to the purposes of the agreement for personal financial gain, the appropriate Federal banking agency with supervisory responsibility over the insured depository institution may impose either or both of the following penalties:

(i) Disgorgement by the offending individual of funds received under the agreement.

(ii) Prohibition of the offending individual from being a party to any agreement described in subsection (a) for a period of not to exceed 10 years.

(2) Designation of successor nongovernmental party.—If an agreement described in subsection (a) is found to be unenforceable under this subsection, the appropriate Federal banking agency may assist the insured depository institution in identifying a successor nongovernmental party to assume the responsibilities of the agreement.

(3) Inadvertent or de minimis reporting errors.—An error in a report filed under subsection (c) that is inadvertent or de minimis shall not subject the filing party to any penalty.

(g) Rule of Construction.—No provision of this section shall be construed as authorizing any appropriate Federal banking agency to enforce the provisions of any agreement described in subsection (a). . . .

§ 1831aa. Enforcement of [Written] Agreements

(a) In General.—Notwithstanding clause (i) or (ii) of § 1818(b)(6)(A) or § 1831o(e)(2)(E)(i), the appropriate Federal banking agency for a depository institution may enforce, under § 1818, the terms of—

(1) any condition imposed in writing by the agency on the depository institution or an institution-affiliated party in connection with any action on any application, notice, or other request concerning the depository institution; or

(2) any written agreement entered into between the agency and the depository institution or an institution-affiliated party.

(b) Receiverships and Conservatorships.—After the appointment of the Corporation as the receiver or conservator for a depository institution, the Corporation may enforce any condition or agreement described in paragraph (1) or (2) of subsection (a) imposed on or entered into with such institution or institution-affiliated party through an action brought in an appropriate United States district court.

BANK HOLDING COMPANY ACT OF 1956

§ 1841. Definitions

(a) Bank Holding Company; Control.—

(1) Bank holding company.—Except as provided in paragraph (5) of this subsection, "bank holding company" means any company which has control over any bank or over any company that is or becomes a bank holding company by virtue of this Act.

(2) Control.—Any company has control over a bank or over any company if—

(A) the company directly or indirectly or acting through one or more other persons owns, controls, or has power to vote 25 per centum or more of any class of voting securities of the bank or company;

(B) the company controls in any manner the election of a majority of the directors or trustees of the bank or company; or

(C) the Board determines, after notice and opportunity for hearing, that the company directly or indirectly exercises a controlling influence over the management or policies of the bank or company.

(3) Presumption against control.—For the purposes of any proceeding under paragraph (2)(C) of this subsection, there is a presumption that any company which directly or indirectly owns, controls, or has power to vote less than 5 per centum of any class of voting securities of a given bank or company does not have control over that bank or company.

(4) Presumption against control.—In any administrative or judicial proceeding under this Act, other than a proceeding under paragraph (2)(C) of this subsection, a company may not be held to have had control over any given bank or company at any given time unless that company, at the time in question, directly or indirectly owned, controlled, or had power to vote 5 per centum or more of any class of voting securities of the bank or company, or had already been found to have control in a proceeding under paragraph (2)(C).

(5) Exceptions.—Notwithstanding any other provision of this subsection—

(A) Fiduciary.—No bank and no company owning or controlling voting shares of a bank is a bank holding company by virtue of its ownership or control of shares in a fiduciary capacity, except as provided in paragraphs (2) and (3) of subsection (g) of this section. For the purpose of the preceding sentence, bank shares shall not be deemed to have been acquired in a fiduciary capacity if the acquiring bank or company has sole discretionary authority to exercise voting rights with respect thereto. . . .

(B) Underwriting.—No company is a bank holding company by virtue of its ownership or control of shares acquired by it in connection with its underwriting of securities if such shares are held only for such period of time as will permit the sale thereof on a reasonable basis.

(C) Proxy solicitation.—No company formed for the sole purpose of participating in a proxy solicitation is a bank holding company by virtue of its control of voting rights of shares acquired in the course of such solicitation.

(D) Securing or collecting debt.—No company is a bank holding company by virtue of its ownership or control of shares acquired in securing or collecting a debt previously contracted in good faith, until two years after the date of acquisition. The Board is authorized upon application by a company to extend, from time to time for not more than one year at a time, the two-year period referred to herein for disposing of any shares acquired by a company in the regular course of securing or collecting a debt previously contracted in good faith, if, in the Board's judgment, such an extension would not be detrimental to the public interest, but no such extension shall in the aggregate exceed three years.

(E) Bank for thrift institutions.—No company is a bank holding company by virtue of its ownership or control of any State-chartered bank or trust company which—

(i) is wholly owned by 1 or more thrift institutions or savings banks; and

(ii) is restricted to accepting—

(I) deposits from thrift institutions or savings banks;

(II) deposits arising out of the corporate business of the thrift institutions or savings banks that own the bank or trust company; or

(III) deposits of public moneys.

(F) Special grandfather rule for bank owning bank.—No trust company or mutual savings bank which is an insured bank under the Federal Deposit Insurance Act is a bank holding company by virtue of its direct or indirect ownership or control of one bank located in the same State, if (i) such ownership or control existed on December 31, 1970, and is specifically authorized by applicable State law, and (ii) the trust company or mutual savings bank does not after that date acquire an interest in any company that, together with any other interest it holds in that company, will exceed 5 per centum of any class of the voting shares of that company, except that this limitation shall not be applicable to investments of the trust company or mutual savings bank, direct and indirect, which are otherwise in accordance with the limitations applicable to national banks under § 24.

(6) Successor.—For the purposes of this Act, any successor to a bank holding company shall be deemed to be a bank holding company from the date on which the predecessor company became a bank holding company.

(b) Company.—"Company" means any corporation, partnership, business trust, association, or similar organization, or any other trust unless by its terms it must terminate within twenty-five years or not later than twenty-one years and ten months after the death of individuals living on the effective date of the trust but shall not include any corporation the majority of the shares of which are owned by the United States or by any State, and shall not include a qualified family partnership. "Company covered in 1970" means a company which becomes a bank holding company as a result of the enactment of the Bank Holding Company Act Amendments of 1970 and which would have been a bank holding company on June 30, 1968, if those amendments had been enacted on that date.

(c) Bank Defined.—For purposes of this Act—

(1) In general.—Except as provided in paragraph (2), the term "bank" means any of the following:

(A) FDIC insurance.—An insured bank as defined in § 1813(h).

(B) Functions.—An institution organized under the laws of the United States, any State of the United States, the District of Columbia, any territory of the United States, Puerto Rico, Guam, American Samoa, or the Virgin Islands which both—

(i) accepts demand deposits or deposits that the depositor may withdraw by check or similar means for payment to third parties or others; and

(ii) is engaged in the business of making commercial loans.

(2) Exceptions.—The term "bank" does not include any of the following:

(A) Foreign bank.—A foreign bank which would be a bank within the meaning of paragraph (1) solely because such bank has an insured or uninsured branch in the United States.

(B) Thrift institution.—An insured institution (as defined in subsection (j) of this section).

(C) Firm with U.S. business incidental to foreign activities.—An organization that does not do business in the United States except as an incident to its activities outside the United States.

(D) Trust company.—An institution that functions solely in a trust or fiduciary capacity, if—

(i) all or substantially all of the deposits of such institution are in trust funds and are received in a bona fide fiduciary capacity,

(ii) no deposits of such institution which are insured by the Federal Deposit Insurance Corporation are offered or marketed by or through an affiliate of such institution;

(iii) such institution does not accept demand deposits or deposits that the depositor may withdraw by check or similar means for payment to third parties or others or make commercial loans; and

(iv) such institution does not—

(I) obtain payment or payment related services from any Federal Reserve bank, including any service referred to in § 248a; or

(II) exercise discount or borrowing privileges pursuant to § 461(b)(7).

(E) Credit union.—A credit union (as described in § 461(b)(1)(A)(iv)).

(F) Credit card bank.—An institution, including an institution that accepts collateral for extensions of credit by holding deposits under $100,000, and by other means which—

(i) engages only in credit card operations;

(ii) does not accept demand deposits or deposits that the depositor may withdraw by check or similar means for payment to third parties or others;

(iii) does not accept any savings or time deposit of less than $100,000;

(iv) maintains only one office that accepts deposits; and

(v) does not engage in the business of making commercial loans, other than credit card loans that are made to businesses that meet the criteria for a small business concern to be eligible for business loans under regulations established by the Small Business Administration under part 121 of title 13, Code of Federal Regulations.

(G) Edge or agreement corporation.—An organization operating under §§ 601-604a or §§ 611-631.

(H) Industrial bank.—An industrial loan company, industrial bank, or other similar institution which is—

(i) an institution organized under the laws of a State which, on March 5, 1987, had in effect or had under consideration in such State's legislature a statute which required or would require such institution to obtain insurance under the Federal Deposit Insurance Act—

(I) which does not accept demand deposits that the depositor may withdraw by check or similar means for payment to third parties;

(II) which has total assets of less than $100,000,000; or

(III) the control of which is not acquired by any company after August 10, 1987; or

(ii) an institution which does not, directly, indirectly, or through an affiliate, engage in any activity in which it was not lawfully engaged as of March 5, 1987, except that this subparagraph shall cease to apply to any institution which permits any overdraft (including any intraday overdraft), or which incurs any such overdraft in such institution's account at a Federal Reserve bank, on behalf of an affiliate if such overdraft is not the result of an inadvertent computer or accounting error that is beyond the control of both the institution and the affiliate, or that is otherwise permissible for a bank controlled by a company described in § 1843(f)(1).

(d) Subsidiary.—"Subsidiary," with respect to a specified bank holding company, means (1) any company 25 per centum or more of whose voting shares . . . is directly or indirectly owned or controlled by such bank holding company, or is held by it with power to vote; (2) any company the election of a majority of whose directors is controlled in any manner by such bank holding company; or (3) any company with respect to the management of policies of which such bank holding company has the power, directly or indirectly, to exercise a controlling influence, as determined by the Board, after notice and opportunity for hearing. . . .

(f) Board.—"Board" means the Board of Governors of the Federal Reserve System.

(g) Attribution Rules.—For the purposes of this Act—

(1) shares owned or controlled by any subsidiary of a bank holding company shall be deemed to be indirectly owned or controlled by such bank holding company; and

(2) shares held or controlled directly or indirectly by trustees for the benefit of (A) a company, (B) the shareholders or members of a company, or (C) the employees (whether exclusively or not) of a company, shall be deemed to be controlled by such company, unless the Board determines that such treatment is not appropriate in light of the facts and circumstances of the case and the purposes of this Act.

(h) Geographic Scope; U.S. Activities of Certain Foreign Companies.—

(1) Geographic scope.—Except as provided by paragraph (2), the application of this Act and of § 371c shall not be affected by the fact that a transaction takes place wholly or partly outside the United States or that a company is organized or operates outside the United States.

(2) Exemption for certain foreign companies.—Except as provided in paragraph (3), the prohibitions of § 1843 shall not apply to shares of any company organized under the laws of a foreign country (or to shares held by such company in any company engaged in the same general line of business as the investor company or in a business related to the business of the investor company) that is principally engaged in business outside the United States if such shares are held or acquired by a bank holding company organized under the laws of a foreign country that is principally engaged in the banking business outside the United States. For the purpose of this subsection, the term "section 2(h)(2) company" means any company whose shares are held pursuant to this paragraph.

(3) Exemption inapplicable to financial companies.—Nothing in paragraph (2) authorizes a section 2(h)(2) company to engage in (or acquire or hold more than 5 percent of the outstanding shares of any class of voting securities of a company engaged in) any banking, securities, insurance, or other financial activities, as defined by the Board, in the United States. This paragraph does not prohibit a section 2(h)(2) company from holding shares that were lawfully acquired before August 10, 1987.

(4) Preferential lending prohibited.—No domestic office or subsidiary of a bank holding company or subsidiary thereof holding shares of a section 2(h)(2) company may extend credit to a domestic office or subsidiary of such section 2(h)(2) company on terms more favorable than those afforded similar borrowers in the United States.

(5) Cross-marketing restricted.—No domestic banking office or bank subsidiary of a bank holding company that controls a section 2(h)(2) company may offer or market products or services of such section 2(h)(2) company, or permit its products or services to be offered or marketed by or through such section 2(h)(2) company, unless such products or services were being so offered or marketed as of March 5, 1987, and then only in the same manner in which they were being offered or marketed as of that date.

(i) Thrift Institution.—For purposes of this Act, the term "thrift institution" means—

(1) any domestic building and loan or savings and loan association;

(2) any cooperative bank without capital stock organized and operated for mutual purposes and without profit; [and]

(3) any Federal savings bank. . . .

(j) Definition of Savings Associations and Related Term.—The term "savings association" or "insured institution" means—

(1) any Federal savings association or Federal savings bank;

(2) any building and loan association, savings and loan association, homestead association, or cooperative bank if such association or cooperative bank is a member of the Deposit Insurance Fund; and

(3) any savings bank or cooperative bank which is deemed by the appropriate Federal banking agency to be a savings association under § 1467a(1).

(k) Affiliate.—For purposes of this Act, the term "affiliate" means any company that controls, is controlled by, or is under common control with another company.

(l) Savings Bank Holding Company.—For purposes of this Act, the term "savings bank holding company" means any company which controls one or more qualified savings banks if the aggregate total assets of such savings banks constitute, upon formation of the holding company and at all times thereafter, at least 70 percent of the total assets of such company. . . .

(n) Incorporated Definitions.—For purposes of this Act, the terms "depository institution," "insured depository institution," "appropriate Federal banking agency," "default," "in danger of default," and "State bank supervisor" have the same meanings as in § 1813.

(o) Other Definitions.—For purposes of this Act, the following definitions shall apply:

(1) Capital terms.—

(A) Insured depository institutions.—With respect to insured depository institutions, the terms "well capitalized," "adequately capitalized," and "undercapitalized" have the same meanings as in § 1831o.

(B) Bank holding company.—

(i) Adequately capitalized.—With respect to a bank holding company, the term "adequately capitalized" means a level of capitalization which meets or exceeds all applicable Federal regulatory capital standards.

(ii) Well capitalized.—A bank holding company is "well capitalized" if it meets the required capital levels for well capitalized bank holding companies established by the Board.

(C) Other capital terms.—The terms "Tier 1" and "risk-weighted assets" have the meanings given those terms in the capital guidelines or regulations established by the Board for bank holding companies.

(2) Antitrust laws.—Except as provided in § 1849, the term "antitrust laws"—

(A) has the same meaning as in the first section of the Clayton Act (15 U.S.C. § 12(a)); and

(B) includes § 45 of title 15 to the extent that such § 45 relates to unfair methods of competition.

(3) Branch.—The term "branch" means a domestic branch (as defined in § 1813 of this title).

(4) Home State.—The term "home State" means—

(A) with respect to a national bank, the State in which the main office of the bank is located;

(B) with respect to a State bank, the State by which the bank is chartered;

(C) with respect to a bank holding company, the State in which the total deposits of all banking subsidiaries of such company are the largest on the later of—

(i) July 1, 1966; or

(ii) the date on which the company becomes a bank holding company under this Act;

(D) with respect to a State savings association, the State by which the savings association is chartered; and

(E) with respect to a Federal savings association, the State in which the home office (as defined by the regulations of the Director of the Office of Thrift Supervision, or, on and after the transfer date, the Comptroller of the Currency) of the Federal savings association is located.

(5) Host State.—The term "host State" means—

(A) with respect to a bank, a State, other than the home State of the bank, in which the bank maintains, or seeks to establish and maintain, a branch; and

(B) with respect to a bank holding company, a State, other than the home State of the company, in which the company controls, or seeks to control, a bank subsidiary.

(6) Out-of-State bank.—The term "out-of-State bank" means, with respect to any State, a bank whose home State is another State.

(7) Out-of-State bank holding company.—The term "out-of-State bank holding company" means, with respect to any State, a bank holding company whose home State is another State.

(8) Lead insured depository institutions.—

(A) **In general.**—The term "lead insured depository institution" means the largest insured depository institution controlled by the subject bank holding company at any time, based on a comparison of the average total risk-weighted assets controlled by each insured depository institution during the previous 12-month period.

(B) Branch or agency.—For purposes of this paragraph and § 1843(j)(4) of this title, the term "insured depository institution" includes any branch or agency operated in the United States by a foreign bank.

(9) Well managed.—The term "well managed" means—

(A) in the case of any company or depository institution which receives examinations, the achievement of—

(i) a CAMEL composite rating of 1 or 2 (or an equivalent rating under an equivalent rating system) in connection with the most recent examination or subsequent review of such company or institution; and

(ii) at least a satisfactory rating for management, if such rating is given; or

(B) in the case of a company or depository institution that has not received an examination rating, the existence and use of managerial resources which the Board determines are satisfactory.

(10) Qualified family partnership.—The term "qualified family partnership" means a general or limited partnership that the Board determines—

(A) does not directly control any bank, except through a registered bank holding company;

(B) does not control more than 1 registered bank holding company;

(C) does not engage in any business activity, except indirectly through ownership of other business entities;

(D) has no investments other than those permitted for a bank holding company pursuant to § 1843(c);

(E) is not obligated on any debt, either directly or as a guarantor;

(F) has partners, all of whom are either—

(i) individuals related to each other by blood, marriage (including former marriage), or adoption; or

(ii) trusts for the primary benefit of individuals related as described in clause (i); and

(G) has filed with the Board a statement that includes—

(i) the basis for the eligibility of the partnership under subparagraph (F);

(ii) a list of the existing activities and investments of the partnership;

(iii) a commitment to comply with this paragraph;

(iv) a commitment to comply with § 1817 with respect to any acquisition of control of an insured depository institution occurring after September 30, 1996; and

(v) a commitment to be subject, to the same extent as if the qualified family partnership were a bank holding company—

(I) to examination by the Board to assure compliance with this paragraph; and

(II) to § 1818.

(p) Financial Holding Company.—For purposes of this Act, the term "financial holding company" means a bank holding company that meets the requirements of § 1843(*l*)(1).

(q) Insurance Company.—For purposes of §§ 1843 and 1844, the term "insurance company" includes any person engaged in the business of insurance to the extent of such activities.

§ 1842. Acquisition of Bank Shares or Assets

(a) Prior Approval of Board as Necessary . . . —It shall be unlawful, except with the prior approval of the Board,

(1) for any action to be taken that causes any company to become a bank holding company;

(2) for any action to be taken that causes a bank to become a subsidiary of a bank holding company;

(3) for any bank holding company to acquire direct or indirect ownership or control of any voting shares of any bank if, after such acquisition, such company will directly or indirectly own or control more than 5 per centum of the voting shares of such bank;

(4) for any bank holding company or subsidiary thereof, other than a bank, to acquire all or substantially all of the assets of a bank; or

(5) for any bank holding company to merge or consolidate with any other bank holding company.

Notwithstanding the foregoing this prohibition shall not apply to

(A) shares acquired by a bank,

(i) in good faith in a fiduciary capacity, except where such shares are held under a trust that constitutes a company as defined in § 1841(b) and except as provided in paragraphs (2) and (3) of § 1841(g), or

(ii) in the regular course of securing or collecting a debt previously contracted in good faith, but any shares acquired after May 9, 1956, in securing or collecting any such previously contracted debt shall be disposed of within a period of two years from the date on which they were acquired;

(B) additional shares acquired by a bank holding company in a bank in which such bank holding company owned or controlled a majority of the voting shares prior to such acquisition. The Board is authorized upon application by a bank to extend, from time to time for not more than one year at a time, the two-year period referred to above for disposing of any shares acquired by a bank in the regular course of securing or collecting a debt previously contracted in good faith, if, in the Board's judgment, such an extension would not be detrimental to the public interest, but no such extension shall in the aggregate exceed three years. For the purpose of the preceding sentence, bank shares acquired after December 31, 1970, shall not be deemed to have been acquired in good faith in a fiduciary capacity if the acquiring bank or company has sole discretionary authority to exercise voting rights with respect thereto, but in such instances acquisitions may be made without prior approval of the Board if the Board, upon application filed within ninety days after the shares are acquired, approves retention or, if retention is disapproved, the acquiring bank disposes of the shares or its sole discretionary voting rights within two years after issuance of the order of disapproval; or

(C) the acquisition, by a company, of control of a bank in a reorganization in which a person or group of persons exchanges their shares of the bank for shares of a newly formed bank holding company and receives after the reorganization substantially the same proportional share interest in the holding company as they held in the bank except for changes in shareholders' interests resulting from the exercise of dissenting shareholders' rights under State or Federal law if—

(i) immediately following the acquisition—

(I) the bank holding company meets the capital and other financial standards prescribed by the Board by regulation for such a bank holding company; and

(II) the bank is adequately capitalized (as defined in § 1831o);

(ii) the holding company does not engage in any activities other than those of managing and controlling banks as a result of the reorganization;

(iii) the company provides 30 days prior notice to the Board and the Board does not object to such transaction during such 30 day period; and

(iv) the holding company will not acquire control of any additional bank as a result of the reorganization.

(b) Application for Approval. . . . —

(1) Notice and hearing requirements.—Upon receiving from a company any application for approval under this section, the Board shall give notice to the Comptroller of the Currency, if the applicant company or any bank the voting shares or assets of which are sought to be required is a national banking association, or to the appropriate supervisory authority of the interested State, if the applicant company or any bank the voting shares or assets of which are sought to be acquired is a State bank, in order to provide for the submission of the views and recommendations of the Comptroller of the Currency or the State supervisory authority, as the case may be. The views and recommendations shall be submitted within thirty calendar days of the date on which notice is given, or within ten calendar days of such date if the Board advises the Comptroller of the Currency or the State supervisory authority that an emergency exists requiring expeditious action. If the thirty-day notice period applies and if the Comptroller of the Currency or the State supervisory authority so notified by the Board disapproves the application in writing within this period, the Board shall forthwith give written notice of that fact to the applicant. Within three days after giving such notice to the applicant, the Board shall notify in writing the applicant and the disapproving authority of the date for commencement of a hearing by it on such application. Any such hearing shall be commenced not less than ten nor more than thirty days after the Board has given written notice to the applicant of the action of the disapproving authority. The length of any such hearing shall be determined by the Board, but it shall afford all interested parties a reasonable opportunity to testify at such hearing. At the conclusion thereof, the Board shall, by order, grant or deny the application on the basis of the record made at such hearing. In the event of the failure of the Board to act on any application for approval under this section within the ninety-one-day period which begins on the date of submission to the Board of the complete record on that application, the application shall be deemed to have been granted. Notwithstanding any other provision of this subsection, if the Board finds that it must act immediately on any application for approval under this section in order to prevent the probable failure of a bank or bank holding company involved in a proposed acquisition, merger, or consolidation transaction, the Board may dispense with the notice requirements of this subsection, and if notice is given, the Board may request that the views and recommendations of the Comptroller of the Currency or the State supervisory authority, as the case may be, be submitted immediately in any form or by any means acceptable to the Board. If the Board has found pursuant to this subsection either that an emergency exists requiring expeditious action or that it must act immediately to prevent probable failure, the Board may grant or deny any such application without a hearing notwithstanding any recommended disapproval by the appropriate supervisory authority.

(2) Waiver in case of bank in danger of closing.—If the Board receives a certification described in § 1823(f)(8)(D) from the appropriate Federal or State chartering authority that a bank is in danger of closing, the Board may dispense with the notice and hearing requirements of paragraph (1) with respect to any application received by the Board relating to the acquisition of such bank, the bank holding company which controls such bank, or any other affiliated bank.

(c) Factors for Consideration by Board.—

(1) Competitive factors.—The Board shall not approve—

(A) any acquisition or merger or consolidation under this section which would result in a monopoly, or which would be in furtherance of any combination or conspiracy to monopolize or to attempt to monopolize the business of banking in any part of the United States, or

(B) any other proposed acquisition or merger or consolidation under this section whose effect in any section of the country may be substantially to lessen competition, or to tend to create a monopoly, or which in any other manner would be in restraint or trade, unless it finds that the anticompetitive effects of the proposed transaction are clearly outweighed in the public interest by the probable effect of the transaction in meeting the convenience and needs of the community to be served.

(2) **Banking and community factors**.—In every case, the Board shall take into consideration the financial and managerial resources and future prospects of the company or companies and the banks concerned, and the convenience and needs of the community to be served.

(3) **Supervisory factors**.—The Board shall disapprove any application under this section by any company if—

(A) the company fails to provide the Board with adequate assurances that the company will make available to the Board such information on the operations or activities of the company, and any affiliate of the company, as the Board determines to be appropriate to determine and enforce compliance with this Act; or

(B) in the case of an application involving a foreign bank, the foreign bank is not subject to comprehensive supervision or regulation on a consolidated basis by the appropriate authorities in the bank's home country. . . .

(5) **Managerial resources**.—Consideration of the managerial resources of a company or bank under paragraph (2) shall include consideration of the competence, experience, and integrity of the officers, directors, and principal shareholders of the company or bank.

(6) **Money laundering**.—In every case, the Board shall take into consideration the effectiveness of the company or companies in combating money laundering activities, including in overseas branches.

(7) **Financial stability**.—In every case, the Board shall take into consideration the extent to which a proposed acquisition, merger, or consolidation would result in greater or more concentrated risks to the stability of the United States banking or financial system.

(d) **Interstate Banking**.—

(1) **Approvals authorized**.—

(A) **Acquisition of banks**.—The Board may approve an application under this section by a bank holding company that is well capitalized and well managed to acquire control of, or acquire all or substantially all of the assets of, a bank located in a State other than the home state of such bank holding company, without regard to whether such transaction is prohibited under the law of any State.

(B) **Preservation of State age laws**.—

(i) **In general**.—Notwithstanding subparagraph (A), the Board may not approve an application pursuant to such subparagraph that would have the effect of permitting an out-of-State bank holding company to acquire a bank in a host State that has not been in existence for the minimum period of time, if any, specified in the statutory law of the host State.

(ii) Special rule for State age laws specifying a period of more than 5 years.—Notwithstanding clause (i), the Board may approve, pursuant to subparagraph (A), the acquisition of a bank that has been in existence for at least 5 years without regard to any longer minimum period of time specified in a statutory law of the host State.

(C) Shell banks.—For purposes of this subsection, a bank that has been chartered solely for the purpose of, and does not open for business prior to, acquiring control of, or acquiring all or substantially all of the assets of, an existing bank shall be deemed to have been in existence for the same period of time as the bank to be acquired. . . .

(2) Concentration limits.—

(A) Nationwide concentration limits.—The Board may not approve an application pursuant to paragraph (1)(A) if the applicant (including all insured depository institutions which are affiliates of the applicant) controls, or upon consummation of the acquisition for which such application is filed would control, more than 10 percent of the total amount of deposits of insured depository institutions in the United States.

(B) Statewide concentration limits other than with respect to initial entries.—The Board may not approve an application pursuant to paragraph (1)(A) if—

(i) immediately before the consummation of the acquisition for which such application is filed, the applicant (including any insured depository institution affiliate of the applicant) controls any insured depository institution or any branch of an insured depository institution in the home State of any bank to be acquired or in any host State in which any such bank maintains a branch; and

(ii) the applicant (including all insured depository institutions which are affiliates of the applicant), upon consummation of the acquisition, would control 30 percent or more of the total amount of deposits of insured depository institutions in any such State.

(C) Effectiveness of State deposit caps.—No provision of this subsection shall be construed as affecting the authority of any State to limit, by statute, regulation, or order, the percentage of the total amount of deposits of insured depository institutions in the State which may be held or controlled by any bank or bank holding company (including all insured depository institutions which are affiliates of the bank or bank holding company) to the extent the application of such limitation does not discriminate against out-of-State banks, out-of-State bank holding companies, or subsidiaries of such banks or holding companies.

(D) Exceptions to subparagraph (B).—The Board may approve an application pursuant to paragraph (1)(A) without regard to the applicability of subparagraph (B) with respect to any State if—

(i) there is a limitation described in subparagraph (C) in a State statute, regulation, or order which has the effect of permitting a bank or bank holding company (including all insured depository institutions which are affiliates of the bank or bank holding company) to control a greater percentage of total deposits of all insured depository institutions in the State than the percentage permitted under subparagraph (B); or

(ii) the acquisition is approved by the appropriate State bank supervisor of such State and the standard on which such approval is based does not have the effect of discriminating against out-of-State banks, out-of-State bank holding companies, or subsidiaries of such banks or holding companies.

(E) "Deposit" defined.—For purposes of this paragraph, the term "deposit" has the same meaning as in § 1813(*l*).

(3) Community reinvestment compliance.—In determining whether to approve an application under paragraph (1)(A), the Board shall—

(A) comply with the responsibilities of the Board regarding such application under § 2903; and

(B) take into account the applicant's record of compliance with applicable State community reinvestment laws.

(4) Applicability of antitrust laws.—No provision of this subsection shall be construed as affecting—

(A) the applicability of the antitrust laws; or

(B) the applicability, if any, of any State law which is similar to the antitrust laws.

(5) Exception for banks in default or in danger of default.—The Board may approve an application pursuant to paragraph (1)(A) which involves—

(A) an acquisition of 1 or more banks in default or in danger of default; or

(B) an acquisition with respect to which assistance is provided under § 1823(c);

without regard to subparagraph (B) or (D) of paragraph (1) or paragraph (2) or (3).

(e) Insured Depository Institution.—Every bank that is a holding company and every bank that is a subsidiary of such a company shall become and remain an insured depository institution as defined in § 1813. . . .

(g) Mutual Bank Holding Company.—

(1) Establishment.—Notwithstanding any provision of Federal law other than this Act, a savings bank or cooperative bank operating in mutual form may reorganize so as to form a holding company.

(2) Regulations.—A bank holding company organized as a mutual holding company shall be regulated on terms, and shall be subject to limitations, comparable to those applicable to any other bank holding company.

§ 1843. Interests in Nonbanking Organizations

(a) General Prohibition.—Except as otherwise provided in this Act, no bank holding company shall—

(1) ... acquire direct or indirect ownership or control of any voting shares of any company which is not a bank, or

(2) after two years from the date as of which it becomes a bank holding company ..., retain direct or indirect ownership or control of any voting shares of any company which is not a bank or bank holding company or engage in any activities other than—

> (A) those of banking or of managing or controlling banks and other subsidiaries authorized under this Act or of furnishing services to or performing services for its subsidiaries, and
>
> (B) those permitted under paragraph (8) of subsection (c) of this section subject to all the conditions specified in such paragraph or in any order or regulation issued by the Board under such paragraph.

Provided, That a company covered in 1970 may also engage in those activities in which directly or through a subsidiary (i) it was lawfully engaged on June 30, 1968, and (ii) it has been continuously engaged since June 30, 1968. ... The Board by order, after opportunity for hearing, may terminate the authority conferred by the preceding proviso on any company to engage directly or through a subsidiary in any activity otherwise permitted by that proviso if it determines, having due regard to the purposes of this Act, that such action is necessary to prevent undue concentration of resources, decreased or unfair competition, conflicts of interest, or unsound banking practices. ...

Nothing in this paragraph shall be construed to authorize any bank holding company referred to in the preceding proviso, or any subsidiary thereof, to engage in activities authorized by that proviso through the acquisition, pursuant to a contract entered into after June 30, 1968, of any interest in or the assets of a going concern engaged in such activities. ...

The Board is authorized, upon application by a bank holding company, to extend the two year period referred to in paragraph (2) above from time to time as to such bank holding company for not more than one year at a time, if, in its judgment, such an extension would not be detrimental to the public interest, but no such extensions shall in the aggregate exceed three years. ... In making its decision whether to grant such extension, the

Board shall consider whether the company has made a good faith effort to divest such interests and whether such extension is necessary to avert substantial loss to the company.

(b) Stapled Stock Prohibited.—[N]o certificate evidencing shares of any bank holding company shall bear any statement purporting to represent shares of any other company except a bank or a bank holding company, nor shall the ownership, sale, or transfer of shares of any bank holding company be conditioned in any manner whatsoever upon the ownership, sale, or transfer of shares of any other company except a bank or a bank holding company.

(c) Exemptions.—The prohibitions in this section shall not . . . apply to—

(1) shares of any company engaged or to be engaged solely in one or more of the following activities:

(A) holding or operating properties used wholly or substantially by any banking subsidiary of such bank holding company in the operations of such banking subsidiary or acquired for such future use; or

(B) conducting a safe deposit business; or

(C) furnishing services to or performing services for such bank holding company or its banking subsidiaries; or

(D) liquidating assets acquired from such bank holding company or its banking subsidiaries or acquired from any other source prior to May 9, 1956, or the date on which such company became a bank holding company, whichever is later;

(2) shares acquired by a bank holding company or any of its subsidiaries in satisfaction of a debt previously contracted in good faith, but such shares shall be disposed of within a period of two years from the date on which they were acquired, except that the Board is authorized upon application by such bank holding company to extend such period of two years from time to time as to such holding company if, in its judgment, such an extension would not be detrimental to the public interest, and, in the case of a bank holding company which has not disposed of such shares within 5 years after the date on which such shares were acquired, the Board may, upon the application of such company, grant additional exemptions if, in the judgment of the Board, such extension would not be detrimental to the public interest and, either the bank holding company has made a good faith attempt to dispose of such shares during such 5-year period, or the disposal of such shares during such 5-year period would have been detrimental to the company, except that the aggregate duration of such extensions shall not extend beyond 10 years after the date on which such shares were acquired;

(3) shares acquired by such bank holding company from any of its subsidiaries which subsidiary has been requested to dispose of such shares by any Federal or State authority having statutory power to examine such subsidiary, but such bank holding company shall dispose of such shares within a period of two years from the date on which they were acquired;

(4) shares held or acquired by a bank in good faith in a fiduciary capacity, except where such shares are held under a trust that constitutes a company as defined in § 1841(b) and except as provided in paragraphs (2) and (3) of § 1841 (g);

(5) shares which are of the kinds and amounts eligible for investment by national banking associations under the provisions of § 24;

(6) shares of any company which do not include more than 5 per centum of the outstanding voting shares of such company;

(7) shares of an investment company which is not a bank holding company and which is not engaged in any business other than investing in securities, which securities do not include more than 5 per centum of the outstanding voting shares of any company;

(8) shares of any company the activities of which had been determined by the Board by regulation or order under this paragraph as of the day before November 12, 1999, to be so closely related to banking as to be a proper incident thereto (subject to such terms and conditions contained in such regulation or order, unless modified by the Board);

(9) shares held or activities conducted by any company organized under the laws of a foreign country the greater part of whose business is conducted outside the United States, if the Board by regulation or order determines that, under the circumstances and subject to the conditions set forth in the regulation or order, the exemption would not be substantially at variance with the purposes of this Act and would be in the public interest;

(10) shares lawfully acquired and owned prior to May 9, 1956, by a bank which is a bank holding company, or by any of its wholly owned subsidiaries;

(11) shares owned directly or indirectly by a company covered in 1970 in a company which does not engage in any activities other than those in which the bank holding company, or its subsidiaries, may engage by virtue of this section, but nothing in this paragraph authorizes any bank holding company, or subsidiary thereof, to acquire any interest in or the assets of any going concern (except pursuant to a binding written contract entered into before June 30, 1968, or pursuant to another provision of this Act) other than one which was a subsidiary on June 30, 1968;

(12) shares retained or acquired, or activities engaged in, by any company which becomes, as a result of the enactment of the Bank Holding Company Act Amendments of 1970, a bank holding company on December 31, 1970, or by any subsidiary thereof, if such company—

(A) within the applicable time limits prescribed in subsection (a)(2) of this section (i) ceases to be a bank holding company, or (ii) ceases to retain direct or indirect ownership or control of those shares and to engage in those activities not authorized under this section; and

(B) complies with such other conditions as the Board may by regulation or order prescribe;

(13) shares of, or activities conducted by, any company which does no business in the United States except as an incident to its international or foreign business, if the Board by regulation or order determines that, under the circumstances and subject to the conditions set forth in the regulation or order, the exemption would not be substantially at variance with the purposes of this Act and would be in the public interest; or

(14) shares of any company which is an export trading company whose acquisition (including each acquisition of shares) or formation by a bank holding company has not been disapproved by the Board pursuant to this paragraph, except that such investments, whether direct or indirect, in such shares shall not exceed 5 per centum of the bank holding company's consolidated capital and surplus. . . .

(F) For purposes of this paragraph—

(i) the term **"export trading company"** means a company which does business under the laws of the United States or any State, which is exclusively engaged in activities related to international trade, and which is organized and operated principally for purposes of exporting goods or services produced in the United States or for purposes of facilitating the exportation of goods or services produced in the United States by unaffiliated persons by providing one or more export trade services.

(ii) the term **"export trade services"** includes, but is not limited to, consulting, international market research, advertising, marketing, insurance (other than acting as principal, agent or broker in the sale of insurance on risks resident or located, or activities performed, in the United States, except for insurance covering the transportation of cargo from any point of origin in the United States to a point of final destination outside the United States), product research and design, legal assistance, transportation, including trade documentation and freight forwarding, communication and processing of foreign orders to and for exporters and foreign purchasers, warehousing, foreign exchange, financing, and taking title to goods, when provided in order to facilitate the export of goods or services produced in the United States. . . .

(f) Certain Companies Not Treated as Bank Holding Companies.—

(1) In general.—[A]ny company which—

(A) on March 5, 1987, controlled an institution which became a bank as a result of the enactment of the Competitive Equality Amendments of 1987; and

(B) was not a bank holding company on the day before August 10, 1987, shall not be treated as a bank holding company for purposes of this Act solely by virtue of such company's control of such institution.

(2) Loss of exemption.—Subject to paragraph (3), a company described in paragraph (1) shall no longer qualify for the exemption provided under that paragraph if—

(A) such company directly or indirectly—

(i) acquires control of an additional bank or an insured institution (other than an insured institution described in paragraph (10) or (12) of this subsection) after March 5, 1987; or

(ii) acquires control of more than 5 percent of the shares or assets of an additional bank or a savings association other than—

(I) shares held as a bona fide fiduciary (whether with or without the sole discretion to vote such shares);

(II) shares held by any person as a bona fide fiduciary solely for the benefit of employees of either the company described in paragraph (1) or any subsidiary of that company and the beneficiaries of those employees;

(III) shares held temporarily pursuant to an underwriting commitment in the normal course of an underwriting business;

(IV) shares held in an account solely for trading purposes;

(V) shares over which no control is held other than control of voting rights acquired in the normal course of a proxy solicitation;

(VI) loans or other accounts receivable acquired in the normal course of business;

(VII) shares or assets acquired in securing or collecting a debt previously contracted in good faith, during the 2-year period beginning on the date of such acquisition or for such additional time (not exceeding 3 years) as the Board may permit if the Board determines that such an extension will not be detrimental to the public interest;

(VIII) shares or assets of a savings association described in paragraph (10) or (12) of this subsection;

(IX) shares of a savings association held by any insurance company, as defined in § 80a-2(a)(17) of title 15, except as provided in paragraph (11);

(X) shares issued in a qualified stock issuance under § 1467a(q) of this title; and

(XI) assets that are derived from, or incidental to, activities in which institutions described in subparagraph (F) or (H) of § 1841(c)(2) of this title are permitted to engage;

except that the aggregate amount of shares held under this clause (other than under subclauses (I), (II), (III), (IV), (V), and (VIII)) may not exceed 15 percent of all outstanding shares or of the voting power of a savings association;

(B) any bank subsidiary of such company—

(i) accepts demand deposits or deposits that the depositor may withdraw by check or similar means for payment to third parties; and

(ii) engages in the business of making commercial loans (except that, for purposes of this clause, loans made in the ordinary course of a credit card operation shall not be treated as commercial loans); or

(C) after August 10, 1987, any bank subsidiary of such company permits any overdraft (including any intraday overdraft), or incurs any such overdraft in the account of the bank at a Federal reserve bank, on behalf of an affiliate, other than an overdraft described in paragraph (3).

(3) Permissible overdrafts described.—For purposes of paragraph (2)(C), an overdraft is described in this paragraph if—

(A) such overdraft results from an inadvertent computer or accounting error that is beyond the control of both the bank and the affiliate;

(B) such overdraft—

(i) is permitted or incurred on behalf of an affiliate that is monitored by, reports to, and is recognized as a primary dealer by the Federal Reserve Bank of New York; and

(ii) is fully secured, as required by the Board, by bonds, notes, or other obligations that are direct obligations of the United States or on which the principal and interest are fully guaranteed by the United States or by securities and obligations eligible for settlement on the Federal Reserve book entry system; or

(C) such overdraft—

(i) is permitted or incurred by, or on behalf of, an affiliate in connection with an activity that is financial in nature or incidental to a financial activity; and

(ii) does not cause the bank to violate any provision of § 371c or § 371c-1, either directly, in the case of a bank that is a member of the Federal Reserve System, or by virtue of § 1828(j), in the case of a bank that is not a member of the Federal Reserve System.

(4) Divestiture in case of loss of exemption.—If any company described in paragraph (1) fails to qualify for the exemption provided under paragraph (1) by operation of paragraph (2), such exemption shall cease to apply to such company and such company shall divest control of each bank it controls before the end of the 180-day period beginning on the date on which the company receives notice from the Board that the company has failed to continue to qualify for such exemption, unless, before the end of such 180-day period, the company has—

(A) either—

(i) corrected the condition or ceased the activity that caused the company to fail to continue to qualify for the exemption; or

(ii) submitted a plan to the Board for approval to cease the activity or correct the condition in a timely manner (which shall not exceed 1 year); and

(B) implemented procedures that are reasonably adapted to avoid the reoccurrence of such condition or activity. . . .

(10) Exemption unaffected by certain emergency acquisitions.—

. . .

(11) Shares held by insurance affiliates.— . . .

(12) Exemption unaffected by certain other acquisitions.— . . .

(14) Foreign bank subsidiaries of limited purpose credit card banks.— . . .

(i) Acquisition of Savings Associations.—

(1) In general.—The Board may approve an application by any bank holding company under subsection (c)(8) of this section to acquire any savings association in accordance with the requirements and limitations of this section.

(2) Prohibition on tandem restrictions.—In approving an application by a bank holding company to acquire a savings association, the Board shall not impose any restriction on transactions between the savings association and its holding company affiliates, except as required under sections 371 and 371c-1 or any other applicable law. . . .

(8) Interstate acquisitions.—

(A) **In general.**—The Board may not approve an application by a bank holding company to acquire an insured depository institution under subsection (c)(8) or any other provision of this Act if—

(i) the home State of such insured depository institution is a State other than the home State of the bank holding company; and

(ii) the applicant (including all insured depository institutions which are affiliates of the applicant) controls, or upon consummation of the transaction would control, more than 10 percent of the total amount of deposits of insured depository institutions in the United States.

(B) **Exception.**—Subparagraph (A) shall not apply to an acquisition that involves an insured depository institution in default or in danger of default, or with respect to which the Federal Deposit Insurance Corporation provides assistance under § 1823.

(j) Notice Procedures for Nonbanking Activities.—

(1) General notice procedure.—

(A) **Notice requirement.**—Except as provided in paragraph (3), no bank holding company may engage in any nonbanking activity or acquire or retain ownership or control of the shares of a company engaged in activities based on subsection (c)(8) or (a)(2) of this section or in any complementary activity under subsection (k)(1)(B) of this section without providing the Board with written notice of the proposed transaction or activity at least 60 days before the transaction or activity is proposed to occur or commence.

(B) **Contents of notice.**—The notice submitted to the Board shall contain such information as the Board shall prescribe by regulation or by specific request in connection with a particular notice.

(C) **Procedure for agency action.**—

(i) **Notice of disapproval.**—Any notice filed under this subsection shall be deemed to be approved by the Board unless, before the end of the 60-day period beginning on the date the Board receives a complete notice under subparagraph (A), the Board issues an order disapproving the transaction or activity and setting forth the reasons for disapproval.

(ii) **Extension of period.**—The Board may extend the 60-day period referred to in clause (i) for an additional 30 days. The Board may further extend the period with the agreement of the bank holding company submitting the notice pursuant to this subsection.

(iii) **Determination of period in case of public hearing.**—In the event a hearing is requested or the Board determines that a hearing is warranted, the Board may extend the notice period provided in this subsection for such time as is reasonably necessary to conduct a hearing and to evaluate the hearing record. Such extension shall not exceed the 91-day period beginning on the date that the hearing record is complete.

(D) **Approval before end of period.**—

(i) **In general.**—Any transaction or activity may commence before the expiration of any period for disapproval established under this paragraph if the Board issues a written notice of approval.

(ii) **Shorter periods by regulation.**—The Board may prescribe regulations which provide for a shorter notice period with respect to particular activities or transactions.

(E) **Extension of period.**—In the case of any notice to engage in, or to acquire or retain ownership or control of shares of any company engaged in, any activity pursuant to subsection (c)(8) or (a)(2) of this section or in any complementary activity under subsection (k)(1)(B) of this section that has not been previously approved by regulation, the Board may extend the notice period under this subsection for an additional 90 days. The Board may further extend the period with the agreement of the bank holding company submitting the notice pursuant to this subsection.

(2) **General standards for review.**—

(A) **Criteria.**—In connection with a notice under this subsection, the Board shall consider whether performance of the activity by a bank holding company or a subsidiary of such company can reasonably be expected to produce benefits to the public, such as greater convenience, increased competition, or gains in efficiency, that outweigh possible adverse effects, such as undue concentration of resources, decreased or unfair competition, conflicts of interests, unsound banking practices, or risk to the stability of the United States banking or financial system.

(B) **Grounds for disapproval.**—The Board may deny any proposed transaction or activity for which notice has been submitted pursuant to this subsection if the bank holding company submitting such notice neglects, fails, or refuses to furnish the Board all the information required by the Board.

(C) Conditional action.—Nothing in this subsection limits the authority of the Board to impose conditions in connection with an action under this section.

(3) No notice required for certain transactions.—No notice under paragraph (1) of this subsection or under subsection (c)(8) or (a)(2)(B) of this section is required for a proposal by a bank holding company to engage in any activity, other than any complementary activity under subsection (k)(1)(B) of this section, or acquire the shares or assets of any company, other than an insured depository institution or a company engaged in any complementary activity under subsection (k)(1)(B) of this section, if the proposal qualifies under paragraph (4).

(4) Criteria for statutory approval.—A proposal qualifies under this paragraph if all of the following criteria are met:

    (A) Financial criteria.—Both before and immediately after the proposed transaction—

        (i) the acquiring bank holding company is well capitalized,

        (ii) the lead insured depository institution of such holding company is well capitalized;

        (iii) well capitalized insured depository institutions control at least 80 percent of the aggregate total risk-weighted assets of insured depository institutions controlled by such holding company; and

        (iv) no insured depository institution controlled by such holding company is undercapitalized.

    (B) Managerial criteria.—

        (i) Well managed.—At the time of the transaction, the acquiring bank holding company, its lead insured depository institution, and insured depository institutions that control at least 90 percent of the aggregate total risk-weighted assets of insured depository institutions controlled by such holding company are well managed.

        (ii) Limitation on poorly managed institutions.—Except as provided in paragraph (6), no insured depository institution controlled by the acquiring bank holding company has received 1 of the 2 lowest composite ratings at the later of the institution's most recent examination or subsequent review.

    (C) Activities permissible.—Following consummation of the proposal, the bank holding company engages directly or through a subsidiary solely in—

        (i) activities that are permissible under subsection (c)(8) of this section, as determined by the Board by regulation or order thereunder, subject to all of the restrictions, terms, and conditions of such subsection and such regulation or order; and

        (ii) such other activities as are otherwise permissible under this section, subject to the restrictions, terms and conditions, including any prior notice or approval requirements, provided in this section.

(D) Size of acquisition.—
   (i) Asset size.—The book value of the total assets to be acquired does not exceed 10 percent of the consolidated total risk-weighted assets of the acquiring bank holding company.
   (ii) Consideration.—The gross consideration to be paid for the securities or assets does not exceed 15 percent of the consolidated Tier 1 capital of the acquiring bank holding company.
(E) Notice not otherwise warranted.—For proposals described in paragraph (5)(B), the Board has not, before the conclusion of the period provided in paragraph (5)(B), advised the bank holding company that a notice under paragraph (1) is required.
(F) Compliance criterion.—During the 12-month period ending on the date on which the bank holding company proposes to commence an activity or acquisition, no administrative enforcement action has been commenced, and no cease and desist order has been issued pursuant to § 1818, against the bank holding company or any depository institution subsidiary of the holding company, and no such enforcement action, order, or other administrative enforcement proceeding is pending as of such date.
(5) Notification.—
(A) Commencement of activities approved by rule.—A bank holding company that qualifies under paragraph (4) and that proposes to engage de novo, directly or through a subsidiary, in any activity that is permissible under subsection (c)(8) of this section, as determined by the Board by regulation, may commence that activity without prior notice to the Board and must provide written notification to the Board not later than 10 business days after commencing the activity.
(B) Activities permitted by order and acquisitions.—
   (i) In general.—At least 12 business days before commencing any activity pursuant to paragraph (3) (other than an activity described in subparagraph (A) of this paragraph) or acquiring shares or assets of any company pursuant to paragraph (3), the bank holding company shall provide written notice of the proposal to the Board, unless the Board determines that no notice or a shorter notice period is appropriate.
   (ii) Description of activities and terms.—A notification under this subparagraph shall include a description of the proposed activities and the terms of any proposed acquisition.
(6) Recently acquired institutions.—Any insured depository institution which has been acquired by a bank holding company during the 12-month period preceding the date on which the company proposes to commence an activity or acquisition pursuant to paragraph (3) may be excluded for purposes of paragraph (4)(B)(ii) if—
   (A) the bank holding company has developed a plan for the institution to restore the capital and management of the institution which is acceptable to the appropriate Federal banking agency; and

(B) all such insured depository institutions represent, in the aggregate, less than 10 percent of the aggregate total risk-weighted assets of all insured depository institutions controlled by the bank holding company.

(7) Adjustment of percentages.—The Board may, by regulation, adjust the percentages and the manner in which the percentages of insured depository institutions are calculated under paragraph (4)(B)(i), (4)(D), or (6)(B) if the Board determines that any such adjustment is consistent with safety and soundness and the purposes of this Act.

(k) Engaging in Activities That Are Financial in Nature.—

(1) In general.—Notwithstanding subsection (a), a financial holding company may engage in any activity, and may acquire and retain the shares of any company engaged in any activity, that the Board, in accordance with paragraph (2), determines (by regulation or order)—

(A) to be financial in nature or incidental to such financial activity; or

(B) is complementary to a financial activity and does not pose a substantial risk to the safety or soundness of depository institutions or the financial system generally.

(2) Coordination between the Board and the Secretary of the Treasury.—

(A) Proposals raised before the Board.—

(i) Consultation.—The Board shall notify the Secretary of the Treasury of, and consult with the Secretary of the Treasury concerning, any request, proposal, or application under this subsection for a determination of whether an activity is financial in nature or incidental to a financial activity.

(ii) Treasury view.—The Board shall not determine that any activity is financial in nature or incidental to a financial activity under this subsection if the Secretary of the Treasury notifies the Board in writing, not later than 30 days after the date of receipt of the notice described in clause (i) (or such longer period as the Board determines to be appropriate under the circumstances) that the Secretary of the Treasury believes that the activity is not financial in nature or incidental to a financial activity or is not otherwise permissible under this section.

(B) Proposals raised by the Treasury.—

(i) Treasury recommendation.—The Secretary of the Treasury may, at any time, recommend in writing that the Board find an activity to be financial in nature or incidental to a financial activity.

(ii) Time period for Board action.—Not later than 30 days after the date of receipt of a written recommendation from the Secretary of the Treasury under clause (i) (or such longer period as the Secretary of the Treasury and the Board determine to be appropriate under the circumstances), the Board shall determine whether to initiate a public rulemaking proposing that the recommended activity be found to be financial in nature or incidental to a financial activity under this subsection, and shall notify the Secretary of the Treasury in writing of the determination of the Board and, if the Board determines not to seek public comment on the proposal, the reasons for that determination.

(3) **Factors to be considered**.—In determining whether an activity is financial in nature or incidental to a financial activity, the Board shall take into account—

(A) the purposes of this Act and the Gramm-Leach-Bliley Act;

(B) changes or reasonably expected changes in the marketplace in which financial holding companies compete;

(C) changes or reasonably expected changes in the technology for delivering financial services; and

(D) whether such activity is necessary or appropriate to allow a financial holding company and the affiliates of a financial holding company to—

(i) compete effectively with any company seeking to provide financial services in the United States;

(ii) efficiently deliver information and services that are financial in nature through the use of technological means, including any application necessary to protect the security or efficacy of systems for the transmission of data or financial transactions; and

(iii) offer customers any available or emerging technological means for using financial services or for the document imaging of data.

(4) **Activities that are financial in nature**.—For purposes of this subsection, the following activities shall be considered to be financial in nature:

(A) Lending, exchanging, transferring, investing for others, or safeguarding money or securities.

(B) Insuring, guaranteeing, or indemnifying against loss, harm, damage, illness, disability, or death, or providing and issuing annuities, and acting as principal, agent, or broker for purposes of the foregoing, in any State.

(C) Providing financial, investment, or economic advisory services, including advising an investment company (as defined in § 80a-3 of title 15).

(D) Issuing or selling instruments representing interests in pools of assets permissible for a bank to hold directly.

(E) Underwriting, dealing in, or making a market in securities.

(F) Engaging in any activity that the Board has determined, by order or regulation that is in effect on November 12, 1999, to be so closely related to banking or managing or controlling banks as to be a proper incident thereto (subject to the same terms and conditions contained in such order or regulation, unless modified by the Board).

(G) Engaging, in the United States, in any activity that—

(i) a bank holding company may engage in outside of the United States; and

(ii) the Board has determined, under regulations prescribed or interpretations issued pursuant to subsection (c)(13) (as in effect on the day before November 12, 1999) to be usual in connection with the transaction of banking or other financial operations abroad.

(H) Directly or indirectly acquiring or controlling, whether as principal, on behalf of 1 or more entities (including entities, other than a depository institution or subsidiary of a depository institution, that the bank holding company controls), or otherwise, shares, assets, or ownership interests (including debt or equity securities, partnership interests, trust certificates, or other instruments representing ownership) of a company or other entity, whether or not constituting control of such company or entity, engaged in any activity not authorized pursuant to this section if—

(i) the shares, assets, or ownership interests are not acquired or held by a depository institution or subsidiary of a depository institution;

(ii) such shares, assets, or ownership interests are acquired and held by—

(I) a securities affiliate or an affiliate thereof, or

(II) an affiliate of an insurance company described in subparagraph (I)(ii) that provides investment advice to an insurance company and is registered pursuant to the Investment Advisers Act of 1940, or an affiliate of such investment adviser;

as part of a bona fide underwriting or merchant or investment banking activity, including investment activities engaged in for the purpose of appreciation and ultimate resale or disposition of the investment;

(iii) such shares, assets, or ownership interests are held for a period of time to enable the sale or disposition thereof on a reasonable basis consistent with the financial viability of the activities described in clause (ii); and

(iv) during the period such shares, assets, or ownership interests are held, the bank holding company does not routinely manage or operate such company or entity except as may be necessary or required to obtain a reasonable return on investment upon resale or disposition.

(I) Directly or indirectly acquiring or controlling, whether as principal, on behalf of 1 or more entities (including entities, other than a depository institution or subsidiary of a depository institution, that the bank holding company controls) or otherwise, shares, assets, or ownership interests (including debt or equity securities, partnership interests, trust certificates or other instruments representing ownership) of a company or other entity, whether or not constituting control of such company or entity, engaged in any activity not authorized pursuant to this section if—

(i) the shares, assets, or ownership interests are not acquired or held by a depository institution or a subsidiary of a depository institution;

(ii) such shares, assets, or ownership interests are acquired and held by an insurance company that is predominantly engaged in underwriting life, accident and health, or property and casualty insurance (other than credit-related insurance) or providing and issuing annuities;

(iii) such shares, assets, or ownership interests represent an investment made in the ordinary course of business of such insurance company in accordance with relevant State law governing such investments; and

(iv) during the period such shares, assets, or ownership interests are held, the bank holding company does not routinely manage or operate such company except as may be necessary or required to obtain a reasonable return on investment.

(5) Actions required.—

(A) In general.—The Board shall, by regulation or order, define, consistent with the purposes of this Act, the activities described in subparagraph (B) as financial in nature, and the extent to which such activities are financial in nature or incidental to a financial activity.

(B) Activities.—The activities described in this subparagraph are as follows:

(i) Lending, exchanging, transferring, investing for others, or safeguarding financial assets other than money or securities.

(ii) Providing any device or other instrumentality for transferring money or other financial assets.

(iii) Arranging, effecting, or facilitating financial transactions for the account of third parties.

(6) Required notification.—

(A) In general.—A financial holding company that acquires any company or commences any activity pursuant to this subsection shall provide written notice to the Board describing the activity commenced or conducted by the company acquired not later than 30 calendar days after commencing the activity or consummating the acquisition, as the case may be.

(B) Approval not required for certain financial activities.—

(i) In general.—Except as provided in subsection (j) with regard to the acquisition of a savings association and clause (ii), a financial holding company may commence any activity, or acquire any company, pursuant to paragraph (4) or any regulation prescribed or order issued under paragraph (5), without prior approval of the Board.

(ii) Exception.—A financial holding company may not acquire a company, without the prior approval of the Board, in a transaction in which the total consolidated assets to be acquired by the financial holding company exceed $10,000,000,000. . . .

(B) **Approval not required for certain financial activities.**—Except as provided in subsection (j) with regard to the acquisition of a savings association, a financial holding company may commence any activity, or acquire any company, pursuant to paragraph (4) or any regulation prescribed or order issued under paragraph (5), without prior approval of the Board.

(7) **Merchant banking activities.**—

(A) **Joint regulations.**—The Board and the Secretary of the Treasury may issue such regulations implementing paragraph (4)(H), including limitations on transactions between depository institutions and companies controlled pursuant to such paragraph, as the Board and the Secretary jointly deem appropriate to assure compliance with the purposes and prevent evasions of this Act and the Gramm-Leach-Bliley Act and to protect depository institutions.

(B) **Sunset of restrictions on merchant banking activities of financial subsidiaries.**—The restrictions contained in paragraph (4)(H) on the ownership and control of shares, assets, or ownership interests by or on behalf of a subsidiary of a depository institution shall not apply to a financial subsidiary (as defined in § 24a) of a bank, if the Board and the Secretary of the Treasury jointly authorize financial subsidiaries of banks to engage in merchant banking activities pursuant to section 122 of the Gramm-Leach-Bliley Act.

(*l*) **Conditions for Engaging in Expanded Financial Activities.**—

(1) **In general.**—Notwithstanding subsection (k), (n), or (o), a bank holding company may not engage in any activity, or directly or indirectly acquire or retain shares of any company engaged in any activity, under subsection (k), (n), or (o), other than activities permissible for any bank holding company under subsection (c)(8), unless—

(A) all of the depository institution subsidiaries of the bank holding company are well capitalized;

(B) all of the depository institution subsidiaries of the bank holding company are well managed;

(C) the bank holding company is well capitalized and well managed; and

(D) the bank holding company has filed with the Board—

(i) a declaration that the company elects to be a financial holding company to engage in activities or acquire and retain shares of a company that were not permissible for a bank holding company to engage in or acquire before the enactment of the Gramm-Leach-Bliley Act; and

(ii) a certification that the company meets the requirements of subparagraphs (A), (B), and (C).

(2) **CRA requirement.**—Notwithstanding subsection (k) or (n) of this section, § 24a of this title, or § 1831w(a) of this title, the appropriate

Federal banking agency shall prohibit a financial holding company or any insured depository institution from—

(A) commencing any new activity under subsection (k) or (n) of this section, § 24a, or § 1831w(a); or

(B) directly or indirectly acquiring control of a company engaged in any activity under subsection (k) or (n) of this section, § 24a of this title, or § 1831w(a) of this title (other than an investment made pursuant to subparagraph (H) or (I) of subsection (k)(4) . . . by an affiliate already engaged in activities under any such provision);

if any insured depository institution subsidiary of such financial holding company, or the insured depository institution or any of its insured depository institution affiliates, has received in its most recent examination under the Community Reinvestment Act of 1977, a rating of less than "satisfactory record of meeting community credit needs."

(3) Foreign banks.—For purposes of paragraph (1), the Board shall apply comparable capital and management standards to a foreign bank that operates a branch or agency or owns or controls a commercial lending company in the United States, giving due regard to the principle of national treatment and equality of competitive opportunity.

(m) Provisions Applicable to Financial Holding Companies That Fail to Meet Certain Requirements.—

(1) In general.—If the Board finds that—

(A) a financial holding company is engaged, directly or indirectly, in any activity under subsection (k), (n), or (o), other than activities that are permissible for a bank holding company under subsection (c)(8); and

(B) such financial holding company is not in compliance with the requirements of subsection (l)(1);

the Board shall give notice to the financial holding company to that effect, describing the conditions giving rise to the notice.

(2) Agreement to correct conditions required.—Not later than 45 days after the date of receipt by a financial holding company of a notice given under paragraph (1) (or such additional period as the Board may permit), the financial holding company shall execute an agreement with the Board to comply with the requirements applicable to a financial holding company under subsection (l)(1).

(3) Board may impose limitations.—Until the conditions described in a notice to a financial holding company under paragraph (1) are corrected, the Board may impose such limitations on the conduct or activities of that financial holding company or any affiliate of that company as the Board determines to be appropriate under the circumstances and consistent with the purposes of this Act.

(4) Failure to correct.—If the conditions described in a notice to a financial holding company under paragraph (1) are not corrected within

180 days after the date of receipt by the financial holding company of a notice under paragraph (1), the Board may require such financial holding company, under such terms and conditions as may be imposed by the Board and subject to such extension of time as may be granted in the discretion of the Board, either—

    (A) to divest control of any subsidiary depository institution; or

    (B) at the election of the financial holding company instead to cease to engage in any activity conducted by such financial holding company or its subsidiaries (other than a depository institution or a subsidiary of a depository institution) that is not an activity that is permissible for a bank holding company under subsection (c)(8).

(5) Consultation.—In taking any action under this subsection, the Board shall consult with all relevant Federal and State regulatory agencies and authorities.

(n) Authority to Retain Limited Nonfinancial Activities and Affiliations.—

(1) In general.—Notwithstanding subsection (a), a company that is not a bank holding company or a foreign bank (as defined in § 3101(b)(7)) and becomes a financial holding company after November 12, 1999, may continue to engage in any activity and retain direct or indirect ownership or control of shares of a company engaged in any activity if—

    (A) the holding company lawfully was engaged in the activity or held the shares of such company on September 30, 1999;

    (B) the holding company is predominantly engaged in financial activities as defined in paragraph (2); and

    (C) the company engaged in such activity continues to engage only in the same activities that such company conducted on September 30, 1999, and other activities permissible under this Act.

(2) Predominantly financial.—For purposes of this subsection, a company is predominantly engaged in financial activities if the annual gross revenues derived by the holding company and all subsidiaries of the holding company (excluding revenues derived from subsidiary depository institutions), on a consolidated basis, from engaging in activities that are financial in nature or are incidental to a financial activity under subsection (k) represent at least 85 percent of the consolidated annual gross revenues of the company.

(3) No expansion of grandfathered commercial activities through merger or consolidation.—A financial holding company that engages in activities or holds shares pursuant to this subsection, or a subsidiary of such financial holding company, may not acquire, in any merger, consolidation, or other type of business combination, assets of any other company that is engaged in any activity that the Board has not determined to be financial in nature or incidental to a financial activity under subsection (k). . . .

(4) Continuing revenue limitation on grandfathered commercial activities.—Notwithstanding any other provision of this subsection, a financial holding company may continue to engage in activities or hold shares in companies pursuant to this subsection only to the extent that the aggregate annual gross revenues derived from all such activities and all such companies does not exceed 15 percent of the consolidated annual gross revenues of the financial holding company (excluding revenues derived from subsidiary depository institutions).

(5) Cross marketing restrictions applicable to commercial activities.—

(A) In general.—A depository institution controlled by a financial holding company shall not—

(i) offer or market, directly or through any arrangement, any product or service of a company whose activities are conducted or whose shares are owned or controlled by the financial holding company pursuant to this subsection or subparagraph (H) or (I) of subsection (k)(4); or

(ii) permit any of its products or services to be offered or marketed, directly or through any arrangement, by or through any company described in clause (i).

(B) Rule of construction.—Subparagraph (A) shall not be construed as prohibiting an arrangement between a depository institution and a company owned or controlled pursuant to subparagraph (H) or (I) of subsection (k)(4) for the marketing of products or services through statement inserts or Internet websites if—

(i) such arrangement does not violate § 1972(1); and

(ii) the Board determines that the arrangement is in the public interest, does not undermine the separation of banking and commerce, and is consistent with the safety and soundness of depository institutions.

(6) Transactions with nonfinancial affiliates.—A depository institution controlled by a financial holding company may not engage in a covered transaction (as defined in § 371c(b)(7)) with any affiliate controlled by the company pursuant to this subsection. . . .

(o) Regulation of Certain Financial Holding Companies.—Notwithstanding subsection (a), a company that is not a bank holding company or a foreign bank (as defined in § 3101(b)(7)) and becomes a financial holding company after November 12, 1999, may continue to engage in, or directly or indirectly own or control shares of a company engaged in, activities related to the trading, sale, or investment in commodities and underlying physical properties that were not permissible for bank holding companies to conduct in the United States as of September 30, 1997, if—

(1) the holding company, or any subsidiary of the holding company, lawfully was engaged, directly or indirectly, in any of such activities as of September 30, 1997, in the United States;

(2) the attributed aggregate consolidated assets of the company held by the holding company pursuant to this subsection, and not otherwise permitted to be held by a financial holding company, are equal to not more than 5 percent of the total consolidated assets of the bank holding company, except that the Board may increase that percentage by such amounts and under such circumstances as the Board considers appropriate, consistent with the purposes of this Act; and

(3) the holding company does not permit—

(A) any company, the shares of which it owns or controls pursuant to this subsection, to offer or market any product or service of an affiliated depository institution; or

(B) any affiliated depository institution to offer or market any product or service of any company, the shares of which are owned or controlled by such holding company pursuant to this subsection.

§ 1844. Administration

(a) **Registration of Bank Holding Company.**—Within one hundred and eighty days . . . after becoming a bank holding company, whichever is later, each bank holding company shall register with the Board on forms prescribed by the Board, which shall include such information with respect to the financial condition and operations, management, and intercompany relationships of the bank holding company and its subsidiaries, and related matters, as the Board may deem necessary or appropriate to carry out the purposes of this Act. The Board may, in its discretion, extend the time within which a bank holding company shall register and file the requisite information. A declaration filed in accordance with § 1843(1)(1)(C) shall satisfy the requirements of this subsection with regard to the registration of a bank holding company but not any requirement to file an application to acquire a bank pursuant to § 1842.

(b) **Regulations and Orders.**—The Board is authorized to issue such regulations and orders, including regulations and orders relating to the capital requirements for bank holding companies, as may be necessary to enable it to administer and carry out the purposes of this Act and prevent evasions thereof. In establishing capital regulations pursuant to this subsection, the Board shall seek to make such requirements countercyclical, so that the amount of capital required to be maintained by a company increases in times of economic expansion and decreases in times of economic contraction, consistent with the safety and soundness of the company.

(c) **Reports and Examinations.**—

(1) **Reports.**— . . .

(2) **Examinations.**—

(A) **In general.**—[T]he Board may make examinations of a bank holding company and each subsidiary of a bank holding company in order to—

(i) inform the Board of—

(I) the nature of the operations and financial condition of the bank holding company and the subsidiary;

(II) the financial, operational, and other risks within the bank holding company system that may pose a threat to—

(aa) the safety and soundness of the bank holding company or of any depository institution subsidiary of the bank holding company; or

(bb) the stability of the financial system of the United States; and

(III) the systems of the bank holding company for monitoring and controlling the risks described in subclause (II); and

(ii) monitor the compliance of the bank holding company and the subsidiary with—

(I) this Act;

(II) Federal laws that the Board has specific jurisdiction to enforce against the company or subsidiary; and

(III) other than in the case of an insured depository institution or functionally regulated subsidiary, any other applicable provisions of Federal law.

(B) **Use of reports to reduce examinations.**—For purposes of this paragraph, the Board shall, to the fullest extent possible, rely on—

(i) examination reports made by other Federal or State regulatory agencies relating to a bank holding company and any subsidiary of a bank holding company; and

(ii) the reports and other information required under paragraph (1).

(C) **Coordination with other regulators.**—The Board shall—

(i) provide reasonable notice to, and consult with, the appropriate Federal banking agency, the Securities and Exchange Commission, the Commodity Futures Trading Commission, or State regulatory agency, as appropriate, for a subsidiary that is a depository institution or a functionally regulated subsidiary of a bank holding company before commencing an examination of the subsidiary under this section; and

(ii) to the fullest extent possible, avoid duplication of examination activities, reporting requirements, and requests for information.

(3) **Capital.**—

(A) **In general.**—The Board may not, by regulation, guideline, order, or otherwise, prescribe or impose any capital or capital adequacy rules, guidelines, standards, or requirements on any functionally regulated subsidiary of a bank holding company that—

(i) is not a depository institution; and

(ii) is—

(I) in compliance with the applicable capital requirements of its Federal regulatory authority (including the Securities and Exchange Commission) or State insurance authority;

(II) properly registered as an investment adviser under the investment Advisers Act of 1940, or with any State; or

(III) is licensed as an insurance agent with the appropriate State insurance authority.

(B) Rule of construction.—Subparagraph (A) shall not be construed as preventing the Board from imposing capital or capital adequacy rules, guidelines, standards, or requirements with respect to—

(i) activities of a registered investment adviser other than with respect to investment advisory activities or activities incidental to investment advisory activities; or

(ii) activities of a licensed insurance agent other than insurance agency activities or activities incidental to insurance agency activities.

(C) Limitations on indirect action.—In developing, establishing, or assessing bank holding company capital or capital adequacy rules, guidelines, standards, or requirements for purposes of this paragraph, the Board may not take into account the activities, operations, or investments of an affiliated investment company registered under the Investment Company Act of 1940, unless the investment company is—

(i) a bank holding company; or

(ii) controlled by a bank holding company by reason of ownership by the bank holding company (including through all of its affiliates) of 25 percent or more of the shares of the investment company, and the shares owned by the bank holding company have a market value equal to more than $1,000,000.

(4) Functional regulation of securities and insurance activities.—

(A) Securities activities.—Securities activities conducted in a functionally regulated subsidiary of a depository institution shall be subject to regulation by the Securities and Exchange Commission, and by relevant State securities authorities, as appropriate, subject to § 6701 of title 15, to the same extent as if they were conducted in a nondepository institution subsidiary of a bank holding company.

(B) Insurance activities.—Subject to § 6701 of title 15, insurance agency and brokerage activities and activities as principal conducted in a functionally regulated subsidiary of a depository institution shall be subject to regulation by a State insurance authority to the same extent as if they were conducted in a nondepository institution subsidiary of a bank holding company.

(5) Definition.—For purposes of this subsection, the term "functionally regulated subsidiary" means any company—

(A) that is not a bank holding company or a depository institution; and

(B) that is—

(i) a broker or dealer that is registered under the Securities Exchange Act of 1934;

(ii) a registered investment adviser, properly registered by or on behalf of either the Securities and Exchange Commission or any State, with respect to the investment advisory activities of such investment adviser and activities incidental to such investment advisory activities;

(iii) an investment company that is registered under the Investment Company Act of 1940;

(iv) an insurance company, with respect to insurance activities of the insurance company and activities incidental to such insurance activities, that is subject to supervision by a State insurance regulator; or

(v) an entity that is subject to regulation by, or registration with, the Commodity Futures Trading Commission, with respect to activities conducted as a futures commission merchant, commodity trading adviser, commodity pool, commodity pool operator, swap execution facility, swap data repository, swap dealer, major swap participant, and activities that are incidental to such commodities and swaps activities. . . .

(e) Termination of Activities or Ownership or Control of Nonbank Subsidiaries Constituting Serious Risk.—

(1) In general.—Notwithstanding any other provision of this Act, the Board may, whenever it has reasonable cause to believe that the continuation by a bank holding company of any activity or of ownership or control of any of its nonbank subsidiaries, other than a nonbank subsidiary of a bank, constitutes a serious risk to the financial safety, soundness, or stability of a bank holding company subsidiary bank and is inconsistent with sound banking principles or with the purposes of this Act or with the Financial Institutions Supervisory Act of 1966 [as reflected, e.g., in 12 U.S.C. § 1818(b)], at the election of the bank holding company—

(A) order the bank holding company or any such nonbank subsidiaries, after due notice and opportunity for hearing, and after considering the views of the bank's primary supervisor, which shall be the Comptroller of the Currency in the case of a national bank or the Federal Deposit Insurance Corporation and the appropriate State supervisory authority in the case of an insured nonmember bank, to terminate such activities or to terminate (within one hundred and twenty days or such longer period as the Board may direct in unusual circumstances) its ownership or control of any such subsidiary either by sale or by distribution of the shares of the subsidiary to the shareholders of the bank holding company; or

(B) order the bank holding company, after due notice and opportunity for hearing, and after consultation with the primary supervisor for the bank, which shall be the Comptroller of the Currency in the case of a national bank, and the Federal Deposit Insurance Corporation and the appropriate State supervisor in the case of an insured nonmember bank, to terminate (within 120 days or such longer period as the Board may direct) the ownership or control of any such bank by such company.

The distribution referred to in subparagraph (A) shall be pro rata with respect to all of the shareholders of the distributing bank holding company, and the holding company shall not make any charge to its shareholders arising out of such a distribution.

(2) **Enforcement.**— . . .

(f) **Powers of Board Respecting Applications, Examinations, or Other Proceedings.**—In the course of or in connection with an application, examination, investigation or other proceeding under this Act, the Board, or any member or designated representative thereof, including any person designated to conduct any hearing under this Act, shall have the power to administer oaths and affirmations, to take . . . depositions, and to issue, revoke, quash, or modify subpoenas and subpoenas duces tecum; and the Board is empowered to make rules and regulations to effectuate the purposes of this subsection. The attendance of witnesses and the production of documents provided for in this subsection may be required from any place in any State or in any territory or other place subject to the jurisdiction of the United States at any designated place where such proceeding is being conducted. Any party to proceedings under this Act may apply to the United States District Court for the District of Columbia, or the United States district court for the judicial district or the United States court in any territory in which such proceeding is being conducted or where the witness resides or carries on business, for the enforcement of any subpoena or subpoena duces tecum issued pursuant to this subsection, and such courts shall have jurisdiction and power to order and require compliance therewith. . . . Any court having jurisdiction of any proceeding instituted under this subsection may allow to any such party such reasonable expenses and attorneys' fees as it deems just and proper. Any person who willfully shall fail or refuse to attend and testify or to answer any lawful inquiry or to produce books, papers, correspondence, memoranda, contracts, agreements, or other records, if in such person's power so to do, in obedience to the subpoena of the Board, shall be guilty of a misdemeanor and, upon conviction, shall be subject to a fine of not more than $1,000 or to imprisonment for a term of not more than one year or both.

(g) **Authority of State Insurance Regulator and the Securities and Exchange Commission.**—

(1) **In general.**—Notwithstanding any other provision of law, any regulation, order, or other action of the Board that requires a bank holding company to provide funds or other assets to a subsidiary depository institution shall not be effective nor enforceable with respect to an entity described in subparagraph (A) if—

(A) such funds or assets are to be provided by—

(i) a bank holding company that is an insurance company, a broker or dealer registered under the Securities Exchange Act of 1934, an investment company registered under the Investment Company Act of 1940, or an investment adviser registered by or on behalf of either the Securities and Exchange Commission or any State; or

(ii) an affiliate of the depository institution that is an insurance company or a broker or dealer registered under the Securities Exchange Act of 1934, an investment company registered under the Investment Company Act of 1940, or an investment adviser registered by or on behalf of either the Securities and Exchange Commission or any State; and

(B) the State insurance authority for the insurance company or the Securities and Exchange Commission for the registered broker, dealer, investment adviser (solely with respect to investment advisory activities or activities incidental thereto), or investment company, as the case may be, determines in writing sent to the holding company and the Board that the holding company shall not provide such funds or assets because such action would have a material adverse effect on the financial condition of the insurance company or the broker, dealer, investment company, or investment adviser, as the case may be.

(2) Notice to State insurance authority or SEC required.—If the Board requires a bank holding company, or an affiliate of a bank holding company, that is an insurance company or a broker, dealer, investment company, or investment adviser described in paragraph (1)(A) to provide funds or assets to a depository institution subsidiary of the holding company pursuant to any regulation, order, or other action of the Board referred to in paragraph (1), the Board shall promptly notify the State insurance authority for the insurance company, the Securities and Exchange Commission, or State securities regulator, as the case may be, of such requirement.

(3) Divestiture in lieu of other action.—If the Board receives a notice described in paragraph (1)(B) from a State insurance authority or the Securities and Exchange Commission with regard to a bank holding company or affiliate referred to in that paragraph, the Board may order the bank holding company to divest the depository institution not later than 180 days after receiving the notice, or such longer period as the Board determines consistent with the safe and sound operation of the depository institution.

(4) Conditions before divestiture.—During the period beginning on the date an order to divest is issued by the Board under paragraph (3) to a bank holding company and ending on the date the divestiture is completed, the Board may impose any conditions or restrictions on the holding company's ownership or operation of the depository institution, including restricting or prohibiting transactions between the depository institution and any affiliate of the institution, as are appropriate under the circumstances.

(5) Rule of construction.—No provision of this subsection may be construed as limiting or otherwise affecting, except to the extent specifically provided in this subsection, the regulatory authority, including the scope of the authority, of any Federal agency or department with regard to any entity that is within the jurisdiction of such agency or department.

§ 1846. Reservation of Rights to States

(a) In General.—No provision of this Act shall be construed as preventing any State from exercising such powers and jurisdiction which it now has or may hereafter have with respect to companies, banks, bank holding companies, and subsidiaries thereof.

(b) State Taxation Authority Not Affected.—No provision of this Act shall be construed as affecting the authority of any State or political subdivision of any State to adopt, apply, or administer any tax or method of taxation to any bank, bank holding company, or foreign bank, or any affiliate of any bank, bank holding company, or foreign bank, to the extent that such tax or tax method is otherwise permissible by or under the Constitution of the United States or other Federal law.

§ 1848. Judicial Review

Any party aggrieved by an order of the Board under this Act may obtain a review of such order in the United States Court of Appeals within any circuit wherein such party has its principal place of business, or in the Court of Appeals in the District of Columbia, by filing in the court, within thirty days after the entry of the Board's order, a petition praying that the order of the Board be set aside. A copy of such petition shall be forthwith transmitted to the Board by the clerk of the court, and thereupon the Board shall file in the court the record made before the Board, as provided in § 2112 of title 28. Upon the filing of such petition the court shall have jurisdiction to affirm, set aside, or modify the order of the Board and to require the Board to take such action with regard to the matter under review as the court deems proper. The findings of the Board as to the facts, if supported by substantial evidence, shall be conclusive.

§ 1850a. Securities Holding Companies

(a) Definitions.—In this section—
(1) the term **"associated person of a securities holding company"** means a person directly or indirectly controlling, controlled by, or under common control with, a securities holding company; . . .

(4) the term **"securities holding company"**—
(A) means—
(i) a person (other than a natural person) that owns or controls 1 or more brokers or dealers registered with the Commission; and
(ii) the associated persons of a person described in clause (i); and
(B) does not include a person that is—
(i) a nonbank financial company supervised by the Board under title I of the Dodd-Frank Wall Street Reform and Consumer Protection Act [i.e., a systemically significant nonbank firm];
(ii) an insured bank (other than an institution described in subparagraphs (D), (F), or (H) of § 1841(c)(2)) or a savings association;
(iii) an affiliate of an insured bank (other than an institution described in subparagraphs (D), (F), or (H) of § 1841(c)(2)) or an affiliate of a savings association;
(iv) a foreign bank[; or]
(vi) subject to comprehensive consolidated supervision by a foreign regulator; [and]

(5) the term **"supervised securities holding company"** means a securities holding company that is supervised by the Board of Governors under this section. . . .

(b) Supervision of a Securities Holding Company Not Having a Bank or Savings Association Affiliate.—

(1) In general.—A securities holding company that is required by a foreign regulator or provision of foreign law to be subject to comprehensive consolidated supervision may register with the Board of Governors . . . to become a supervised securities holding company. Any securities holding company filing such a registration shall be supervised in accordance with this section, and shall comply with the rules and orders prescribed by the Board of Governors applicable to supervised securities holding companies. . . .

(c) Supervision of Securities Holding Companies.—

(1) Recordkeeping and reporting.—[Each supervised securities holding company and each affiliate of a supervised securities holding company shall keep records and make reports as required by the Board of Governors. The Board may require a balance sheet, an income statement, an assessment of consolidated capital and liquidity, a report on the extent to which the company has complied with the Board's rules under this section, and an independent auditor's report attesting to the company's compliance with its internal risk management and internal control objectives.]

(3) Examination authority.— . . . The Board of Governors may make examinations of any supervised securities holding company and any affiliate of a supervised securities holding company to carry out this subsection, to prevent evasions thereof, and to monitor compliance by the supervised securities holding company or affiliate with applicable provisions of law. . . .

(d) Capital and Risk Management.—

(1) In general.—The Board of Governors shall, by regulation or order, prescribe capital adequacy and other risk management standards for supervised securities holding companies that are appropriate to protect the safety and soundness of the supervised securities holding companies and address the risks posed to financial stability by supervised securities holding companies.

(2) Differentiation.—In imposing standards under this subsection, the Board of Governors may differentiate among supervised securities holding companies on an individual basis, or by category, taking into consideration the requirements under paragraph (3).

(3) Content.—Any standards imposed on a supervised securities holding company under this subsection shall take into account—

(A) the differences among types of business activities carried out by the supervised securities holding company;

(B) the amount and nature of the financial assets of the supervised securities holding company;

(C) the amount and nature of the liabilities of the supervised securities holding company, including the degree of reliance on short-term funding;

(D) the extent and nature of the off-balance sheet exposures of the supervised securities holding company;

(E) the extent and nature of the transactions and relationships of the supervised securities holding company with other financial companies;

(F) the importance of the supervised securities holding company as a source of credit for households, businesses, and State and local governments, and as a source of liquidity for the financial system; and

(G) the nature, scope, and mix of the activities of the supervised securities holding company. . . .

(e) Other Provisions of Law Applicable to Supervised Securities Holding Companies.— . . .

(2) Bank Holding Company Act of 1956.—Except as the Board of Governors may otherwise provide by regulation or order, a supervised securities holding company shall be subject to the provisions of the Bank Holding Company Act of 1956 in the same manner and to the same extent a bank holding company is subject to such provisions, except that a supervised securities holding company may not, by reason of this paragraph, be deemed to be a bank holding company for purposes of § 1843.

§ 1851. Prohibitions on Proprietary Trading and Certain Relationships with Hedge Funds and Private Equity Funds

(a) In General.—

(1) Prohibition.—Unless otherwise provided in this section, a banking entity shall not—

(A) engage in proprietary trading; or

(B) acquire or retain any equity, partnership, or other ownership interest in or sponsor a hedge fund or a private equity fund. . . .

(b)(2)(B) Coordinated rulemaking.— . . .

(ii) **Coordination, consistency, and comparability.**—In developing and issuing regulations pursuant to this section, the appropriate Federal banking agencies, the Securities and Exchange Commission, and the Commodity Futures Trading Commission shall consult and coordinate with each other, as appropriate, for the purposes of assuring, to the extent possible, that such regulations are comparable and provide for consistent application and implementation of the applicable provisions of this section to avoid providing advantages or imposing disadvantages to the companies affected by this subsection and to protect the safety and soundness of banking entities and nonbank financial companies supervised by the Board.

(d) Permitted Activities.—

(1) In general.—Notwithstanding the restrictions under subsection (a), to the extent permitted by any other provision of Federal or State law, and subject to the limitations under paragraph (2) and any restrictions or limitations that the appropriate Federal banking agencies, the Securities and Exchange Commission, and the Commodity Futures Trading Commission, may determine, the following activities (in this section referred to as "permitted activities") are permitted:

(A) The purchase, sale, acquisition, or disposition of obligations of the United States or any agency thereof, obligations, participations, or other instruments of or issued by [Ginnie Mae or a government-sponsored enterprise], and obligations of any State or of any political subdivision thereof.

(B) The purchase, sale, acquisition, or disposition of securities and other instruments described in subsection (h)(4) in connection with underwriting or market-making-related activities, to the extent that any such activities permitted by this subparagraph are designed not to exceed the reasonably expected near term demands of clients, customers, or counterparties.

(C) Risk-mitigating hedging activities in connection with and related to individual or aggregated positions, contracts, or other holdings of a banking entity that are designed to reduce the specific risks to the banking entity in connection with and related to such positions, contracts, or other holdings.

(D) The purchase, sale, acquisition, or disposition of securities and other instruments described in subsection (h)(4) on behalf of customers.

(E) Investments in one or more small business investment companies, ... investments designed primarily to promote the public welfare, of the type permitted under 12 U.S.C. § 24, or investments that are qualified rehabilitation expenditures with respect to a qualified rehabilitated building or certified historic structure, ... or a similar State historic tax credit program.

(F) The purchase, sale, acquisition, or disposition of securities and other instruments described in subsection (h)(4) by a regulated insurance company directly engaged in the business of insurance for the general account of the company and by any affiliate of such regulated insurance company, provided that such activities by any affiliate are solely for the general account of the regulated insurance company. ...

(G) Organizing and offering a private equity or hedge fund, including serving as a general partner, managing member, or trustee of the fund and in any manner selecting or controlling (or having employees, officers, directors, or agents who constitute) a majority of the directors, trustees, or management of the fund, including any necessary expenses for the foregoing, only if—

(i) the banking entity provides bona fide trust, fiduciary, or investment advisory services;

(ii) the fund is organized and offered only in connection with the provision of bona fide trust, fiduciary, or investment advisory services and only to persons that are customers of such services of the banking entity;

(iii) the banking entity does not acquire or retain an equity interest, partnership interest, or other ownership interest in the funds except for a de minimis investment subject to and in compliance with paragraph (4);

(iv) [even if the banking entity is not an insured depository institution, the banking entity's transactions with the affiliate comply with §§ 371 and 371c-1 as if the institution were an insured depository institution];

(v) the banking entity does not, directly or indirectly, guarantee, assume, or otherwise insure the obligations or performance of the hedge fund or private equity fund or of any hedge fund or private equity fund in which such hedge fund or private equity fund invests;

(vi) the banking entity does not share with the hedge fund or private equity fund, for corporate, marketing, promotional, or other purposes, the same name or a variation of the same name;

(vii) no director or employee of the banking entity takes or retains an equity interest, partnership interest, or other ownership interest in the hedge fund or private equity fund, except for any director or employee of the banking entity who is directly engaged in providing investment advisory or other services to the hedge fund or private equity fund; and

(viii) the banking entity discloses to prospective and actual investors in the fund, in writing, that any losses in such hedge fund or private equity fund are borne solely by investors in the fund and not by the banking entity, and otherwise complies with any additional rules . . . designed to ensure that losses in such hedge fund or private equity fund are borne solely by investors in the fund and not by the banking entity.

(H) Proprietary trading conducted by a banking entity pursuant to paragraph (9) or (13) of § 1843(c), provided that the trading occurs solely outside of the United States and that the banking entity is not directly or indirectly controlled by a banking entity that is organized under the laws of the United States or of one or more States.

(I) The acquisition or retention of any equity, partnership, or other ownership interest in, or the sponsorship of, a hedge fund or a private equity fund by a banking entity pursuant to paragraph (9) or (13) of § 1843(c) solely outside of the United States, provided that no ownership interest in such hedge fund or private equity fund is offered for sale or sold to a resident of the United States and that the banking entity is not directly or indirectly controlled by a banking entity that is organized under the laws of the United States or of one or more States.

(J) Such other activity as the appropriate Federal banking agencies, the Securities and Exchange Commission, and the Commodity Futures Trading Commission determine, by rule, . . . would promote and protect the safety and soundness of the banking entity and the financial stability of the United States.

(2) Limitation on permitted activities.—

(A) **In general.**—No transaction, class of transactions, or activity may be deemed a permitted activity under paragraph (1) if the transaction, class of transactions, or activity—

(i) would involve or result in a material conflict of interest . . . between the banking entity and its clients, customers, or counterparties;

(ii) would result, directly or indirectly, in a material exposure by the banking entity to high-risk assets or high-risk trading strategies . . . ;

(iii) would pose a threat to the safety and soundness of such banking entity; or

(iv) would pose a threat to the financial stability of the United States. . . .

(f) Limitations on Relationships with Hedge Funds and Private Equity Funds.—

(1) In general.—No banking entity that serves, directly or indirectly, as the investment manager, investment adviser, or sponsor to a hedge fund or private equity fund, or that organizes and offers a hedge fund or private equity fund pursuant to paragraph (d)(1)(G), and no affiliate of such entity, may enter into a transaction with the fund, or with any other hedge fund or private equity fund that is controlled by such fund, that would be a covered transaction, as defined in § 371c, with the hedge fund or private equity fund, as if such banking entity and the affiliate thereof were a member bank and the hedge fund or private equity fund were an affiliate thereof. . . .

(3) Permitted services.—

(A) In general.—Notwithstanding paragraph (1), the Board may permit a banking entity to enter into any prime brokerage transaction with any hedge fund or private equity fund in which a hedge fund or private equity fund managed, sponsored, or advised by such banking entity has taken an equity, partnership, or other ownership interest, if—

(i) the banking entity is in compliance with each of the limitations set forth in subsection (d)(1)(G) with regard to a hedge fund or private equity fund organized and offered by such banking entity;

(ii) the chief executive officer . . . of the banking entity certifies in writing annually . . . that the conditions specified in subsection (d)(1)(G)(v) are satisfied; and

(iii) the Board has determined that such transaction is consistent with the safe and sound operation and condition of the banking entity.

(4) De minimis investment.—

(A) In general.—A banking entity may make and retain an investment in a hedge fund or private equity fund that the banking entity organizes and offers . . . for the purposes of—

(i) establishing the fund and providing the fund with sufficient initial equity for investment to permit the fund to attract unaffiliated investors; or

(ii) making a de minimis investment.

(B) Limitations and restrictions on investments.—

(i) Requirement to seek other investors.—A banking entity shall actively seek unaffiliated investors to reduce or dilute the investment of the banking entity to the amount permitted under clause (ii).

(ii) Limitations on size of investments.—Notwithstanding any other provision of law, investments by a banking entity in a hedge fund or private equity fund shall—

(I) not later than 1 year after the date of establishment of the fund, be reduced through redemption, sale, or dilution to an amount that is not more than 3 percent of the total ownership interests of the fund;

(II) be immaterial to the banking entity, as defined, by rule, pursuant to subsection (b)(2), but in no case may the aggregate of all of the interests of the banking entity in all such funds exceed 3 percent of the Tier 1 capital of the banking entity.

(iii) Capital.—For purposes of determining compliance with applicable capital standards under paragraph (3), the aggregate amount of the outstanding investments by a banking entity under this paragraph, including retained earnings, shall be deducted from the assets and tangible equity of the banking entity, and the amount of the deduction shall increase commensurate with the leverage of the hedge fund or private equity fund.

(C) Extension.—Upon an application by a banking entity, the Board may extend the period of time to meet the requirements under subparagraph (B)(ii)(I) for 2 additional years, if the Board finds that an extension would be consistent with safety and soundness and in the public interest.

(h) Definitions.—In this section, the following definitions shall apply:

(1) Banking entity.—The term "banking entity" means any insured depository institution (as defined in § 1813), any company that controls an insured depository institution . . . , and any affiliate or subsidiary of any such entity.

(2) Hedge fund; private equity fund.—The terms "hedge fund" and "private equity fund" mean an issuer that would be [subject to investment company regulation but for 15 U.S.C. § 80a-3(c)(1) or (7), which respectively exempt a fund with no more than 100 investors that makes no public offering of its securities and a fund that permits only wealthy people to invest] . . . .

(4) Proprietary trading.—The term "proprietary trading", when used with respect to a banking entity or nonbank financial company supervised by the Board, means engaging as a principal for the trading account of the banking entity or nonbank financial company supervised by the Board in any transaction to purchase or sell, or otherwise acquire or dispose of, any security, any derivative, any contract of sale of a commodity for future delivery, any option on any such security, derivative, or contract, or any other security or financial instrument that the appropriate Federal banking agencies, the Securities and Exchange Commission, and the Commodity Futures Trading Commission may, by rule as provided in subsection (b)(2), determine.

(5) Sponsor.—The term to "sponsor" a fund means—

(A) to serve as a general partner, managing member, or trustee of a fund;

(B) in any manner to select or to control (or to have employees, officers, or directors, or agents who constitute) a majority of the directors, trustees, or management of a fund; or

(C) to share with a fund, for corporate, marketing, promotional, or other purposes, the same name or a variation of the same name.

(6) Trading account.—The term "trading account" means any account used for acquiring or taking positions in the securities and instruments described in paragraph (4) principally for the purpose of selling in the near term (or otherwise with the intent to resell in order to profit from short-term price movements), and any such other accounts as the [agencies may by rule determine] . . . .

§ 1852. Concentration Limits on Large Financial Firms

(a) Definitions.—In this section—
(1) the term **"Council"** means the Financial Stability Oversight Council;
  (2) the term **"financial company"** means—
    (A) an insured depository institution;
    (B) a bank holding company;
    (C) a savings and loan holding company;
    (D) a company that controls an insured depository institution;
    (E) a nonbank financial company supervised by the Board under title I of the Dodd-Frank Wall Street Reform and Consumer Protection Act [i.e., a systemically significant nonbank firm]; and
    (F) a foreign bank or company that is treated as a bank holding company for purposes of this Act; and
  (3) the term **"liabilities"** means—
    (A) with respect to a United States financial company—
      (i) the total risk-weighted assets of the financial company, as determined under the risk-based capital rules applicable to bank holding companies, as adjusted to reflect exposures that are deducted from regulatory capital; less
      (ii) the total regulatory capital of the financial company under the risk-based capital rules applicable to bank holding companies;
    (B) with respect to a foreign-based financial company—
      (i) the total risk-weighted assets of the United States operations of the financial company, as determined under the applicable risk-based capital rules, as adjusted to reflect exposures that are deducted from regulatory capital; less
      (ii) the total regulatory capital of the United States operations of the financial company, as determined under the applicable risk-based capital rules; and
    (C) with respect to an insurance company or other nonbank financial company supervised by the Board, such assets of the company as the Board shall specify by rule, in order to provide for consistent and equitable treatment of such companies.

(b) Concentration Limit.—Subject to the recommendations by the Council under subsection (e) [under which the Council may adjust the limit], a financial company may not merge or consolidate with, acquire all or substantially all of the assets of, or otherwise acquire control of, another company, if the total consolidated liabilities of the acquiring financial company upon consummation of the transaction would exceed 10 percent of the aggregate consolidated liabilities of all financial companies at the end of the calendar year preceding the transaction.

(c) Exception to Concentration Limit.—With the prior written consent of the Board, the concentration limit under subsection (b) shall not apply to an acquisition—

(1) of a bank in default or in danger of default;

(2) with respect to which assistance is provided by the Federal Deposit Insurance Corporation under § 1823; or

(3) that would result only in a de minimis increase in the liabilities of the financial company. . . .

BANK HOLDING COMPANY ACT AMENDMENTS OF 1970

§ 1971. Definitions

As used in this Act, the terms "bank," "bank holding company," "subsidiary," and "Board" have the meaning ascribed to such terms in § 1841. . . . The term "trust service" means any service customarily performed by a bank trust department. For purposes of this Act, a financial subsidiary of a national bank engaging in activities pursuant to § 24a(a) shall be deemed to be a subsidiary of a bank holding company, and not a subsidiary of a bank.

§ 1972. Certain Tying Arrangements Prohibited; Correspondent Accounts

(1) Certain tying arrangements prohibited.—A bank shall not in any manner extend credit, lease or sell property of any kind, or furnish any service, or fix or vary the consideration for any of the foregoing, on the condition or requirement—

(A) that the customer shall obtain some additional credit, property, or service from such bank other than a loan, discount, deposit, or trust service;

(B) that the customer shall obtain some additional credit, property, or service from a bank holding company of such bank, or from any other subsidiary of such bank holding company;

(C) that the customer provide some additional credit, property, or service to such bank, other than those related to and usually provided in connection with a loan, discount, deposit, or trust service;

(D) that the customer provide some additional credit, property, or service to a bank holding company of such bank, or to any other subsidiary of such bank holding company; or

(E) that the customer shall not obtain some other credit, property, or service from a competitor of such bank, a bank holding company of such bank, or any subsidiary of such bank holding company, other than a condition or requirement that such bank shall reasonably impose in a credit transaction to assure the soundness of the credit.

The Board may issue such regulations as are necessary to carry out this section, and, in consultation with the Comptroller of the Currency and the Federal Deposit Insurance Company, may by regulation or order permit such exceptions to the foregoing prohibition and the prohibitions of § 1843(f)(9) and (h)(2) as it considers will not be contrary to the purposes of this section.

(2) **Preferential lending to correspondent bank's insiders prohibited**.—

(A) **Bank holding other bank's correspondent account may not make preferential loans to other bank's insiders**.—No bank which maintains a correspondent account in the name of another bank shall make an extension of credit to an executive officer or director of, or to any person who directly or indirectly or acting through or in concert with one or more persons owns, controls, or has the power to vote more than 10 per centum of any class of voting securities of, such other bank or to any related interest of such person unless such extension of credit is made on substantially the same terms, including interest rates and collateral as those prevailing at the time for comparable transactions with other persons and does not involve more than the normal risk of repayment or present other unfavorable features.

(B) **Bank whose insider has preferential loan from other bank may not open correspondent account at other bank**.—No bank shall open a correspondent account at another bank while such bank has outstanding an extension of credit to an executive officer or director of, or other person who directly or indirectly or acting through or in concert with one or more persons owns, controls, or has the power to vote more than 10 per centum of any class of voting securities of, the bank desiring to open the account or to any related interest of such person, unless such extension of credit was made on substantially the same terms, including interest rates and collateral as those prevailing at the time for comparable transactions with other persons and does not involve more than the normal risk of repayment or present other unfavorable features.

(C) **Bank having correspondent account at other bank may not make preferential loans to other bank's insiders**.—No bank which maintains a correspondent account at another bank shall make an extension of credit to an executive officer or director of, or to any person who directly or indirectly acting through or in concert with one or more persons owns, controls, or has the power to vote more than 10 per centum of any class of voting securities of, such other bank or to any related interest of such person, unless such extension of credit is made on substantially the same terms, including interest rates and collateral as those prevailing at the time for comparable transactions with other persons and does not involve more than the normal risk of repayment or present other unfavorable features.

(D) Bank with preferential loan to other bank's insider may not open correspondent account at other bank.—No bank which has outstanding an extension of credit to an executive officer or director of, or to any person who directly or indirectly or acting through or in concert with one or more persons owns, controls, or has the power to vote more than 10 per centum of any class of voting securities of, another bank or to any related interest of such person shall open a correspondent account at such other bank, unless such extension of credit was made on substantially the same terms, including interest rates and collateral as those prevailing at the time for comparable transactions with other persons and does not involve more than the normal risk of repayment or present other unfavorable features.

(E) Extension of credit and executive officer defined.—For purposes of this paragraph, the term "extension of credit" shall have the meaning prescribed by the Board pursuant to § 375b, and the term "executive officer" shall have the same meaning given it under § 375a.

(F) Civil money penalty. . . .

(G) Additional definitions.—For the purpose of this paragraph— . . .

(ii) the term **"related interests of such persons"** includes any company controlled by such executive officer, director, or person, or any political or campaign committee the funds or services of which will benefit such executive officer, director, or person or which is controlled by such executive officer, director, or person; and

(iii) the terms **"control of a company"** and **"company"** have the same meaning as under § 375b. . . .

§ 1975. Civil Actions by Persons Injured

Any person who is injured in his business or property by reason of anything forbidden in § 1972 may sue therefor in any district court of the United States in which the defendant resides or is found or has an agent, without regard to the amount in controversy, and shall be entitled to recover three times the amount of the damages sustained by him, and the cost of suit, including a reasonable attorney's fee.

§ 1976. Injunctive Relief

Any person may sue for and have injunctive relief, in any court of the United States having jurisdiction over the parties, against threatened loss or damage by reason of a violation of § 1972. . . .

COMMUNITY REINVESTMENT ACT OF 1978

§ 2901. Congressional Findings and Statement of Purpose

(a) **Findings**.—The Congress finds that—

(1) regulated financial institutions are required by law to demonstrate that their deposit facilities serve the convenience and needs of the communities in which they are chartered to do business;

(2) the convenience and needs of communities include the need for credit services as well as deposit services; and

(3) regulated financial institutions have continuing and affirmative obligation to help meet the credit needs of the local communities in which they are chartered.

(b) **Purpose**.—It is the purpose of this Act to require each appropriate Federal financial supervisory agency to use its authority when examining financial institutions, to encourage such institutions to help meet the credit needs of the local communities in which they are chartered consistent with the safe and sound operation of such institutions.

§ 2902. Definitions

For the purposes of this Act—

(1) the term **"appropriate Federal financial supervisory agency"** means—

(A) the Comptroller of the Currency with respect to national banks and Federal savings associations (the deposits of which are insured by the Federal Deposit Insurance Corporation);

(B) the Board of Governors of the Federal Reserve System with respect to State chartered banks which are members of the Federal Reserve System, bank holding companies, and savings and loan holding companies; [and]

(C) the Federal Deposit Insurance Corporation with respect to State chartered banks and savings banks which are not members of the Federal Reserve System and the deposits of which are insured by the Corporation, and State savings associations (the deposits of which are insured by the Federal Deposit Insurance Corporation).

(2) the term **"regulated financial institution"** means an insured depository institution (as defined in § 1813); and

(3) the term **"application for a deposit facility"** means an application to the appropriate Federal financial supervisory agency otherwise required under Federal law or regulations thereunder for—

(A) a charter for a national bank or Federal savings and loan association;

(B) deposit insurance in connection with a newly chartered State bank, savings bank, savings and loan association or similar institution;

(C) the establishment of a domestic branch or other facility with the ability to accept deposits of a regulated financial institution;

(D) the relocation of the home office or a branch office of a regulated financial institution;

(E) the merger or consolidation with, or the acquisition of the assets, or the assumption of the liabilities of a regulated financial institution requiring approval under § 1828(c) or under regulations issued under the authority of title IV of the National Housing Act; or

(F) the acquisition of shares in, or the assets of, a regulated financial institution requiring approval under § 1842. . . .

(4) A financial institution whose business predominately consists of serving the needs of military personnel who are not located within a defined geographic area may define its **"entire community"** to include its entire deposit customer base without regard to geographic proximity.

§ 2903. Assessing Record of Meeting Community Credit Needs

(a) In General.—In connection with its examination of a financial institution, the appropriate Federal financial supervisory agency shall—

(1) assess the institution's record of meeting the credit needs of its entire community, including low- and moderate-income neighborhoods, consistent with the safe and sound operation of such institution; and

(2) take such record into account in its evaluation of an application for a deposit facility by such institution. . . .

(c) Financial Holding Company Requirement.—

(1) In general.—An election by a bank holding company to become a financial holding company under § 1843 shall not be effective if—

(A) the Board finds that, as of the date the declaration of such election and the certification is filed by such holding company under § 1843(*l*)(1)(C), not all of the subsidiary insured depository institutions of the bank holding company had achieved a rating of "satisfactory record of meeting community credit needs," or better, at the most recent examination of each such institution; and

(B) the Board notifies the company of such finding before the end of the 30-day period beginning on such date.

(2) Limited exclusions for newly acquired insured depository institutions.—Any insured depository institution acquired by a bank holding company during the 12-month period preceding the date of the submission to the Board of the declaration and certification under § 1843(*l*)(1)(C) may be excluded for purposes of paragraph (1) during the 12-month period beginning on the date of such acquisition if—

(A) the bank holding company has submitted an affirmative plan to the appropriate Federal financial supervisory agency to take such action as may be necessary in order for such institution to achieve a rating of "satisfactory record of meeting community credit needs," or better, at the next examination of the institution; and

(B) the plan has been accepted by such agency. . . .

§ 2906. Written Evaluations

(a) Required.—

(1) In general.—Upon the conclusion of each examination of an insured depository institution under § 2903, the appropriate Federal financial supervisory agency shall prepare a written evaluation of the institution's record of meeting the credit needs of its entire community, including low and moderate-income neighborhoods.

(2) Public and confidential sections.—Each written evaluation required under paragraph (1) shall have a public section and a confidential section.

(b) Public Section of Report.—

(1) Findings and conclusions.—

(A) **Contents of written evaluation.**—The public section of the written evaluation shall—

(i) state the appropriate Federal financial supervisory agency's conclusions for each assessment factor identified in the regulations prescribed by the Federal financial supervisory agencies to implement this Act;

(ii) discuss the facts and data supporting such conclusions; and

(iii) contain the institution's rating and a statement describing the basis for the rating.

(B) **Metropolitan area distinctions.**—The information required by clauses (i) and (ii) of subparagraph (A) shall be presented separately for each metropolitan area in which a regulated depository institution maintains one or more domestic branch offices.

(2) Assigned rating.—The institution's rating referred to in paragraph (1)(C) shall be 1 of the following:

(A) "Outstanding record of meeting community credit needs."

(B) "Satisfactory record of meeting community credit needs."

(C) "Needs to improve record of meeting community credit needs."

(D) "Substantial noncompliance in meeting community credit needs."

Such ratings shall be disclosed to the public on and after July 1, 1990.

(c) Confidential Section of Report.—

(1) Privacy of named individuals.—The confidential section of the written evaluation shall contain all references that identify any customer of the institution, any employee or officer of the institution, or any person or organization that has provided information in confidence to a Federal or State financial supervisory agency.

(2) Topics not suitable for disclosure.—The confidential section shall also contain any statements obtained or made by the appropriate Federal financial supervisory agency in the course of an examination which, in the judgment of the agency, are too sensitive or speculative in nature to disclose to the institution or the public.

(3) Disclosure to depository institution.—The confidential section may be disclosed, in whole or part, to the institution, if the appropriate Federal financial supervisory agency determines that such disclosure will promote the objectives of this Act. However, disclosure under this paragraph shall not identify a person or organization that has provided information in confidence to a Federal or State financial supervisory agency.

(d) Institutions with Interstate Branches.—

(1) State-by-State evaluation.—In the case of a regulated financial institution that maintains domestic branches in 2 or more States, the appropriate Federal financial supervisory agency shall prepare—

(A) a written evaluation of the entire institution's record of performance under this Act, as required by subsections (a), (b), and (c) of this section; and

(B) for each State in which the institution maintains 1 or more domestic branches, a separate written evaluation of the institution's record of performance within such State under this Act, as required by subsections (a), (b), and (c) of this section.

(2) Multistate metropolitan areas.—In the case of a regulated financial institution that maintains domestic branches in 2 or more States within a multistate metropolitan area, the appropriate Federal financial supervisory agency shall prepare a separate written evaluation of the institution's record of performance within such metropolitan area under this Act, as required by subsections (a), (b), and (c) of this section. If the agency prepares a written evaluation pursuant to this paragraph, the scope of the written evaluation required under paragraph (1)(B) shall be adjusted accordingly.

(3) Content of State level evaluation.—A written evaluation prepared pursuant to paragraph (1)(B) shall—

(A) present the information required by subparagraphs (A) and (B) of subsection (b)(1) of this section separately for each metropolitan area in which the institution maintains 1 or more domestic branch offices and separately for the remainder of the nonmetropolitan area of the State if the institution maintains 1 or more domestic branch offices in such nonmetropolitan area; and

(B) describe how the Federal financial supervisory agency has performed the examination of the institution, including a list of the individual branches examined. . . .

§ 2908. Small Bank Regulatory Relief

(a) **In General**.—Except as provided in subsections (b) and (c), any regulated financial institution with aggregate assets of not more than $250,000,000 shall be subject to routine examination under this Act—

(1) not more than once every 60 months for an institution that has achieved a rating of "outstanding record of meeting community credit needs" at its most recent examination under § 2903;

(2) not more than once every 48 months for an institution that has received a rating of "satisfactory record of meeting community credit needs" at its most recent examination under § 2903; and

(3) as deemed necessary by the appropriate Federal financial supervisory agency, for an institution that has received a rating of less than "satisfactory record of meeting community credit needs" at its most recent examination under § 2903.

(b) **No Exception from CRA Examinations in Connection with Applications for Deposit Facilities**.—A regulated financial institution described in subsection (a) shall remain subject to examination under this Act in connection with an application for a deposit facility.

(c) **Discretion**.—A regulated financial institution described in subsection (a) may be subject to more frequent or less frequent examinations for reasonable cause under such circumstances as may be determined by the appropriate Federal financial supervisory agency.

DEPOSITORY INSTITUTION MANAGEMENT INTERLOCKS ACT

§ 3202. Interlocks in Same Locality Prohibited

A management official [i.e., a director or an employee or officer with management functions] of a depository institution or a depository holding company may not serve as a management official of any other depository institution or depository holding company not affiliated therewith if an office of one of the institutions or any depository institution that is an affiliate of such institutions is located within either—

(1) the same primary metropolitan statistical area, the same metropolitan statistical area, or the same consolidated metropolitan statistical area that is not comprised of designated primary metropolitan statistical areas as defined by the Office of Management and Budget, except in the case of depository institutions with less than $50,000,000 in assets in which case the provision of paragraph (2) shall apply, as that in which an office of the other institution or any depository institution that is an affiliate of such other institution is located, or

(2) the same city, town, or village as that in which an office of the other institution or any depository institution that is an affiliate of such other institution is located, or in any city, town, or village contiguous or adjacent thereto.

§ 3203. Certain Interlocks Prohibited Nationwide

If a depository institution or a depository holding company has total assets exceeding $2,500,000,000, a management official of such institution or any affiliate thereof may not serve as a management official of any other non-affiliated depository institution or depository holding company having total assets exceeding $1,500,000,000 or as a management official of any affiliate of such other institution. . . .

§ 3204. Exceptions

The prohibitions contained in §§ 3202 and 3203 shall not apply in the case of [a savings and loan holding company that meets certain criteria; a credit union served by a management official of another credit union; a bank organized specifically to serve other depository institutions [e.g., a bankers' bank]; a depository institution or other firm that does business in the United States only as an incident to its activities abroad; a depository institution in receivership; and a failed or failing depository institution acquired by another depository institution, during the 5-year period beginning on the date of acquisition].

INTERNATIONAL LENDING SUPERVISION ACT OF 1983

§ 3907. Capital Adequacy

(a) Requiring Adequate Capital.—
(1) In general.—Each appropriate Federal banking agency shall cause banking institutions to achieve and maintain adequate capital by establishing minimum levels of capital for such banking institutions and by using

such other methods as the appropriate Federal banking agency deems appropriate. Each appropriate Federal banking agency shall seek to make the capital standards required under this section or other provisions of Federal law for insured depository institutions countercyclical so that the amount of capital required to be maintained by an insured depository institution increases in times of economic expansion and decreases in times of economic contraction, consistent with the safety and soundness of the insured depository institution.

(2) **Capital standards.**—Each appropriate Federal banking agency shall have the authority to establish such minimum level of capital for a banking institution as the appropriate Federal banking agency, in its discretion, deems to be necessary or appropriate in light of the particular circumstances of the banking institution.

(b) Undercapitalization.—

(1) **Unsafe and unsound practice.**—Failure of a banking institution to maintain capital at or above its minimum level as established pursuant to subsection (a) of this section may be deemed by the appropriate Federal banking agency, in its discretion, to constitute an unsafe and unsound practice within the meaning of § 1818.

(2) **Capital directive.—**

(A) **Agency authority.**—In addition to, or in lieu of, any other action authorized by law, including paragraph (1), the appropriate Federal banking agency may issue a directive to a banking institution that fails to maintain [capital] at or above its required level as established pursuant to subsection (a) of this section.

(B) **Effect of directive.—**

(i) **Plan.**—Such directive may require the banking institution to submit and adhere to a plan acceptable to the appropriate Federal banking agency describing the means and timing by which the banking institution shall achieve its required capital level.

(ii) **Enforcement.**—Any such directive issued pursuant to this paragraph, including plans submitted pursuant thereto, shall be enforceable under the provisions of § 1818(i) to the same extent as an effective and outstanding order issued pursuant to § 1818(b) which has become final.

(3) **Regulatory applications; international progress.—**

(A) **Agency may consider capital in evaluating application.**—Each appropriate Federal banking agency may consider such banking institution's progress in adhering to any plan required under this subsection whenever such banking institution, or an affiliate thereof, or the holding company which controls such banking institution, seeks the requisite approval of such appropriate Federal banking agency for any proposal which would divert earnings, diminish capital, or otherwise impede such banking institution's progress in achieving its minimum capital level.

(B) Denying application.—Such appropriate Federal banking agency may deny such approval where it determines that such proposal would adversely affect the ability of the banking institution to comply with such plan.

(C) International progress.—The Chairman of the Board of Governors of the Federal Reserve System and the Secretary of the Treasury shall encourage governments, central banks, and regulatory authorities of other major banking countries to work toward maintaining and, where appropriate, strengthening the capital bases of banking institutions involved in international lending.

DODD-FRANK WALL STREET REFORM AND CONSUMER PROTECTION ACT

§ 5301. Definitions

As used in this Act, the following definitions shall apply, except as the context otherwise requires or as otherwise specifically provided in this Act . . .

(3) Board of Governors.—The term "Board of Governors" means the Board of Governors of the Federal Reserve System.

(4) Bureau.—The term "Bureau" means the Bureau of Consumer Financial Protection. . . .

(5) Commission.—The term "Commission" means the Securities and Exchange Commission, except in the context of the Commodity Futures Trading Commission. . . .

(7) Corporation.—The term "Corporation" means the Federal Deposit Insurance Corporation.

(8) Council.—The term "Council" means the Financial Stability Oversight Council established under title I. . . .

(11) Functionally regulated subsidiary.—The term "functionally regulated subsidiary" has the same meaning as in § 1844(c)(5).

(12) Primary financial regulatory agency.—The term "primary financial regulatory agency" means—

(A) the appropriate Federal banking agency, with respect to institutions described in § 1813(q), except to the extent that an institution is or the activities of an institution are otherwise described in subparagraph (B), (C), (D), or (E);

(B) the Securities and Exchange Commission, with respect to—

(i) [any securities broker or dealer, clearing agency, national securities association, national securities exchange, nationally recognized statistical rating organization, securities information processor, transfer agent, security-based swap execution facility, security-based swap data repository, security-based swap dealer, or major security-based swap participant that is registered with the Commission under the Securities Exchange Act of 1934, with respect to the activities requiring the entity to be registered under that Act; the Municipal Securities Rulemaking Board; the Public Company Accounting Oversight Board; and the Securities Investor Protection Corporation];

(ii) any investment company that is registered with the Commission under the Investment Company Act of 1940, with respect to the activities of the investment company that require the investment company to be registered under that Act;

(iii) any investment adviser that is registered with the Commission under the Investment Advisers Act of 1940, with respect to the investment advisory activities of such company and activities that are incidental to such advisory activities;

(C) the Commodity Futures Trading Commission, with respect to [any futures commission merchant, commodity pool operator, commodity trading advisor or introducing broker, derivatives clearing organization, futures association, retail foreign exchange dealer, swap execution facility, swap data repository, swap dealer, or major swap participant that is registered with the Commodity Futures Trading Commission under the Commodity Exchange Act, with respect to the activities requiring the entity to be registered under that Act; and any commodity pool, as defined in that Act];

(D) the State insurance authority of the State in which an insurance company is domiciled, with respect to the insurance activities and activities that are incidental to such insurance activities of an insurance company that is subject to supervision by the State insurance authority under State insurance law; and

(E) the Federal Housing Finance Agency, with respect to Federal Home Loan Banks or the Federal Home Loan Bank System, and with respect to the Federal National Mortgage Association or the Federal Home Loan Mortgage Corporation.

(13) Prudential standards.—The term "prudential standards" means enhanced supervision and regulatory standards developed by the Board of Governors under § 5365.

(14) Secretary.—The term "Secretary" means the Secretary of the Treasury. . . .

Title I—Financial Stability Act of 2010

§ 5311. Definitions

(a) In General.—For purposes of this title, unless the context otherwise requires, the following definitions shall apply:

(1) **Bank holding company.**—The term "bank holding company" has the same meaning as in § 1841. . . .

(2) **Chairperson.**—The term "Chairperson" means the Chairperson of the Council.

(3) **Member agency.**—The term "member agency" means an agency represented by a voting member of the Council.

(4) **Nonbank financial company definitions.**

(A) **Foreign nonbank financial company.**—The term "foreign nonbank financial company" means a company (other than a company that is, or is treated in the United States as, a bank holding company) that is—

(i) incorporated or organized in a country other than the United States; and

(ii) predominantly engaged in, including through a branch in the United States, financial activities, as defined in paragraph (6).

(B) **U.S. nonbank financial company.**—The term "U.S. nonbank financial company" means a company (other than a bank holding company, a Farm Credit System institution chartered and subject to the provisions of the Farm Credit Act of 1971, or a national securities exchange (or parent thereof), clearing agency (or parent thereof, unless the parent is a bank holding company), security-based swap execution facility, or security-based swap data repository registered with the Commission, or a board of trade designated as a contract market (or parent thereof), or a derivatives clearing organization (or parent thereof, unless the parent is a bank holding company), swap execution facility or a swap data repository registered with the Commodity Futures Trading Commission), that is—

(i) incorporated or organized under the laws of the United States or any State; and

(ii) predominantly engaged in financial activities, as defined in paragraph (6).

(C) **Nonbank financial company.**—The term "nonbank financial company" means a U.S. nonbank financial company and a foreign nonbank financial company.

(D) **Nonbank financial company supervised by the Board of Governors.**—The term "nonbank financial company supervised by the Board of Governors" means a nonbank financial company that the Council has determined under § 5323 shall be supervised by the Board of Governors. . . .

(6) **Predominantly engaged.**—A company is "predominantly engaged in financial activities" if—

(A) the annual gross revenues derived by the company and all of its subsidiaries from activities that are financial in nature (as defined in § 1843(k) and, if applicable, from the ownership or control of one or more insured depository institutions, represents 85 percent or more of the consolidated annual gross revenues of the company; or

(B) the consolidated assets of the company and all of its subsidiaries related to activities that are financial in nature (as defined in § 1843(k)) and, if applicable, related to the ownership or control of one or more insured depository institutions, represents 85 percent or more of the consolidated assets of the company.

(7) **Significant institutions.**—The terms "significant nonbank financial company" and "significant bank holding company" have the meanings given those terms by rule of the Board of Governors, but in no instance shall the term "significant nonbank financial company" include those entities that are excluded under paragraph (4)(B).

(b) **Definitional Criteria.**—The Board of Governors shall establish, by regulation, the requirements for determining if a company is predominantly engaged in financial activities, as defined in subsection (a)(6). . . .

§ 5321. Financial Stability Oversight Council Established

(a) **Establishment.**—[T]here is established the Financial Stability Oversight Council.

(b) **Membership.**—The Council shall consist of the following members:

(1) **Voting members.**—The voting members, who shall each have 1 vote on the Council shall be—

(A) the Secretary of the Treasury, who shall serve as Chairperson of the Council;

(B) the Chairman of the Board of Governors [of the Federal Reserve System];

(C) the Comptroller of the Currency;

(D) the Director of the Bureau [of Consumer Financial Protection];

(E) the Chairman of the [Securities and Exchange] Commission;

(F) the Chairperson of the [Federal Deposit Insurance] Corporation;

(G) the Chairperson of the Commodity Futures Trading Commission;

(H) the Director of the Federal Housing Finance Agency [i.e., the regulator of Fannie Mae, Freddie Mac, and the Federal Home Loan Bank System];

(I) the Chairman of the National Credit Union Administration Board; and

(J) an independent member appointed [for a 6-year term] by the President, by and with the advice and consent of the Senate, having insurance expertise.

(2) **Nonvoting members.**—The nonvoting members, who shall serve in an advisory capacity as a nonvoting member of the Council, shall be—

(A) the Director of the Office of Financial Research;

(B) the Director of the Federal Insurance Office;

(C) a State insurance commissioner, to be designated by a selection process determined by the State insurance commissioners;

(D) a State banking supervisor, to be designated by a selection process determined by the State banking supervisors; and

(E) a State securities commissioner (or an officer performing like functions), to be designated by a selection process determined by such State securities commissioners. . . .

(e) Meetings.— . . . The Council shall meet at the call of the Chairperson or a majority of the members then serving, but not less frequently than quarterly. . . .

(f) Voting.—Unless otherwise specified, the Council shall make all decisions that it is authorized or required to make by a majority vote of the voting members then serving. . . .

§ 5322. Council Authority

(a) Purposes and Duties of the Council.—

(1) In general.—The purposes of the Council are—

(A) to identify risks to the financial stability of the United States that could arise from the material financial distress or failure, or ongoing activities, of large, interconnected bank holding companies or nonbank financial companies, or that could arise outside the financial services marketplace;

(B) to promote market discipline, by eliminating expectations on the part of shareholders, creditors, and counterparties of such companies that the Government will shield them from losses in the event of failure; and

(C) to respond to emerging threats to the stability of the United States financial system.

(2) Duties.—The Council shall, in accordance with this title—

(A) collect information from member agencies, other Federal and State financial regulatory agencies, the Federal Insurance Office and, if necessary to assess risks to the United States financial system, direct the Office of Financial Research to collect information from bank holding companies and nonbank financial companies;

(B) provide direction to, and request data and analyses from, the Office of Financial Research to support the work of the Council;

(C) monitor the financial services marketplace in order to identify potential threats to the financial stability of the United States;

(D) to monitor domestic and international financial regulatory proposals and developments, including insurance and accounting issues, and to advise Congress and make recommendations in such areas that will enhance the integrity, efficiency, competitiveness, and stability of the U.S. financial markets;

(E) facilitate information sharing and coordination among the member agencies and other Federal and State agencies regarding domestic financial services policy development, rulemaking, examinations, reporting requirements, and enforcement actions;

(F) recommend to the member agencies general supervisory priorities and principles reflecting the outcome of discussions among the member agencies;

(G) identify gaps in regulation that could pose risks to the financial stability of the United States;

(H) require supervision by the Board of Governors for nonbank financial companies that may pose risks to the financial stability of the United States in the event of their material financial distress or failure, or because of their activities pursuant to § 5323;

(I) make recommendations to the Board of Governors concerning the establishment of heightened prudential standards for risk-based capital, leverage, liquidity, contingent capital, resolution plans and credit exposure reports, concentration limits, enhanced public disclosures, and overall risk management for nonbank financial companies and large, interconnected bank holding companies supervised by the Board of Governors;

(J) identify systemically important financial market utilities and payment, clearing, and settlement activities;

(K) make recommendations to primary financial regulatory agencies to apply new or heightened standards and safeguards for financial activities or practices that could create or increase risks of significant liquidity, credit, or other problems spreading among bank holding companies, nonbank financial companies, and United States financial markets;

(L) review and, as appropriate, may submit comments to the Commission and any standard-setting body with respect to an existing or proposed accounting principle, standard, or procedure;

(M) provide a forum for—

(i) discussion and analysis of emerging market developments and financial regulatory issues; and

(ii) resolution of jurisdictional disputes among the members of the Council; and

(N) annually report to and testify before Congress on—

(i) the activities of the Council;

(ii) significant financial market and regulatory developments, including insurance and accounting regulations and standards, along with an assessment of those developments on the stability of the financial system;

(iii) potential emerging threats to the financial stability of the United States;

(iv) all determinations made under § 5323 or the Payment, Clearing, and Settlement Supervision Act of 2010, and the basis for such determinations;

(v) all recommendations made [for resolving certain types of jurisdictional disputes] and the result of such recommendations; and

(vi) recommendations—

(I) to enhance the integrity, efficiency, competitiveness, and stability of United States financial markets;

(II) to promote market discipline; and

(III) to maintain investor confidence.

(b) Statements by Voting Members of the Council.—[When the Council submits its annual report to Congress], each voting member of the Council shall—

(1) if such member believes that the Council, the Government, and the private sector are taking all reasonable steps to ensure financial stability and to mitigate systemic risk that would negatively affect the economy, submit a signed statement to Congress stating such belief; or

(2) if such member does not believe that all reasonable steps described under paragraph (1) are being taken, submit a signed statement to Congress stating what actions such member believes need to be taken in order to ensure that all reasonable steps described under paragraph (1) are taken. . . .

§ 5323. Authority to Require Supervision and Regulation of Certain Nonbank Financial Companies

(a) U.S. Nonbank Financial Companies Supervised by the Board of Governors.—

(1) **Determination.**—The Council, on a nondelegable basis and by a vote of not fewer than 2/3 of the voting members then serving, including an affirmative vote by the Chairperson, may determine that a U.S. nonbank financial company shall be supervised by the Board of Governors and shall be subject to prudential standards, in accordance with this title, if the Council determines that material financial distress at the U.S. nonbank financial company, or the nature, scope, size, scale, concentration, interconnectedness, or mix of the activities of the U.S. nonbank financial company, could pose a threat to the financial stability of the United States.

(2) **Considerations.**—In making a determination under paragraph (1), the Council shall consider—

(A) the extent of the leverage of the company;

(B) the extent and nature of the off-balance-sheet exposures of the company;

(C) the extent and nature of the transactions and relationships of the company with other significant nonbank financial companies and significant bank holding companies;

(D) the importance of the company as a source of credit for households, businesses, and State and local governments and as a source of liquidity for the United States financial system;

(E) the importance of the company as a source of credit for low-income, minority, or underserved communities, and the impact that the failure of such company would have on the availability of credit in such communities;

(F) the extent to which assets are managed rather than owned by the company, and the extent to which ownership of assets under management is diffuse;

(G) the nature, scope, size, scale, concentration, interconnectedness, and mix of the activities of the company;

(H) the degree to which the company is already regulated by 1 or more primary financial regulatory agencies;

(I) the amount and nature of the financial assets of the company;

(J) the amount and types of the liabilities of the company, including the degree of reliance on short-term funding; and

(K) any other risk-related factors that the Council deems appropriate. . . .

(c) Antievasion.—

(1) Determinations.—In order to avoid evasion of this title, the Council, on its own initiative or at the request of the Board of Governors, may determine, on a nondelegable basis and by a vote of not fewer than 2/3 of the voting members then serving, including an affirmative vote by the Chairperson, that—

(A) material financial distress related to, or the nature, scope, size, scale, concentration, interconnectedness, or mix of, the financial activities conducted directly or indirectly by a company incorporated or organized under the laws of the United States or any State or the financial activities in the United States of a company incorporated or organized in a country other than the United States would pose a threat to the financial stability of the United States, based on consideration of the factors in subsection (a)(2) . . . ;

(B) the company is organized or operates in such a manner as to evade the application of this title; and

(C) such financial activities of the company shall be supervised by the Board of Governors and subject to prudential standards in accordance with this title, consistent with paragraph (3). . . .

(3) Consolidated supervision of only financial activities; establishment of an intermediate holding company.—

(A) **Establishment of an intermediate holding company.**—Upon a determination under paragraph (1), the company that is the subject of the determination may establish an intermediate holding company in which the financial activities of such company and its subsidiaries [other than internal financial activities] shall be conducted . . . in compliance with any regulations or guidance provided by the Board of Governors. Such intermediate holding company shall be subject to the supervision of the Board of Governors and to prudential standards under this title as if the intermediate holding company were a nonbank financial company supervised by the Board of Governors.

(B) **Action of the Board of Governors.**—To facilitate the supervision of the financial activities subject to the determination in paragraph (1), the Board of Governors may require a company to establish an intermediate holding company, as provided for in § 5367, which would be subject to the supervision of the Board of Governors and to prudential standards under this title, as if the intermediate holding company were a nonbank financial company supervised by the Board of Governors. . . .

(5) **Covered financial activities.**—For purposes of this subsection, the term "financial activities"—

(A) means activities that are financial in nature (as defined in § 1843(k));

(B) includes the ownership or control of one or more insured depository institutions; and

(C) does not include internal financial activities conducted for the company or any affiliate thereof, including internal treasury, investment, and employee benefit functions.

(6) **Only financial activities subject to prudential supervision.**—Nonfinancial activities of the company shall not be subject to supervision by the Board of Governors and prudential standards of the Board. For purposes of this title, the financial activities that are the subject of the determination in paragraph (1) shall be subject to the same requirements as a nonbank financial company supervised by the Board of Governors. Nothing in this paragraph shall prohibit or limit the authority of the Board of Governors to apply prudential standards under this title to the financial activities that are subject to the determination in paragraph (1). . . .

(d) **Reevaluation and Rescission.**—The Council shall—

(1) not less frequently than annually, reevaluate each determination made under [subsection (a)]; and

(2) rescind any such determination, if the Council, by a vote of not fewer than 2/3 of the voting members then serving, including an affirmative vote by the Chairperson, determines that the nonbank financial company no longer meets the standards under subsection (a). . . .

(e) **Notice and Opportunity for Hearing** . . .

(f) Emergency Exception. . . . The Council may waive or modify the requirements of subsection (e) with respect to a nonbank financial company, if the Council determines, by a vote of not fewer than 2/3 of the voting members then serving, including an affirmative vote by the Chairperson, that such waiver or modification is necessary or appropriate to prevent or mitigate threats posed by the nonbank financial company to the financial stability of the United States. . . .

(h) Judicial Review.—If the Council makes a final determination under this section with respect to a nonbank financial company, such nonbank financial company may . . . bring an action in the United States district court for the judicial district in which the home office of such nonbank financial company is located, or in the United States District Court for the District of Columbia, for an order requiring that the final determination be rescinded, and the court shall, upon review, dismiss such action or direct the final determination to be rescinded. Review of such an action shall be limited to whether the final determination made under this section was arbitrary and capricious. . . .

§ 5325. Enhanced Supervision and Prudential Standards for Nonbank Financial Companies Supervised by the Board of Governors and Certain Bank Holding Companies

(a) In General.—
  (1) Purpose.—In order to prevent or mitigate risks to the financial stability of the United States that could arise from the material financial distress, failure, or ongoing activities of large, interconnected financial institutions, the Council may make recommendations to the Board of Governors concerning the establishment and refinement of prudential standards and reporting and disclosure requirements applicable to nonbank financial companies supervised by the Board of Governors and large, interconnected bank holding companies, that—
    (A) are more stringent than those applicable to other nonbank financial companies and bank holding companies that do not present similar risks to the financial stability of the United States; and
    (B) increase in stringency, based on the considerations identified in subsection (b)(3).
  (2) Recommended application of required standards.—In making recommendations under this section, the Council may—
    (A) differentiate among companies that are subject to heightened standards on an individual basis or by category, taking into consideration their capital structure, riskiness, complexity, financial activities (including the financial activities of their subsidiaries), size, and any other risk-related factors that the Council deems appropriate; or

(B) recommend an asset threshold that is higher than $50,000,000,000. . . .

(b) Development of Prudential Standards.—

(1) In general.—The recommendations of the Council under subsection (a) may include—

(A) risk-based capital requirements;

(B) leverage limits;

(C) liquidity requirements;

(D) resolution plan and credit exposure report requirements;

(E) concentration limits;

(F) a contingent capital requirement;

(G) enhanced public disclosures;

(H) short-term debt limits; and

(I) overall risk management requirements. . . .

(3) Considerations.—In making recommendations concerning prudential standards under paragraph (1), the Council shall—

(A) take into account differences among nonbank financial companies supervised by the Board of Governors and bank holding companies described in subsection (a), based on—

(i) the factors described in [§ 5323(a)];

(ii) whether the company owns an insured depository institution;

(iii) nonfinancial activities and affiliations of the company; and

(iv) any other factors that the Council determines appropriate;

(B) to the extent possible, ensure that small changes in the factors listed in [§ 5323(a)] would not result in sharp, discontinuous changes in the prudential standards established under § 5365; and

(C) adapt its recommendations as appropriate in light of any predominant line of business of such company, including assets under management or other activities for which particular standards may not be appropriate. . . .

(e) Concentration Limits.—In order to limit the risks that the failure of any individual company could pose to nonbank financial companies supervised by the Board of Governors or bank holding companies described in subsection (a), the Council may make recommendations to the Board of Governors to prescribe standards to limit such risks, as set forth in § 5365. . . .

§ 5327. Treatment of Certain Companies That Cease to Be Bank Holding Companies

(a) Applicability.—This section shall apply to—

(1) any entity that—

(A) was a bank holding company having total consolidated assets equal to or greater than $50,000,000,000 as of January 1, 2010; and

(B) received financial assistance under or participated in the Capital Purchase Program established under the Troubled Asset Relief Program authorized by the Emergency Economic Stabilization Act of 2008; and

(2) any successor entity . . . to an entity described in paragraph (1).

(b) Treatment.—If an entity described in subsection (a) ceases to be a bank holding company at any time after January 1, 2010, then such entity shall be treated as a nonbank financial company supervised by the Board of Governors, as if the Council had made a determination under § 5323 with respect to that entity.

(c) Appeal.—

(1) Request for hearing.—An entity may request, in writing, an opportunity for a written or oral hearing before the Council to appeal its treatment as a nonbank financial company supervised by the Board of Governors in accordance with this section. . . .

(2) Decision.—

(A) **Proposed decision.**—A Council decision to grant an appeal under this subsection shall be made by a vote of not fewer than 2/3 of the voting members then serving, including an affirmative vote by the Chairperson. Not later than 60 days after the date of a hearing under paragraph (1), the Council shall submit a report [on its proposed decision to the appropriate Senate and House committees].

(B) **Notice of final decision.**—The Council shall notify the subject entity of the final decision of the Council regarding an appeal under paragraph (1), which notice shall contain a statement of the basis for the final decision of the Council, not later than 60 days after the later of—

(i) the date of the submission of the report under subparagraph (A); or

(ii) [the last hearing held on the report by one of those committees during the year after the submission of the report].

(C) **Considerations.**—In making a decision regarding an appeal under paragraph (1), the Council shall consider whether the company meets the standards under § 5323(a) . . . and the definition of the term "nonbank financial company" under § 5311. The decision of the Council shall be final, subject to the review under paragraph (3).

(3) Review.—If the Council denies an appeal under this subsection, the Council shall, not less frequently than annually, review and reevaluate the decision.

§ 5330. Additional Standards Applicable to Activities or Practices for Financial Stability Purposes

(a) In General.—The Council may provide for more stringent regulation of a financial activity by issuing recommendations to the primary financial regulatory agencies to apply new or heightened standards and safeguards, including standards enumerated in § 5325, for a financial activity or practice conducted by bank holding companies or nonbank financial companies under their respective jurisdictions, if the Council determines that the conduct, scope, nature, size, scale, concentration, or interconnectedness of such activity or practice could create or increase the risk of significant liquidity, credit, or other problems spreading among bank holding companies and nonbank financial companies, financial markets of the United States, or low-income, minority, or underserved communities. . . .

(c) Implementation of Recommended Standards.— . . . The primary financial regulatory agency shall impose the standards recommended by the Council in accordance with subsection (a), or similar standards that the Council deems acceptable, or shall explain in writing to the Council, not later than 90 days after the date on which the Council issues the recommendation, why the agency has determined not to follow the recommendation of the Council. . . .

§ 5331. Mitigation of Risks to Financial Stability

(a) Mitigatory Actions.—If the Board of Governors determines that a bank holding company with total consolidated assets of $50,000,000,000 or more, or a nonbank financial company supervised by the Board of Governors, poses a grave threat to the financial stability of the United States, the Board of Governors, upon an affirmative vote of not fewer than 2/3 of the voting members of the Council then serving, shall [after notice and hearing]—

(1) limit the ability of the company to merge with, acquire, consolidate with, or otherwise become affiliated with another company;

(2) restrict the ability of the company to offer a financial product or products;

(3) require the company to terminate one or more activities;

(4) impose conditions on the manner in which the company conducts 1 or more activities; or

(5) if the Board of Governors determines that the actions described in paragraphs (1) through (4) are inadequate to mitigate a threat to the financial stability of the United States in its recommendation, require the company to sell or otherwise transfer assets or off-balance-sheet items to unaffiliated entities. . . .

§ 5342. Office of Financial Research Established

(a) Establishment.—There is established within the Department of the Treasury the Office of Financial Research.

(b) Director.—

(1) **In general.**—The Office shall be headed by a Director, who shall be appointed by the President, by and with the advice and consent of the Senate.

(2) **Term of service.**—The Director shall serve for a term of 6 years . . .

§ 5343. Purpose and Duties of the Office

(a) **Purpose and Duties.**—The purpose of the Office is to support the Council in fulfilling the purposes and duties of the Council, . . . and to support member agencies, by—

(1) collecting data on behalf of the Council, and providing such data to the Council and member agencies;

(2) standardizing the types and formats of data reported and collected;

(3) performing applied research and essential long-term research;

(4) developing tools for risk measurement and monitoring;

(5) performing other related services;

(6) making the results of the activities of the Office available to financial regulatory agencies; and

(7) assisting such member agencies in determining the types and formats of data authorized by this title to be collected by such member agencies. . . .

§ 5363. Acquisitions

(a) **Acquisitions of Banks; Treatment as a Bank Holding Company.**—For purposes of § 1842, a nonbank financial company supervised by the Board of Governors shall be deemed to be, and shall be treated as, a bank holding company.

(b) **Acquisition of Nonbank Companies.—**

(1) **Prior notice for large acquisitions.**—Notwithstanding § 1843(k)(6)(B), a bank holding company with total consolidated assets equal to or greater than $50,000,000,000 or a nonbank financial company supervised by the Board of Governors shall not acquire direct or indirect ownership or control of any voting shares of any company (other than an insured depository institution) that is engaged in activities described in § 1843(k) having total consolidated assets of $10,000,000,000 or more, without providing written notice to the Board of Governors in advance of the transaction. . . .

§ 5365. Enhanced Supervision and Prudential Standards for Nonbank Financial Companies Supervised by the Board of Governors and Certain Bank Holding Companies

(a) In General.—

(1) Purpose.—In order to prevent or mitigate risks to the financial stability of the United States that could arise from the material financial distress or failure, or ongoing activities, of large, interconnected financial institutions, the Board of Governors shall . . . establish prudential standards for nonbank financial companies supervised by the Board of Governors and bank holding companies with total consolidated assets equal to or greater than $50,000,000,000 that . . . are more stringent than the standards and requirements applicable to nonbank financial companies and bank holding companies that do not present similar risks to the financial stability of the United States. . . .

(b) Development of Prudential Standards.—

(1) In general.—

(A) Required standards.—The Board of Governors shall establish prudential standards for nonbank financial companies supervised by the Board of Governors and bank holding companies described in subsection (a), that shall include—

(i) risk-based capital requirements and leverage limits, unless the Board of Governors, in consultation with the Council, determines that such requirements are not appropriate for a company subject to more stringent prudential standards because of the activities of such company (such as investment company activities or assets under management) or structure, in which case, the Board of Governors shall apply other standards that result in similarly stringent risk controls;

(ii) liquidity requirements;

(iii) overall risk management requirements;

(iv) resolution plan and credit exposure report requirements; and

(v) concentration limits.

(B) Additional standards authorized.—The Board of Governors may establish additional prudential standards for nonbank financial companies supervised by the Board of Governors and bank holding companies described in subsection (a), that include—

(i) a contingent capital requirement;

(ii) enhanced public disclosures;

(iii) short-term debt limits; and

(iv) such other prudential standards as the Board or Governors, on its own or pursuant to a recommendation made by the Council in accordance with § 5325, determines are appropriate. . . .

§ 5366. Early Remediation Requirements

(a) In General.—The Board of Governors, in consultation with the Council and the Corporation, shall prescribe regulations establishing requirements to provide for the early remediation of financial distress of a nonbank financial company supervised by the Board of Governors or a bank holding company described in § 5365(a), except that nothing in this subsection authorizes the provision of financial assistance from the Federal Government.

(b) Purpose of the Early Remediation Requirements.—The purpose of the early remediation requirements under subsection (a) shall be to establish a series of specific remedial actions to be taken by a nonbank financial company supervised by the Board of Governors or a bank holding company described in § 5365(a) that is experiencing increasing financial distress, in order to minimize the probability that the company will become insolvent and the potential harm of such insolvency to the financial stability of the United States.

(c) Remediation Requirements.—The regulations prescribed by the Board of Governors under subsection (a) shall—

(1) define measures of the financial condition of the company, including regulatory capital, liquidity measures, and other forward-looking indicators; and

(2) establish requirements that increase in stringency as the financial condition of the company declines, including—

(A) requirements in the initial stages of financial decline, including limits on capital distributions, acquisitions, and asset growth; and

(B) requirements at later stages of financial decline, including a capital restoration plan and capital-raising requirements, limits on transactions with affiliates, management changes, and asset sales.

§ 5367. Affiliations

(a) Affiliations.—Nothing in [§§ 5361-5374] shall be construed to require a nonbank financial company supervised by the Board of Governors, or a company that controls a nonbank financial company supervised by the Board of Governors, to conform the activities thereof to the requirements of § 1843.

(b) Requirement.—

(1) In general.—

(A) **Board authority.**—If a nonbank financial company supervised by the Board of Governors conducts activities other than those that are determined to be financial in nature or incidental thereto under § 1843(k), the Board of Governors may require such company to establish and conduct all or a portion of such activities that are determined to be financial in nature or incidental thereto in or through an intermediate holding company established pursuant to regulation of the Board of

Governors, not later than 90 days (or such longer period as the Board of Governors may deem appropriate) after the date on which the nonbank financial company supervised by the Board of Governors is notified of the determination of the Board of Governors under this section.

(B) Necessary actions.—Notwithstanding subparagraph (A), the Board of Governors shall require a nonbank financial company supervised by the Board of Governors to establish an intermediate holding company if the Board of Governors makes a determination that the establishment of such intermediate holding company is necessary to—

(i) appropriately supervise activities that are determined to be financial in nature or incidental thereto; or

(ii) . . . ensure that supervision by the Board of Governors does not extend to the commercial activities of such nonbank financial company.

(2) Internal financial activities.—For purposes of this subsection, activities that are determined to be financial in nature or incidental thereto under § 1843(k) . . . shall not include internal financial activities, including internal treasury, investment, and employee benefit functions. With respect to any internal financial activity engaged in for the company or an affiliate and a non-affiliate of such company during the year prior to July 21, 2010, such company (or an affiliate that is not an intermediate holding company or subsidiary of an intermediate holding company) may continue to engage in such activity, as long as not less than 2/3 of the assets or 2/3 of the revenues generated from the activity are from or attributable to such company or an affiliate, subject to review by the Board of Governors, to determine whether engaging in such activity presents undue risk to such company or to the financial stability of the United States.

(3) Source of strength.—A company that directly or indirectly controls an intermediate holding company established under this section shall serve as a source of strength to its subsidiary intermediate holding company.

(4) Parent company reports.—The Board of Governors may, from time to time, require reports under oath from a company that controls an intermediate holding company . . . solely for purposes of ensuring compliance with the provisions of this section, including assessing the ability of the company to serve as a source of strength to its subsidiary intermediate holding company pursuant to paragraph (3). . . .

(c) Regulations.—The Board of Governors—

(1) shall promulgate regulations to establish the criteria for determining whether to require a nonbank financial company supervised by the Board of Governors to establish an intermediate holding company under subsection (b); and

(2) may promulgate regulations to establish any restrictions or limitations on transactions between an intermediate holding company or a nonbank financial company supervised by the Board of Governors and its

affiliates, as necessary to prevent unsafe and unsound practices in connection with transactions between such company, or any subsidiary thereof, and its parent company or affiliates that are not subsidiaries of such company, except that such regulations shall not restrict or limit any transaction in connection with the bona fide acquisition or lease by an unaffiliated person of assets, goods, or services.

§ 5370. Safe Harbor

(a) Regulations.—The Board of Governors shall promulgate regulations on behalf of, and in consultation with, the Council setting forth the criteria for exempting certain types or classes of U.S. nonbank financial companies . . . from supervision by the Board of Governors.

(b) Considerations.—In developing the criteria under subsection (a), the Board of Governors shall take into account the factors for consideration described in . . . § 5323[(a)] in determining whether a U.S. nonbank financial company . . . shall be supervised by the Board of Governors. . . .

§ 5371. Leverage and Risk-Based Capital Requirements

(a) Definitions.—For purposes of this section, the following definitions shall apply:

(1) Generally applicable leverage capital requirements.—The term "generally applicable leverage capital requirements" means—

(A) the minimum ratios of tier 1 capital to average total assets, as established by the appropriate Federal banking agencies to apply to insured depository institutions under the prompt corrective action regulations implementing § 1831o, regardless of total consolidated asset size or foreign financial exposure; and

(B) includes the regulatory capital components in the numerator of that capital requirement, average total assets in the denominator of that capital requirement, and the required ratio of the numerator to the denominator.

(2) Generally applicable risk-based capital requirements.—The term "generally applicable risk-based capital requirements" means—

(A) the risk-based capital requirements, as established by the appropriate Federal banking agencies to apply to insured depository institutions under the prompt corrective action regulations implementing § 1831o, regardless of total consolidated asset size or foreign financial exposure; and

(B) includes the regulatory capital components in the numerator of those capital requirements, the risk-weighted assets in the denominator of those capital requirements, and the required ratio of the numerator to the denominator.

(3) Definition of depository institution holding company.—The term "depository institution holding company" means a bank holding company or a savings and loan holding company (as those terms are defined in § 1813) that is organized in the United States, including any bank or savings and loan holding company that is owned or controlled by a foreign organization, but does not include the foreign organization.

(b) Minimum Capital Requirements.—

(1) Minimum leverage capital requirements.—The appropriate Federal banking agencies shall establish minimum leverage capital requirements on a consolidated basis for insured depository institutions, depository institution holding companies, and nonbank financial companies supervised by the Board of Governors. The minimum leverage capital requirements established under this paragraph shall not be less than the generally applicable leverage capital requirements, which shall serve as a floor for any capital requirements that the agency may require, nor quantitatively lower than the generally applicable leverage capital requirements that were in effect for insured depository institutions as of July 21, 2010.

(2) Minimum risk-based capital requirements.—The appropriate Federal banking agencies shall establish minimum risk-based capital requirements on a consolidated basis for insured depository institutions, depository institution holding companies, and nonbank financial companies supervised by the Board of Governors. The minimum risk-based capital requirements established under this paragraph shall not be less than the generally applicable risk-based capital requirements, which shall serve as a floor for any capital requirements that the agency may require, nor quantitatively lower than the generally applicable risk-based capital requirements that were in effect for insured depository institutions as of July 21, 2010.

(3) Investments in financial subsidiaries.—For purposes of this section, investments in financial subsidiaries that insured depository institutions are required to deduct from regulatory capital under § 25a or § 1831w(a)(2) need not be deducted from regulatory capital by depository institution holding companies or nonbank financial companies supervised by the Board of Governors, unless such capital deduction is required by the Board of Governors or the primary financial regulatory agency in the case of nonbank financial companies supervised by the Board of Governors. . . .

(7) Capital requirements to address activities that pose risks to the financial system.—

(A) In general.—Subject to the recommendations of the Council, in accordance with § 5330, the Federal banking agencies shall develop capital requirements applicable to insured depository institutions, depository institution holding companies, and nonbank financial companies supervised by the Board of Governors that address the risks that the activities of such institutions pose, not only to the institution engaging in the activity, but to other public and private stakeholders in the event of adverse performance, disruption, or failure of the institution or the activity.

(B) Content.—Such rules shall address, at a minimum, the risks arising from—

(i) significant volumes of activity in derivatives, securitized products purchased and sold, financial guarantees purchased and sold, securities borrowing and lending, and repurchase agreements and reverse repurchase agreements;

(ii) concentrations in assets for which the values presented in financial reports are based on models rather than historical cost or prices deriving from deep and liquid 2-way markets; and

(iii) concentrations in market share for any activity that would substantially disrupt financial markets if the institution is forced to unexpectedly cease the activity.

§ 5374. Rule of Construction

No regulation or standard imposed under this title may be construed in a manner that would lessen the stringency of the requirements of any applicable primary financial regulatory agency or any other Federal or State agency that are otherwise applicable. This title, and the rules and regulations or orders prescribed pursuant to this title, do not divest any such agency of any authority derived from any other applicable law.

Title II—Orderly Liquidation Authority

§ 5381. Definitions

(a) In General.—In this title, the following definitions shall apply . . .

(3) Bridge financial company.—The term "bridge financial company" means a new financial company organized by the Corporation in accordance with § 5390(h) for the purpose of resolving a covered financial company.

(4) Claim.—The term "claim" means any right to payment, whether or not such right is reduced to judgment, liquidated, unliquidated, fixed, contingent, matured, unmatured, disputed, undisputed, legal, equitable, secured, or unsecured. . . .

(6) Court.—The term "Court" means the United States District Court for the District of Columbia, unless the context otherwise requires.

(7) Covered broker or dealer.—The term "covered broker or dealer" means a covered financial company that is a broker or dealer that—

(A) is registered with the Commission under 15 U.S.C. § 78o(b); and

(B) is a member of SIPC.

(8) Covered financial company.—The term "covered financial company"—

(A) means a financial company for which a determination has been made under 12 U.S.C. § 5383(b); and

(B) does not include an insured depository institution.

(9) Covered subsidiary.—The term "covered subsidiary" means a subsidiary of a covered financial company, other than—

(A) an insured depository institution;

(B) an insurance company; or

(C) a covered broker or dealer. . . .

(11) Financial company.—The term "financial company" means any company that—

(A) is incorporated or organized under any provision of Federal law or the laws of any State;

(B) is—

(i) a bank holding company, as defined in § 1841(a);

(ii) a nonbank financial company supervised by the Board of Governors;

(iii) any company that is predominantly engaged in activities that the Board of Governors has determined are financial in nature or incidental thereto for purposes of § 1843(k) other than a company described in clause (i) or (ii) [of this subparagraph]; or

(iv) any subsidiary of any company described in any of clauses (i) through (iii) that is predominantly engaged in activities that the Board of Governors has determined are financial in nature or incidental thereto for purposes of § 1843(k) (other than a subsidiary that is an insured depository institution or an insurance company); and

(C) is not a [government-sponsored enterprise].

(12) Fund.—The term "Fund" means the Orderly Liquidation Fund established under § 5390(n).

(13) Insurance company.—The term "insurance company" means any entity that is—

(A) engaged in the business of insurance;

(B) subject to regulation by a State insurance regulator; and

(C) covered by a State law that is designed to specifically deal with the rehabilitation, liquidation, or insolvency of an insurance company.

(14) Nonbank financial company.—The term "nonbank financial company" has the same meaning as in § 5311(a)(4)(C).

(15) Nonbank financial company supervised by the Board of Governors.—The term "nonbank financial company supervised by the Board of Governors" has the same meaning as in § 5311(a)(4)(D).

(16) SIPC.—The term "SIPC" means the Securities Investor Protection Corporation.

(b) Definitional Criteria.—For purpose of the definition of the term "financial company" under subsection (a)(11), no company shall be deemed to be predominantly engaged in activities that the Board of Governors has determined are financial in nature or incidental thereto for purposes of § 1843(k), if the consolidated revenues of such company from such activities constitute less than 85 percent of the total consolidated revenues of such company, as the Corporation, in consultation with the Secretary, shall establish by regulation. In determining whether a company is a financial company under this title, the consolidated revenues derived from the ownership or control of a depository institution shall be included.

§ 5382. [Appointment of Receiver;] Judicial Review

(a) Commencement of Orderly Liquidation.—
  (1) Petition to district court.—
    (A) District court review.—
      (i) Petition to district court.—Subsequent to a determination by the Secretary under § 5383 that a financial company satisfies the criteria in § 5383(b), the Secretary shall notify the Corporation and the covered financial company. If the board of directors (or body performing similar functions) of the covered financial company acquiesces or consents to the appointment of the Corporation as receiver, the Secretary shall appoint the Corporation as receiver. If the board of directors (or body performing similar functions) of the covered financial company does not acquiesce or consent to the appointment of the Corporation as receiver, the Secretary shall petition the United States District Court for the District of Columbia for an order authorizing the Secretary to appoint the Corporation as receiver.

      (ii) Form and content of order.—The Secretary shall present all relevant findings and the recommendation made pursuant to § 5383(a) to the Court. The petition shall be filed under seal.

      (iii) Determination.—On a strictly confidential basis, and without any prior public disclosure, the Court, after notice to the covered financial company and a hearing in which the covered financial company may oppose the petition, shall determine whether the determination of the Secretary that the covered financial company is in default or in danger of default and satisfies the definition of a financial company under § 5381(a)(11) is arbitrary and capricious.

(iv) Issuance of order.—If the Court determines that the determination of the Secretary that the covered financial company is in default or in danger of default and satisfies the definition of a financial company under § 5381(a)(11)—

(I) is not arbitrary and capricious, the Court shall issue an order immediately authorizing the Secretary to appoint the Corporation as receiver of the covered financial company; or

(II) is arbitrary and capricious, the Court shall immediately provide to the Secretary a written statement of each reason supporting its determination, and afford the Secretary an immediate opportunity to amend and refile the petition under clause (i).

(v) Petition granted by operation of law.—If the Court does not make a determination within 24 hours of receipt of the petition—

(I) the petition shall be granted by operation of law;

(II) the Secretary shall appoint the Corporation as receiver; and

(III) liquidation under this title shall automatically and without further notice or action be commenced and the Corporation may immediately take all actions authorized under this title.

(B) Effect of determination.—The determination of the Court under subparagraph (A) shall be final, and shall be subject to appeal only in accordance with paragraph (2). The decision shall not be subject to any stay or injunction pending appeal. Upon conclusion of its proceedings under subparagraph (A), the Court shall provide immediately for the record a written statement of each reason supporting the decision of the Court, and shall provide copies thereof to the Secretary and the covered financial company.

(C) Criminal penalties.—A person who recklessly discloses a determination of the Secretary under § 5383(b) or a petition of the Secretary under subparagraph (A), or the pendency of court proceedings as provided for under subparagraph (A), shall be fined not more than $250,000, or imprisoned for not more than 5 years, or both.

(2) Appeal of decisions of the district court.—

(A) Appeal to Court of Appeals.—

(i) In general.—[T]he United States Court of Appeals for the District of Columbia Circuit shall have jurisdiction of an appeal of a final decision of the Court filed by the Secretary or a covered financial company, through its board of directors, notwithstanding § 5390(a)(1)(A)(i), not later than 30 days after the date on which the decision of the Court is rendered or deemed rendered under this subsection. . . .

(iii) Expedition.—The Court of Appeals shall consider any appeal under this subparagraph on an expedited basis.

(iv) Scope of review.—For an appeal taken under this subparagraph, review shall be limited to whether the determination of the

Secretary that a covered financial company is in default or in danger of default and satisfies the definition of a financial company under § 5381(a)(11) is arbitrary and capricious.

(B) Appeal to the Supreme Court.—[The Supreme Court may review a decision of the Court of Appeals, subject to the same limits on the scope of review as apply under subparagraph (A)(iv).]

(c) Provisions Applicable to Financial Companies.—

(1) Bankruptcy Code.—Except as provided in this subsection, the provisions of the Bankruptcy Code and rules issued thereunder or otherwise applicable insolvency law, and not the provisions of this title, shall apply to financial companies that are not covered financial companies for which the Corporation has been appointed as receiver.

(2) This title.—The provisions of this title shall exclusively apply to and govern all matters relating to covered financial companies for which the Corporation is appointed as receiver, and no provisions of the Bankruptcy Code or the rules issued thereunder shall apply in such cases, except as expressly provided in this title.

(d) Time Limit on Receivership Authority.—[Receivership normally terminates after 3 years but may be extended for up to 2 years under some circumstances.]

§ 5383. Systemic Risk Determination

(a) Written Recommendation and Determination.—

(1) Vote required.—

(A) In general.—On their own initiative, or at the request of the Secretary, the Corporation and the Board of Governors shall consider whether to make a written recommendation described in paragraph (2) with respect to whether the Secretary should appoint the Corporation as receiver for a financial company. Such recommendation shall be made upon a vote of not fewer than 2/3 of the members of the Board of Governors then serving and 2/3 of the members of the board of directors of the Corporation then serving.

(B) Cases involving brokers or dealers.—In the case of a broker or dealer, or in which the largest United States subsidiary (as measured by total assets as of the end of the previous calendar quarter) of a financial company is a broker or dealer, the Commission and the Board of Governors, at the request of the Secretary, or on their own initiative, shall consider whether to make the written recommendation described in paragraph (2) with respect to the financial company. Subject to the requirements in paragraph (2), such recommendation shall be made upon a vote of not fewer than 2/3 of the members of the Board of Governors then serving and 2/3 of the members of the Commission then serving, and in consultation with the Corporation.

(C) Cases involving insurance companies.—In the case of an insurance company, or in which the largest United States subsidiary . . . of a financial company is an insurance company, the Director of the Federal Insurance Office and the Board of Governors, at the request of the Secretary or on their own initiative, shall consider whether to make the written recommendation described in paragraph (2) with respect to the financial company. Subject to the requirements in paragraph (2), such recommendation shall be made upon a vote of not fewer than 2/3 of the Board of Governors then serving and the affirmative approval of the Director of the Federal Insurance Office, and in consultation with the Corporation.

(2) Recommendation required.—Any written recommendation pursuant to paragraph (1) shall contain—

(A) an evaluation of whether the financial company is in default or in danger of default;

(B) a description of the effect that the default of the financial company would have on financial stability in the United States;

(C) a description of the effect that the default of the financial company would have on economic conditions or financial stability for low income, minority, or underserved communities;

(D) a recommendation regarding the nature and the extent of actions to be taken under this title regarding the financial company;

(E) an evaluation of the likelihood of a private sector alternative to prevent the default of the financial company;

(F) an evaluation of why a case under the Bankruptcy Code is not appropriate for the financial company;

(G) an evaluation of the effects on creditors, counterparties, and shareholders of the financial company and other market participants; and

(H) an evaluation of whether the company satisfies the definition of a financial company under § 5381.

(b) Determination by the Secretary.—Notwithstanding any other provision of Federal or State law, the Secretary shall take action in accordance with § 5382(a)(1)(A), if, upon the written recommendation under subsection (a), the Secretary (in consultation with the President) determines that—

(1) the financial company is in default or in danger of default;

(2) the failure of the financial company and its resolution under otherwise applicable Federal or State law would have serious adverse effects on financial stability in the United States;

(3) no viable private sector alternative is available to prevent the default of the financial company;

(4) any effect on the claims or interests of creditors, counterparties, and shareholders of the financial company and other market participants as a

result of actions to be taken under this title is appropriate, given the impact that any action taken under this title would have on financial stability in the United States;

(5) any action under § 5384 would avoid or mitigate such adverse effects, taking into consideration the effectiveness of the action in mitigating potential adverse effects on the financial system, the cost to the general fund of the Treasury, and the potential to increase excessive risk taking on the part of creditors, counterparties, and shareholders in the financial company;

(6) a Federal regulatory agency has ordered the financial company to convert all of its convertible debt instruments that are subject to the regulatory order; and

(7) the company satisfies the definition of a financial company under § 5381.

(c) Documentation and Review.—

(1) In general.—The Secretary shall—

(A) document any determination under subsection (b);

(B) retain the documentation for review under paragraph (2); and

(C) notify the covered financial company and the Corporation of such determination.

(2) Report to Congress.—Not later than 24 hours after the date of appointment of the Corporation as receiver for a covered financial company, the Secretary shall provide written notice of the recommendations and determinations reached in accordance with subsections (a) and (b) to the Majority Leader and the Minority Leader of the Senate and the Speaker and the Minority Leader of the House of Representatives, the Committee on Banking, Housing, and Urban Affairs of the Senate, and the Committee on Financial Services of the House of Representatives, which shall consist of a summary of the basis for the determination, including, to the extent available at the time of the determination—

(A) the size and financial condition of the covered financial company;

(B) the sources of capital and credit support that were available to the covered financial company;

(C) the operations of the covered financial company that could have had a significant impact on financial stability, markets, or both;

(D) identification of the banks and financial companies which may be able to provide the services offered by the covered financial company;

(E) any potential international ramifications of resolution of the covered financial company under other applicable insolvency law;

(F) an estimate of the potential effect of the resolution of the covered financial company under other applicable insolvency law on the financial stability of the United States;

(G) the potential effect of the appointment of a receiver by the Secretary on consumers;

(H) the potential effect of the appointment of a receiver by the Secretary on the financial system, financial markets, and banks and other financial companies; and

(I) whether resolution of the covered financial company under other applicable insolvency law would cause banks or other financial companies to experience severe liquidity distress.

(3) Reports to Congress and the public.—

(A) In general.—Not later than 60 days after the date of appointment of the Corporation as receiver for a covered financial company, the Corporation shall file a report with the Committee on Banking, Housing, and Urban Affairs of the Senate and the Committee on Financial Services of the House of Representatives—

(i) setting forth information on the financial condition of the covered financial company as of the date of the appointment, including a description of its assets and liabilities;

(ii) describing the plan of, and actions taken by, the Corporation to wind down the covered financial company;

(iii) explaining each instance in which the Corporation waived any applicable requirements of part 366 of title 12, Code of Federal Regulations (or any successor thereto) with respect to conflicts of interest by any person in the private sector who was retained to provide services to the Corporation in connection with such receivership;

(iv) describing the reasons for the provision of any funding to the receivership out of the Fund;

(v) setting forth the expected costs of the orderly liquidation of the covered financial company;

(vi) setting forth the identity of any claimant that is treated in a manner different from other similarly situated claimants under subsection (b)(4), (d)(4), or (h)(5)(E) [of § 5390], the amount of any additional payment to such claimant under subsection (d)(4), and the reason for any such action; and

(vii) which report the Corporation shall publish on an online website maintained by the Corporation, subject to maintaining appropriate confidentiality.

(B) Amendments.—The Corporation shall, on a timely basis, not less frequently than quarterly, amend or revise and resubmit the reports prepared under this paragraph, as necessary.

(C) Congressional testimony.—The Corporation and the primary financial regulatory agency, if any, of the financial company for which the Corporation was appointed receiver under this title shall appear before Congress, if requested, not later than 30 days after the date on which the Corporation first files the reports required under subparagraph (A).

(4) **Default or in danger of default**.—For purposes of this title, a financial company shall be considered to be in default or in danger of default if, as determined in accordance with subsection (b)—

(A) a case has been, or likely will promptly be, commenced with respect to the financial company under the Bankruptcy Code;

(B) the financial company has incurred, or is likely to incur, losses that will deplete all or substantially all of its capital, and there is no reasonable prospect for the company to avoid such depletion;

(C) the assets of the financial company are, or are likely to be, less than its obligations to creditors and others; or

(D) the financial company is, or is likely to be, unable to pay its obligations (other than those subject to a bona fide dispute) in the normal course of business.

(5) **GAO review**.—The Comptroller General of the United States shall review and report to Congress on any determination under subsection (b), that results in the appointment of the Corporation as receiver, including—

(A) the basis for the determination;

(B) the purpose for which any action was taken pursuant thereto;

(C) the likely effect of the determination and such action on the incentives and conduct of financial companies and their creditors, counterparties, and shareholders; and

(D) the likely disruptive effect of the determination and such action on the reasonable expectations of creditors, counterparties, and shareholders, taking into account the impact any action under this title would have on financial stability in the United States, including whether the rights of such parties will be disrupted.

(d) **Corporation Policies and Procedures**.—As soon as is practicable after the date of enactment of this Act, the Corporation shall establish policies and procedures that are acceptable to the Secretary governing the use of funds available to the Corporation to carry out this title, including the terms and conditions for the provision and use of funds under §§ 5384(d), 5390(h)(2)(G)(iv), and 5390(h)(9).

(e) **Treatment of Insurance Companies and Insurance Company Subsidiaries**.—

(1) **In general**.—Notwithstanding subsection (b), if an insurance company is a covered financial company or a subsidiary or affiliate of a covered financial company, the liquidation or rehabilitation of such insurance company, and any subsidiary or affiliate of such company that is not excepted under paragraph (2), shall be conducted as provided under applicable State law.

(2) **Exception for subsidiaries and affiliates**.—The requirement of paragraph (1) shall not apply with respect to any subsidiary or affiliate of an insurance company that is not itself an insurance company.

(3) **Backup authority**.—Notwithstanding paragraph (1), with respect to a covered financial company described in paragraph (1), if, after the end of

the 60-day period beginning on the date on which a determination is made under § 5382(a) with respect to such company, the appropriate regulatory agency has not filed the appropriate judicial action in the appropriate State court to place such company into orderly liquidation under the laws and requirements of the State, the Corporation shall have the authority to stand in the place of the appropriate regulatory agency and file the appropriate judicial action in the appropriate State court to place such company into orderly liquidation under the laws and requirements of the State.

§ 5384. Orderly Liquidation of Covered Financial Companies

(a) Purpose of Orderly Liquidation Authority.—It is the purpose of this title to provide the necessary authority to liquidate failing financial companies that pose a significant risk to the financial stability of the United States in a manner that mitigates such risk and minimizes moral hazard. The authority provided in this title shall be exercised in the manner that best fulfills such purpose, so that—

(1) creditors and shareholders will bear the losses of the financial company;

(2) management responsible for the condition of the financial company will not be retained; and

(3) the Corporation and other appropriate agencies will take all steps necessary and appropriate to assure that all parties, including management, directors, and third parties, having responsibility for the condition of the financial company bear losses consistent with their responsibility, including actions for damages, restitution, and recoupment of compensation and other gains not compatible with such responsibility.

(b) Corporation as Receiver.—Upon the appointment of the Corporation under § 5382, the Corporation shall act as the receiver for the covered financial company, with all of the rights and obligations set forth in this title. . . .

(d) Funding for Orderly Liquidation.—Upon its appointment as receiver for a covered financial company, and thereafter as the Corporation may, in its discretion, determine to be necessary or appropriate, the Corporation may make available to the receivership, subject to the conditions set forth in § 5386 and subject to the plan described in § 5390(n)(9), funds for the orderly liquidation of the covered financial company. All funds provided by the Corporation under this subsection shall have a priority of claims under subparagraph (A) or (B) of § 5390(b)(1), as applicable, including funds used for—

(1) making loans to, or purchasing any debt obligation of, the covered financial company or any covered subsidiary;

(2) purchasing or guaranteeing against loss the assets of the covered financial company or any covered subsidiary, directly or through an entity established by the Corporation for such purpose;

(3) assuming or guaranteeing the obligations of the covered financial company or any covered subsidiary to 1 or more third parties;

(4) taking a lien on any or all assets of the covered financial company or any covered subsidiary, including a first priority lien on all unencumbered assets of the covered financial company or any covered subsidiary to secure repayment of any transactions conducted under this subsection;

(5) selling or transferring all, or any part, of such acquired assets, liabilities, or obligations of the covered financial company or any covered subsidiary; and

(6) making payments pursuant to subsections (b)(4), (d)(4), and (h)(5)(E) of § 5390.

§ 5385. Orderly Liquidation of Covered Brokers and Dealers

(a) **Appointment of SIPC as Trustee.**— . . . Upon the appointment of the Corporation as receiver for any covered broker or dealer, the Corporation shall appoint, without any need for court approval, the Securities Investor Protection Corporation to act as trustee for the liquidation under the Securities Investor Protection Act of 1970 of the covered broker or dealer. . . .

(g) **Priorities.**—

(1) **Customer property.**—As trustee for a covered broker or dealer, SIPC shall allocate customer property and deliver customer name securities in accordance with . . . the Securities Investor Protection Act of 1970.

(2) **Other claims.**—All claims other than those described in paragraph (1) (including any unpaid claim by a customer for the allowed net equity claim of such customer from customer property) shall be paid in accordance with the priorities in § 5390(b). . . .

§ 5386. Mandatory Terms and Conditions for All Orderly Liquidation Actions

In taking action under this title, the Corporation shall—

(1) determine that such action is necessary for purposes of the financial stability of the United States, and not for the purpose of preserving the covered financial company;

(2) ensure that the shareholders of a covered financial company do not receive payment until after all other claims and the Fund are fully paid;

(3) ensure that unsecured creditors bear losses in accordance with the priority of claim provisions in § 5390;

(4) ensure that management responsible for the failed condition of the covered financial company is removed (if such management has not already been removed at the time at which the Corporation is appointed receiver);

(5) ensure that the members of the board of directors (or body performing similar functions) responsible for the failed condition of the covered financial company are removed, if such members have not already been removed at the time the Corporation is appointed as receiver; and

(6) not take an equity interest in or become a shareholder of any covered financial company or any covered subsidiary. . . .

§ 5388. Dismissal and Exclusion of Other Actions

(a) In General.—Effective as of the date of the appointment of the Corporation as receiver for the covered financial company under § 5382 or the appointment of SIPC as trustee for a covered broker or dealer under § 5385, as applicable, any case or proceeding commenced with respect to the covered financial company under the Bankruptcy Code or the Securities Investor Protection Act of 1970 shall be dismissed . . . and no such case or proceeding may be commenced with respect to a covered financial company at any time while the orderly liquidation is pending. . . .

(c) Limitation.—[A]ny order entered or other relief granted by a bankruptcy court prior to the date of appointment of the Corporation as receiver shall continue with the same validity as if an orderly liquidation had not been commenced.

§ 5389. Rulemaking; Non-Conflicting Law

The Corporation shall, in consultation with the Council, prescribe such rules or regulations as the Corporation considers necessary or appropriate to implement this title, including rules and regulations with respect to the rights, interests, and priorities of creditors, counterparties, security entitlement holders, or other persons with respect to any covered financial company or any assets or other property of or held by such covered financial company, and address the potential for conflicts of interest between or among individual receiverships established under this title or under the Federal Deposit Insurance Act. To the extent possible, the Corporation shall seek to harmonize applicable rules and regulations promulgated under this section with the insolvency laws that would otherwise apply to a covered financial company.

§ 5390. Powers and Duties of the Corporation

[This section largely parallels § 1821, which governs the FDIC's powers and duties as receiver for a failed FDIC-insured depository institution.]
(a) Powers and Authorities.—

(1) General powers.—

(A) Successor to covered financial company.—The Corporation shall, upon appointment as receiver for a covered financial company under this title, succeed to—

(i) all rights, titles, powers, and privileges of the covered financial company and its assets, and of any stockholder, member, officer, or director of such company; and

(ii) title to the books, records, and assets of any previous receiver or other legal custodian of such covered financial company.

(B) Operation of the covered financial company during the period of orderly liquidation.—The Corporation, as receiver for a covered financial company, may—

(i) take over the assets of and operate the covered financial company with all of the powers of the members or shareholders, the directors, and the officers of the covered financial company, and conduct all business of the covered financial company;

(ii) collect all obligations and money owed to the covered financial company;

(iii) perform all functions of the covered financial company, in the name of the covered financial company;

(iv) manage the assets and property of the covered financial company, consistent with maximization of the value of the assets in the context of the orderly liquidation; and

(v) provide by contract for assistance in fulfilling any function, activity, action, or duty of the Corporation as receiver.

(C) Functions of covered financial company officers, directors, and shareholders.—The Corporation may provide for the exercise of any function by any member or stockholder, director, or officer of any covered financial company for which the Corporation has been appointed as receiver under this title.

(D) Additional powers as receiver.—The Corporation shall, as receiver for a covered financial company, and subject to all legally enforceable and perfected security interests and all legally enforceable security entitlements in respect of assets held by the covered financial company, liquidate, and wind-up the affairs of a covered financial company, including taking steps to realize upon the assets of the covered financial company, in such manner as the Corporation deems appropriate, including through the sale of assets, the transfer of assets to a bridge financial company established under subsection (h), or the exercise of any other rights or privileges granted to the receiver under this section.

(E) Additional powers with respect to failing subsidiaries of a covered financial company.—

(i) **In general.**—In any case in which a receiver is appointed for a covered financial company under §5382, the Corporation may appoint itself as receiver of any covered subsidiary of the covered financial company that is organized under Federal law or the laws of any State, if the Corporation and the Secretary jointly determine that—

(I) the covered subsidiary is in default or in danger of default;

(II) such action would avoid or mitigate serious adverse effects on the financial stability or economic conditions of the United States; and

(III) such action would facilitate the orderly liquidation of the covered financial company.

(ii) Treatment as covered financial company.—If the Corporation is appointed as receiver of a covered subsidiary of a covered financial company under clause (i), the covered subsidiary shall thereafter be considered a covered financial company under this title, and the Corporation shall thereafter have all the powers and rights with respect to that covered subsidiary as it has with respect to a covered financial company under this title.

(F) Organization of bridge companies.—The Corporation, as receiver for a covered financial company, may organize a bridge financial company under subsection (h).

(G) Merger; transfer of assets and liabilities.—

(i) In general.—[T]he Corporation, as receiver for a covered financial company, may—

(I) merge the covered financial company with another company; or

(II) transfer any asset or liability of the covered financial company (including any assets and liabilities held by the covered financial company for security entitlement holders, any customer property, or any assets and liabilities associated with any trust or custody business) without obtaining any approval, assignment, or consent with respect to such transfer. . . .

(H) Payment of valid obligations.—The Corporation, as receiver for a covered financial company, shall, to the extent that funds are available, pay all valid obligations of the covered financial company that are due and payable at the time of the appointment of the Corporation as receiver, in accordance with the prescriptions and limitations of this title. . . .

(K) Incidental powers.—The Corporation, as receiver for a covered financial company, may exercise all powers and authorities specifically granted to receivers under this title, and such incidental powers as shall be necessary to carry out such powers under this title. . . .

(M) Shareholders and creditors of covered financial company.—Notwithstanding any other provision of law, the Corporation, as receiver for a covered financial company, shall succeed by operation of law to the rights, titles, powers, and privileges described in subparagraph (A), and shall terminate all rights and claims that the stockholders and creditors of the covered financial company may have against the assets of the covered financial company or the Corporation arising out of their status as stockholders or creditors, except for their right to payment, resolution, or other satisfaction of their claims, as permitted under this section. The Corporation shall ensure that shareholders and unsecured creditors bear losses, consistent with the priority of claims provisions under this section. . . .

(2) Determination of claims.—

   (A) In general.—The Corporation, as receiver for a covered financial company, shall report on claims, as set forth in § 5383(c)(3). Subject to paragraph (4) of this subsection, the Corporation, as receiver for a covered financial company, shall determine claims in accordance with the requirements of this subsection and regulations prescribed under § 5389. . . .

(3) Procedures for resolution of claims.—

   (A) Decision period.—

      (i) In general.—Prior to the 180th day after the date on which a claim against a covered financial company is filed with the Corporation as receiver . . . , the Corporation shall notify the claimant whether it allows or disallows the claim. . . .

   (B) Allowance of proven claim.—The receiver shall allow any [timely claim that] is proved to the satisfaction of the receiver. . . .

   (D) Authority to disallow claims.—

      (i) In general.—The Corporation may disallow any portion of any claim by a creditor or claim of a security, preference, setoff, or priority which is not proved to the satisfaction of the Corporation.

      (ii) Payments to undersecured creditors.—In the case of a claim against a covered financial company that is secured by any property or other asset of such covered financial company, the receiver—

         (I) may treat the portion of such claim which exceeds an amount equal to the fair market value of such property or other asset as an unsecured claim; and

         (II) may not make any payment with respect to such unsecured portion of the claim, other than in connection with the disposition of all claims of unsecured creditors of the covered financial company. . . .

(4) Judicial determination of claims.—[A] claimant may file suit on a claim (or continue an action commenced before the date of appointment of the Corporation as receiver) in the district . . . court of the United States for the district within which the principal place of business of the covered financial company is located. . . .

(7) Payment of claims.—

(A) In general.—[T]he Corporation as receiver may, in its discretion and to the extent that funds are available, pay creditor claims, in such manner and amounts as are authorized under this section, which are—

(i) allowed by the receiver;

(ii) approved by the receiver pursuant to a final determination pursuant to paragraph (3) or (5), as applicable; or

(iii) determined by the final judgment of a court of competent jurisdiction. . . .

(b) Priority of Expenses and Unsecured Claims.—

(1) In general.—Unsecured claims against a covered financial company, or the Corporation as receiver for such covered financial company under this section, that are proven to the satisfaction of the receiver shall have priority in the following order:

(A) Administrative expenses of the receiver.

(B) Any amounts owed to the United States, unless the United States agrees or consents otherwise.

(C) Wages, salaries, or commissions, including vacation, severance, and sick leave pay earned by an individual (other than an individual described in subparagraph (G)), but only to the extent of $11,725 for each individual . . . earned not later than 180 days before the date of appointment of the Corporation as receiver.

(D) Contributions owed to employee benefit plans arising from services rendered not later than 180 days before the date of appointment of the Corporation as receiver, to the extent of the number of employees covered by each such plan, multiplied by $11,725 . . . , less the aggregate amount paid to such employees under subparagraph (C), plus the aggregate amount paid by the receivership on behalf of such employees to any other employee benefit plan.

(E) Any other general or senior liability of the covered financial company (which is not a liability described under subparagraph (F), (G), or (H)).

(F) Any obligation subordinated to general creditors (which is not an obligation described under subparagraph (G) or (H)).

(G) Any wages, salaries, or commissions, including vacation, severance, and sick leave pay earned, owed to senior executives and directors of the covered financial company.

(H) Any obligation to shareholders, members, general partners, limited partners, or other persons, with interests in the equity of the covered financial company arising as a result of their status as shareholders, members, general partners, limited partners, or other persons with interests in the equity of the covered financial company.

(2) Post-receivership financing priority.—In the event that the Corporation, as receiver for a covered financial company, is unable to obtain unsecured credit for the covered financial company from commercial sources, the Corporation as receiver may obtain credit or incur debt on the part of the covered financial company, which shall have priority over any or all administrative expenses of the receiver under paragraph (1)(A).

(3) **Claims of the United States.**—Unsecured claims of the United States shall, at a minimum, have a higher priority than liabilities of the covered financial company that count as regulatory capital.

(4) **Creditors similarly situated.**—All claimants of a covered financial company that are similarly situated under paragraph (1) shall be treated in a similar manner, except that the Corporation may take any action (including making payments, subject to subsection (o)(1)(D)(i)) that does not comply with this subsection, if—

(A) the Corporation determines that such action is necessary—

(i) to maximize the value of the assets of the covered financial company;

(ii) to initiate and continue operations essential to implementation of the receivership or any bridge financial company;

(iii) to maximize the present value return from the sale or other disposition of the assets of the covered financial company; or

(iv) to minimize the amount of any loss realized upon the sale or other disposition of the assets of the covered financial company; and

(B) all claimants that are similarly situated under paragraph (1) receive not less than the amount provided in paragraphs (2) and (3) of subsection (d).

(5) **Secured claims unaffected.**—This section shall not affect secured claims or security entitlements in respect of assets or property held by the covered financial company, except to the extent that the security is insufficient to satisfy the claim, and then only with regard to the difference between the claim and the amount realized from the security. . . .

(h) **Bridge Financial Companies.**—

(1) **Organization.**—

(A) **Purpose.**—The Corporation, as receiver for one or more covered financial companies or in anticipation of being appointed receiver for one or more covered financial companies, may organize one or more bridge financial companies in accordance with this subsection.

(B) **Authorities.**—Upon the creation of a bridge financial company under subparagraph (A) with respect to a covered financial company, such bridge financial company may—

(i) assume such liabilities . . . of such covered financial company as the Corporation may, in its discretion, determine to be appropriate;

(ii) purchase such assets . . . of such covered financial company as the Corporation may, in its discretion, determine to be appropriate; and

(iii) perform any other temporary function which the Corporation may, in its discretion, prescribe in accordance with this section.

(2) Charter and establishment.—

(A) Establishment.—[T]he Corporation, as receiver for a covered financial company, may grant a Federal charter to and approve articles of association for one or more bridge financial company or companies, with respect to such covered financial company which shall, by operation of law and immediately upon issuance of its charter and approval of its articles of association, be established and operate in accordance with, and subject to, such charter, articles, and this section.

(B) Management.—Upon its establishment, a bridge financial company shall be under the management of a board of directors appointed by the Corporation.

(C) Articles of association.—The articles of association and organization certificate of a bridge financial company shall have such terms as the Corporation may provide, and shall be executed by such representatives as the Corporation may designate.

(D) Terms of charter; rights and privileges.—Subject to and in accordance with the provisions of this subsection, the Corporation shall—

(i) establish the terms of the charter of a bridge financial company and the rights, powers, authorities, and privileges of a bridge financial company granted by the charter or as an incident thereto; and

(ii) provide for, and establish the terms and conditions governing, the management (including the bylaws and the number of directors of the board of directors) and operations of the bridge financial company.

(E) Transfer of rights and privileges of covered financial company.—

(i) **In general.**—Notwithstanding any other provision of Federal or State law, the Corporation may provide for a bridge financial company to succeed to and assume any rights, powers, authorities, or privileges of the covered financial company with respect to which the bridge financial company was established and, upon such determination by the Corporation, the bridge financial company shall immediately and by operation of law succeed to and assume such rights, powers, authorities, and privileges. . . .

(G) Capital.— . . . Notwithstanding any other provision of Federal or State law, a bridge financial company may, if permitted by the Corporation, operate without any capital or surplus, or with such capital or surplus as the Corporation may in its discretion determine to be appropriate. . . .

(H) Bridge brokers or dealers.—

(i) In general.—The Corporation, as receiver for a covered broker or dealer, may approve articles of association for one or more bridge financial companies with respect to such covered broker or dealer, which bridge financial company or companies shall, by operation of law and immediately upon approval of its articles of association—

(I) be established and deemed registered with the Commission under the Securities Exchange Act of 1934 and a member of SIPC;

(II) operate in accordance with such articles and this section; and

(III) succeed to any and all registrations and memberships of the covered financial company with or in any self-regulatory organizations. . . .

(3) Interests in and assets and obligations of covered financial company.—Notwithstanding paragraph (1) or (2) or any other provision of law—

(A) a bridge financial company shall assume, acquire, or succeed to the assets or liabilities of a covered financial company . . . only to the extent that such assets or liabilities are transferred by the Corporation to the bridge financial company in accordance with, and subject to the restrictions set forth in, paragraph (1)(B); and

(B) a bridge financial company shall not assume, acquire, or succeed to any obligation that a covered financial company for which the Corporation has been appointed receiver may have to any shareholder, member, general partner, limited partner, or other person with an interest in the equity of the covered financial company that arises as a result of the status of that person having an equity claim in the covered financial company. . . .

(5) Transfer of assets and liabilities.—

(A) Authority of Corporation.—The Corporation, as receiver for a covered financial company, may transfer any assets and liabilities of a covered financial company . . . to one or more bridge financial companies, in accordance with and subject to the restrictions of paragraph (1). . . .

(C) Treatment of trust or custody business.—For purposes of this paragraph, the trust or custody business, including fiduciary appointments, held by any covered financial company is included among its assets and liabilities. . . .

(E) Equitable treatment of similarly situated creditors.—The Corporation shall treat all creditors of a covered financial company that are similarly situated under subsection (b)(1), in a similar manner in exercising the authority of the Corporation under this subsection to transfer any assets or liabilities of the covered financial company to one or more bridge financial companies established with respect to such covered financial company, except that the Corporation may take any action (including making payments, subject to subsection (o)(1)(D)(i)) that does not comply with this subparagraph, if—

(i) the Corporation determines that such action is necessary—

(I) to maximize the value of the assets of the covered financial company;

(II) to maximize the present value return from the sale or other disposition of the assets of the covered financial company; or

(III) to minimize the amount of any loss realized upon the sale or other disposition of the assets of the covered financial company; and

(ii) all creditors that are similarly situated under subsection (b)(1) receive not less than the amount provided under paragraphs (2) and (3) of subsection (d).

(F) Limitation on transfer of liabilities.—Notwithstanding any other provision of law, the aggregate amount of liabilities of a covered financial company that are transferred to, or assumed by, a bridge financial company from a covered financial company may not exceed the aggregate amount of the assets of the covered financial company that are transferred to, or purchased by, the bridge financial company from the covered financial company. . . .

(9) Funding authorized.—The Corporation may, subject to the plan described in subsection (n)(9), provide funding to facilitate any transaction described in subparagraph (A), (B), (C), or (D) of paragraph (13) with respect to any bridge financial company, or facilitate the acquisition by a bridge financial company of any assets, or the assumption of any liabilities, of a covered financial company for which the Corporation has been appointed receiver. . . .

(12) Duration of bridge financial company.—Subject to paragraphs (13) and (14), the status of a bridge financial company as such shall terminate at the end of the 2-year period following the date on which it was granted a charter. The Corporation may, in its discretion, extend the status of the bridge financial company as such for no more than 3 additional 1-year periods.

(13) Termination of bridge financial company status.—The status of any bridge financial company as such shall terminate upon the earliest of—

(A) the date of the merger or consolidation of the bridge financial company with a company that is not a bridge financial company;

(B) at the election of the Corporation, the sale of a majority of the capital stock of the bridge financial company to a company other than the Corporation and other than another bridge financial company;

(C) the sale of 80 percent, or more, of the capital stock of the bridge financial company to a person other than the Corporation and other than another bridge financial company;

(D) at the election of the Corporation, either the assumption of all or substantially all of the liabilities of the bridge financial company by a company that is not a bridge financial company, or the acquisition of all or substantially all of the assets of the bridge financial company by a company that is not a bridge financial company, or other entity as permitted under applicable law; and

(E) the expiration of the period provided in paragraph (12), or the earlier dissolution of the bridge financial company, as provided in paragraph (15). . . .

(16) Authority to obtain credit.—

(A) In general.—A bridge financial company may obtain unsecured credit and issue unsecured debt.

(B) Inability to obtain credit.—If a bridge financial company is unable to obtain unsecured credit or issue unsecured debt, the Corporation may authorize the obtaining of credit or the issuance of debt by the bridge financial company—

(i) with priority over any or all of the obligations of the bridge financial company;

(ii) secured by a lien on property of the bridge financial company that is not otherwise subject to a lien; or

(iii) secured by a junior lien on property of the bridge financial company that is subject to a lien.

(C) Limitations.—

(i) In general.—The Corporation, after notice and a hearing, may authorize the obtaining of credit or the issuance of debt by a bridge financial company that is secured by a senior or equal lien on property of the bridge financial company that is subject to a lien, only if—

(I) the bridge financial company is unable to otherwise obtain such credit or issue such debt; and

(II) there is adequate protection of the interest of the holder of the lien on the property with respect to which such senior or equal lien is proposed to be granted.

(ii) Hearing.—The hearing required pursuant to this subparagraph shall be before a court of the United States, which shall have jurisdiction to conduct such hearing and to authorize a bridge financial company to obtain secured credit under clause (i).

(D) Burden of proof.—In any hearing under this paragraph, the Corporation has the burden of proof on the issue of adequate protection. . . .

(*l*) Prohibition on Entering Secrecy Agreements and Protective Orders.—The Corporation may not enter into any agreement or approve any protective order which prohibits the Corporation from disclosing the terms of any settlement of an administrative or other action for damages or restitution brought by the Corporation in its capacity as receiver for a covered financial company. . . .

(n) Orderly Liquidation Fund.—

(1) Establishment.—There is established in the Treasury of the United States a separate fund to be known as the "Orderly Liquidation Fund", which shall be available to the Corporation to carry out the authorities contained in this title, for the cost of actions authorized by this title, including the orderly liquidation of covered financial companies, payment of administrative expenses, the payment of principal and interest by the Corporation on obligations issued under paragraph (5), and the exercise of the authorities of the Corporation under this title.

(2) **Proceeds.**—Amounts received by the Corporation, including assessments received under subsection (o), proceeds of obligations issued under paragraph (5), interest and other earnings from investments, and repayments to the Corporation by covered financial companies, shall be deposited into the Fund. . . .

(5) **Authority to issue obligations.**—[The Corporation may issue obligations to the Secretary (and thus borrow from the Treasury) under such terms and conditions as the Secretary may require.]

(6) **Maximum obligation limitation.**—The Corporation may not, in connection with the orderly liquidation of a covered financial company, issue or incur any obligation, if, after issuing or incurring the obligation, the aggregate amount of such obligations outstanding under this subsection for each covered financial company would exceed—

(A) an amount that is equal to 10 percent of the total consolidated assets of the covered financial company, based on the most recent financial statement available, during the 30-day period immediately following the date of appointment of the Corporation as receiver (or a shorter time period if the Corporation has calculated the amount described under subparagraph (B)); and

(B) the amount that is equal to 90 percent of the fair value of the total consolidated assets of each covered financial company that are available for repayment, after the time period described in subparagraph (A). . . .

(8) **Rule of construction.**—

(A) **In general.**—Nothing in this section shall be construed to affect the [Corporation's borrowing authority under the Federal Deposit Insurance Act], provided that—

(i) the authorities of the Corporation contained in this title shall not be used to assist the Deposit Insurance Fund or to assist any financial company under applicable law other than this Act;

(ii) the authorities of the Corporation relating to the Deposit Insurance Fund, or any other responsibilities of the Corporation under applicable law other than this title, shall not be used to assist a covered financial company pursuant to this title; and

(iii) the Deposit Insurance Fund may not be used in any manner to otherwise circumvent the purposes of this title.

(B) **Valuation.**—For purposes of determining the amount of obligations under this subsection—

(i) the Corporation shall include as an obligation any contingent liability of the Corporation pursuant to this title; and

(ii) the Corporation shall value any contingent liability at its expected cost to the Corporation.

(9) Orderly liquidation and repayment plans.—

(A) Orderly liquidation plan.—Amounts in the Fund shall be available to the Corporation with regard to a covered financial company for which the Corporation is appointed receiver after the Corporation has developed an orderly liquidation plan that is acceptable to the Secretary with regard to such covered financial company, including the provision and use of funds, including taking any actions specified under § 5384(d) and subsection (h)(2)(G)(iv) and (h)(9) of this section, and payments to third parties. The orderly liquidation plan shall take into account actions to avoid or mitigate potential adverse effects on low income, minority, or underserved communities affected by the failure of the covered financial company, and shall provide for coordination with the primary financial regulatory agencies, as appropriate, to ensure that such actions are taken. The Corporation may, at any time, amend any orderly liquidation plan approved by the Secretary with the concurrence of the Secretary.

(B) Mandatory repayment plan.—

(i) **In general.**—No amount authorized under paragraph (6)(B) may be provided by the Secretary to the Corporation under paragraph (5), unless an agreement is in effect between the Secretary and the Corporation that—

(I) provides a specific plan and schedule to achieve the repayment of the outstanding amount of any borrowing under paragraph (5); and

(II) demonstrates that income to the Corporation from the liquidated assets of the covered financial company and assessments under subsection (o) will be sufficient to amortize the outstanding balance within the period established in the repayment schedule and pay the interest accruing on such balance within the time provided in subsection (o)(1)(B). . . .

(o) Assessments.—

(1) Risk-based assessments.—

(A) Eligible financial companies defined.—For purposes of this subsection, the term "eligible financial company" means any bank holding company with total consolidated assets equal to or greater than $50,000,000,000 and any nonbank financial company supervised by the Board of Governors.

(B) Assessments.—The Corporation shall charge one or more risk-based assessments in accordance with the provisions of subparagraph (D), if such assessments are necessary to pay in full the obligations issued by the Corporation to the Secretary under this title within 60 months of the date of issuance of such obligations.

(C) **Extensions authorized**.—The Corporation may, with the approval of the Secretary, extend the time period under subparagraph (B), if the Corporation determines that an extension is necessary to avoid a serious adverse effect on the financial system of the United States.

(D) **Application of assessments**.—To meet the requirements of subparagraph (B), the Corporation shall—

(i) impose assessments, as soon as practicable, on any claimant that received additional payments or amounts from the Corporation pursuant to subsection (b)(4), (d)(4), or (h)(5)(E), except for payments or amounts necessary to initiate and continue operations essential to implementation of the receivership or any bridge financial company, to recover on a cumulative basis, the entire difference between—

(I) the aggregate value the claimant received from the Corporation on a claim pursuant to this title (including pursuant to subsection (b)(4), (d)(4), and (h)(5)(E)), as of the date on which such value was received; and

(II) the value the claimant was entitled to receive from the Corporation on such claim solely from the proceeds of the liquidation of the covered financial company under this title; and

(ii) if the amounts to be recovered on a cumulative basis under clause (i) are insufficient to meet the requirements of subparagraph (B), after taking into account the considerations set forth in paragraph (4), impose assessments on—

(I) eligible financial companies; and

(II) financial companies with total consolidated assets equal to or greater than $50,000,000,000 that are not eligible financial companies.

(E) **Provision of financing**.—Payments or amounts necessary to initiate and continue operations essential to implementation of the receivership or any bridge financial company described in subparagraph (D)(i) shall not include the provision of financing, as defined by rule of the Corporation, to third parties.

(2) **Graduated assessment rate**.—The Corporation shall impose assessments on a graduated basis, with financial companies having greater assets and risk being assessed at a higher rate. . . .

(4) **Risk-based assessment considerations**.—In imposing assessments under paragraph (1)(D)(ii), the Corporation shall use a risk matrix. The Council shall make a recommendation to the Corporation on the risk matrix to be used in imposing such assessments, and the Corporation shall take into account any such recommendation in the establishment of the risk matrix to be used to impose such assessments. In recommending or establishing such risk matrix, the Council and the Corporation, respectively, shall take into account—

(A) economic conditions generally affecting financial companies so as to allow assessments to increase during more favorable economic conditions and to decrease during less favorable economic conditions;

(B) any assessments imposed on a financial company or an affiliate of a financial company that—

(i) is an insured depository institution, assessed pursuant to § 1817 or § 1823(c)(4)(G) of the Federal Deposit Insurance Act;

(ii) is a member of the Securities Investor Protection Corporation, assessed pursuant to 15 U.S.C. § 78ddd;

(iii) is an insured credit union, assessed pursuant to . . . the Federal Credit Union Act; or

(iv) is an insurance company, assessed pursuant to applicable State law to cover (or reimburse payments made to cover) the costs of the rehabilitation, liquidation, or other State insolvency proceeding with respect to 1 or more insurance companies;

(C) the risks presented by the financial company to the financial system and the extent to which the financial company has benefitted, or likely would benefit, from the orderly liquidation of a financial company under this title, including—

(i) the amount, different categories, and concentrations of assets of the financial company and its affiliates, including both on-balance sheet and off-balance sheet assets;

(ii) the activities of the financial company and its affiliates;

(iii) the relevant market share of the financial company and its affiliates;

(iv) the extent to which the financial company is leveraged;

(v) the potential exposure to sudden calls on liquidity precipitated by economic distress;

(vi) the amount, maturity, volatility, and stability of the company's financial obligations to, and relationship with, other financial companies;

(vii) the amount, maturity, volatility, and stability of the liabilities of the company, including the degree of reliance on short-term funding, taking into consideration existing systems for measuring a company's risk-based capital;

(viii) the stability and variety of the company's sources of funding;

(ix) the company's importance as a source of credit for households, businesses, and State and local governments and as a source of liquidity for the financial system;

(x) the extent to which assets are simply managed and not owned by the financial company and the extent to which ownership of assets under management is diffuse; and

(xi) the amount, different categories, and concentrations of liabilities, both insured and uninsured, contingent and noncontingent, including both on-balance sheet and off-balance sheet liabilities, of the financial company and its affiliates;

(D) any risks presented by the financial company during the 10-year period immediately prior to the appointment of the Corporation as receiver for the covered financial company that contributed to the failure of the covered financial company; and

(E) such other risk-related factors as the Corporation, or the Council, as applicable, may determine to be appropriate. . . .

(6) **Rulemaking**.—The Corporation shall prescribe regulations to carry out this subsection. . . . The regulations . . . shall take into account the differences in risks posed to the financial stability of the United States by financial companies, the differences in the liability structures of financial companies, and the different bases for other assessments that such financial companies may be required to pay, to ensure that assessed financial companies are treated equitably and that assessments under this subsection reflect such differences. . . .

§ 5392. Prohibition of Circumvention and Prevention of Conflicts of Interest

(a) **No Other Funding**.—Funds for the orderly liquidation of any covered financial company under this title shall only be provided as specified under this title.

(b) **Limit on Governmental Actions**.—No governmental entity may take any action to circumvent the purposes of this title.

(c) **Conflict of Interest**.—In the event that the Corporation is appointed receiver for more than 1 covered financial company or is appointed receiver for a covered financial company and receiver for any insured depository institution that is an affiliate of such covered financial company, the Corporation shall take appropriate action, as necessary to avoid any conflicts of interest that may arise in connection with multiple receiverships. . . .

§ 5394. Prohibition on Taxpayer Funding

(a) **Liquidation Required**.—All financial companies put into receivership under this title shall be liquidated. No taxpayer funds shall be used to prevent the liquidation of any financial company under this title.

(b) **Recovery of Funds**.—All funds expended in the liquidation of a financial company under this title shall be recovered from the disposition of assets of such financial company, or shall be the responsibility of the financial sector, through assessments.

(c) **No Losses to Taxpayers**.—Taxpayers shall bear no losses from the exercise of any authority under this title. . . .

[Other Provisions]

§ 5491. Establishment of the Bureau of Consumer Financial Protection

(a) Bureau Established.—There is established in the Federal Reserve System, an independent bureau to be known as the "Bureau of Consumer Financial Protection", which shall regulate the offering and provision of consumer financial products or services under the Federal consumer financial laws. The Bureau shall be considered an Executive agency. . . .

(b) Director . . .

(1) In general.—There is established the position of the Director, who shall serve as the head of the Bureau.

(2) Appointment.—[T]he Director shall be appointed by the President, by and with the advice and consent of the Senate. . . .

(c) Term.—

(1) In general.—The Director shall serve for a term of 5 years.

(2) Expiration of term.—An individual may serve as Director after the expiration of the term for which appointed, until a successor has been appointed and qualified.

(3) Removal for cause.—The President may remove the Director for inefficiency, neglect of duty, or malfeasance in office. . . .

§ 5611. Liquidity Event Determination

(a) Determination and Written Recommendation.—

(1) Determination request.—The Secretary may request the Corporation and the Board of Governors to determine whether a liquidity event exists that warrants use of the guarantee program authorized under § 5612.

(2) Requirements of determination.—Any determination pursuant to paragraph (1) shall—

(A) be written; and

(B) contain an evaluation of the evidence that—

(i) a liquidity event exists;

(ii) failure to take action would have serious adverse effects on financial stability or economic conditions in the United States; and

(iii) actions authorized under § 5612 are needed to avoid or mitigate potential adverse effects on the United States financial system or economic conditions.

(b) Procedures.—Notwithstanding any other provision of Federal or State law, upon the determination of both the Corporation (upon a vote of not fewer than 2/3 of the members of the Corporation then serving) and the Board of Governors (upon a vote of not fewer than 2/3 of the members of the Board of Governors then serving) under subsection (a) that a liquidity event exists that warrants use of the guarantee program authorized under § 5612, and with the written consent of the Secretary—

(1) the Corporation shall take action in accordance with § 5612(a); and

(2) the Secretary (in consultation with the President) shall take action in accordance with § 5612(c).

(c) Documentation and Review.—

(1) Documentation.—The Secretary shall—

(A) maintain the written documentation of each determination of the Corporation and the Board of Governors under this section; and

(B) provide the documentation for review under paragraph (2).

(2) GAO review.—The Comptroller General of the United States shall review and report to Congress on any determination of the Corporation and the Board of Governors under subsection (a), including—

(A) the basis for the determination; and

(B) the likely effect of the actions taken.

(d) Report to Congress.—On the earlier of the date of a submission made to Congress under § 5612(c), or within 30 days of the date of a determination under subsection (a), the Secretary shall provide written notice of the determination of the Corporation and the Board of Governors to the Committee on Banking, Housing, and Urban Affairs of the Senate and the Committee on Financial Services of the House of Representatives, including a description of the basis for the determination.

§ 5612. Emergency Financial Stabilization

(a) In General.—Upon the written determination of the Corporation and the Board of Governors under § 5611, the Corporation shall create a widely available program to guarantee obligations of solvent insured depository institutions or solvent depository institution holding companies (including any affiliates thereof) during times of severe economic distress, except that a guarantee of obligations under this section may not include the provision of equity in any form. . . .

(c) Determination of Guaranteed Amount.—

(1) In general.—In connection with any program established pursuant to subsection **(a)** and subject to paragraph (2) of this subsection, the Secretary (in consultation with the President) shall determine the maximum amount of debt outstanding that the Corporation may guarantee under this section, and the President may transmit to Congress a written report on the plan of the Corporation to exercise the authority under this section to issue guarantees up to that maximum amount and a request for approval of such plan. The Corporation shall exercise the authority under this section to issue guarantees up to that specified maximum amount upon passage of the joint resolution of approval, as provided in subsection (d). Absent such approval, the Corporation shall issue no such guarantees.

(2) **Additional debt guarantee authority**.—If the Secretary (in consultation with the President) determines, after a submission to Congress under paragraph (1), that the maximum guarantee amount should be raised, and the Council concurs with that determination, the President may transmit to Congress a written report on the plan of the Corporation to exercise the authority under this section to issue guarantees up to the increased maximum debt guarantee amount. The Corporation shall exercise the authority under this section to issue guarantees up to that specified maximum amount upon passage of the joint resolution of approval, as provided in subsection (d). Absent such approval, the Corporation shall issue no such guarantees.

(d) **Resolution of Approval**.—

(1) **Additional debt guarantee authority**.—A request by the President under this section shall be considered granted by Congress upon adoption of a joint resolution approving such request. Such joint resolution shall be considered in the Senate under expedited procedures. . . .

(e) **Funding**.—

(1) **Fees and other charges**.—The Corporation shall charge fees and other assessments to all participants in the program established pursuant to this section, in such amounts as are necessary to offset projected losses and administrative expenses . . . and such amounts shall be available to the Corporation. . . .

(4) **Backup special assessments**.—To the extent that the funds collected pursuant to paragraph (1) are insufficient to cover any losses or expenses . . . arising from a program established pursuant to this section, the Corporation shall impose a special assessment solely on participants in the program, in amounts necessary to address such insufficiency, and which shall be available to the Corporation to cover such losses or expenses. . . .

(g) **Definitions**.—For purposes of this section, the following definitions shall apply . . .

(3) **Liquidity event**.—The term "liquidity event" means—

(A) an exceptional and broad reduction in the general ability of financial market participants—

(i) to sell financial assets without an unusual and significant discount; or

(ii) to borrow using financial assets as collateral without an unusual and significant increase in margin; or

(B) an unusual and significant reduction in the ability of financial market participants to obtain unsecured credit.

(4) Solvent.—The term "solvent" means that the value of the assets of an entity exceed[s] its obligations to creditors.

TITLE 15—COMMERCE AND TRADE

SHERMAN AND CLAYTON ACTS

§ 1. Combinations in Restraint of Trade Unlawful

Every contract, combination in the form of trust or otherwise, or conspiracy, in restraint of trade or commerce among the several States, or with foreign nations, is hereby declared to be illegal. . . .

§ 2. Monopolization Unlawful

Every person who shall monopolize, or attempt to monopolize, or combine or conspire with any other person or persons, to monopolize any part of the trade or commerce among the several States, or with foreign nations, shall be deemed guilty of a felony. . . .

§ 18. Acquisition by One Corporation of Stock of Another

No person engaged in commerce or in any activity affecting commerce shall acquire, directly or indirectly, the whole or any part of the stock or other share capital and no person subject to the jurisdiction of the Federal Trade Commission shall acquire the whole or any part of the assets of another person engaged also in commerce or in any activity affecting commerce, where in any line of commerce or in any activity affecting commerce in any section of the country, the effect of such acquisition may be substantially to lessen competition, or to tend to create a monopoly.

No person shall acquire, directly or indirectly, the whole or any part of the stock or other share capital and no person subject to the jurisdiction of the Federal Trade Commission shall acquire the whole or any part of the assets of one or more persons engaged in commerce or in any activity affecting commerce, where in any line of commerce or in any activity affecting commerce in any section of the country, the effect of such acquisition, of such stocks or assets, or of the use of such stock by the voting or granting of proxies or otherwise, may be substantially to lessen competition, or to tend to create a monopoly. . . .

FEDERAL TRADE COMMISSION ACT

§ 45. Unfair Methods of Competition Unlawful

(a) Declaration of Unlawfulness; Power to Prohibit Unfair Practices. . . . —

(1) Unfair methods of competition in or affecting commerce, and unfair or deceptive acts or practices in or affecting commerce, are hereby declared unlawful.

(2) The Commission is hereby empowered and directed to prevent persons, partnerships, or corporations, except banks, savings and loan institutions . . . , [and] Federal credit unions . . . , from using unfair methods of competition in or affecting commerce and unfair or deceptive acts or practices in or affecting commerce. . . .

SECURITIES ACT OF 1933

§ 77b. Definitions

(a) Definitions.—When used in this Act unless the context otherwise requires— . . .

(4) The term **"issuer"** means every person who issues or proposes to issue any security; except that with respect to certificates of deposit, voting-trust certificates, or collateral-trust certificates, or with respect to certificates of interest or shares in an unincorporated investment trust not having a board of directors (or persons performing similar functions) or of the fixed, restricted management, or unit type, the term "issuer" means the person or persons performing the acts and assuming the duties of depositor or manager pursuant to the provisions of the trust or other agreement or instrument under which such securities are issued; except that in the case of an unincorporated association which provides by its articles for limited liability of any or all of its members, or in the case of a trust, committee, or other legal entity, the trustees or members thereof shall not be individually liable as issuers of any security issued by the association, trust, committee, or other legal entity. . . .

(11) The term **"underwriter"** means any person who has purchased from an issuer with a view to, or offers or sells for an issuer in connection with, the distribution of any security, or participates or has a direct or indirect participation in any such undertaking, or participates or has a participation in the direct or indirect underwriting of any such undertaking; but such term shall not include a person whose interest is limited to a commission from an underwriter or dealer not in excess of the usual and customary distributors' or sellers' commission. As used in this

paragraph the term "issuer" shall include, in addition to an issuer, any person directly or indirectly controlling or controlled by the issuer, or any person under direct or indirect common control with the issuer....

(b) Rulemaking Considerations.—Whenever pursuant to this Act the Commission is engaged in rulemaking and is required to consider or determine whether an action is necessary or appropriate in the public interest, the Commission shall also consider, in addition to the protection of investors, whether the action will promote efficiency, competition, and capital formation.

§ 77c. Classes of Securities Under This Act

(a) Exempted Securities.—Except as hereinafter expressly provided, the provisions of this Act shall not apply to any of the following classes of securities: ...

(2) Any security issued or guaranteed by the United States or any territory thereof, or by the District of Columbia, or by any State of the United States, or by any political subdivision of a State or territory, or by any public instrumentality of one or more States or territories, or by any person controlled or supervised by and acting as an instrumentality of the Government of the United States pursuant to authority granted by the Congress of the United States; or any certificate of deposit for any of the foregoing; or any security issued or guaranteed by any bank; or any security issued by or representing an interest in or a direct obligation of a Federal Reserve bank; or any interest or participation in any common trust fund or similar fund that is excluded from the definition of the term "investment company" under § 80a-3(c)(3); or any security which is an industrial development bond (as defined in § 103(c)(2) of the Internal Revenue Code of 1954 the interest on which is excludable from gross income under § 103(a)(1) of such Code if [the security meets certain additional criteria]; or any interest or participation in a single trust fund, or in a collective trust fund maintained by a bank, or any security arising out of a contract issued by an insurance company, which interest, participation, or security is issued in connection with (A) a stock bonus, pension, or profit-sharing plan which meets the requirements for qualification under § 401 of the Internal Revenue Code of 1954, (B) an annuity plan which meets the requirements for the deduction of the employer's contributions under § 404(a)(2) of such Code, (C) a governmental plan as defined in § 414(d) of such Code which has been established by an employer for the exclusive benefit of its employees or their beneficiaries for the purpose of distributing to such employees or their beneficiaries the corpus and income of the funds accumulated under such plan, if under such plan it is impossible, prior to the satisfaction of all liabilities with respect to such employees and their beneficiaries, for any part of the corpus or income to

be used for, or diverted to, purposes other than the exclusive benefit of such employees or their beneficiaries, or (D) a church plan, company, or account that is excluded from the definition of an investment company under § 80a-3(c)(14), other than any plan described in subparagraph (A), (B), (C), or (D) of this paragraph (i) the contributions under which are held in a single trust fund or in a separate account maintained by an insurance company for a single employer and under which an amount in excess of the employer's contribution is allocated to the purchase of securities (other than interests or participations in the trust or separate account itself) issued by the employer or any company directly or indirectly controlling, controlled by, or under common control with the employer, (ii) which covers employees some or all of whom are employees within the meaning of § 401(c)(1) of such Code, or (iii) which is a plan funded by an annuity contract described in § 403(b) of such Code. The Commission, by rules and regulations or order, shall exempt from the provisions of § 77e any interest or participation issued in connection with a stock bonus, pension, profit-sharing, or annuity plan which covers employees some or all of whom are employees within the meaning of § 401(c)(1) of the Internal Revenue Code of 1954, if and to the extent that the Commission determines this to be necessary or appropriate in the public interest and consistent with the protection of investors and the purposes fairly intended by the policy and provisions of this Act. For purposes of this paragraph, a security issued or guaranteed by a bank shall not include any interest or participation in any collective trust fund maintained by a bank; and the term "bank" means any national bank, or any banking institution organized under the laws of any State, territory, or the District of Columbia, the business of which is substantially confined to banking and is supervised by the State or territorial banking commission or similar official; except that in the case of a common trust fund or similar fund, or a collective trust fund, the term "bank" has the same meaning as in the Investment Company Act of 1940;

(3) Any note, draft, bill of exchange, or banker's acceptance which arises out of a current transaction or the proceeds of which have been or are to be used for current transactions, and which has a maturity at the time of issuance of not exceeding nine months, exclusive of days of grace, or any renewal thereof the maturity of which is likewise limited;

(4) Any security issued by a person organized and operated exclusively for religious, educational, benevolent, fraternal, charitable, or reformatory purposes and not for pecuniary profit, and no part of the net earnings of which inures to the benefit of any person, private stockholder, or individual, or any security of a fund that is excluded from the definition of an investment company under § 80a-3(c)(10)(B);

(5) Any security issued (A) by a savings and loan association, building and loan association, cooperative bank, homestead association, or similar institution, which is supervised and examined by State or Federal authority

having supervision over any such institution; or (B) by (i) a farmer's cooperative organization exempt from tax under § 521 of the Internal Revenue Code of 1954, (ii) a corporation described in § 501(c)(16) of such Code and exempt from tax under § 501(a) of such Code, or (iii) a corporation described in § 501(c)(2) of such Code which is exempt from tax under § 501(a) of such Code and is organized for the exclusive purpose of holding title to property, collecting income therefrom, and turning over the entire amount thereof, less expenses, to an organization or corporation described in clause (i) or (ii);

(6) Any interest in a railroad equipment trust. For purposes of this paragraph "interest in a railroad equipment trust" means any interest in an equipment trust, lease, conditional sales contract, or other similar arrangement entered into, issued, assumed, guaranteed by, or for the benefit of, a common carrier to finance the acquisition of rolling stock, including motive power;

(7) Certificates issued by a receiver or by a trustee or debtor in possession in a case under title 11 of the United States Code, with the approval of the court;

(8) Any insurance or endowment policy or annuity contract or optional annuity contract, issued by a corporation subject to the supervision of the insurance commissioner, bank commissioner, or any agency or officer performing like functions, of any State or Territory of the United States or the District of Columbia;

(9) Except with respect to a security exchanged in a case under title 11 of the United States Code, any security exchanged by the issuer with its existing security holders exclusively where no commission or other remuneration is paid or given directly or indirectly for soliciting such exchange;

(10) Except with respect to a security exchanged in a case under title 11 of the United States Code, any security which is issued in exchange for one or more bona fide outstanding securities, claims or property interests, or partly in such exchange and partly for cash, where the terms and conditions of such issuance and exchange are approved, after a hearing upon the fairness of such terms and conditions at which all persons to whom it is proposed to issue securities in such exchange shall have the right to appear, by any court, or by any official or agency of the United States, or by any State or Territorial banking or insurance commission or other governmental authority expressly authorized by law to grant such approval;

(11) Any security which is a part of an issue offered and sold only to persons resident within a single State or Territory, where the issuer of such security is a person resident and doing business within or, if a corporation, incorporated by and doing business within, such State or Territory.

(12) Any equity security issued in connection with the acquisition by a holding company of a bank under § 1842(a) of title 12 or [an FDIC-insured] savings association under § 1467a(e) of that title, if—

(A) the acquisition occurs solely as part of a reorganization in which security holders exchange their shares of a bank or savings association for shares of a newly formed holding company with no significant assets other than securities of the bank or savings association and the existing subsidiaries of the bank or savings association;

(B) the security holders receive, after that reorganization, substantially the same proportional share interests in the holding company as they held in the bank or savings association, except for nominal changes in shareholders' interests resulting from lawful elimination of fractional interests and the exercise of dissenting shareholders' rights under State or Federal law;

(C) the rights and interests of security holders in the holding company are substantially the same as those in the bank or savings association prior to the transaction, other than as may be required by law; and

(D) the holding company has substantially the same assets and liabilities, on a consolidated basis, as the bank or savings association had prior to the transaction. . . .

(13) Any security issued by or any interest or participation in any church plan, company or account that is excluded from the definition of an investment company under § 80a-3(c)(14).

(14) Any security futures product that is—

(A) cleared by a clearing agency registered under § 78q-1 or exempt from registration under § 78q-1(b)(7); and

(B) traded on a national securities exchange or a national securities association registered pursuant to § 78o-3(a).

(b) Additional Exemptions.—The Commission may from time to time by its rules and regulations, and subject to such terms and conditions as may be prescribed therein, add any class of securities to the securities exempted as provided in this section, if it finds that the enforcement of this Act with respect to such securities is not necessary in the public interest and for the protection of investors by reason of the small amount involved or the limited character of the public offering; but no issue of securities shall be exempted under this subsection where the aggregate amount at which such issue is offered to the public exceeds $5,000,000.

§ 77d. Exempted Transactions

The provisions of § 77e shall not apply to—

(1) transactions by any person other than an issuer, underwriter, or dealer.

(2) transactions by an issuer not involving any public offering.

(3) transactions by a dealer (including an underwriter no longer acting as an underwriter in respect of the security involved in such transaction), except—

Securities Act of 1933   15 U.S.C. § 77d

    (A) transactions taking place prior to the expiration of forty days after the first date upon which the security was bona fide offered to the public by the issuer or by or through an underwriter,

    (B) transactions in a security as to which a registration statement has been filed taking place prior to the expiration of forty days after the effective date of such registration statement or prior to the expiration of forty days after the first date upon which the security was bona fide offered to the public by the issuer or by or through an underwriter after such effective date, which ever is later (excluding in the computation of such forty days any time during which a stop order issued under 77h is in effect as to the security), or such shorter period as the Commission may specify by rules and regulations or order, and

    (C) transactions as to securities constituting the whole or a part of an unsold allotment to or subscription by such dealer as a participant in the distribution of such securities by the issuer or by or through an underwriter. . . .

(4) brokers' transactions executed upon customers' orders on any exchange or in the over-the-counter market but not the solicitation of such orders.

(5) (A) Transactions involving offers or sales of one or more promissory notes directly secured by a first lien on a single parcel of real estate upon which is located a dwelling or other residential or commercial structure, and participation interests in such notes—

    (i) where such securities are originated by a savings and loan association, savings bank, commercial bank, or similar banking institution which is supervised and examined by a Federal or State authority, and are offered and sold subject to the following conditions:

(a) the minimum aggregate sales price per purchaser shall not be less than $250,000;

(b) the purchaser shall pay cash either at the time of the sale or within sixty days thereof; and

(c) each purchaser shall buy for his own account only; or

    (ii) where such securities are originated by a mortgagee approved by the Secretary of Housing and Urban Development pursuant to §§ 1709 and 1715b of title 12 and are offered or sold subject to the three conditions specified in subparagraph (A)(i) to any institution described in such subparagraph or to any insurance company subject to the supervision of the insurance commissioner, or any agency or officer performing like function, of any State or territory of the United States or the District of Columbia, or the Federal Home Loan Mortgage Corporation, the Federal National Mortgage Association, or the Government National Mortgage Association.

(B) Transactions between any of the entities described in subparagraph (A)(i) or (A)(ii) hereof involving non-assignable contracts to buy or sell the foregoing securities which are to be completed within two years, where the seller of the foregoing securities pursuant to any such contract is one of the parties described in subparagraph (A)(i) or (A)(ii) who may originate such securities and the purchaser of such securities pursuant to any such contract is any institution described in subparagraph (A)(i) or any insurance company described in subparagraph (A)(ii), the Federal Home Loan Mortgage Corporation, Federal National Mortgage Association, or the Government National Mortgage Association and where the foregoing securities are subject to the three conditions for sale set forth in subparagraphs (A)(i) (a) through (c).

(C) The exemption provided by subparagraphs (A) and (B) hereof shall not apply to resales of the securities acquired pursuant thereto, unless each of the conditions for sale contained in subparagraphs (A)(1) (a) through (c) are satisfied.

(6) transactions involving offers or sales by an issuer solely to one or more accredited investors, if the aggregate offering price of an issue of securities offered in reliance on his paragraph does not exceed the amount allowed under § 77c(b), if there is no advertising or public solicitation in connection with the transaction by the issuer or anyone acting on the issuer's behalf, and if the issuer files such notice with the Commission as the Commission shall prescribe.

§ 77e. Prohibitions Relating to Interstate Commerce and the Mails

(a) Sale or Delivery After Sale of Unregistered Securities.—Unless a registration statement is in effect as to a security, it shall be unlawful for any person, directly or indirectly—

(1) to make use of any means or instruments of transportation or communication in interstate commerce or of the mails to sell such security through the use or medium of any prospectus or otherwise; or

(2) to carry or cause to be carried through the mails or in interstate commerce, by any means or instruments of transportation, any such security for the purpose of sale or for delivery after sale.

(b) Necessity of Prospectus Meeting Requirements of § 77j.—It shall be unlawful for any person, directly or indirectly—

(1) to make use of any means or instruments of transportation or communication in interstate commerce or of the mails to carry or transmit any prospectus relating to any security with respect to which a registration statement has been filed under this Act, unless such prospectus meets the requirements of § 77j; or

(2) to carry or cause to be carried through the mails or in interstate commerce any such security for the purpose of sale or for delivery after sale, unless accompanied or preceded by a prospectus that meets the requirements of § 77j(a).

(c) Necessity of Filing Registration Statement.—It shall be unlawful for any person, directly or indirectly, to make use of any means or instruments of transportation or communication in interstate commerce or of the mails to offer to sell or offer to buy through the use or medium of any prospectus or otherwise any security, unless a registration statement has been filed as to such security, or while the registration statement is the subject of a refusal order or stop order or (prior to the effective date of the registration statement) any public proceeding or examination under § 77h.

§ 77f. Registration of Securities

(a) Method of Registration.—Any security may be registered with the Commission under the terms and conditions hereinafter provided, by filing a registration statement in triplicate, at least one of which shall be signed by each issuer, its principal executive officer or officers, its principal financial officer, its comptroller or principal accounting officer, and the majority of its board of directors or persons performing similar functions (or, if there is no board of directors or persons performing similar functions, by the majority of the persons or board having the power of management of the issuer), and in case the issuer is a foreign or Territorial person by its duly authorized representative in the United States; except that when such registration statement relates to a security issued by a foreign government, or political subdivision thereof, it need be signed only by the underwriter of such security. . . . A registration statement shall be deemed effective only as to securities specified therein as proposed to be offered. . . .

§ 77k. Civil Liabilities on Account of False Registration Statement

(a) Persons Possessing Cause of Action; Persons Liable.—In case any part of the registration statement, when such part became effective, contained an untrue statement of a material fact or omitted to state a material fact required to be stated therein or necessary to make the statements therein not misleading, any person acquiring such security (unless it is proved that at the time of such acquisition he knew of such untruth or omission) may, either at law or in equity, in any court of competent jurisdiction, sue—

(1) every person who signed the registration statement;

(2) every person who was a director of (or person performing similar functions) or partner in, the issuer at the time of the filing of the part of the registration statement with respect to which his liability is asserted;

(3) every person who, with his consent, is named in the registration statement as being or about to become a director, person performing similar functions, or partner;

(4) every accountant, engineer, or appraiser, or any person whose profession gives authority to a statement made by him, who has with his consent been named as having prepared or certified any part of the registration statement, or as having prepared or certified any report or valuation which is used in connection with the registration statement, with respect to the statement, in such registration statement, report, or valuation, which purports to have been prepared or certified by him;

(5) every underwriter with respect to such security.

If such person acquired the security after the issuer has made generally available to its security holders an earning statement covering a period of at least twelve months beginning after the effective date of the registration statement, then the right of recovery under this subsection shall be conditioned on proof that such person acquired the security relying upon such untrue statement in the registration statement or relying upon the registration statement and not knowing of such omission, but such reliance may be established without proof of the reading of the registration statement by such person.

(b) Persons Conditionally Exempt from Liability.—Notwithstanding the provisions of subsection (a) no person, other than the issuer, shall be liable as provided therein who shall sustain the burden of proof—

(1) that before the effective date of the part of the registration statement with respect to which his liability is asserted (A) he had resigned from or had taken steps as are permitted by law to resign from, or ceased or refused to act in, every office, capacity, or relationship in which he was described in the registration statement as acting or agreeing to act, and (B) he had advised the Commission and the issuer in writing that he had taken such action and that he would not be responsible for such part of the registration statement; or

(2) that if such part of the registration statement became effective without his knowledge, upon becoming aware of such fact he forthwith acted and advised the Commission, in accordance with paragraph (1), and, in addition, gave reasonable public notice that such part of the registration statement had become effective without his knowledge; or

(3) that (A) as regards any part of the registration statement not purporting to be made on the authority of an expert, and not purporting to be a copy of or extract from a report or valuation of an expert, and not purporting to be made on the authority of a public official document or statement, he had, after reasonable investigation, reasonable ground to believe and did believe, at the time such part of the registration statement became effective, that the statements therein were true and that there was no omission to state a material fact required to be stated therein or necessary to make the statements therein not misleading; and (B) as regards any part of the registration statement purporting to be made upon his authority as an expert or purporting to be a copy of or extract from a report or valuation of himself as an expert, (i) he had, after reasonable investigation, reasonable ground to believe and did believe, at the time such part of the registration

statement became effective, that the statements therein were true and that there was no omission to state a material fact required to be stated therein or necessary to make the statements therein not misleading, or (ii) such part of the registration statement did not fairly represent his statement as an expert or was not a fair copy of or extract from his report or valuation as an expert; and (C) as regards any part of the registration statement purporting to be made on the authority of an expert (other than himself) or purporting to be a copy of or extract from a report or valuation of an expert (other than himself), he had no reasonable ground to believe and did not believe, at the time such part of the registration statement became effective, that the statements therein were untrue or that there was an omission to state a material fact required to be stated therein or necessary to make the statements therein not misleading, or that such part of the registration statement did not fairly represent the statement of the expert or was not a fair copy of or extract from the report or valuation of the expert; and (D) as regards any part of the registration statement purporting to be a statement made by an official person or purporting to be a copy of or extract from a public official document, he had no reasonable ground to believe and did not believe, at the time such part of the registration statement became effective, that the statements therein were untrue, or that there was an omission to state a material fact required to be stated therein or necessary to make the statements therein not misleading, or that such part of the registration statement did not fairly represent the statement made by the official person or was not a fair copy of or extract from the public official document.

(c) Standard of Reasonableness.—In determining, for the purpose of paragraph (3) of subsection (b) of this section, what constitutes reasonable investigation and reasonable ground for belief, the standard of reasonableness shall be that required of a prudent man in the management of his own property. . . .

(f) Joint and Several Liability.—

(1) Except as provided in paragraph (2) [relating to outside directors], all or any one or more of the persons specified in subsection (a) shall be jointly and severally liable, and every person who becomes liable to make any payment under this section may recover contribution as in cases of contract from any person who, if sued separately, would have been liable to make the same payment, unless the person who has become liable was, and the other was not, guilty of fraudulent misrepresentation. . . .

§ 77r. Exemption from State Regulation of Securities Offerings

(a) Scope of Exemption.—Except as otherwise provided in this section, no law, rule, regulation, or order, or other administrative action of any State or any political subdivision thereof—

(1) requiring, or with respect to, registration or qualification of securities, or registration or qualification of securities transactions, shall directly or indirectly apply to a security that—

(A) is a covered security; or

(B) will be a covered security upon completion of the transaction;

(2) shall directly or indirectly prohibit, limit, or impose any conditions upon the use of—

(A) with respect to a covered security described in subsection (b), any offering document that is prepared by or on behalf of the issuer; or

(B) any proxy statement, report to shareholders, or other disclosure document relating to a covered security or the issuer thereof that is required to be and is filed with the Commission or any national securities organization registered under § 78o-3, except that this subparagraph does not apply to the laws, rules, regulations, or orders, or other administrative actions of the State of incorporation of the issuer; or

(3) shall directly or indirectly prohibit, limit, or impose conditions, based on the merits of such offering or issuer, upon the offer or sale of any security described in paragraph (1).

(b) Covered Securities.—For purposes of this section, the following are covered securities:

(1) Exclusive Federal registration of nationally traded securities.—A security is a covered security if such security is—

(A) listed, or authorized for listing, on the New York Stock Exchange or the American Stock Exchange, or listed, or authorized for listing, on the National Market System of the Nasdaq Stock Market (or any successor to such entities);

(B) listed, or authorized for listing, on a national securities exchange (or tier or segment thereof) that has listing standards that the Commission determines by rule (on its own initiative or on the basis of a petition) are substantially similar to the listing standards applicable to securities described in subparagraph (A); or

(C) a security of the same issuer that is equal in seniority or that is a senior security to a security described in subparagraph (A) or (B).

(2) Exclusive Federal registration of investment companies.—A security is a covered security if such security is a security issued by an investment company that is registered, or that has filed a registration statement, under the Investment Company Act of 1940.

(3) Sales to qualified purchasers.—A security is a covered security with respect to the offer or sale of the security to qualified purchasers, as defined by the Commission by rule. In prescribing such rule, the Commission may define the term "qualified purchaser" differently with respect to different categories of securities, consistent with the public interest and the protection of investors.

(4) Exemption in connection with certain exempt offerings.—A security is a covered security with respect to a transaction that is exempt from registration under this Act pursuant to—

(A) paragraph (1) or (3) of § 77d(1), and the issuer of such security files reports with the Commission pursuant to § 78m or § 78o(d);

(B) § 77d(4);

(C) § 77c(a), other than the offer or sale of a security that is exempt from such registration pursuant to paragraph (4), (10), or (11) of such section, except that a municipal security that is exempt from such registration pursuant to paragraph (2) of such section is not a covered security with respect to the offer or sale of such security in the State in which the issuer of such security is located; or

(D) Commission rules or regulations issued under § 77d(2), except that this subparagraph does not prohibit a State from imposing notice filing requirements that are substantially similar to those required by rule or regulation under § 77d(2) that are in effect on September 1, 1996.

(c) Preservation of Authority.—

(1) Fraud authority.—Consistent with this section, the securities commission (or any agency or office performing like functions) of any State shall retain jurisdiction under the laws of such State to investigate and bring enforcement actions with respect to fraud or deceit, or unlawful conduct by a broker or dealer, in connection with securities or securities transactions.

(2) Preservation of filing requirements.—

(A) **Notice filings permitted.**—Nothing in this section prohibits the securities commission (or any agency or office performing like functions) of any State from requiring the filing of any document filed with the Commission pursuant to this Act, together with annual or periodic reports of the value of securities sold or offered to be sold to persons located in the State (if such sales data is not included in documents filed with the Commission), solely for notice purposes and the assessment of any fee, together with a consent to service of process and any required fee.

(B) **Preservation of [state-imposed] fees.**— ...

(D) **Fees not permitted on listed securities.**—Notwithstanding subparagraphs (A), (B), and (C), no filing or fee may be required with respect to any security that is a covered security pursuant to subsection (b)(1), or will be such a covered security upon completion of the transaction, or is a security of the same issuer that is equal in seniority or that is a senior security to a security that is a covered security pursuant to subsection (b)(1).

(3) Enforcement of requirements.—Nothing in this section shall prohibit the securities commission (or any agency or office performing like functions) of any State from suspending the offer or sale of securities within such State as a result of the failure to submit any filing or fee required under law and permitted under this section.

(d) Definitions.—For purposes of this section, the following definitions shall apply:

(1) Offering document.—The term "offering document"—

(A) has the meaning given the term "prospectus" in § 77b(a)(10), but without regard to the provisions of subparagraphs (a) and (b) of that section; and

(B) includes a communication that is not deemed to offer a security pursuant to a rule of the Commission. . . .

(4) Senior security.—The term "senior security" means any bond, debenture, note, or similar obligation or instrument constituting a security and evidencing indebtedness, and any stock of a class having priority over any other class as to distribution of assets or payment of dividends. . . .

§ 77z-2a. Conflicts of Interest Relating to Certain Securitizations

(a) In General.—An underwriter, placement agent, initial purchaser, or sponsor, or any affiliate or subsidiary of any such entity, of an asset-backed security (as such term is defined in § 78c, which for the purposes of this section shall include a synthetic asset-backed security), shall not, at any time for a period ending on the date that is one year after the date of the first closing of the sale of the asset-backed security, engage in any transaction that would involve or result in any material conflict of interest with respect to any investor in a transaction arising out of such activity. . . .

(c) Exception.—The prohibitions of subsection (a) shall not apply to—

(1) risk-mitigating hedging activities in connection with positions or holdings arising out of the underwriting, placement, initial purchase, or sponsorship of an asset-backed security, provided that such activities are designed to reduce the specific risks to the underwriter, placement agent, initial purchaser, or sponsor associated with positions or holdings arising out of such underwriting, placement, initial purchase, or sponsorship; or

(2) purchases or sales of asset-backed securities made pursuant to and consistent with—

(A) commitments of the underwriter, placement agent, initial purchaser, or sponsor, or any affiliate or subsidiary of any such entity, to provide liquidity for the asset-backed security, or

(B) bona fide market-making in the asset backed security. . . .

§ 77z-3. General Exemptive Authority

The Commission, by rule or regulation, may conditionally or unconditionally exempt any person, security, or transaction, or any class or classes of persons, securities, or transactions, from any provision or provisions of this Act or of any rule or regulation issued under this Act, to the extent that such exemption is necessary or appropriate in the public interest, and is consistent with the protection of investors.

SECURITIES AND EXCHANGE ACT OF 1934

§ 78c. Definitions and Application

(a) **Definitions.**—When used in this Act, unless the context otherwise requires— . . .

(4) **Broker.**—

(A) **In general.**—The term "broker" means any person engaged in the business of effecting transactions in securities for the account of others.

(B) **Exception for certain bank activities.**—A bank shall not be considered to be a broker because the bank engages in any one or more of the following activities under the conditions described:

(i) **Third party brokerage arrangements.**—The bank enters into a contractual or other written arrangement with a broker or dealer registered under this Act under which the broker or dealer offers brokerage services on or off the premises of the bank if—

(I) such broker or dealer is clearly identified as the person performing the brokerage services;

(II) the broker or dealer performs brokerage services in an area that is clearly marked and, to the extent practicable, physically separate from the routine deposit taking activities of the bank;

(III) any materials used by the bank to advertise or promote generally the availability of brokerage services under the arrangement clearly indicate that the brokerage services are being provided by the broker or dealer and not by the bank;

(IV) any materials used by the bank to advertise or promote generally the availability of brokerage services under the arrangement are in compliance with the Federal securities laws before distribution;

(V) bank employees (other than associated persons of a broker or dealer who are qualified pursuant to the rules of a self-regulatory organization) perform only clerical or ministerial functions in connection with brokerage transactions including scheduling appointments with the associated persons of a broker or dealer, except that bank employees may forward customer funds or securities and may describe in general terms the types of investment vehicles available from the bank and the broker or dealer under the arrangement;

(VI) bank employees do not receive incentive compensation for any brokerage transaction unless such employees are associated persons of a broker or dealer and are qualified pursuant to the rules of a self-regulatory organization, except that the bank employees may receive compensation for the referral of any customer if the compensation is a nominal one-time cash fee of a fixed dollar amount and the payment of the fee is not contingent on whether the referral results in a transaction;

(VII) such services are provided by the broker or dealer on a basis in which all customers that receive any services are fully disclosed to the broker or dealer;

(VIII) the bank does not carry a securities account of the customer except as permitted under clause (ii) or (viii) of this subparagraph; and

(IX) the bank, broker, or dealer informs each customer that the brokerage services are provided by the broker or dealer and not by the bank and that the securities are not deposits or other obligations of the bank, are not guaranteed by the bank, and are not insured by the Federal Deposit Insurance Corporation.

(ii) Trust activities.—The bank effects transactions in a trustee capacity, or effects transactions in a fiduciary capacity in its trust department or other department that is regularly examined by bank examiners for compliance with fiduciary principles and standards, and—

(I) is chiefly compensated for such transactions, consistent with fiduciary principles and standards, on the basis of an administration or annual fee (payable on a monthly, quarterly, or other basis), a percentage of assets under management, or a flat or capped per order processing fee equal to not more than the cost incurred by the bank in connection with executing securities transactions for trustee and fiduciary customers, or any combination of such fees; and

(II) does not publicly solicit brokerage business, other than by advertising that it effects transactions in securities in conjunction with advertising its other trust activities.

(iii) Permissible securities transactions.—The bank effects transactions in—

(I) commercial paper, bankers acceptances, or commercial bills;

(II) exempted securities;

(III) qualified Canadian government obligations as defined in § 24 of title 12, in conformity with § 78o-5 of this title and the rules and regulations thereunder, or obligations of the North American Development Bank; or

(IV) any standardized, credit enhanced debt security issued by a foreign government pursuant to the March 1989 plan of then

Secretary of the Treasury Brady, used by such foreign government to retire outstanding commercial bank loans.

(iv) **Certain stock purchase plans.**—

(I) **Employee benefit plans.**—The bank effects transactions, as part of its transfer agency activities, in the securities of an issuer as part of any pension, retirement, profit-sharing, bonus, thrift, savings, incentive, or other similar benefit plan for the employees of that issuer or its affiliates (as defined in § 1841 of title 12, if the bank does not solicit transactions or provide investment advice with respect to the purchase or sale of securities in connection with the plan.

(II) **Dividend reinvestment plans.**—The bank effects transactions, as part of its transfer agency activities, in the securities of an issuer as part of that issuer's dividend reinvestment plan, if—

(aa) the bank does not solicit transactions or provide investment advice with respect to the purchase or sale of securities in connection with the plan; and

(bb) "the bank does not net shareholders" buy and sell orders, other than for programs for odd-lot holders or plans registered with the Commission.

(III) **Issuer plans.**—The bank effects transactions, as part of its transfer agency activities, in the securities of an issuer as part of a plan or program for the purchase or sale of that issuer's shares, if—

(aa) the bank does not solicit transactions or provide investment advice with respect to the purchase or sale of securities in connection with the plan or program; and

(bb) the bank does not net shareholders' buy and sell orders, other than for programs for odd-lot holders or plans registered with the Commission.

(IV) **Permissible delivery of materials.**—The exception to being considered a broker for a bank engaged in activities described in subclauses (I), (II), and (III) will not be affected by delivery of written or electronic plan materials by a bank to employees of the issuer, shareholders of the issuer, or members of affinity groups of the issuer, so long as such materials are—

(aa) comparable in scope or nature to that permitted by the Commission as of the date of the enactment of the Gramm-Leach-Bliley Act; or

(bb) otherwise permitted by the Commission.

(v) **Sweep accounts.**—The bank effects transactions as part of a program for the investment or reinvestment of deposit funds into any no-load, open-end management investment company registered under the Investment Company Act of 1940 that holds itself out as a money market fund.

(vi) Affiliate transactions.—The bank effects transactions for the account of any affiliate of the bank (as defined in § 1841 of title 12) other than—

(I) a registered broker or dealer; or

(II) an affiliate that is engaged in merchant banking, as described in § 1843(k)(4)(H) of title 12.

(vii) Private securities offerings.—The bank—

(I) effects sales as part of a primary offering of securities not involving a public offering, pursuant to § 77c(b), § 77d(4), or § 77d(6) or the rules and regulations issued thereunder;

(II) ... is not affiliated with a broker or dealer that has been registered for more than 1 year in accordance with this Act, and engages in dealing, market making, or underwriting activities, other than with respect to exempted securities; and

(III) if the bank is not affiliated with a broker or dealer, does not effect any primary offering described in subclause (1) the aggregate amount of which exceeds 25 percent of the capital of the bank, except that the limitation of this subclause shall not apply with respect to any sale of government securities or municipal securities.

(viii) Safekeeping and custody activities.—

(I) In general.—The bank, as part of customary banking activities—

(aa) provides safekeeping or custody services with respect to securities, including the exercise of warrants and other rights on behalf of customers;

(bb) facilitates the transfer of funds or securities, as a custodian or a clearing agency, in connection with the clearance and settlement of its customers' transactions in securities;

(cc) effects securities lending or borrowing transactions with or on behalf of customers as part of services provided to customers pursuant to division (aa) or (bb) or invests cash collateral pledged in connection with such transactions;

(dd) holds securities pledged by a customer to another person or securities subject to purchase or resale agreements involving a customer, or facilitates the pledging or transfer of such securities by book entry or as otherwise provided under applicable law, if the bank maintains records separately identifying the securities and the customer; or

(ee) serves as a custodian or provider of other related administrative services to any individual retirement account, pension, retirement, profit sharing, bonus, thrift savings, incentive, or other similar benefit plan.

(II) Exception for carrying broker activities.—The exception to being considered a broker for a bank engaged in activities described in subclause (I) shall not apply if the bank, in connection with such activities, acts in the United States as a carrying broker (as such term, and different formulations thereof, are used in § 78o and the rules and regulations thereunder) for any broker or dealer, unless such carrying broker activities are engaged in with respect to government securities (as defined in paragraph (42) of this subsection).

(ix) **Identified banking products**.—The bank effects transactions in identified banking products as defined in section 206 of the Gramm-Leach-Bliley Act [*see pages* 339–340].

(x) **Municipal securities**.—The bank effects transactions in municipal securities.

(xi) **De minimis exception**.—The bank effects, other than in transactions referred to in clauses (i) through (x), not more than 500 transactions in securities in any calendar year, and such transactions are not effected by an employee of the bank who is also an employee of a broker or dealer.

(C) **Execution by broker or dealer**.—The exception to being considered a broker for a bank engaged in activities described in clauses (ii), (iv), and (viii) of subparagraph (B) shall not apply if the activities described in such provisions result in the trade in the United States of any security that is a publicly traded security in the United States, unless—

(i) the bank directs such trade to a registered broker or dealer for execution;

(ii) the trade is a cross trade or other substantially similar trade of a security that—

(I) is made by the bank or between the bank and an affiliated fiduciary; and

(II) is not in contravention of fiduciary principles established under applicable Federal or State law; or

(iii) the trade is conducted in some other manner permitted under rules, regulations, or orders as the Commission may prescribe or issue.

(D) **Fiduciary capacity**.—For purposes of subparagraph (B)(ii), the term "fiduciary capacity" means—

(i) in the capacity as trustee, executor, administrator, registrar of stocks and bonds, transfer agent, guardian, assignee, receiver, or custodian under a uniform gift to minor act, or as an investment adviser if the bank receives a fee for its investment advice;

(ii) in any capacity in which the bank possesses investment discretion on behalf of another; or

(iii) in any other similar capacity.

(E) **Exception for entities subject to § 77o(e)**.—The term **"broker"** does not include a bank that—

(i) was, on November 11, 1999, subject to § 77o(e); and

(ii) is subject to such restrictions and requirements as the Commission considers appropriate.

(F) Joint rulemaking required.—The Commission and the Board of Governors of the Federal Reserve System shall jointly adopt a single set of rules or regulations to implement the exceptions in subparagraph (B).

(5) Dealer.—

(A) In general.—The term **"dealer"** means any person engaged in the business of buying and selling securities for such person's own account through a broker or otherwise.

(B) Exception for person not engaged in the business of dealing.—The term "dealer" does not include a person that buys or sells securities for such person's own account, either individually or in a fiduciary capacity, but not as a part of a regular business.

(C) Exception for certain bank activities.—A bank shall not be considered to be a dealer because the bank engages in any of the following activities under the conditions described:

(i) Permissible securities transactions.—The bank buys or sells—

(I) commercial paper, bankers acceptances, or commercial bills;

(II) exempted securities;

(III) qualified Canadian government obligations as defined in § 24 of title 12, in conformity with § 78o-5 of this title and the rules and regulations thereunder, or obligations of the North American Development Bank; or

(IV) any standardized, credit enhanced debt security issued by a foreign government pursuant to the March 1989 plan of then Secretary of the Treasury Brady, used by such foreign government to retire outstanding commercial bank loans.

(ii) Investment, trustee, and fiduciary transactions.—The bank buys or sells securities for investment purposes—

(I) for the bank; or

(II) for accounts for which the bank acts as a trustee or fiduciary.

(iii) Asset-backed transactions.—The bank engages in the issuance or sale to qualified investors, through a grantor trust or other separate entity, of securities backed by or representing an interest in notes, drafts, acceptances, loans, leases, receivables, other obligations (other than securities of which the bank is not the issuer), or pools of any such obligations predominantly originated by

(I) the bank;

(II) an affiliate of any such bank other than a broker or dealer; or

(III) a syndicate of banks of which the bank is a member, if the obligations or pool of obligations consists of mortgage obligations or consumer-related receivables.

(iv) Identified banking products.—The bank buys or sells identified banking products, as defined in section 206 of the Gramm-Leach-Bliley Act *[see pages 339–340]*.

(6) The term **"bank"** means (A) a banking institution organized under the laws of the United States or a Federal savings association, as defined in § 1462(5) of title 12, (B) a member bank of the Federal Reserve System, (C) any other banking institution or savings association, as defined in § 1462(4) of that title, whether incorporated or not, doing business under the laws of any State or of the United States, a substantial portion of the business of which consists of receiving deposits or exercising fiduciary powers similar to those permitted to national banks . . . , and which is supervised and examined by State or Federal authority having supervision over banks or savings associations, and which is not operated for the purpose of evading the provisions of this Act, and (D) a receiver, conservator, or other liquidating agent of any institution or firm included in clauses (A), (B), or (C) of this paragraph. . . .

(8) The term **"issuer"** means any person who issues or proposes to issue any security; except that with respect to certificates of deposit for securities, voting-trust certificates, or collateral-trust certificates, or with respect to certificates of interest or shares in an unincorporated investment trust not having a board of directors or of the fixed, restricted management, or unit type, the term "issuer" means the person or persons performing the acts and assuming the duties of depositor or manager pursuant to the provisions of the trust or other agreement or instrument under which such securities are issued; and except that with respect to equipment-trust certificates or like securities, the term "issuer" means the person by whom the equipment or property is, or is to be, used. . . .

(12) (A) The term **"exempted security"** or "exempted securities" includes—

> (i) government securities, as defined in paragraph (42) of this subsection;
>
> (ii) municipal securities, as defined in paragraph (29) of this subsection;
>
> (iii) any interest or participation in any common trust fund or similar fund that is excluded from the definition of the term 'investment company' under § 80a-3(c)(3);
>
> (iv) any interest or participation in a single trust fund, or a collective trust fund maintained by a bank, or any security arising out of a contract issued by an insurance company, which interest, participation, or security is issued in connection with a qualified plan as defined in subparagraph (C) of this paragraph;
>
> (v) any security issued by or any interest or participation in any pooled income fund, collective trust fund, collective investment fund,

or similar fund that is excluded from the definition of an investment company under § 80a-3(c)(10)(B);

(vi) solely for purposes of §§ 78*l*, 78m, 78n, and 78p, any security issued by or any interest or participation in any church plan, company, or account that is excluded from the definition of an investment company under § 80a-3(c)(14); and

(vii) such other securities (which may include, among others, unregistered securities, the market in which is predominantly intrastate) as the Commission may, by such rules and regulations as it deems consistent with the public interest and the protection of investors, either unconditionally or upon specified terms and conditions or for stated periods, exempt from the operation of any one or more provisions of this Act which by their terms do not apply to an "exempted security" or to "exempted securities". . . .

(18) The term **"person associated with a broker or dealer"** or "associated person of a broker or dealer" means any partner, officer, director, or branch manager of such broker or dealer (or any person occupying a similar status or performing similar functions), any person directly or indirectly controlling, controlled by, or under common control with such broker or dealer, or any employee of such broker or dealer, except that any person associated with a broker or dealer whose functions are solely clerical or ministerial shall not be included in the meaning of such term for purposes of § 78o(b) (other than paragraph (6) thereof). . . .

(21) The term **"person associated with a member"** or "associated person of a member" when used with respect to a member of a national securities exchange or registered securities association means any partner, officer, director, or branch manager of such member (or any person occupying a similar status or performing similar functions), any person directly or indirectly controlling, controlled by, or under common control with such member, or any employee of such member. . . .

(26) The term **"self-regulatory organization"** means any national securities exchange, registered securities association, or registered clearing agency. . . .

(38) The term **"market maker"** means any specialist permitted to act as a dealer, any dealer acting in the capacity of block positioner, and any dealer who, with respect to a security, holds himself out (by entering quotations in an inter-dealer communications system or otherwise) as being willing to buy and sell such security for his own account on a regular or continuous basis.

(42) The term **"government securities"** means—

(A) securities which are direct obligations of, or obligations guaranteed as to principal or interest by, the United States;

(B) securities which are issued or guaranteed by the Tennessee Valley Authority or by corporations in which the United States has a direct or indirect interest and which are designated by the Secretary of the

Treasury for exemption as necessary or appropriate in the public interest or for the protection of investors;

(C) securities issued or guaranteed as to principal or interest by any corporation the securities of which are designated, by statute specifically naming such corporation, to constitute exempt securities within the meaning of the laws administered by the Commission;

(D) for purposes of §§ 78o-5 and 78q-1, any put, call, straddle, option, or privilege on a security described in subparagraph (A), (B), or (C) other than a put, call, straddle, option, or privilege—

(i) that is traded on one or more national securities exchanges; or

(ii) for which quotations are disseminated through an automated quotation system operated by a registered securities association; or

(E) for purposes of §§ 78o, 78o-5, and 78q-1 as applied to a bank, a qualified Canadian government obligation . . . as defined in § 24 of title 12. . . .

(46) The term **"financial institution"** means—

(A) a bank (as defined in paragraph (6) of this subsection);

(B) a foreign bank (as such term is used in the International Banking Act of 1978); and

(C) a savings association (as defined in § 1813(b) of title 12) the deposits of which are insured by the Federal Deposit Insurance Corporation.

(47) The term **"securities laws"** means the Securities Act of 1933, the Securities Exchange Act of 1934, the Sarbanes-Oxley Act of 2002, the Public Utility Holding Company Act of 1935, the Trust Indenture Act of 1939, the Investment Company Act of 1940, the Investment Advisers Act of 1940, and the Securities Investor Protection Act of 1970.

(54) Qualified investor.—

(A) **Definition.**—Except as provided in subparagraph (B), for purposes of this Act, the term "qualified investor" means—

(i) any investment company registered with the Commission under § 80a-8;

(ii) any issuer eligible for an exclusion from the definition of investment company pursuant to § 80a-3;

(iii) any bank . . . , savings association . . . , broker, dealer, insurance company. ., or business development company . . . ;

(iv) any small business investment company licensed by the United States Small Business Administration . . . ;

(v) any State sponsored employee benefit plan, or any other employee benefit plan, within the meaning of the Employee Retirement Income Security Act of 1974, other than an individual retirement account, if the investment decisions are made by a plan fiduciary . . . which is either a bank, savings and loan association, insurance company, or registered investment adviser;

(vi) any trust whose purchases of securities are directed by a person described in clauses (i) through (v) of this subparagraph;

(vii) any market intermediary exempt under § 80a-3(c)(2);

(viii) any associated person of a broker or dealer other than a natural person;

(ix) any foreign bank . . . ;

(x) the government of any foreign country;

(xi) any corporation, company, or partnership that owns and invests on a discretionary basis, not less than $25,000,000 in investments;

(xii) any natural person who owns and invests on a discretionary basis, not less than $25,000,000 in investments;

(xiii) any government or political subdivision, agency, or instrumentality of a government who owns and invests on a discretionary basis not less than $50,000,000 in investments; or

(xiv) any multinational or supranational entity or any agency or instrumentality thereof.

(B) Altered thresholds for asset-backed securities and loan participations.—For purposes of subsection 3(a)(5)(C)(iii) of this section and section 206(a)(5) of the Gramm-Leach-Bliley Act, the term "qualified investor" has the meaning given such term by subparagraph (A) of this paragraph except that clauses (xi) and (xii) shall be applied by substituting "$10,000,000" for "$25,000,000."

(C) Additional authority.—The Commission may, by rule or order, define a "qualified investor" as any other person, taking into consideration such factors as the financial sophistication of the person, net worth, and knowledge and experience in financial matters. . . .

(77) Asset-backed security.—The term "asset-backed security"—

(A) means a fixed-income or other security collateralized by any type of self-liquidating financial asset (including a loan, a lease, a mortgage, or a secured or unsecured receivable) that allows the holder of the security to receive payments that depend primarily on cash flow from the asset, including—

(i) a collateralized mortgage obligation;

(ii) a collateralized debt obligation;

(iii) a collateralized bond obligation;

(iv) a collateralized debt obligation of asset-backed securities;

(v) a collateralized debt obligation of collateralized debt obligations; and

(vi) a security that the Commission, by rule, determines to be an asset-backed security for purposes of this section; and

(B) does not include a security issued by a finance subsidiary held by the parent company or a company controlled by the parent company, if none of the securities issued by the finance subsidiary are held by an entity that is not controlled by the parent company. . . .

(f) Rulemaking Considerations.—Whenever pursuant to this Act the Commission is engaged in rulemaking, or in the review of a rule of a self-regulatory organization, and is required to consider or determine whether an action is necessary or appropriate in the public interest, the Commission shall also consider, in addition to the protection of investors, whether the action will promote efficiency, competition, and capital formation.

§ 78d. Securities and Exchange Commission

(a) **Establishment; Members; Term of Office**.—There is hereby established a Securities and Exchange Commission (hereinafter referred to as the "Commission") to be composed of five commissioners to be appointed by the President by and with the advice and consent of the Senate. Not more than three of such commissioners shall be members of the same political party, and in making appointments members of different political parties shall be appointed alternately as nearly as may be practicable. No commissioner shall engage in any other business, vocation, or employment than that of serving as commissioner, nor shall any commissioner participate, directly or indirectly, in any stock-market operations or transactions of a character subject to regulation by the Commission pursuant to this Act. Each commissioner shall hold office for a term of five years and until his successor is appointed and has qualified, except that he shall not so continue to serve beyond the expiration of the next session of Congress subsequent to the expiration of said fixed term of office, and except (1) any commissioner appointed to fill a vacancy occurring prior to the expiration of the term for which his predecessor was appointed shall be appointed for the remainder of such term. . . .

§ 78j. Manipulative and Deceptive Devices

It shall be unlawful for any person, directly or indirectly, by the use of any means or instrumentality of interstate commerce or of the mails, or of any facility of any national securities exchange— . . .

(b) To use or employ, in connection with the purchase or sale of any security registered on a national securities exchange or any security not so registered . . . any manipulative or deceptive device or contrivance in contravention of such rules and regulations as the Commission may prescribe as necessary or appropriate in the public interest or for the protection of investors. . . .

§ 78l. Registration Requirements for Securities

(a) **General Requirement of Registration**.—It shall be unlawful for any member, broker, or dealer to effect any transaction in any security (other than an exempted security) on a national securities exchange unless a registration is effective as to such security for such exchange in accordance with the provisions of this Act and the rules and regulations thereunder. The provisions of this subsection shall not apply in respect of a security futures product traded on a national securities exchange. . . .

§ 78m. Periodical and Other Reports

(a) Reports by Issuer of Security; Contents.—Every issuer of a security registered pursuant to § 78*l* shall file with the Commission, in accordance with such rules and regulations as the Commission may prescribe as necessary or appropriate for the proper protection of investors and to insure fair dealing in the security—

(1) such information and documents . . . as the Commission shall require to keep reasonably current the information and documents required to be included in or filed with an application or registration statement filed pursuant to § 78*l* [; and]

(2) such annual reports . . . , certified if required by the rules and regulations of the Commission by independent public accountants, and such quarterly reports . . . , as the Commission may prescribe. . . .

§ 78o. Registration and Regulation of Brokers and Dealers

(a) Registration of All Persons Utilizing Exchange Facilities to Effect Transactions; Exemptions.—

(1) It shall be unlawful for any broker or dealer which is either a person other than a natural person or a natural person not associated with a broker or dealer which is a person other than a natural person (other than such a broker or dealer whose business is exclusively intrastate and who does not make use of any facility of a national securities exchange) to make use of the mails or any means or instrumentality of interstate commerce to effect any transactions in, or to induce or attempt to induce the purchase or sale of, any security (other than an exempted security or commercial paper, bankers' acceptances, or commercial bills) unless such broker or dealer is registered in accordance with subsection (b) of this section.

(2) The Commission, by rule or order, as it deems consistent with the public interest and the protection of investors, may conditionally or unconditionally exempt from paragraph (1) of this subsection any broker or dealer or class of brokers or dealers specified in such rule or order.

(b) Manner of Registration of Brokers and Dealers.—

(1) A broker or dealer may be registered by filing with the Commission an application for registration in such form and containing such

Securities and Exchange Act of 1934 15 U.S.C. § 78o

information and documents concerning such broker or dealer and any persons associated with such broker or dealer as the Commission, by rule, may prescribe as necessary or appropriate in the public interest or for the protection of investors. Within forty-five days of the date of the filing of such application . . . , the Commission shall—

    (A) by order grant registration, or

    (B) institute proceedings to determine whether registration should be denied. . . .

(c) Use of Manipulative or Deceptive Devices; Contravention of Rules and Regulations.—

(1) (A) No broker or dealer shall make use of the mails or any means or instrumentality of interstate commerce to effect any transaction in, or to induce or attempt to induce the purchase or sale of, any security (other than commercial paper, bankers' acceptances, or commercial bills) otherwise than on a national securities exchange of which it is a member, . . . by means of any manipulative, deceptive, or other fraudulent device or contrivance.

(2) (A) No broker or dealer shall make use of the mails or any means or instrumentality of interstate commerce to effect any transaction in, or to induce or attempt to induce the purchase or sale of, any security (other than an exempted security or commercial paper, bankers' acceptances, or commercial bills) otherwise than on a national securities exchange of which it is a member, in connection with which such broker or dealer engages in any fraudulent, deceptive, or manipulative act or practice, or makes any fictitious quotation. . . .

(3) (A) No broker or dealer . . . shall make use of the mails or any means or instrumentality of interstate commerce to effect any transaction in, or to induce or attempt to induce the purchase or sale of, any security (other than an exempted security (except a government security) or commercial paper, bankers' acceptances, or commercial bills) in contravention of such rules and regulations as the Commission shall prescribe as necessary or appropriate in the public interest or for the protection of investors to provide safeguards with respect to the financial responsibility and related practices of brokers and dealers including, but not limited to, the acceptance of custody and use of customers' securities and the carrying and use of customers' deposits or credit balances. Such rules and regulations shall (A) require the maintenance of reserves with respect to customers' deposits or credit balances, and (B) . . . establish minimum financial responsibility requirements for all brokers and dealers. . . .

(5) No dealer (other than a specialist registered on a national securities exchange) acting in the capacity of market maker or otherwise shall make use of the mails or any means or instrumentality of interstate commerce to effect any transaction in, or to induce or attempt to induce the purchase or sale of, any security (other than an exempted security or a municipal

security) in contravention of such specified and appropriate standards with respect to dealing as the Commission, by rule, shall prescribe as necessary or appropriate in the public interest and for the protection of investors, to maintain fair and orderly markets, or to remove impediments to and perfect the mechanism of a national market system. Under the rules of the Commission a dealer in a security may be prohibited from acting as a broker in that security. . . .

(f) Prevention of Misuse of Material, Nonpublic Information.—Every registered broker or dealer shall establish, maintain, and enforce written policies and procedures reasonably designed, taking into consideration the nature of such broker's or dealer's business, to prevent the misuse in violation of this Act, or the rules or regulations thereunder, of material, nonpublic information by such broker or dealer or any person associated with such broker or dealer. The Commission, as it deems necessary or appropriate in the public interest or for the protection of investors, shall adopt rules or regulations to require specific policies or procedures reasonably designed to prevent misuse in violation of this Act (or the rules or regulations thereunder) of material, nonpublic information. . . .

(h) Limitations on State Law.—

(1) Capital, margin, books and records, bonding, and reports.—No law, rule, regulation, or order, or other administrative action of any State or political subdivision thereof shall establish capital, custody, margin, financial responsibility, making and keeping records, bonding, or financial or operational reporting requirements for brokers, dealers, municipal securities dealers, government securities brokers, or government securities dealers that differ from, or are in addition to, the requirements in those areas established under this Act. The Commission shall consult periodically the securities commissions (or any agency or office performing like functions) of the States concerning the adequacy of such requirements as established under this Act.

(2) De minimis transactions by associated persons.—No law, rule, regulation, or order, or other administrative action of any State or political subdivision thereof may prohibit an associated person of a broker or dealer from effecting a transaction described in paragraph (3) for a customer in such State if—

(A) such associated person is not ineligible to register with such State for any reason other than such a transaction;

(B) such associated person is registered with a registered securities association and at least one State; and

(C) the broker or dealer with which such person is associated is registered with such State.

(3) Described transactions.—

(A) **In general.**—A transaction is described in this paragraph if—

(i) such transaction is effected—

(I) on behalf of a customer that, for 30 days prior to the day of the transaction, maintained an account with the broker or dealer; and

(II) by an associated person of the broker or dealer—

(aa) to which the customer was assigned for 14 days prior to the day of the transaction; and

(bb) who is registered with a State in which the customer was a resident or was present for at least 30 consecutive days during the 1-year period prior to the day of the transaction; or

(ii) the transaction is effected—

(I) on behalf of a customer that, for 30 days prior to the day of the transaction, maintained an account with the broker or dealer; and

(II) during the period beginning on the date on which such associated person files an application for registration with the State in which the transaction is effected and ending on the earlier of—

(aa) 60 days after the date on which the application is filed; or

(bb) the date on which such State notifies the associated person that it has denied the application for registration or has stayed the pendency of the application for cause.

(B) Rules of construction.—For purposes of subparagraph (A)(i)(II)—

(i) each of up to 3 associated persons of a broker or dealer who are designated to effect transactions during the absence or unavailability of the principal associated person for a customer may be treated as an associated person to which such customer is assigned; and

(ii) if the customer is present in another State for 30 or more consecutive days or has permanently changed his or her residence to another State, a transaction is not described in this paragraph, unless the associated person of the broker or dealer files an application for registration with such State not later than 10 business days after the later of the date of the transaction, or the date of the discovery of the presence of the customer in the other State for 30 or more consecutive days or the change in the customer's residence. . . .

§ 78o-3. Registered Securities Associations

(a) Registration; Application.—An association of brokers and dealers may be registered as a national securities association pursuant to subsection (b), or as an affiliated securities association pursuant to subsection (d), under the terms and conditions hereinafter provided in this section and in accordance with the provisions of § 78s(a), by filing with the Commission an application for registration in such form as the Commission, by rule, may prescribe containing the rules of the association and such other information and documents as the Commission, by rule, may prescribe as necessary or appropriate in the public interest or for the protection of investors.

(b) Determinations by Commission Requisite to Registration of Applicant as National Securities Association.—An association of brokers and dealers shall not be registered as a national securities association unless the Commission determines that—

(1) By reason of the number and geographical distribution of its members and the scope of their transactions, such association will be able to carry out the purposes of this section.

(2) Such association is so organized and has the capacity to be able to carry out the purposes of this Act and to comply, and (subject to any rule or order of the Commission pursuant to § 78q(d) or § 78s(g)(2)) to enforce compliance by its members and persons associated with its members, with the provisions of this Act, the rules and regulations thereunder, . . . and the rules of the association.

(3) Subject to the provisions of subsection (g) of this section, the rules of the association provide that any registered broker or dealer may become a member of such association and any person may become associated with a member thereof.

(4) The rules of the association assure a fair representation of its members in the selection of its directors and administration of its affairs and provide that one or more directors shall be representative of issuers and investors and not be associated with a member of the association, broker, or dealer.

(5) The rules of the association provide for the equitable allocation of reasonable dues, fees, and other charges among members and issuers and other persons using any facility or system which the association operates or controls.

(6) The rules of the association are designed to prevent fraudulent and manipulative acts and practices, to promote just and equitable principles of trade, to foster cooperation and coordination with persons engaged in regulating, clearing, settling, processing information with respect to, and facilitating transactions in securities, to remove impediments to and perfect the mechanism of a free and open market and a national market system, and, in general, to protect investors and the public interest; and are not designed to permit unfair discrimination between customers, issuers, brokers, or dealers, to fix minimum profits, to impose any schedule or fix rates of commissions, allowances, discounts, or other fees to be charged by its members, or to regulate by virtue of any authority conferred by this Act matters not related to the purposes of this Act or the administration of the association.

(7) The rules of the association provide that (subject to any rule or order of the Commission pursuant to § 78q(d) or § 78s(g)(2)) its members and persons associated with its members shall be appropriately disciplined for violation of any provision of this Act, the rules or regulations

thereunder, ... or the rules of the association, by expulsion, suspension, limitation of activities, functions, and operations, fine, censure, being suspended or barred from being associated with a member, or any other fitting sanction.

(8) The rules of the association are in accordance with the provisions of subsection (h) of this section, and, in general, provide a fair procedure for the disciplining of members and persons associated with members, the denial of membership to any person seeking membership therein, the barring of any person from becoming associated with a member thereof, and the prohibition or limitation by the association of any person with respect to access to services offered by the association or a member thereof.

(9) The rules of the association do not impose any burden on competition not necessary or appropriate in furtherance of the purposes of this Act.

(10) The requirements of subsection (c), insofar as these may be applicable, are satisfied.

(11) The rules of the association include provisions governing the form and content of quotations relating to securities sold otherwise than on a national securities exchange which may be distributed or published by any member or person associated with a member, and the persons to whom such quotations may be supplied. Such rules relating to quotations shall be designed to produce fair and informative quotations, to prevent fictitious or misleading quotations, and to promote orderly procedures for collecting, distributing, and publishing quotations. . . .

Note to § 78c on the Definition of "Identified Banking Product"

15 U.S.C. § 78c twice refers to "identified banking products as defined in section 206 of the Gramm-Leach-Bliley Act." 15 U.S.C. § 78c(a)(4)(B)(ix), (5)(B)(iv).

Gramm-Leach-Bliley Act § 206, which is not codified in the U.S. Code, reads as follows:

(a) Definition of Identified Banking Product.—For purposes of § 78c(a)(4) and (5), the term "identified banking product" means—

(1) a deposit account, savings account, certificate of deposit, or other deposit instrument issued by a bank;

(2) a banker's acceptance;

(3) a letter of credit issued or loan made by a bank;

(4) a debit account at a bank arising from a credit card or similar arrangement;

(5) a participation in a loan which the bank or an affiliate of the bank (other than a broker or dealer) funds, participates in, or owns that is sold—

(A) to qualified investors; or

(B) to other persons that—

(i) have the opportunity to review and assess any material information, including information regarding the borrower's credit worthiness; and

(ii) based on such factors as financial sophistication, net worth, and knowledge and experience in financial matters, have the capability to evaluate the information available, as determined under generally applicable banking standards or guidelines; or

(6) any swap agreement, including credit and equity swaps, except that an equity swap that is sold directly to any person other than a qualified investor . . . shall not be treated as an identified banking product.

(b) Definition of Swap Agreement.—For purposes of subsection (a)(6), the term "swap agreement" means any individually negotiated contract, agreement, warrant, note, or option that is based, in whole or in part, on the value of, any interest in, or any quantitative measure or the occurrence of any event relating to, one or more commodities, securities, currencies, interest or other rates, indices, or other assets, but does not include any other identified banking product, as defined in paragraphs (1) through (5) of subsection (a).

(c) Classification Limited.—Classification of a particular product as an identified banking product pursuant to this section shall not be construed as finding or implying that such product is or is not a security for any purpose under the securities laws, or is or is not an account, agreement, contract, or transaction for any purpose under the Commodity Exchange Act. . . .

INVESTMENT COMPANY ACT OF 1940

§ 80a-2. General Definitions

(a) Definitions.—When used in this Act, unless the context otherwise requires— . . .

(2) **"Affiliated company"** means a company which is an affiliated person.

(3) **"Affiliated person"** of another person means (A) any person directly or indirectly owning, controlling, or holding with power to vote, 5 per centum or more of the outstanding voting securities of such other person; (B) any person 5 per centum or more of whose outstanding voting securities are directly or indirectly owned, controlled, or held with power to vote, by such other person; (C) any person directly or indirectly controlling, controlled by, or under common control with, such other person; (D) any officer, director, partner, copartner, or employee of such other person; (E) if such other person is an investment company, any investment adviser thereof or any member of an advisory board thereof; and (F) if such other person is an unincorporated investment company not having a board of directors, the depositor thereof. . . .

(7) **"Commission"** means the Securities and Exchange Commission.

(8) **"Company"** means a corporation, a partnership, an association, a joint-stock company, a trust, a fund, or any organized group of persons whether incorporated or not. . . .

(9) **"Control"** means the power to exercise a controlling influence over the management or policies of a company, unless such power is solely the result of an official position with such company. Any person who owns beneficially, either directly or through one or more controlled companies, more than 25 per centum of the voting securities of a company shall be presumed to control such company. Any person who does not so own more than 25 per centum of the voting securities of any company shall be presumed not to control such company. A natural person shall be presumed not to be a controlled person within the meaning of this Act. Any such presumption may be rebutted by evidence, but except as hereinafter provided, shall continue until a determination to the contrary made by the Commission. . . .

(19) **"Interested person"** of another person means—

(A) when used with respect to an investment company—

(i) any affiliated person of such company,

(ii) any member of the immediate family of any natural person who is an affiliated person of such company,

(iii) any interested person of any investment adviser of or principal underwriter for such company,

(iv) any person or partner or employee of any person who at any time since the beginning of the last two completed fiscal years of such company has acted as legal counsel for such company,

(v) any person or any affiliated person of a person (other than a registered investment company) that, at any time during the 6-month period preceding the date of the determination of whether that person or affiliated person is an interested person, has executed any portfolio transactions for, engaged in any principal transactions with, or distributed shares for—

(I) the investment company;

(II) any other investment company having the same investment adviser as such investment company or holding itself out to investors as a related company for purposes of investment or investor services; or

(III) any account over which the investment company's investment adviser has brokerage placement discretion,

(vi) any person or any affiliated person of a person (other than a registered investment company) that, at any time during the 6-month period preceding the date of the determination of whether that person or affiliated person is an interested person, has loaned money or other property to—

(I) the investment company;

(II) any other investment company having the same investment adviser as such investment company or holding itself out to investors as a related company for purposes of investment or investor services; or

(III) any account for which the investment company's investment adviser has borrowing authority, [and]

(vii) any natural person whom the Commission by order shall have determined to be an interested person by reason of having had, at any time since the beginning of the last two completed fiscal years of such company, a material business or professional relationship with such company or with the principal executive officer of such company or with any other investment company having the same investment adviser or principal underwriter or with the principal executive officer of such other investment company:

Provided, That no person shall be deemed to be an interested person of an investment company solely by reason of (aa) his being a member of its board of directors or advisory board or an owner of its securities, or (bb) his membership in the immediate family of any person specified in clause (aa) of this proviso; and

(B) when used with respect to an investment adviser of or principal underwriter for any investment company—

(i) any affiliated person of such investment adviser or principal underwriter,

(ii) any member of the immediate family of any natural person who is an affiliated person of such investment advisor or principal underwriter,

(iii) any person who knowingly has any direct or indirect beneficial interest in, or who is designated as trustee, executor, or guardian of any legal interest in, any security issued either by such investment adviser or principal underwriter or by a controlling person of such investment adviser or principal underwriter,

(iv) any person or partner or employee of any person who at any time since the beginning of the last two completed fiscal years of such investment company has acted as legal counsel for such investment adviser or principal underwriter,

(v) any person or any affiliated person of a person (other than a registered investment company) that, at any time during the 6-month period preceding the date of the determination of whether that person or affiliated person is an interested person, has executed any portfolio transactions for, engaged in any principal transactions with, or distributed shares for—

(I) any investment company for which the investment adviser or principal underwriter serves as such;

(II) any investment company holding itself out to investors, for purposes of investment or investor services, as a company related to any investment company for which the investment adviser or principal underwriter serves as such; or

(III) any account over which the investment adviser has brokerage placement discretion,

(vi) any person or any affiliated person of a person (other than a registered investment company) that, at any time during the 6-month period preceding the date of the determination of whether that person or affiliated person is an interested person, has loaned money or other property to—

(I) any investment company for which the investment adviser or principal underwriter serves as such;

(II) any investment company holding itself out to investors, for purposes of investment or investor services, as a company related to any investment company for which the investment adviser or principal underwriter serves as such; or

(III) any account for which the investment adviser has borrowing authority,

(vii) any natural person whom the Commission by order shall have determined to be an interested person by reason of having had at any time since the beginning of the last two completed fiscal years of such investment company a material business or professional relationship with such investment adviser or principal underwriter or with the principal executive officer or any controlling person of such investment adviser or principal underwriter.

For the purposes of this paragraph (19), "member of the immediate family" means any parent, spouse of a parent, child, spouse of a child, spouse, brother, or sister, and includes step and adoptive relationships. . . .

(20) "Investment adviser" of an investment company means (A) any person (other than a bona fide officer, director, trustee, member of an advisory board, or employee of such company, as such) who pursuant to contract with such company regularly furnishes advice to such company with respect to the desirability of investing in, purchasing or selling securities or other property, or is empowered to determine what securities or other property shall be purchased or sold by such company, and (B) any other person who pursuant to contract with a person described in clause (A) regularly performs substantially all of the duties undertaken by such person described in clause (A); but does not include (i) a person whose advice is furnished solely through uniform publications distributed to subscribers thereto, (ii) a person who furnishes only statistical and other factual information, advice regarding economic factors and trends, or advice as to occasional transactions in specific securities, but without generally furnishing advice or making recommendations regarding the purchase or sale of securities, (iii) a company furnishing such services at cost to one or more investment companies, insurance companies, or other financial institutions, (iv) any person the character and amount of whose compensation for such services must be approved by a court, or (v) such other persons as the Commission may by rules and regulations or order determine not to be within the intent of this definition. . . .

(23) **"Lend"** includes a purchase coupled with an agreement by the vendor to repurchase; "borrow" includes a sale coupled with a similar agreement. . . .

(29) **"Principal underwriter"** of or for any investment company other than a closed-end company, or of any security issued by such a company, means any underwriter who as principal purchases from such company . . . any such security for distribution, or who as agent for such company sells or has the right to sell any such security to a dealer or to the public or both, but does not include a dealer who purchases from such company through a principal underwriter acting as agent for such company. . . .

(30) **"Promoter"** of a company or a proposed company means a person who, acting alone or in concert with other persons, is initiating or directing, or has within one year initiated or directed, the organization of such company.

(32) **"Redeemable security"** means any security, other than short-term paper, under the terms of which the holder, upon its presentation to the issuer or to a person designated by the issuer, is entitled . . . to receive approximately his proportionate share of the issuer's current net assets, or the cash equivalent thereof.

(34) **"Sale,"** "sell", "offer to sell", or "offer for sale" includes every contract of sale or disposition of, attempt or offer to dispose of, or solicitation of an offer to buy, a security or interest in a security, for value.

(35) **"Sales load"** means the difference between the price of a security to the public and that portion of the proceeds from its sale which is received and invested or held for investment by the issuer (or in the case of a unit investment trust, by the depositor or trustee), less any portion of such difference deducted for trustee's or custodian's fee, insurance premiums, issue taxes, or administrative expenses or fees which are not properly chargeable to sales or promotional activities. . . .

(36) **"Security"** means any note, stock, treasury stock, security future, bond, debenture, evidence of indebtedness, certificate of interest or participation in any profit-sharing agreement, collateral-trust certificate, pre-organization certificate or subscription, transferable share, investment contract, voting-trust certificate, certificate of deposit for a security, fractional undivided interest in oil, gas, or other mineral rights, any put, call, straddle, option, or privilege on any security (including a certificate of deposit) or on any group or index of securities (including any interest

therein or based on the value thereof), or any put, call, straddle, option, or privilege entered into on a national securities exchange relating to foreign currency, or, in general, any interest or instrument commonly known as a "security," or any certificate of interest or participation in, temporary or interim certificate for, receipt for, guarantee of, or warrant or right to subscribe to or purchase, any of the foregoing.

(37) **"Separate account"** means an account established and maintained by an insurance company ... under which income, gains and losses, whether or not realized, from assets allocated to such account, are, in accordance with the applicable contract, credited to or charged against such account without regard to other income, gains, or losses of the insurance company.

(38) **"Short-term paper"** means any note, draft, bill of exchange, or banker's acceptance payable on demand or having a maturity at the time of issuance of not exceeding nine months, exclusive of days of grace, or any renewal thereof payable on demand or having a maturity likewise limited; and such other classes of securities, of a commercial rather than an investment character, as the Commission may designate by rules and regulations.

(40) **"Underwriter"** means any person who has purchased from an issuer with a view to, or sells for an issuer in connection with, the distribution of any security, or participates or has a direct or indirect participation in any such undertaking, or participates or has a participation in the direct or indirect underwriting of any such undertaking; but such term shall not include a person whose interest is limited to a commission from an underwriter or dealer not in excess of the usual and customary distributor's or seller's commission. As used in this paragraph the term "issuer" shall include, in addition to an issuer, any person directly or indirectly controlling or controlled by the issuer, or any person under direct or indirect common control with the issuer. When the distribution of the securities in respect of which any person is an underwriter is completed such person shall cease to be an underwriter in respect of such securities or the issuer thereof. . . .

(42) **"Voting security"** means any security presently entitling the owner or holder thereof to vote for the election of directors of a company. . . . The vote of a majority of the outstanding voting securities of a company means the vote, at the annual or a special meeting of the security holders of such company duly called, (A) of 67 per centum or more of the voting securities present at such meeting, if the holders of more than 50 per centum of the outstanding voting securities of such company are present or represented by proxy; or (B) of more than 50 per centum of the outstanding voting securities of such company, whichever is the less.

(43) **"Wholly-owned subsidiary"** of a person means a company 95 per centum or more of the outstanding voting securities of which are owned by

such person, or by a company which, within the meaning of this paragraph, is a wholly-owned subsidiary of such person. . . .
  (51) (A) "Qualified purchaser" means—
    (i) any natural person . . . who owns not less than $5,000,000 in investments, as defined by the Commission; [or]
    (iv) any person, acting for its own account or the accounts of other qualified purchasers, who in the aggregate owns and invests on a discretionary basis, not less than $25,000,000 in investments. . . .
  (c) Rulemaking Considerations.—Whenever pursuant to this Act the Commission is engaged in rulemaking and is required to consider or determine whether an action is consistent with the public interest, the Commission shall also consider, in addition to the protection of investors, whether the action will promote efficiency, competition, and capital formation.

§ 80a-3. Definition of Investment Company

(a) Definitions.—
  (1) When used in this Act, **"investment company"** means any issuer which—
    (A) First prima facie definition.—is or holds itself out as being engaged primarily, or proposes to engage primarily, in the business of investing, reinvesting, or trading in securities; [or]
    (C) Second prima facie definition.—is engaged or proposes to engage in the business of investing, reinvesting, owning, holding, or trading in securities, and owns or proposes to acquire investment securities having a value exceeding 40 per centum of the value of such issuer's total assets (exclusive of Government securities and cash items) on an unconsolidated basis.
  (2) As used in this section, **"investment securities"** includes all securities except (A) Government securities, (B) securities issued by employees' securities companies, and (C) securities issued by majority-owned subsidiaries of the owner which (i) are not investment companies, and (ii) are not relying on the exception from the definition of investment company in paragraph (1) or (7) of subsection (c).
  (b) Exemptions from Second Prima Facie Definition.—Notwithstanding paragraph (1)(C) of subsection (a), none of the following persons is an investment company within the meaning of this Act:
    (1) Any issuer primarily engaged, directly or through a wholly-owned subsidiary or subsidiaries, in a business or businesses other than that of investing, reinvesting, owning, holding, or trading in securities.
    (2) Any issuer which the Commission, upon application by such issuer, finds and by order declares to be primarily engaged in a business or businesses other than that of investing, reinvesting, owning, holding, or trading

Investment Company Act of 1940   15 U.S.C. § 80a-3

in securities either directly or (A) through majority-owned subsidiaries or (B) through controlled companies conducting similar types of businesses. . . .

(3) Any issuer all the outstanding securities of which (other than short-term paper and directors' qualifying shares) are directly or indirectly owned by a company excepted from the definition of investment company by paragraph (1) or (2) of this subsection.

(c) Full Exemptions.—Notwithstanding subsection (a), none of the following persons is an investment company within the meaning of this Act:

(1) Any issuer whose outstanding securities (other than short-term paper) are beneficially owned by not more than one hundred persons and which is not making and does not presently propose to make a public offering of its securities. Such issuer shall be deemed to be an investment company for purposes of the limitations set forth in subparagraphs (A)(i) and (B)(i) of § 80a–12(d)(1) governing the purchase or other acquisition by such issuer of any security issued by any registered investment company and the sale of any security issued by any registered open-end investment company to any such issuer. For purposes of this paragraph:

(A) Beneficial ownership by a company shall be deemed to be beneficial ownership by one person, except that, if the company owns 10 per centum or more of the outstanding voting securities of the issuer, and is or, but for the exception provided for in this paragraph or paragraph (7), would be an investment company, the beneficial ownership shall be deemed to be that of the holders of such company's outstanding securities (other than short-term paper). . . .

(2) (A) Any person primarily engaged in the business of underwriting and distributing securities issued by other persons, selling securities to customers, acting as broker, and acting as market intermediary, or any one or more of such activities, whose gross income normally is derived principally from such business and related activities. . . .

(3) Any bank or insurance company; any savings and loan association, building and loan association, cooperative bank, homestead association, or similar institution, or any receiver, conservator, liquidator, liquidating agent, or similar official or person thereof or therefor; or any common trust fund or similar fund maintained by a bank exclusively for the collective investment and reinvestment of moneys contributed thereto by the bank in its capacity as a trustee, executor, administrator, or guardian, if—

(A) such fund is employed by the bank solely as an aid to the administration of trusts, estates, or other accounts created and maintained for a fiduciary purpose;

(B) except in connection with the ordinary advertising of the bank's fiduciary services, interests in such fund are not—

(i) advertised; or

(ii) offered for sale to the general public; and

(C) fees and expenses charged by such fund are not in contravention of fiduciary principles established under applicable Federal or State law.

(4) Any person substantially all of whose business is confined to making small loans, industrial banking, or similar businesses.

(5) Any person who is not engaged in the business of issuing redeemable securities, face-amount certificates of the installment type or periodic payment plan certificates, and who is primarily engaged in one or more of the following businesses: (A) Purchasing or otherwise acquiring notes, drafts, acceptances, open accounts receivable, and other obligations representing part or all of the sales price of merchandise, insurance, and services; (B) making loans to manufacturers, wholesalers, and retailers of, and to prospective purchasers of, specified merchandise, insurance, and services; and (C) purchasing or otherwise acquiring mortgages and other liens on and interests in real estate.

(6) Any company primarily engaged, directly or through majority-owned subsidiaries, in one or more of the businesses described in paragraphs (3), (4), and (5), or in one or more of such businesses (from which not less than 25 centum of such company's gross income during its last fiscal year was derived) together with an additional business or businesses other than investing, reinvesting, owning, holding, or trading in securities.

(7) (A) Any issuer, the outstanding securities of which are owned exclusively by persons who, at the time of acquisition of such securities, are qualified purchasers, and which is not making and does not at that time propose to make a public offering of such securities. Securities that are owned by persons who received the securities from a qualified purchaser as a gift or bequest, or in a case in which the transfer was caused by legal separation, divorce, death, or other involuntary event, shall be deemed to be owned by a qualified purchaser, subject to such rules, regulations, and orders as the Commission may prescribe as necessary or appropriate in the public interest or for the protection of investors. . . .

(B) Notwithstanding subparagraph (A), an issuer is within the exception provided by this paragraph if—

(i) in addition to qualified purchasers, outstanding securities of that issuer are beneficially owned by not more than 100 persons who are not qualified purchasers, if—

(I) such persons acquired any portion of the securities of such issuer on or before September 1, 1996; and

(II) at the time at which such persons initially acquired the securities of such issuer, the issuer was excepted by paragraph (1); and

(ii) prior to availing itself of the exception provided by this paragraph—

(I) such issuer has disclosed to each beneficial owner, as determined under paragraph (1), that future investors will be limited to qualified purchasers, and that ownership in such issuer is no longer limited to not more than 100 persons; and

(II) concurrently with or after such disclosure, such issuer has provided each beneficial owner, as determined under paragraph (1), with a reasonable opportunity to redeem any part or all of their interests in the issuer, notwithstanding any agreement to the contrary between the issuer and such persons, for that person's proportionate share of the issuer's net assets.

(C) Each person that elects to redeem under subparagraph (B)(ii)(II) shall receive an amount in cash equal to that person's proportionate share of the issuer's net assets, unless the issuer elects to provide such person with the option of receiving, and such person agrees to receive, all or a portion of such person's share in assets of the issuer. If the issuer elects to provide such persons with such an opportunity, disclosure concerning such opportunity shall be made in the disclosure required by subparagraph (B)(ii)(I).

(D) An issuer that is excepted under this paragraph shall nonetheless be deemed to be an investment company for purposes of the limitations set forth in subparagraphs (A)(i) and (B)(i) of § 80a–12(d)(1) relating to the purchase or other acquisition by such issuer of any security issued by any registered investment company and the sale of any security issued by any registered open-end investment company to any such issuer.

(E) For purposes of determining compliance with this paragraph and paragraph (1), an issuer that is otherwise excepted under this paragraph and an issuer that is otherwise excepted under paragraph (1) shall not be treated by the Commission as being a single issuer for purposes of determining whether the outstanding securities of the issuer excepted under paragraph (1) are beneficially owned by not more than 100 persons or whether the outstanding securities of the issuer excepted under this paragraph are owned by persons that are not qualified purchasers. Nothing in this subparagraph shall be construed to establish that a person is a bona fide qualified purchaser for purposes of this paragraph or a bona fide beneficial owner for purposes of paragraph (1).

(8) Any company subject to regulation under the Public Utility Holding Company Act of 1935.

(9) Any person substantially all of whose business consists of owning or holding oil, gas, or other mineral royalties or leases, or fractional interests therein, or certificates of interest or participation in or investment contracts relative to such royalties, leases, or fractional interests.

(10) (A) Any company organized and operated exclusively for religious, educational, benevolent, fraternal, charitable, or reformatory purposes—

(i) no part of the net earnings of which inures to the benefit of any private shareholder or individual; or

(ii) which is or maintains a fund described in subparagraph (B).

(B) For the purposes of subparagraph (A)(ii), a fund is described in this subparagraph if such fund is a pooled income fund, collective trust fund, collective investment fund, or similar fund maintained by a charitable organization exclusively for the collective investment and reinvestment of one or more of the following:

(i) assets of the general endowment fund or other funds of one or more charitable organizations;

(ii) assets of a pooled income fund;

(iii) assets contributed to a charitable organization in exchange for the issuance of charitable gift annuities;

(iv) assets of a charitable remainder trust or of any other trust, the remainder interests of which are irrevocably dedicated to any charitable organization;

(v) assets of a charitable lead trust;

(vi) assets of a trust, the remainder interests of which are revocably dedicated to or for the benefit of 1 or more charitable organizations, if the ability to revoke the dedication is limited to circumstances involving—

(I) an adverse change in the financial circumstances of a settlor or an income beneficiary of the trust;

(II) a change in the identity of the charitable organization or organizations having the remainder interest, provided that the new beneficiary is also a charitable organization; or

(III) both the changes described in subclauses (I) and (II);

(vii) assets of a trust not described in clauses (i) through (v), the remainder interests of which are revocably dedicated to a charitable organization, subject to subparagraph (C); or

(viii) such assets as the Commission may prescribe by rule, regulation, or order in accordance with § 80a–6(c).

(C) A fund that contains assets described in clause (vii) of subparagraph (B) shall be excluded from the definition of an investment company for a period of 3 years after the date of enactment of this subparagraph, but only if—

(i) such assets were contributed before the date which is 60 days after the date of enactment of this subparagraph; and

(ii) such assets are commingled in the fund with assets described in one or more of clauses (i) through (vi) and (viii) of subparagraph (B). . . .

(11) Any employee's stock bonus, pension, or profit-sharing trust which meets the requirements for qualification under § 401 of the Internal Revenue Code of 1986; or any governmental plan described in § 77c(a)(2)(C) of this title; or any collective trust fund maintained by a bank consisting

solely of assets of such trusts or governmental plans, or both; or any separate account the assets of which are derived solely from (A) contributions under pension or profit-sharing plans which meet the requirements of § 401 of the Internal Revenue Code of 1986 or the requirements for deduction of the employer's contribution under § 404(a)(2) of such Code, (B) contributions under governmental plans in connection with which interests, participations, or securities are exempted from the registration provisions of § 77 of this title by § 77(a)(2)(C), and (C) advances made by an insurance company in connection with the operation of such separate account.

(12) Any voting trust the assets of which consist exclusively of securities of a single issuer which is not an investment company.

(13) Any security holders' protective committee or similar issuer having outstanding and issuing no securities other than certificates of deposit and short-term paper.

(14) Any church plan described in § 414(e) of the Internal Revenue Code of 1986, if, under any such plan, no part of the assets may be used for, or diverted to, purposes other than the exclusive benefit of plan participants or beneficiaries. . . .

§ 80a-4. Classification of Investment Companies

For the purposes of this Act, investment companies are divided into three principal classes, defined as follows:

(1) **"Face-amount certificate company"** means an investment company which is engaged or proposes to engage in the business of issuing face-amount certificates of the installment type, or which has been engaged in such business and has any such certificate outstanding.

(2) **"Unit investment trust"** means an investment company which (A) is organized under a trust indenture, contract of custodianship or agency, or similar instrument, (B) does not have a board of directors, and (C) issues only redeemable securities, each of which represents an undivided interest in a unit of specified securities; but does not include a voting trust.

(3) **"Management company"** means any investment company other than a face-amount certificate company or a unit investment trust.

§ 80a-5. Subclassification of Management Companies

(a) **Open-End and Closed-End Companies.**—For the purposes of this Act, management companies are divided into open-end and closed-end companies, defined as follows:

(1) **"Open-end company"** means a management company which is offering for sale or has outstanding any redeemable security of which it is the issuer.

(2) "Closed-end company" means any management company other than an open-end company.

(b) **Diversified and Non-Diversified Companies.**—Management companies are further divided into diversified companies and non-diversified companies, defined as follows:

(1) "**Diversified company**" means a management company which meets the following requirements: At least 75 per centum of the value of its total assets is represented by cash and cash items (including receivables), Government securities, securities of other investment companies, and other securities for the purposes of this calculation limited in respect of any one issuer to an amount not greater in value than 5 per centum of the value of the total assets of such management company and to not more than 10 per centum of the outstanding voting securities of such issuer.

(2) "**Non-diversified company**" means any management company other than a diversified company. . . .

§ 80a-6. Exemptions . . .

(c) **Commission's General Exemptive Authority.**—The Commission, by rules and regulations upon its own motion, or by order upon application, may conditionally or unconditionally exempt any person, security, or transaction, or any class or classes of persons, securities, or transactions, from any provision or provisions of this Act or of any rule or regulation thereunder, if and to the extent that such exemption is necessary or appropriate in the public interest and consistent with the protection of investors and the purposes fairly intended by the policy and provisions of this Act. . . .

(e) **Application of Certain Specified Provisions of This Act to Otherwise Exempt Companies.**—If, in connection with any rule, regulation, or order under this section exempting any investment company from any provision of § 80a-7, the Commission deems it necessary or appropriate in the public interest or for the protection of investors that certain specified provisions of this Act pertaining to registered investment companies shall be applicable in respect of such company, the provisions so specified shall apply to such company, and to other persons in their transactions and relations with such company, as though such company were a registered investment company. . . .

§ 80a-7. Transactions by Unregistered Investment Companies

(a) **Interstate Transactions by Unregistered Management Company Prohibited.**—No investment company organized or otherwise created under the laws of the United States or of a State and having a board of directors, unless registered under § 80a–8, shall directly or indirectly—

Investment Company Act of 1940 15 U.S.C. § 80a-8

(1) offer for sale, sell, or deliver after sale, by the use of the mails or any means or instrumentality of interstate commerce, any security or any interest in a security, whether the issuer of such security is such investment company or another person; or offer for sale, sell, or deliver after sale any such security or interest, having reason to believe that such security or interest will be made the subject of a public offering by use of the mails or any means or instrumentality of interstate commerce;

(2) purchase, redeem, retire, or otherwise acquire or attempt to acquire, by use of the mails or any means or instrumentality of interstate commerce, any security or any interest in a security, whether the issuer of such security is such investment company or another person;

(3) control any investment company which does any of the acts enumerated in paragraphs (1) and (2);

(4) engage in any business in interstate commerce; or

(5) control any company which is engaged in any business in interstate commerce. . . .

(b) Interstate Transactions for Unregistered Unit Investment Trust.— No depositor or trustee of or underwriter for any investment company, organized or otherwise created under the laws of the United States or of a State and not having a board of directors, unless such company is registered under § 80a–8 or exempt under § 80a–6], shall directly or indirectly—

(1) offer for sale, sell, or deliver after sale, by use of the mails or any means or instrumentality of interstate commerce, any security or any interest in a security of which such company is the issuer; or offer for sale, sell, or deliver after sale any such security or interest, having reason to believe that such security or interest will be made the subject of a public offering by use of the mails or any means or instrumentality of interstate commerce;

(2) purchase, redeem, or otherwise acquire or attempt to acquire, by use of the mails or any means or instrumentality of interstate commerce, any security or any interest in a security of which such company is the issuer; or

(3) sell or purchase for the account of such company, by use of the mails or any means or instrumentality of interstate commerce, any security or interest in a security, by whomever issued. . . .

§ 80a-8. Registration of Investment Companies

(a) Notification of Registration.—Any investment company organized or otherwise created under the laws of the United States or of a State may register for the purposes of this Act by filing with the Commission a notification of registration, in such form as the Commission shall by rules and regulations prescribe as necessary or appropriate in the public interest or for the protection of investors. An investment company shall be deemed to be registered upon receipt by the Commission of such notification of registration.

(b) Registration Statement.—Every registered investment company shall file with the Commission . . . a registration statement, in such form and containing such . . . information and documents as the Commission shall by rules and regulations prescribe as necessary or appropriate in the public interest or for the protection of investors. . . .

§ 80a-10. Affiliations of Directors

(a) Proportion of Interested Directors Limited.—No registered investment company shall have a board of directors more than 60 per centum of the members of which are persons who are interested persons of such registered company.

(b) Certain Persons Disqualified.—No registered investment company shall—

(1) employ as regular broker any director, officer, or employee of such registered company, or any person of which any such director, officer, or employee is an affiliated person, unless a majority of the board of directors of such registered company shall be persons who are not such brokers or affiliated persons of any of such brokers;

(2) use as a principal underwriter of securities issued by it any director, officer, or employee of such registered company or any person of which any such director, officer, or employee is an interested person, unless a majority of the board of directors of such registered company shall be persons who are not such principal underwriters or interested persons of any of such principal underwriters; or

(3) have as director, officer, or employee any investment banker, or any affiliated person of any investment banker, unless a majority of the board of directors of such registered company shall be persons who are not investment bankers or affiliated persons of any investment banker. . . .

(c) Bank-Affiliated Directors.—No registered investment company shall have a majority of its board of directors consisting of persons who are officers, directors, or employees of any one bank (together with its affiliates and subsidiaries) or any one bank holding company (together with its affiliates and subsidiaries) . . . or any one savings and loan holding company, together with its affiliates and subsidiaries. . . .

(d) Exception for Certain No-Load, Open-End Companies.—Notwithstanding subsections (a) and (b)(2) of this section, a registered investment company may have a board of directors all the members of which, except one, are interested persons of the investment adviser of such company, or are officers or employees of such company, if—

(1) such investment company is an open-end company;

(2) such investment adviser is registered under [the Investment Advisers Act] and is engaged principally in the business of rendering investment supervisory services as defined in [that Act];

(3) no sales load is charged on securities issued by such investment company;

(4) any premium over net asset value charged by such company upon the issuance of any such security, plus any discount from net asset value charged on redemption thereof, shall not in the aggregate exceed 2 per centum;

(5) no sales or promotion expenses are incurred by such registered company; but expenses incurred in complying with laws regulating the issue or sale of securities shall not be deemed sales or promotion expenses;

(6) such investment adviser is the only investment adviser to such investment company, and such investment adviser does not receive a management fee exceeding 1 per centum per annum of the value of such company's net assets averaged over the year or taken as of a definite date or dates within the year;

(7) all executive salaries and executive expenses and office rent of such investment company are paid by such investment adviser; and

(8) such investment company has only one class of securities outstanding, each unit of which has equal voting rights with every other unit. . . .

(f) Purchasing Underwritten Security.—No registered investment company shall knowingly purchase or otherwise acquire, during the existence of any underwriting or selling syndicate, any security (except a security of which such company is the issuer) a principal underwriter of which is an officer, director, member of an advisory board, investment adviser, or employee of such registered company, or is a person (other than a company of the character described in § 80a–12(d)(3)(A) and (B)) of which any such officer, director, member of an advisory board, investment adviser, or employee is an affiliated person, unless in acquiring such security such registered company is itself acting as a principal underwriter for the issuer. The Commission, by rules and regulations upon its own motion or by order upon application, may conditionally or unconditionally exempt any transaction or classes of transactions from any of the provisions of this subsection, if and to the extent that such exemption is consistent with the protection of investors. . . .

§ 80a-12. Functions and Activities of Investment Companies

(a) Margin Purchases, Trading Accounts, and Short Sales.—It shall be unlawful for any registered investment company, in contravention of such rules and regulations or orders as the Commission may prescribe as necessary or appropriate in the public interest or for the protection of investors—

(1) to purchase any security on margin, except such short-term credits as are necessary for the clearance of transactions;

(2) to participate on a joint or a joint and several basis in any trading account in securities, except in connection with an underwriting in which such registered company is a participant; or

(3) to effect a short sale of any security. . . .

(b) Distributing Own Securities.—It shall be unlawful for any registered open-end company (other than a company complying with the provisions of § 80a–10(d)) to act as a distributor of securities of which it is the issuer, except through an underwriter, in contravention of such rules and regulations as the Commission may prescribe as necessary or appropriate in the public interest or for the protection of investors. . . .

(d) Limits on Acquiring Securities of Certain Types of Firms.—

(1) Securities of Other Investment Companies.—

(A) In general.—It shall be unlawful for any registered investment company (the "acquiring company") and any company or companies controlled by such acquiring company to purchase or otherwise acquire any security issued by any other investment company (the "acquired company"), and for any investment company (the "acquiring company") and any company or companies controlled by such acquiring company to purchase or otherwise acquire any security issued by any registered investment company (the "acquired company"), if the acquiring company and any company or companies controlled by it immediately after such purchase or acquisition own in the aggregate—

(i) more than 3 per centum of the total outstanding voting stock of the acquired company;

(ii) securities issued by the acquired company having an aggregate value in excess of 5 per centum of the value of the total assets of the acquiring company; or

(iii) securities issued by the acquired company and all other investment companies (other than treasury stock of the acquiring company) having an aggregate value in excess of 10 per centum of the value of the total assets of the acquiring company.

(B) Disposition restricted.—It shall be unlawful for any registered open-end investment company (the "acquired company"), any principal underwriter therefor, or any broker or dealer registered under the Securities Exchange Act of 1934, knowingly to sell or otherwise dispose of any security issued by the acquired company to any other investment company (the "acquiring company") or any company or companies controlled by the acquiring company, if immediately after such sale or disposition—

(i) more than 3 per centum of the total outstanding voting stock of the acquired company is owned by the acquiring company and any company or companies controlled by it; or

(ii) more than 10 per centum of the total outstanding voting stock of the acquired company is owned by the acquiring company and other investment companies and companies controlled by them.

(C) Closed-end company.—It shall be unlawful for any investment company (the "acquiring company") and any company or companies controlled by the acquiring company to purchase or otherwise acquire any security issued by a registered closed-end investment company, if immediately after such purchase or acquisition the acquiring company, other investment companies having the same investment adviser, and companies controlled by such investment companies, own more than 10 per centum of the total outstanding voting stock of such closed-end company. . . .

(J) Exemptions.—The Commission, by rule or regulation, upon its own motion or by order upon application, may conditionally or unconditionally exempt any person, security, or transaction, or any class or classes of persons, securities, or transactions from any provision of this subsection, if and to the extent that such exemption is consistent with the public interest and the protection of investors. . . .

§ 80a-13. Changes in Investment Policy

(a) No registered investment company shall, unless authorized by the vote of a majority of its outstanding voting securities—

(1) change its subclassification as defined in § 80a–5(a)(1) and (2) of this Act or its subclassification from a diversified to a non-diversified company;

(2) borrow money, issue senior securities, underwrite securities issued by other persons, purchase or sell real estate or commodities or make loans to other persons, except in each case in accordance with the recitals of policy contained in its registration statement in respect thereto;

(3) deviate from its policy in respect of concentration of investments in any particular industry or group of industries as recited in its registration statement, deviate from any investment policy which is changeable only if authorized by shareholder vote, or deviate from any policy recited in its registration statement pursuant to § 80a–8(b)(3); [or]

(4) change the nature of its business so as to cease to be an investment company. . . .

§ 80a-15. Investment Advisory and Underwriting Contracts

(a) Investment Adviser Must Have Written Contract.—It shall be unlawful for any person to serve or act as investment adviser of a registered investment company, except pursuant to a written contract, which contract ... has been approved by the vote of a majority of the outstanding voting securities of such registered company, and—

(1) precisely describes all compensation to be paid thereunder;

(2) shall continue in effect for a period more than two years from the date of its execution, only so long as such continuance is specifically approved at least annually by the board of directors by vote of a majority of the outstanding voting securities of such company;

(3) provides, in substance, that it may be terminated at any time, without the payment of any penalty, by the board of directors ... or by vote of a majority of the outstanding voting securities ... ; and

(4) provides, in substance, for its automatic termination in the event of its assignment.

(b) Principal Underwriter Must Have Written Contract.—It shall be unlawful for any principal underwriter for a registered open-end company to offer for sale, sell, or deliver after sale any security of which such company is the issuer, except pursuant to a written contract with such company, which contract—

(1) shall continue in effect for a period more than two years from the date of its execution, only so long as such continuance is specifically approved at least annually by the board of directors or by vote of a majority of the outstanding voting securities of such company; and

(2) provides, in substance, for its automatic termination in the event of its assignment.

(c) Approval by Noninterested Directors Required.—In addition to the requirements of subsections (a) and (b) of this section, it shall be unlawful for any registered investment company having a board of directors to enter into, renew, or perform any contract or agreement, written or oral, whereby a person undertakes regularly to serve or act as investment adviser of or principal underwriter for such company, unless the terms of such contract or agreement and any renewal thereof have been approved by the vote of a majority of directors, who are not parties to such contract or agreement or interested persons of any such party, cast in person at a meeting called for the purpose of voting on such approval. It shall be the duty of the directors of a registered investment company to request and evaluate, and the duty of an investment adviser to such company to furnish, such information as may reasonably be necessary to evaluate the terms of any contract whereby a person undertakes regularly to serve or act as investment adviser of such company. . . .

§ 80a-16. Changes in Board of Directors

(a) Election of Directors.—No person shall serve as a director of a registered investment company unless elected to that office by the holders of the outstanding voting securities of such company, at an annual or a special meeting duly called for that purpose; except that vacancies occurring between such meetings may be filled in any otherwise legal manner if immediately after filling any such vacancy at least two-thirds of the directors then holding office shall have been elected to such office by the holders of the outstanding voting securities of the company at such an annual or special meeting. In the event that at any time less than a majority of the directors of such company holding office at that time were so elected by the holders of the outstanding voting securities, the board of directors or proper officer of such company shall forthwith cause to be held as promptly as possible and in any event within sixty days a meeting of such holders for the purpose of electing directors to fill any existing vacancies in the board of directors unless the Commission shall by order extend such period. . . .

Nothing herein shall, however, preclude a registered investment company from dividing its directors into classes if its charter, certificate of incorporation, articles of association, by-laws, trust indenture, or other instrument or the law under which it is organized, so provides and prescribes the tenure of office of the several classes: *Provided,* That no class shall be elected for a shorter period than one year or for a longer period than five years and the term of office of at least one class shall expire each year. . . .

§ 80a-17. Transactions of Certain Affiliated Persons and Underwriters

(a) Prohibited Transactions.—It shall be unlawful for any affiliated person or promoter of or principal underwriter for a registered investment company (other than a company of the character described in § 80a–12(d)(3)(A) and (B)), or any affiliated person of such a person, promoter, or principal underwriter, acting as principal—

(1) knowingly to sell any security or other property to such registered company or to any company controlled by such registered company, unless such sale involves solely (A) securities of which the buyer is the issuer, (B) securities of which the seller is the issuer and which are part of a general offering to the holders of a class of its securities, or (C) securities deposited with the trustee of a unit investment trust . . . by the depositor thereof;

(2) knowingly to purchase from such registered company, or from any company controlled by such registered company, any security or other property (except securities of which the seller is the issuer);

(3) to borrow money or other property from such registered company or from any company controlled by such registered company (unless the borrower is controlled by the lender) except as permitted in § 80a–21(b); or

(4) to loan money or other property to such registered company, or to any company controlled by such registered company,

in contravention of such rules, regulations, or orders as the Commission may, after consultation with and taking into consideration the views of the Federal banking agencies ..., prescribe or issue consistent with the protection of investors.

(b) Application for Exemption.—Notwithstanding subsection (a), any person may file with the Commission an application for an order exempting a proposed transaction of the applicant from one or more provisions of that subsection. The Commission shall grant such application and issue such order of exemption if evidence establishes that—

(1) the terms of the proposed transaction, including the consideration to be paid or received, are reasonable and fair and do not involve overreaching on the part of any person concerned;

(2) the proposed transaction is consistent with the policy of each registered investment company concerned, as recited in its registration statement and reports filed under this Act; and

(3) the proposed transaction is consistent with the general purposes of this Act.

(c) Sale or Purchase of Merchandise.—Notwithstanding subsection (a), a person may, in the ordinary course of business, sell to or purchase from any company merchandise or may enter into a lessor-lessee relationship with any person and furnish the services incident thereto.

(d) Joint Transactions Prohibited.—It shall be unlawful for any affiliated person of or principal underwriter for a registered investment company (other than a company of the character described in § 80a–12(d)(3)(A) and (B)), or any affiliated person of such a person or principal underwriter, acting as principal to effect any transaction in which such registered company, or a company controlled by such registered company, is a joint or a joint and several participant with such person, principal underwriter, or affiliated person, in contravention of such rules and regulations as the Commission may prescribe for the purpose of limiting or preventing participation by such registered or controlled company on a basis different from or less advantageous than that of such other participant. ...

(e) Compensation Limited.—It shall be unlawful for any affiliated person of a registered investment company, or any affiliated person of such person—

(1) acting as agent, to accept from any source any compensation (other than a regular salary or wages from such registered company) for the purchase or sale of any property to or for such registered company or any controlled company thereof, except in the course of such person's business as an underwriter or broker; or

(2) acting as broker, in connection with the sale of securities to or by such registered company or any controlled company thereof, to receive from any source a commission, fee, or other remuneration for effecting

such transaction which exceeds (A) the usual and customary broker's commission if the sale is effected on a securities exchange, or (B) 2 per centum of the sales price if the sale is effected in connection with a secondary distribution of such securities, or (C) 1 per centum of the purchase or sale price of such securities if the sale is otherwise effected unless the Commission shall, by rules and regulations or order in the public interest and consistent with the protection of investors, permit a larger commission.

(f) Custody of Securities.—

(1) Custodian required.—Every registered management company shall place and maintain its securities and similar investments in the custody of (A) a bank or banks having the qualifications prescribed in paragraph (1) of § 80a–26(a) for the trustees of unit investment trusts; or (B) a company which is a member of a national securities exchange as defined in the Securities Exchange Act of 1934, subject to such rules and regulations as the Commission may from time to time prescribe for the protection of investors; or (C) such registered company, but only in accordance with such rules and regulations or orders as the Commission may from time to time prescribe for the protection of investors.

(2) Central handling system as custodian.—Subject to such rules, regulations, and orders as the Commission may adopt as necessary or appropriate for the protection of investors, a registered management company or any such custodian ... may deposit all or any part of the securities owned by such registered management company in a system for the central handling of securities established by a national securities exchange or national securities association registered with the Commission under the Securities Exchange Act of 1934, or such other person as may be permitted by the Commission, pursuant to which system all securities of any particular class or series of any issuer deposited within the system are treated as fungible and may be transferred or pledged by bookkeeping entry without physical delivery of such securities. ...

(4) Dealer disqualified.—No such member which trades in securities for its own account may act as custodian except in accordance with rules and regulations prescribed by the Commission for the protection of investors.

(5) Custody of cash.—If a registered company maintains its securities and similar investments in the custody of a qualified bank or banks, the cash proceeds from the sale of such securities and similar investments and other cash assets of the company shall likewise be kept in the custody of such a bank or banks, or in accordance with such rules and regulations or orders as the Commission may from time to time prescribe for the protection of investors, except that such a registered company may maintain a checking account in a bank or banks having the qualifications prescribed in paragraph (1) of § 80a–26(a) for the trustees of unit investment trusts with the balance of such account or the aggregate balances of such accounts at no time in excess of the amount of the fidelity bond, maintained pursuant to § 80a–17(g), covering the officers or employees authorized to draw on such account or accounts.

(6) Affiliated bank as custodian.—The Commission may, after consultation with and taking into consideration the views of the Federal banking agencies . . . , adopt rules and regulations, and issue orders, consistent with the protection of investors, prescribing the conditions under which a bank, or an affiliated person of a bank, either of which is an affiliated person, promoter, organizer, or sponsor of, or principal underwriter for, a registered management company may serve as custodian of that registered management company.

(g) Fidelity Bond.—The Commission is authorized to require . . . that any officer or employee of a registered management investment company who may . . . have access to securities or funds of any registered company . . . be bonded by a reputable fidelity insurance company against larceny and embezzlement in such reasonable minimum amounts as the Commission may prescribe.

(h) Exculpation of Directors and Officers Limited.—[N]either the charter, certificate of incorporation, articles of association, indenture of trust, nor the by-laws of any registered investment company, nor any other instrument pursuant to which such a company is organized or administered, shall contain any provision which protects or purports to protect any director or officer of such company against any liability to the company or to its security holders to which he would otherwise be subject by reason of willful misfeasance, bad faith, gross negligence or reckless disregard of the duties involved in the conduct of his office.

(i) Exculpation of Investment Adviser Limited.—[N]o contract or agreement under which any person undertakes to act as investment adviser of, or principal underwriter for, a registered investment company shall contain any provision which protects or purports to protect such person against any liability to such company or its security holders to which he would otherwise be subject by reason of willful misfeasance, bad faith, or gross negligence, in the performance of his duties, or by reason of his reckless disregard of his obligations and duties under such contract or agreement.

(j) Fraudulent, Deceptive, and Manipulative Practices Prohibited.— It shall be unlawful for any affiliated person of or principal underwriter for a registered investment company or any affiliated person of an investment adviser of or principal underwriter for a registered investment company, to engage in any act, practice, or course of business in connection with the purchase or sale . . . by such person of any security held or to be acquired by such registered investment company in contravention of such rules and regulations as the Commission may adopt to define, and prescribe means reasonably necessary to prevent, such acts, practices, or courses of business as are fraudulent, deceptive or manipulative. Such rules and regulations may include requirements for the adoption of codes of ethics by registered investment companies and investment advisers of, and principal underwriters for, such investment companies establishing such standards as are reasonably necessary to prevent such acts, practices, or courses of business.

§ 80a-18. Capital Structure

(a) Issuing Senior Securities.—It shall be unlawful for any registered closed-end company to issue any class of senior security, or to sell any such security of which it is the issuer, unless—
  (1) if such class of senior security represents an indebtedness—
    (A) immediately after such issuance or sale, it will have an asset coverage of at least 300 per centum;
    (B) provision is made to prohibit the declaration of any dividend . . . , or the declaration of any other distribution, upon any class of the capital stock of such investment company, or the purchase of any such capital stock, unless, in every such case, such class of senior securities has at the time of the declaration of any such dividend or distribution or at the time of any such purchase an asset coverage of at least 300 per centum after deducting the amount of such dividend, distribution, or purchase price, as the case may be, except that dividends may be declared upon any preferred stock if such senior security representing indebtedness has an asset coverage of at least 200 per centum at the time of declaration thereof after deducting the amount of such dividend; and
    (C) provision is made either—
      (i) that, if on the last business day of each of twelve consecutive calendar months such class of senior securities shall have an asset coverage of less than 100 per centum, the holders of such securities voting as a class shall be entitled to elect at least a majority of the members of the board of directors of such registered company, such voting right to continue until such class of senior security shall have an asset coverage of 110 per centum or more on the last business day of each of three consecutive calendar months, or
      (ii) that, if on the last business day of each of twenty-four consecutive calendar months such class of senior securities shall have an asset coverage of less than 100 per centum, an event of default shall be deemed to have occurred;
  (2) if such class of senior security is a stock—
    (A) immediately after such issuance or sale it will have an asset coverage of at least 200 per centum;

(B) provision is made to prohibit the declaration of any dividend . . . , or the declaration of any other distribution, upon the common stock of such investment company, or the purchase of any such common stock, unless in every such case such class of senior security has at the time of the declaration of any such dividend or distribution or at the time of any such purchase an asset coverage of at least 200 per centum after deducting the amount of such dividend, distribution or purchase price, as the case may be;

(C) provision is made to entitle the holders of such senior securities, voting as a class, to elect at least two directors at all times, and, subject to the prior rights, if any, of the holders of any other class of senior securities outstanding, to elect a majority of the directors if at any time dividends on such class of securities shall be unpaid in an amount equal to two full years' dividends on such securities, and to continue to be so represented until all dividends in arrears shall have been paid or otherwise provided for;

(D) provision is made requiring approval by the vote of a majority of such securities, voting as a class, of any plan of reorganization adversely affecting such securities or of any action requiring a vote of security holders as in § 80a–13(a) provided; and

(E) such class of stock shall have complete priority over any other class as to distribution of assets and payment of dividends, which dividends shall be cumulative. . . .

(c) No More Than One Class of Debt Securities and One Class of Senior Equity Securities Allowed.—Notwithstanding the provisions of subsection (a) it shall be unlawful for any registered closed-end investment company to issue or sell any senior security representing indebtedness if immediately thereafter such company will have outstanding more than one class of senior security representing indebtedness, or to issue or sell any senior security which is a stock if immediately thereafter such company will have outstanding more than one class of senior security which is a stock. . . .

(e) Exception for Refunding and Reorganization.—The provisions of this § 80a–18 shall not apply to any senior securities issued or sold by any registered closed-end company—

(1) for the purpose of refunding through payment, purchase, redemption, retirement, or exchange, any senior security of such registered investment company except that no senior security representing indebtedness shall be so issued or sold for the purpose of refunding any senior security which is a stock; or

(2) pursuant to [a qualifying plan of reorganization].

(f) Open-End Company.—

(1) Senior Securities Prohibited.—It shall be unlawful for any registered open-end company to issue any class of senior security or to sell any senior security of which it is the issuer, except that any such registered company shall be permitted to borrow from any bank: *Provided,* That immediately after any such borrowing there is an asset coverage of at least 300 per centum for all borrowings of such registered company. . . .

(g) Senior Security Defined.—Unless otherwise provided: "Senior security" means any bond, debenture, note, or similar obligation or instrument constituting a security and evidencing indebtedness, and any stock of a class having priority over any other class as to distribution of assets or payment of dividends; and "senior security representing indebtedness" means any senior security other than stock. The term "senior security," when used in subparagraphs (B) and (C) of paragraph (1) of subsection (a), shall not include any promissory note or other evidence of indebtedness issued in consideration of any loan, extension, or renewal thereof, made by a bank or other person and privately arranged, and not intended to be publicly distributed; nor shall such term, when used in this § 80a–18, include any such promissory note or other evidence of indebtedness in any case where such a loan is for temporary purposes only and in an amount not exceeding 5 per centum of the value of the total assets of the issuer at the time when the loan is made. A loan shall be presumed to be for temporary purposes if it is repaid within sixty days and is not extended or renewed; otherwise it shall be presumed not to be for temporary purposes. Any such presumption may be rebutted by evidence.

(h) Asset Coverage Defined.—"Asset coverage" of a class of senior security representing an indebtedness of an issuer means the ratio which the value of the total assets of such issuer, less all liabilities and indebtedness not represented by senior securities, bears to the aggregate amount of senior securities representing indebtedness of such issuer. "Asset coverage" of a class of senior security of an issuer which is a stock means the ratio which the value of the total assets of such issuer, less all liabilities and indebtedness not represented by senior securities, bears to the aggregate amount of senior securities representing indebtedness of such issuer plus the aggregate of the involuntary liquidation preference of such class of senior security which is a stock. The involuntary liquidation preference of a class of senior security which is a stock shall be deemed to mean the amount to which such class of senior security would be entitled on involuntary liquidation of the issuer in preference to a security junior to it.

(i) Voting Rights.—Except as provided in subsection (a) of this section, or as otherwise required by law, every share of stock hereafter issued by a registered management company . . . shall be a voting stock and have equal voting rights with every other outstanding voting stock: *Provided,* That this subsection shall not apply to . . . shares issued in accordance with any rules, regulations, or orders which the Commission may make permitting such issue. . . .

§ 80a-20. ... Circular Ownership ...

(c) Prohibition on Purchase of Securities Knowingly Resulting in Cross-Ownership or Circular Ownership.—No registered investment company shall purchase any voting security if, to the knowledge of such registered company, cross-ownership or circular ownership exists, or after such acquisition will exist, between such registered company and the issuer of such security. Cross-ownership shall be deemed to exist between two companies when each of such companies beneficially owns more than 3 per centum of the outstanding voting securities of the other company. Circular ownership shall be deemed to exist between two companies if such companies are included within a group of three or more companies, each of which—

(1) beneficially owns more than 3 per centum of the outstanding voting securities of one or more other companies of the group; and

(2) has more than 3 per centum of its own outstanding voting securities beneficially owned by another company, or by each of two or more other companies, of the group. ...

§ 80a-21. Loans

It shall be unlawful for any registered management company to lend money or property to any person, directly or indirectly, if—

(a) the investment policies of such registered company, as recited in its registration statement and reports filed under this Act, do not permit such a loan; or

(b) such person controls or is under common control with such registered company. ...

§ 80a-22. Distribution, Redemption, and Repurchase of Redeemable Securities ...

(d) Distribution.—No registered investment company shall sell any redeemable security issued by it to any person except either to or through a principal underwriter for distribution or at a current public offering price described in the prospectus, and, if such class of security is being currently offered to the public by or through an underwriter, no principal underwriter of such security and no dealer shall sell any such security to any person except a dealer, a principal underwriter, or the issuer, except at a current public offering price described in the prospectus. Nothing in this subsection shall prevent a sale made ... (iii) in accordance with rules and regulations of the Commission made pursuant to subsection (b) of § 80a–12.

(e) Suspending Right of Redemption.—No registered investment company shall suspend the right of redemption, or postpone the date of payment or satisfaction upon redemption of any redeemable security in accordance with its terms for more than seven days after the tender of such security to the company or its agent designated for that purpose for redemption. . . .

(g) Consideration for Shares.—No registered open-end company shall issue any of its securities (1) for services; or (2) for property other than cash or securities (including securities of which such registered company is the issuer), except as a dividend or distribution to its security holders or in connection with a reorganization.

§ 80a-23. Distribution and Repurchase of Securities: Closed-End Companies

(a) Consideration for Shares.—No registered closed-end company shall issue any of its securities (1) for services; or (2) for property other than cash or securities (including securities of which such registered company is the issuer), except as a dividend or distribution to its security holders or in connection with a reorganization.

(b) Distribution.—No registered closed-end company shall sell any common stock of which it is the issuer at a price below the current net asset value of such stock, exclusive of any distributing commission or discount . . . , except (1) in connection with an offering to the holders of one or more classes of its capital stock; (2) with the consent of a majority of its common stockholders; . . . or (5) under such other circumstances as the Commission may permit by rules and regulations or orders for the protection of investors.

(c) Repurchase.—No registered closed-end company shall purchase any securities of any class of which it is the issuer except—

(1) on a securities exchange or such other open market as the Commission may designate by rules and regulations or orders: *Provided,* That if such securities are stock, such registered company shall, within the preceding six months, have informed stockholders of its intention to purchase stock of such class by letter or report addressed to stockholders of such class; or

(2) pursuant to tenders, after reasonable opportunity to submit tenders given to all holders of securities of the class to be purchased; or

(3) under such other circumstances as the Commission may permit by rules and regulations or orders for the protection of investors in order to insure that such purchases are made in a manner or on a basis which does not unfairly discriminate against any holders of the class or classes of securities to be purchased. . . .

§ 80a-34. Unlawful Representations and Names

(a) **Misrepresentation of Guarantees.**—

(2) **Disclosures.**—Any person issuing or selling the securities of a registered investment company that is advised by, or sold through, a bank shall prominently disclose that an investment in the company is not insured by the Federal Deposit Insurance Corporation or any other government agency. . . .

§ 80a-35. Breach of Fiduciary Duty

(a) **Civil Actions by Commission.**—The Commission is authorized to bring an action . . . alleging that a person who is, or at the time of the alleged misconduct was, serving or acting in one or more of the following capacities has engaged . . . or is about to engage in any act or practice constituting a breach of fiduciary duty involving personal misconduct in respect of any registered investment company for which such person so serves or acts, or at the time of the alleged misconduct, so served or acted—

(1) as officer, director, . . . investment adviser, or depositor; or

(2) as principal underwriter, if such registered company is an open-end company [or] unit investment trust. . . .

(b) **Investment Adviser's Compensation.**—For the purposes of this subsection, the investment adviser of a registered investment company shall be deemed to have a fiduciary duty with respect to the receipt of compensation for services, or of payments of a material nature, paid by such registered investment company, or by the security holders thereof, to such investment adviser or any affiliated person of such investment adviser. An action may be brought under this subsection by the Commission, or by a security holder of such registered investment company on behalf of such company, against such investment adviser, or any affiliated person of such investment adviser, or any other person enumerated in subsection (a) of this section who has a fiduciary duty concerning such compensation or payments, for breach of fiduciary duty in respect of such compensation or payments paid by such registered investment company or by the security holders thereof to such investment adviser or person. With respect to any such action the following provisions shall apply:

(1) It shall not be necessary to allege or prove that any defendant engaged in personal misconduct, and the plaintiff shall have the burden of proving a breach of fiduciary duty.

(2) In any such action approval by the board of directors of such investment company of such compensation or payments, or of contracts or other arrangements providing for such compensation or payments, and ratification or approval of such compensation or payments, or of contracts

or other arrangements providing for such compensation or payments, by the shareholders of such investment company, shall be given such consideration by the court as is deemed appropriate under all the circumstances. . . .

§ 80a-37. Rules, Regulations, and Orders

(a) Powers of Commission.—The Commission shall have authority . . . to make, issue, amend, and rescind such rules and regulations and such orders as are necessary or appropriate to the exercise of the powers conferred upon the Commission elsewhere in this Act. . . .

§ 80a-46. Validity of Contracts

(a) Waiver of Compliance as Void.—Any condition, stipulation, or provision binding any person to waive compliance with any provision of this Act or with any rule, regulation, or order thereunder shall be void. . . .

INVESTMENT ADVISERS ACT OF 1940

§ 80b-2. Definitions

(a) In General.—When used in this Act, unless the context otherwise requires, the following definitions shall apply: . . .

(11) **"Investment adviser"** means any person who, for compensation, engages in the business of advising others, either directly or through publications or writings, as to the value of securities or as to the advisability of investing in, purchasing, or selling securities, or who, for compensation and as part of a regular business, issues or promulgates analyses or reports concerning securities; but does not include (A) a bank, or any bank holding company . . . , which is not an investment company, except that the term "investment adviser" includes any bank or bank holding company to the extent that such bank or bank holding company serves or acts as an investment adviser to a registered investment company, but if, in the case of a bank, such services or actions are performed through a separately identifiable department or division, the department or division, and not the bank itself, shall be deemed to be the investment adviser; (B) any lawyer, accountant, engineer, or teacher whose performance of such services is solely incidental to the practice of his profession; (C) any broker or dealer whose performance of such

services is solely incidental to the conduct of his business as a broker or dealer and who receives no special compensation therefor; (D) the publisher of any bona fide newspaper, news magazine or business or financial publication of general and regular circulation; (E) any person whose advice, analyses, or reports relate to no securities other than securities which are direct obligations of or obligations guaranteed as to principal or interest by the United States . . . ; (F) any nationally recognized statistical rating organization . . . unless such organization engages in issuing recommendations as to purchasing, selling, or holding securities or in managing assets, consisting in whole or in part of securities, on behalf of others; (G) any family office, as defined by . . . the Commission, in accordance with the purposes of this Act; or (H) such other persons not within the intent of this paragraph, as the Commission may designate by rules and regulations or order. . . .

(25) **"Supervised person"** means any partner, officer, director (or other person occupying a similar status or performing similar functions), or employee of an investment adviser, or other person who provides investment advice on behalf of the investment adviser and is subject to the supervision and control of the investment adviser.

(26) The term **"separately identifiable department or division"** of a bank means a unit—

(A) that is under the direct supervision of an officer or officers designated by the board of directors of the bank as responsible for the day-to-day conduct of the bank's investment adviser activities for one or more investment companies, including the supervision of all bank employees engaged in the performance of such activities; and

(B) for which all of the records relating to its investment adviser activities are separately maintained in or extractable from such unit's own facilities or the facilities of the bank, and such records are so maintained or otherwise accessible as to permit independent examination and enforcement by the Commission of this Act or the Investment Company Act of 1940. . . .

(29) The term **"private fund"** means an issuer that would be an investment company, as defined in section 3 of the Investment Company Act of 1940, but for section 3(c)(1) or 3(c)(7) of that Act [i.e., the private-issuer exemptions].

(30) The term **"foreign private adviser"** means any investment adviser who—

(A) has no place of business in the United States;

(B) has, in total, fewer than 15 clients and investors in the United States in private funds advised by the investment adviser;

(C) has aggregate assets under management attributable to clients in the United States and investors in the United States in private funds advised by the investment adviser of less than $25,000,000, or such

higher amount as the Commission may, by rule, deem appropriate in accordance with the purposes of this Act; and
  (D) neither—
    (i) holds itself out generally to the public in the United States as an investment adviser; nor
    (ii) acts as . . . an investment adviser to any investment company registered under the Investment Company Act of 1940. . . .

(c) Rulemaking Considerations.—Whenever pursuant to this Act the Commission is engaged in rulemaking and is required to consider or determine whether an action is necessary or appropriate in the public interest, the Commission shall also consider, in addition to the protection of investors, whether the action will promote efficiency, competition, and capital formation.

§ 80b-3. Registration of Investment Advisers

(a) Registration Required.—Except as provided in subsection (b) and § 80b-3a, it shall be unlawful for any investment adviser, unless registered under this section, to make use of the mails or any means or instrumentality of interstate commerce in connection with his or its business as an investment adviser.

(b) Exemptions.—The provisions of subsection (a) shall not apply to—
  (1) any investment adviser, other than an investment adviser who acts as an investment adviser to any private fund, all of whose clients are residents of the State within which such investment adviser maintains his or its principal office and place of business, and who does not furnish advice or issue analyses or reports with respect to securities listed or admitted to unlisted trading privileges on any national securities exchange;
  (2) any investment adviser whose only clients are insurance companies;
  (3) any investment adviser that is a foreign private adviser;
  (4) any investment adviser that is a charitable organization, as defined in § 80a-3(c)(10)(D), or is a trustee, director, officer, employee, or volunteer of such a charitable organization acting within the scope of such person's employment or duties with such organization; . . .
  (6) any investment adviser that is registered with the Commodity Futures Trading Commission as a commodity trading advisor whose business does not consist primarily of acting as an investment adviser, as defined in § 80b-2(a)(11), and that does not act as an investment adviser to [a registered investment company; or]
  (7) any investment adviser . . . who solely advises . . . small business investment companies that are licensees under the Small Business Investment Act of 1958. . . .

(*l*) Exemption of venture capital fund advisers.—No investment adviser that acts as an investment adviser solely to 1 or more venture capital funds shall be subject to the registration requirements of this Act with respect to the provision of investment advice relating to a venture capital fund. . . . The Commission shall require such advisers to maintain such records and provide to the Commission such annual or other reports as the Commission determines necessary or appropriate in the public interest or for the protection of investors.

(m) Exemption of and reporting by certain private fund advisers—

    (1) In general.—The Commission shall provide an exemption from the registration requirements under this section to any investment adviser of private funds, if each of such investment adviser acts solely as an adviser to private funds and has assets under management in the United States of less than $150,000,000.

    (2) Reporting.—The Commission shall require investment advisers exempted by reason of this subsection to maintain such records and provide to the Commission such annual or other reports as the Commission determines necessary or appropriate in the public interest or for the protection of investors.

(n) Registration and examination of mid-sized private fund advisers.—In prescribing regulations to carry out the requirements of this section with respect to investment advisers acting as investment advisers to mid-sized private funds, the Commission shall take into account the size, governance, and investment strategy of such funds to determine whether they pose systemic risk, and shall provide for registration and examination procedures with respect to the investment advisers of such funds which reflect the level of systemic risk posed by such funds.

§ 80b-3a. State and Federal Responsibilities

(a) Advisers Subject to State Authorities.—

    (1) In general.—No investment adviser that is regulated or required to be regulated as an investment adviser in the State in which it maintains its principal office and place of business shall register under § 80b-3, unless the investment adviser—

        (A) has assets under management of not less than $25,000,000, or such higher amount as the Commission may, by rule, deem appropriate in accordance with the purposes of this Act; or

        (B) is an adviser to [a registered investment company].

    (2) Treatment of mid-sized investment advisers.—

        (A) In general.—No investment adviser described in subparagraph (B) shall register under § 80b-3, unless the investment adviser is an adviser to an investment company registered under the Investment

Company Act of 1940, . . . except that, if by effect of this paragraph an investment adviser would be required to register with 15 or more States, then the adviser may register under § 80b-3.

(B) Covered persons.—An investment adviser described in this subparagraph is an investment adviser that—

(i) is required to be registered as an investment adviser with the securities commissioner (or any agency or office performing like functions) of the State in which it maintains its principal office and place of business and, if registered, would be subject to examination as an investment adviser by any such commissioner, agency, or office; and

(ii) has assets under management between—

(I) the amount specified under subparagraph (A) of paragraph (1), as such amount may have been adjusted by the Commission pursuant to that subparagraph; and

(II) $100,000,000, or such higher amount as the Commission may, by rule, deem appropriate in accordance with the purposes of this Act.

(3) Definition.—For purposes of this subsection, the term **"assets under management"** means the securities portfolios with respect to which an investment adviser provides continuous and regular supervisory or management services.

(b) Advisers Subject to Commission Authority.—

(1) In general.—No law of any State or political subdivision thereof requiring the registration, licensing, or qualification as an investment adviser or supervised person of an investment adviser shall apply to any person—

(A) that is registered under § 80b-3 as an investment adviser, or that is a supervised person of such person, except that a State may license, register, or otherwise qualify any investment adviser representative who has a place of business located within that State; or

(B) that is not registered under § 80b-3 because that person is excepted from the definition of an investment adviser under § 80b-2(a)(11).

(2) Limitation.—Nothing in this subsection shall prohibit the securities commission (or any agency or office performing like functions) of any State from investigating and bringing enforcement actions with respect to fraud or deceit against an investment adviser or person associated with an investment adviser.

(c) Exemptions.—Notwithstanding subsection (a), the Commission, by rule or regulation upon its own motion, or by order upon application, may permit the registration with the Commission of any person or class of persons to which the application of subsection (a) would be unfair, a burden on interstate commerce, or otherwise inconsistent with the purposes of this section. . . .

§ 80b-4a. Prevention of Misuse of Nonpublic Information

Every investment adviser . . . shall establish, maintain, and enforce written policies and procedures reasonably designed, taking into consideration the nature of such investment adviser's business, to prevent the misuse in violation of this Act or the Securities Exchange Act of 1934, or the rules or regulations thereunder, of material, nonpublic information by such investment adviser or any person associated with such investment adviser. The Commission, as it deems necessary or appropriate in the public interest or for the protection of investors, shall adopt rules or regulations to require specific policies or procedures reasonably designed to prevent misuse . . . of material, nonpublic information.

§ 80b-5. Investment Advisory Contracts

(a) Compensation and Assignment.—No investment adviser, unless exempt from registration pursuant to § 80b-3(b), shall make use of the mails or any means or instrumentality of interstate commerce, directly or indirectly, to enter into, extend, or renew any investment advisory contract, or in any way to perform any investment advisory contract entered into, extended, or renewed on or after the effective date of this Act, if such contract—

(1) provides for compensation to the investment adviser on the basis of a share of capital gains upon or capital appreciation of the funds or any portion of the funds of the client; [or]

(2) fails to provide, in substance, that no assignment of such contract shall be made by the investment adviser without the consent of the other party by the contract. . . .

(b) Exceptions to Compensation Prohibition.—Paragraph (1) of subsection (a) shall not—

(1) be construed to prohibit an investment advisory contract which provides for compensation based upon the total value of a fund averaged over a definite period, or as of definite dates, or taken as of a definite date;

(2) apply to an investment advisory contract with—

(A) [a registered investment company], or

(B) any other person (except a trust, governmental plan, collective trust fund, or separate account referred to in § 80a-3(c)(11), provided that the contract relates to the investment of assets in excess of $1 million, if the contract provides for compensation based on the asset value of the company or fund under management averaged over a specified period and increasing and decreasing proportionately with the investment performance of the company or fund over a specified period in relation to the investment record of an appropriate index of securities prices or such other measure of investment performance as the Commission by rule, regulation, or order may specify; . . .

(4) apply to an investment advisory contract with a company excepted from the definition of an investment company under § 80a-3(c)(7); or

(5) apply to an investment advisory contract with a person who is not a resident of the United States.

(c) Measuring Changes in Compensation.—For purposes of paragraph (2) of subsection (b), the point from which increases and decreases in compensation are measured shall be the fee which is paid or earned when the investment performance of such company or fund is equivalent to that of the index or other measure of performance, and an index of securities prices shall be deemed appropriate unless the Commission by order shall determine otherwise.

(d) Investment Advisory Contract Defined.—As used in paragraphs (2) and (3) of subsection (a), "investment advisory contract" means any contract or agreement whereby a person agrees to act as investment adviser to or to manage any investment or trading account of another person other than [a registered investment company].

(e) Exemptions.—The Commission, by rule or regulation, upon its own motion, or by order upon application, may conditionally or unconditionally exempt any person or transaction, or any class or classes of persons or transactions, from subsection (a)(1), if and to the extent that the exemption relates to an investment advisory contract with any person that the Commission determines does not need the protections of subsection (a)(1), on the basis of such factors as financial sophistication, net worth, knowledge of and experience in financial matters, amount of assets under management, relationship with a registered investment adviser, and such other factors as the Commission determines are consistent with this section.

§ 80b-6. Prohibited Transactions by Registered Investment Advisers

It shall be unlawful for any investment adviser, by use of the mails or any means or instrumentality of interstate commerce, directly or indirectly—

(1) to employ any device, scheme, or artifice to defraud any client or prospective client;

(2) to engage in any transaction, practice, or course of business which operates as a fraud or deceit upon any client or prospective client;

(3) acting as principal for his own account, knowingly to sell any security to or purchase any security from a client, or acting as broker for a

person other than such client, knowingly to effect any sale or purchase of any security for the account of such client, without disclosing to such client in writing before the completion of such transaction the capacity in which he is acting and obtaining the consent of the client to such transaction. The prohibitions of this paragraph (3) shall not apply to any transaction with a customer of a broker or dealer if such broker or dealer is not acting as an investment adviser in relation to such transaction; [or]

(4) to engage in any act, practice, or course of business which is fraudulent, deceptive, or manipulative. The Commission shall, for the purposes of this paragraph (4) by rules and regulations define, and prescribe means reasonably designed to prevent, such acts, practices, and courses of business as are fraudulent, deceptive, or manipulative.

§ 80b-11. Rules, Regulations, and Orders of Commission

(a) Power of Commission.—The Commission shall have authority from time to time to make, issue, amend, and rescind such rules and regulations and such orders as are necessary or appropriate to the exercise of the functions and powers conferred upon the Commission elsewhere in this title, including rules and regulations defining technical, trade, and other terms used in this title, except that the Commission may not define the term "client" for purposes of paragraphs (1) and (2) of § 80b-6 to include an investor in a private fund managed by an investment adviser, if such private fund has entered into an advisory contract with such adviser. For the purposes of its rules or regulations the Commission may classify persons and matters within its jurisdiction and prescribe different requirements for different classes of persons or matters. . . .

(g) Standard of Conduct.—

(1) In general.—The Commission may promulgate rules to provide that the standard of conduct for all brokers, dealers, and investment advisers, when providing personalized investment advice about securities to retail customers (and such other customers as the Commission may by rule provide), shall be to act in the best interest of the customer without regard to the financial or other interest of the broker, dealer, or investment adviser providing the advice. In accordance with such rules, any material conflicts of interest shall be disclosed and may be consented to by the customer. Such rules shall provide that such standard of conduct shall be no less stringent than the standard applicable to investment advisers under § 80b-6(1)-(2) when providing personalized investment advice about securities, except the Commission shall not ascribe a meaning to the term "customer" that would include an investor in a private fund managed by an investment adviser, where such private fund has entered into an advisory contract with such adviser. The receipt of compensation based on commission or fees shall not, in and of itself, be considered a violation of such standard applied to a broker, dealer, or investment adviser.

(2) Retail customer defined.—For purposes of this subsection, the term "retail customer" means a natural person, or the legal representative of such natural person, who—

(A) receives personalized investment advice about securities from a broker, dealer, or investment adviser; and

(B) uses such advice primarily for personal, family, or household purposes.

(h) Other matters.—The Commission shall—

(1) facilitate the provision of simple and clear disclosures to investors regarding the terms of their relationships with brokers, dealers, and investment advisers, including any material conflicts of interest; and

(2) examine and, where appropriate, promulgate rules prohibiting or restricting certain sales practices, conflicts of interest, and compensation schemes for brokers, dealers, and investment advisers that the Commission deems contrary to the public interest and the protection of investors. . . .

§ 80b-15. Validity of Contracts

(a) Waiver of Compliance as Void.—Any condition, stipulation, or provision binding any person to waive compliance with any provision of this Act or with any rule, regulation, or order thereunder shall be void.

(b) Rights Affected by Invalidity.—Every contract made in violation of any provision of this Act and every contract heretofore or hereafter made, the performance of which involves the violation of, or the continuance of any relationship or practice in violation of any provision of this Act, or any rule, regulation, or order thereunder, shall be void (1) as regards the rights of any person who, in violation of any such provision, rule, regulation, or order, shall have made or engaged in the performance of any such contract, and (2) as regards the rights of any person who, not being a party to such contract, shall have acquired any right thereunder with actual knowledge of the facts by reason of which the making or performance of such contract was in violation of any such provision. . . .

§ 80b-18a. State Regulation of Investment Advisers

(a) Jurisdiction of State Regulators.—Nothing in this Act shall affect the jurisdiction of the securities commissioner (or any agency or officer performing like functions) of any State over any security or any person insofar as it does not conflict with the provisions of this Act or the rules and regulations thereunder.

(b) Dual Compliance Purposes.—No State may enforce any law or regulation that would require an investment adviser to maintain any books or records in addition to those required under the laws of the State in which it maintains its principal place of business, if the investment adviser—

(1) is registered or licensed as such in the State in which it maintains its principal place of business; and

(2) is in compliance with the applicable books and records requirements of the State in which it maintains its principal place of business.

(c) Limitation on Capital and Bond Requirements.—No State may enforce any law or regulation that would require an investment adviser to maintain a higher minimum net capital or to post any bond in addition to any that is required under the laws of the State in which it maintains its principal place of business, if the investment adviser—

(1) is registered or licensed as such in the State in which it maintains its principal place of business; and

(2) is in compliance with the applicable net capital or bonding requirements of the State in which it maintains its principal place of business.

(d) National De Minimis Standard.—No law of any State or political subdivision thereof requiring the registration, licensing, or qualification as an investment adviser shall require an investment adviser to register with the securities commissioner of the State (or any agency or officer performing like functions) or to comply with such law (other than any provision thereof prohibiting fraudulent conduct) if the investment adviser—

(1) does not have a place of business located within the State; and

(2) during the preceding 12-month period, has had fewer than 6 clients who are residents of that State.

§ 80b-18b. Custody of Client Accounts

An investment adviser registered under this Act shall take such steps to safeguard client assets over which such adviser has custody, including, without limitation, verification of such assets by an independent public accountant, as the Commission may, by rule, prescribe.

MCCARRAN-FERGUSON ACT

§ 1011. Declaration of Policy

Congress hereby declares that the continued regulation and taxation by the several States of the business of insurance is in the public interest, and that silence on the part of the Congress shall not be construed to impose any barrier to the regulation or taxation of such business by the several States.

§ 1012. Nonpreemption

(a) State Regulation.—The business of insurance, and every person engaged therein, shall be subject to the laws of the several States which relate to the regulation or taxation of such business.

(b) Federal Regulation.—No Act of Congress shall be construed to invalidate, impair, or supersede any law enacted by any State for the purpose of regulating the business of insurance, or which imposes a fee or tax upon such business, unless such Act specifically relates to the business of insurance. . . .

FAIR CREDIT REPORTING ACT

§ 1681. Congressional Findings and Statement of Purpose

(a) Accuracy and Fairness of Credit Reporting.—The Congress makes the following findings:

(1) The banking system is dependent upon fair and accurate credit reporting. Inaccurate credit reports directly impair the efficiency of the banking system, and unfair credit reporting methods undermine the public confidence which is essential to the continued functioning of the banking system.

(2) An elaborate mechanism has been developed for investigating and evaluating the creditworthiness, credit standing, credit capacity, character, and general reputation of consumers.

(3) Consumer reporting agencies have assumed a vital role in assembling and evaluating consumer credit and other information on consumers.

(4) There is a need to insure that consumer reporting agencies exercise their grave responsibilities with fairness, impartiality, and a respect for the consumer's right to privacy.

(b) Reasonable Procedures.—It is the purpose of this Act to require that consumer reporting agencies adopt reasonable procedures for meeting the needs of commerce for consumer credit, personnel, insurance, and other information in a manner which is fair and equitable to the consumer, with regard to the confidentiality, accuracy, relevancy, and proper utilization of such information in accordance with the requirements of this Act.

§ 1681a. Definitions; Rules of Construction . . .

(a) Applicability.—Definitions and rules of construction set forth in this section are applicable for the purposes of this Act.

(b) Person.—The term "person" means any individual, partnership, corporation, trust, estate, cooperative, association, government or governmental subdivision or agency, or other entity.

(c) Consumer.—The term "consumer" means an individual.

(d) Consumer Report.—

(1) In general.—The term "consumer report" means any written, oral, or other communication of any information by a consumer reporting agency bearing on a consumer's credit worthiness, credit standing, credit capacity, character, general reputation, personal characteristics, or mode of living which is used or expected to be used or collected in whole or in part for the purpose of serving as a factor in establishing the consumer's eligibility for—

(A) credit or insurance to be used primarily for personal, family, or household purposes;

(B) employment purposes; or

(C) any other purpose authorized under section 1681b.

(2) Exclusions.—Except as provided in paragraph (3), the term "consumer report" does not include—

(A) subject to section 1681s-3 [relating to sharing information with affiliates], any—

(i) report containing information solely as to transactions or experiences between the consumer and the person making the report;

(ii) communication of that information among persons related by common ownership or affiliated by corporate control; or

(iii) communication of other information among persons related by common ownership or affiliated by corporate control, if it is clearly and conspicuously disclosed to the consumer that the information may be communicated among such persons and the consumer is given the opportunity, before the time that the information is initially communicated, to direct that such information not be communicated among such persons;

(B) any authorization or approval of a specific extension of credit directly or indirectly by the issuer of a credit card or similar device;

(C) any report in which a person who has been requested by a third party to make a specific extension of credit directly or indirectly to a consumer conveys his or her decision with respect to such request, if the third party advises the consumer of the name and address of the person to whom the request was made, and such person makes the disclosures to the consumer required under section 1681m; or

(D) a communication described in subsection (o) or (x) of this section [relating respectively to recruitment and to investigation of employee misconduct]. . . .

(e) Investigative Consumer Report.—The term "investigative consumer report" means a consumer report or portion thereof in which information on a consumer's character, general reputation, personal characteristics, or mode of living is obtained through personal interviews with neighbors, friends, or associates of the consumer reported on or with others with whom he is acquainted or who may have knowledge concerning any such items of information. However, such information shall not include specific factual information on a consumer's credit record obtained directly from a creditor of the consumer or from a consumer reporting agency when such information was obtained directly from a creditor of the consumer or from the consumer.

(f) Consumer Reporting Agency.—The term "consumer reporting agency" means any person which, for monetary fees, dues, or on a cooperative nonprofit basis, regularly engages in whole or in part in the practice of assembling or evaluating consumer credit information or other information on consumers for the purpose of furnishing consumer reports to third parties, and which uses any means or facility of interstate commerce for the purpose of preparing or furnishing consumer reports.

(g) File.—The term "file," when used in connection with information on any consumer, means all of the information on that consumer recorded and retained by a consumer reporting agency regardless of how the information is stored.

(h) Employment Purposes.—The term "employment purposes" when used in connection with a consumer report means a report used for the purpose of evaluating a consumer for employment, promotion, reassignment or retention as an employee. . . .

(k) Adverse Action.—

    (1) Actions included.—The term "adverse action" . . .

        (B) means—

            (i) a denial or cancellation of, an increase in any charge for, or a reduction or other adverse or unfavorable change in the terms of coverage or amount of, any insurance, existing or applied for, in connection with the underwriting of insurance;

            (ii) a denial of employment or any other decision for employment purposes that adversely affects any current or prospective employee;

            (iii) a denial or cancellation of, an increase in any charge for, or any other adverse or unfavorable change in the terms of, any license or benefit described in section 1681b(a)(3)(D); and

            (iv) an action taken or determination that is—

                (I) made in connection with an application that was made by, or a transaction that was initiated by, any consumer, or in connection with a review of an account under section 1681b(a)(3)(F)(ii); and

                (II) adverse to the interests of the consumer. . . .

(*l*) Firm Offer of Credit or Insurance.—The term "firm offer of credit or insurance" means any offer of credit or insurance to a consumer that will be honored if the consumer is determined, based on information in a consumer report on the consumer, to meet the specific criteria used to select the consumer for the offer. . . .

(p) Consumer Reporting Agency That Compiles and Maintains Files on Consumers on a Nationwide Basis.—The term "consumer reporting agency that compiles and maintains files on consumers on a nationwide basis" means a consumer reporting agency that regularly engages in the practice of assembling or evaluating, and maintaining, for the purpose of furnishing consumer reports to third parties bearing on a consumer's credit worthiness [*sic: "credit worthiness" is two words here*], credit standing, or credit capacity, each of the following regarding consumers residing nationwide:

(1) Public record information.

(2) Credit account information from persons who furnish that information regularly and in the ordinary course of business.

(q) Definitions Relating to Fraud Alerts.— . . .

(2) Fraud alert; active duty alert.—The terms "fraud alert" and "active duty alert" mean a statement in the file of a consumer that—

(A) notifies all prospective users of a consumer report relating to the consumer that the consumer may be a victim of fraud, including identity theft, or is an active duty military consumer, as applicable. . . .

(3) Identity theft.—The term "identity theft" means a fraud committed using the identifying information of another person, subject to such further definition as the Bureau may prescribe, by regulation. . . .

(t) Financial Institution.—The term "financial institution" means a State or National bank, a State or Federal savings and loan association, a mutual savings bank, a State or Federal credit union, or any other person that, directly or indirectly, holds a transaction account . . . belonging to a consumer.

(u) Reseller.—The term "reseller" means a consumer reporting agency that—

(1) assembles and merges information contained in the database of another consumer reporting agency or multiple consumer reporting agencies concerning any consumer for purposes of furnishing such information to any third party, to the extent of such activities; and

(2) does not maintain a database of the assembled or merged information from which new consumer reports are produced. . . .

(w) Bureau.—The term "Bureau" means the Bureau of Consumer Financial Protection.

(x) Nationwide Specialty Consumer Reporting Agency.—The term "nationwide specialty consumer reporting agency" means a consumer reporting agency that compiles and maintains files on consumers on a nationwide basis relating to—

(1) medical records or payments;

(2) residential or tenant history;

(3) check writing history;

(4) employment history; or

(5) insurance claims. . . .

§ 1681b. Permissible Purposes of Consumer Reports

(a) In General.—Subject to subsection (c) of this section, any consumer reporting agency may furnish a consumer report under the following circumstances and no other:

(1) In response to the order of a court having jurisdiction to issue such an order, or a subpoena issued in connection with proceedings before a Federal grand jury.

(2) In accordance with the written instructions of the consumer to whom it relates.

(3) To a person which it has reason to believe—

(A) intends to use the information in connection with a credit transaction involving the consumer on whom the information is to be furnished and involving the extension of credit to, or review or collection of an account of, the consumer; or

(B) intends to use the information for employment purposes; or

(C) intends to use the information in connection with the underwriting of insurance involving the consumer; or

(D) intends to use the information in connection with a determination of the consumer's eligibility for a license or other benefit granted by a governmental instrumentality required by law to consider an applicant's financial responsibility or status; or

(E) intends to use the information, as a potential investor or servicer, or current insurer, in connection with a valuation of, or an assessment of the credit or prepayment risks associated with, an existing credit obligation; or

(F) otherwise has a legitimate business need for the information—

(i) in connection with a business transaction that is initiated by the consumer; or

(ii) to review an account to determine whether the consumer continues to meet the terms of the account. . . .

(b) Conditions for Furnishing and Using Consumer Reports for Employment Purposes.—

(1) Certification from user.—A consumer reporting agency may furnish a consumer report for employment purposes only if—

(A) the person who obtains such report from the agency certifies to the agency that—

(i) the person has complied with paragraph (2) with respect to the consumer report, and the person will comply with paragraph (3) with respect to the consumer report if paragraph (3) becomes applicable; and

(ii) information from the consumer report will not be used in violation of any applicable Federal or State equal employment opportunity law or regulation; and

(B) the consumer reporting agency provides with the report, or has previously provided, a summary of the consumer's rights under this Act. . . .

(2) Disclosure to consumer.—

(A) **In general**.—[A] person may not procure a consumer report, or cause a consumer report to be procured, for employment purposes with respect to any consumer, unless—

(i) a clear and conspicuous disclosure has been made in writing to the consumer at any time before the report is procured or caused to be procured, in a document that consists solely of the disclosure, that a consumer report may be obtained for employment purposes; and

(ii) the consumer has authorized in writing (which authorization may be made on the document referred to in clause (i)) the procurement of the report by that person. . . .

(3) Conditions on use for adverse actions.—

(A) **In general**.—[I]n using a consumer report for employment purposes, before taking any adverse action based in whole or in part on the report, the person intending to take such adverse action shall provide to the consumer to whom the report relates [a copy of the report and a written description of the consumer's rights]. . . .

(c) Furnishing Reports in Connection with Credit or Insurance Transactions That Are Not Initiated by the Consumer.—

(1) In general.—A consumer reporting agency may furnish a consumer report relating to any consumer pursuant to subparagraph (A) or (C) of subsection (a)(3) in connection with any credit or insurance transaction that is not initiated by the consumer only if—

(A) the consumer authorizes the agency to provide such report to such person; or

(B)

(i) the transaction consists of a firm offer of credit or insurance;

(ii) the consumer reporting agency has complied with subsection (e);

(iii) there is not in effect an election by the consumer, made in accordance with subsection (e), to have the consumer's name and address excluded from lists of names provided by the agency pursuant to this paragraph; and

(iv) the consumer report does not contain a date of birth that shows that the consumer has not attained the age of 21. . . .

(2) Limits on information received under paragraph (1)(b).—A person may receive pursuant to paragraph (1)(B) only—

(A) the name and address of a consumer;

(B) an identifier that is not unique to the consumer and that is used by the person solely for the purpose of verifying the identity of the consumer; and

(C) other information pertaining to a consumer that does not identify the relationship or experience of the consumer with respect to a particular creditor or other entity. . . .

(e) Election of Consumer to Be Excluded from Lists.—

(1) In general.—A consumer may elect to have the consumer's name and address excluded from any list provided by a consumer reporting agency under subsection (c)(1)(B) in connection with a credit or insurance transaction that is not initiated by the consumer by notifying the agency . . . that the consumer does not consent to any use of a consumer report relating to the consumer in connection with any credit or insurance transaction that is not initiated by the consumer. . . .

(f) Certain Use or Obtaining of Information Prohibited.—A person shall not use or obtain a consumer report for any purpose unless—

(1) the consumer report is obtained for a purpose for which the consumer report is authorized to be furnished under this section; and

(2) the purpose is certified in accordance with section 1681e by a prospective user of the report through a general or specific certification. . . .

§ 1681c. Requirements Relating to Information Contained in Consumer Reports

(a) Information Excluded from Consumer Reports.—Except as authorized under subsection (b) of this section, no consumer reporting agency may make any consumer report containing any of the following items of information:

(1) Cases under [the Bankruptcy Code that] antedate the report by more than 10 years.

(2) Civil suits, civil judgments, and records of arrest that, from date of entry, antedate the report by more than seven years or until the governing statute of limitations has expired, whichever is the longer period.

(3) Paid tax liens which, from date of payment, antedate the report by more than seven years.

(4) Accounts placed for collection or charged to profit and loss which antedate the report by more than seven years.

(5) Any other adverse item of information, other than records of convictions of crimes, which antedates the report by more than seven years.

(6) The name, address, and telephone number of any medical information furnisher that has notified the agency of its status, unless—

(A) such name, address, and telephone number are restricted or reported using codes that do not identify, or provide information sufficient to infer, the specific provider or the nature of such services, products, or devices to a person other than the consumer; or

(B) the report is being provided to an insurance company for a purpose relating to engaging in the business of insurance other than property and casualty insurance.

(b) Exempted Cases.—The provisions of paragraphs (1) through (5) of subsection (a) of this section are not applicable in the case of any consumer credit report to be used in connection with—

(1) a credit transaction involving, or which may reasonably be expected to involve, a principal amount of $150,000 or more;

(2) the underwriting of life insurance involving, or which may reasonably be expected to involve, a face amount of $150,000 or more; or

(3) the employment of any individual at an annual salary which equals, or which may reasonably be expected to equal $75,000, or more. . . .

(d) Information Required to Be Disclosed.—

(1) Title 11 information.—Any consumer reporting agency that furnishes a consumer report that contains information regarding any case involving the consumer that arises under Title 11 [i.e., the Bankruptcy Code], shall include in the report an identification of the chapter of such Title 11 under which such case arises if provided by the source of the information. If any case arising or filed under Title 11 . . . is withdrawn by the consumer before a final judgment, the consumer reporting agency shall include in the report that such case or filing was withdrawn upon receipt of documentation certifying such withdrawal.

(2) Key factor in credit score information.—Any consumer reporting agency that furnishes a consumer report that contains any credit score or any other risk score or predictor on any consumer shall include in the report a clear and conspicuous statement that a key factor (as defined in section 1681g(f)(2)(B)) that adversely affected such score or predictor was the number of enquiries, if such a predictor was in fact a key factor that adversely affected such score. . . .

(e) Indication of Closure of Account by Consumer.—If a consumer reporting agency is notified pursuant to section 1681s-2(a)(4) that a credit account of a consumer was voluntarily closed by the consumer, the agency shall indicate that fact in any consumer report that includes information related to the account.

(f) Indication of Dispute by Consumer.—If a consumer reporting agency is notified pursuant to section 1681s-2(a)(3) that information regarding a consumer who was furnished to the agency is disputed by the consumer, the agency shall indicate that fact in each consumer report that includes the disputed information.

(g) Truncation of Credit Card and Debit Card Numbers.—

(1) In general.—[N]o person that accepts credit cards or debit cards for the transaction of business shall print more than the last 5 digits of the card number or the expiration date upon any receipt provided to the cardholder at the point of the sale or transaction. . . .

§ 1681c-1. Identity Theft Prevention; Fraud Alerts . . .

(a) One-Call Fraud Alerts.—

(1) **Initial alerts.**—Upon the direct request of a consumer . . . who asserts in good faith a suspicion that the consumer has been or is about to become a victim of fraud or related crime, including identity theft, a consumer reporting agency described in section 1681a(p) that maintains a file on the consumer and has received appropriate proof of the identity of the requester shall—

(A) include a fraud alert in the file of that consumer, and also provide that alert along with any credit score generated in using that file, for a period of not less than 90 days . . . ; and

(B) refer the information regarding the fraud alert under this paragraph to each of the other consumer reporting agencies described in section 603(p). . . .

(b) Extended Alerts.—

(1) **In general.**—Upon the direct request of a consumer . . . who submits an identity theft report to a consumer reporting agency described in section 1681a(p) that maintains a file on the consumer, if the agency has received appropriate proof of the identity of the requester, the agency shall—

(A) include a fraud alert in the file of that consumer, and also provide that alert along with any credit score generated in using that file, during the 7-year period beginning on the date of such request . . . ;

(B) during the 5-year period beginning on the date of such request, exclude the consumer from any list of consumers prepared by the consumer reporting agency and provided to any third party to offer credit or insurance to the consumer as part of a transaction that was not initiated by the consumer . . . ; and

(C) refer the information regarding the extended fraud alert under this paragraph to each of the other consumer reporting agencies described in section 1681a(p). . . .

(h) Limitations on Use of Information for Credit Extensions.—

(1) **Requirements for initial and active duty alerts.—** . . .

(B) **Limitation on users.—** . . . No prospective user of a consumer report that includes an initial fraud alert or an active duty alert in accordance with this section may establish a new credit plan or extension of credit, other than under an open-end credit plan . . . , in the name of the consumer, or issue an additional card on an existing credit account requested by a consumer, or grant any increase in credit limit on an existing credit account requested by a consumer, unless the user utilizes reasonable policies and procedures to form a reasonable belief that the user knows the identity of the person making the request. . . .

(2) Requirements for extended alerts.— . . .

(B) Limitation on users.—No prospective user of a consumer report or of a credit score generated using the information in the file of a consumer that includes an extended fraud alert in accordance with this section may establish a new credit plan or extension of credit, other than under an open-end credit plan . . . , in the name of the consumer, or issue an additional card on an existing credit account requested by a consumer, or any increase in credit limit on an existing credit account requested by a consumer, unless the user contacts the consumer in person or using the contact method [designated by the consumer] to confirm that the application for a new credit plan or increase in credit limit, or request for an additional card is not the result of identity theft.

§ 1681c-2. Block of Information Resulting from Identity Theft

(a) Block.—Except as otherwise provided in this section, a consumer reporting agency shall block the reporting of any information in the file of a consumer that the consumer identifies as information that resulted from an alleged identity theft, not later than 4 business days after the date of receipt by such agency of—

(1) appropriate proof of the identity of the consumer;

(2) a copy of an identity theft report;

(3) the identification of such information by the consumer; and

(4) a statement by the consumer that the information is not information relating to any transaction by the consumer. . . .

(b) Notification.—A consumer reporting agency shall promptly notify the furnisher of information identified by the consumer under subsection (a)—

(1) that the information may be a result of identity theft;

(2) that an identity theft report has been filed;

(3) that a block has been requested under this section; and

(4) of the effective dates of the block. . . .

§ 1681d. Disclosure of Investigative Consumer Reports

(a) Disclosure of Fact of Preparation.—A person may not procure or cause to be prepared an investigative consumer report on any consumer unless—

(1) it is clearly and accurately disclosed to the consumer that an investigative consumer report including information as to his character, general reputation, personal characteristics, and mode of living, whichever are applicable, may be made, and such disclosure (A) is made in a writing mailed, or otherwise delivered, to the consumer, not later than three days after the date

on which the report was first requested, and (B) includes a statement informing the consumer of his right to request the additional disclosures provided for under subsection (b) of this section and the written summary of the rights of the consumer prepared pursuant to section 1681g(c); and

(2) the person certifies or has certified to the consumer reporting agency that—

(A) the person has made the disclosures to the consumer required by paragraph (1); and

(B) the person will comply with subsection (b) of this section.

(b) Disclosure on Request of Nature and Scope of Investigation.—Any person who procures or causes to be prepared an investigative consumer report on any consumer shall, upon written request made by the consumer within a reasonable period of time after the receipt by him of the disclosure required by subsection (a)(1), make a complete and accurate disclosure of the nature and scope of the investigation requested. This disclosure shall be made in a writing mailed, or otherwise delivered, to the consumer not later than five days after the date on which the request for such disclosure was received from the consumer or such report was first requested, whichever is the later.

(c) Limitation on Liability upon Showing of Reasonable Procedures for Compliance with Provisions.—No person may be held liable for any violation of subsection (a) or (b) of this section if he shows by a preponderance of the evidence that at the time of the violation he maintained reasonable procedures to assure compliance with subsection (a) or (b) of this section.

(d) Prohibitions.—

(1) Certification.—A consumer reporting agency shall not prepare or furnish an investigative consumer report unless the agency has received a certification under subsection (a)(2) from the person who requested the report.

(2) Inquiries.—A consumer reporting agency shall not make an inquiry for the purpose of preparing an investigative consumer report on a consumer for employment purposes if the making of the inquiry by an employer or prospective employer of the consumer would violate any applicable Federal or State equal employment opportunity law or regulation.

(3) Certain public record information.—Except as otherwise provided in section 1681k, a consumer reporting agency shall not furnish an investigative consumer report that includes information that is a matter of public record and that relates to an arrest, indictment, conviction, civil judicial action, tax lien, or outstanding judgment, unless the agency has verified the accuracy of the information during the 30-day period ending on the date on which the report is furnished.

(4) Certain adverse information.—A consumer reporting agency shall not prepare or furnish an investigative consumer report on a consumer that contains information that is adverse to the interest of the consumer and that is obtained through a personal interview with a neighbor, friend, or associate of the consumer or with another person with whom the consumer is acquainted or who has knowledge of such item of information, unless—

(A) the agency has followed reasonable procedures to obtain confirmation of the information, from an additional source that has independent and direct knowledge of the information; or

(B) the person interviewed is the best possible source of the information.

§ 1681e. Compliance Procedures

(a) **Identity and Purposes of Credit Users**.—Every consumer reporting agency shall maintain reasonable procedures designed to avoid violations of section 1681c [relating to prohibited and required content] and to limit the furnishing of consumer reports to the purposes listed under section 1681b. These procedures shall require that prospective users of the information identify themselves, certify the purposes for which the information is sought, and certify that the information will be used for no other purpose. Every consumer reporting agency shall make a reasonable effort to verify the identity of a new prospective user and the uses certified by such prospective user prior to furnishing such user a consumer report. No consumer reporting agency may furnish a consumer report to any person if it has reasonable grounds for believing that the consumer report will not be used for a purpose listed in section 1681b.

(b) **Accuracy of Report**.—Whenever a consumer reporting agency prepares a consumer report it shall follow reasonable procedures to assure maximum possible accuracy of the information concerning the individual about whom the report relates.

(c) **Disclosure of Consumer Reports by Users Allowed**.—A consumer reporting agency may not prohibit a user of a consumer report furnished by the agency on a consumer from disclosing the contents of the report to the consumer, if adverse action against the consumer has been taken by the user based in whole or in part on the report.

(d) **Notice to Users and Furnishers of Information**.—

(1) **Notice requirement**.—A consumer reporting agency shall provide to any person—

(A) who regularly and in the ordinary course of business furnishes information to the agency with respect to any consumer; or

(B) to whom a consumer report is provided by the agency;

a notice of such person's responsibilities under this Act. . . .

(e) **Procurement of Consumer Report for Resale**.—

(1) **Disclosure**.—A person may not procure a consumer report for purposes of reselling the report (or any information in the report) unless the person discloses to the consumer reporting agency that originally furnishes the report—

(A) the identity of the end-user of the report (or information); and

(B) each permissible purpose under section 1681b for which the report is furnished to the end-user of the report (or information).

(2) Responsibilities of procurers for resale.—A person who procures a consumer report for purposes of reselling the report (or any information in the report) shall—

(A) establish and comply with reasonable procedures designed to ensure that the report (or information) is resold by the person only for a purpose for which the report may be furnished under section 1681b, including by requiring that each person to which the report (or information) is resold and that resells or provides the report (or information) to any other person—

(i) identifies each end user of the resold report (or information);

(ii) certifies each purpose for which the report (or information) will be used; and

(iii) certifies that the report (or information) will be used for no other purpose; and

(B) before reselling the report, make reasonable efforts to verify the identifications and certifications made under subparagraph (A).

§ 1681f. Disclosures to Governmental Agencies

Notwithstanding the provisions of section 1681b, a consumer reporting agency may furnish identifying information respecting any consumer, limited to his name, address, former addresses, places of employment, or former places of employment, to a governmental agency.

§ 1681g. Disclosures to Consumers

(a) Information on File; Sources; Report Recipients.—Every consumer reporting agency shall, upon request, and subject to section 1681h(a)(1), clearly and accurately disclose to the consumer:

(1) All information. All information in the consumer's file at the time of the request, except that . . .

(B) nothing in this paragraph shall be construed to require a consumer reporting agency to disclose to a consumer any information concerning credit scores or any other risk scores or predictors relating to the consumer.

(2) Sources. The sources of the information; except that the sources of information acquired solely for use in preparing an investigative consumer report and actually used for no other purpose need not be disclosed: *Provided*, That in the event an action is brought under this Act, such sources shall be available to the plaintiff under appropriate discovery procedures in the court in which the action is brought.

(3) **Users.**

(A) Identification of each person (including each end-user identified under section 1681e(e)(1)) that procured a consumer report—

(i) for employment purposes, during the 2-year period preceding the date on which the request is made; or

(ii) for any other purpose, during the 1-year period preceding the date on which the request is made.

(B) An identification of a person under subparagraph (A) shall include—

(i) the name of the person or, if applicable, the trade name (written in full) under which such person conducts business; and

(ii) upon request of the consumer, the address and telephone number of the person.

(C) Subparagraph (A) does not apply if—

(i) the end user is an agency or department of the United States Government that procures the report from the person for purposes of determining the eligibility of the consumer to whom the report relates to receive access or continued access to classified information (as defined in section 1681b(b)(4)(E)(i)); and

(ii) the head of the agency or department makes a written finding as prescribed under section 1681b(b)(4)(A).

(4) **Checks.** The dates, original payees, and amounts of any checks upon which is based any adverse characterization of the consumer, included in the file at the time of the disclosure.

(5) **Inquiries.** A record of all inquiries received by the agency during the 1-year period preceding the request that identified the consumer in connection with a credit or insurance transaction that was not initiated by the consumer.

(6) **Credit score.** If the consumer requests the credit file and not the credit score, a statement that the consumer may request and obtain a credit score.

(b) **Exempt Information.**—The requirements of subsection (a) of this section respecting the disclosure of sources of information and the recipients of consumer reports do not apply to information received or consumer reports furnished prior to the effective date of this Act except to the extent that the matter involved is contained in the files of the consumer reporting agency on that date.

(c) **Summary of Rights to Obtain and Dispute Information in Consumer Reports and to Obtain Credit Scores.**—

(1) **Bureau summary of rights required.**—

(A) **In general.**—The Bureau shall prepare a model summary of the rights of consumers under this title. . . .

(2) Summary of rights required to be included with agency disclosures.—A consumer reporting agency shall provide to a consumer, with each written disclosure by the agency to the consumer under this section—

(A) the summary of rights prepared by the Bureau under paragraph (1); [and]

(B) in the case of a consumer reporting agency described in section 1681a(p), a toll-free telephone number established by the agency, at which personnel are accessible to consumers during normal business hours. . . .

(d) Summary of Rights of Identity Theft Victims.— . . .

(e) Information Available to Victims.—

(1) In general.—For the purpose of documenting fraudulent transactions resulting from identity theft, not later than 30 days after the date of receipt of a request from a victim in accordance with paragraph (3), and subject to verification of the identity of the victim and the claim of identity theft in accordance with paragraph (2), a business entity that has provided credit to, provided for consideration products, goods, or services to, accepted payment from, or otherwise entered into a commercial transaction for consideration with, a person who has allegedly made unauthorized use of the means of identification of the victim, shall provide a copy of application and business transaction records in the control of the business entity, whether maintained by the business entity or by another person on behalf of the business entity, evidencing any transaction alleged to be a result of identity theft to—

(A) the victim;

(B) any Federal, State, or local government law enforcement agency or officer specified by the victim in such a request; or

(C) any law enforcement agency investigating the identity theft and authorized by the victim to take receipt of records provided under this subsection. . . .

(f) Disclosure of Credit Scores.—

(1) In general.—Upon the request of a consumer for a credit score, a consumer reporting agency shall supply to the consumer a statement indicating that the information and credit scoring model may be different than the credit score that may be used by the lender, and a notice which shall include—

(A) the current credit score of the consumer or the most recent credit score of the consumer that was previously calculated by the credit reporting agency for a purpose related to the extension of credit;

(B) the range of possible credit scores under the model used;

(C) all of the key factors that adversely affected the credit score of the consumer in the model used, the total number of which shall not exceed 4, subject to paragraph (9);

(D) the date on which the credit score was created; and

(E) the name of the person or entity that provided the credit score or credit file upon which the credit score was created.

(2) **Definitions.**—For purposes of this subsection, the following definitions shall apply:

(A) **Credit score.**—The term "credit score"—

(i) means a numerical value or a categorization derived from a statistical tool or modeling system used by a person who makes or arranges a loan to predict the likelihood of certain credit behaviors, including default (and the numerical value or the categorization derived from such analysis may also be referred to as a "risk predictor" or "risk score"). . . .

(B) **Key factors.**—The term "key factors" means all relevant elements or reasons adversely affecting the credit score for the particular individual, listed in the order of their importance based on their effect on the credit score. . . .

(6) **Maintenance of credit scores not required.**—This subsection shall not be construed to require a consumer reporting agency to maintain credit scores in its files.

(7) **Compliance in certain cases.**—In complying with this subsection, a consumer reporting agency shall—

(A) supply the consumer with a credit score that is derived from a credit scoring model that is widely distributed to users by that consumer reporting agency in connection with residential real property loans or with a credit score that assists the consumer in understanding the credit scoring assessment of the credit behavior of the consumer and predictions about the future credit behavior of the consumer; and

(B) a statement indicating that the information and credit scoring model may be different than that used by the lender.

(8) **Fair and reasonable fee.**—A consumer reporting agency may charge a fair and reasonable fee, as determined by the Bureau, for providing the information required under this subsection.

(9) **Use of enquiries as a key factor.**—If a key factor that adversely affects the credit score of a consumer consists of the number of enquiries made with respect to a consumer report, that factor shall be included in the disclosure pursuant to paragraph (1)(C) without regard to the numerical limitation in such paragraph. . . .

§ 1681i. Procedure in Case of Disputed Accuracy

(a) **Reinvestigations of Disputed Information.**—

(1) **Reinvestigation required.**—

(A) **In general.**—Subject to subsection (f), if the completeness or accuracy of any item of information contained in a consumer's file at a consumer reporting agency is disputed by the consumer and the consumer notifies the agency directly, or indirectly through a reseller, of such dispute, the agency shall, free of charge, conduct a reasonable reinvestigation to determine whether the disputed information is inaccurate and record the current status of the disputed information, or delete the item from the file in accordance with paragraph (5), before the end of the 30-day period beginning on the date on which the agency receives the notice of the dispute from the consumer or reseller.

(B) **Extension of period to reinvestigate**.—Except as provided in subparagraph (C), the 30-day period described in subparagraph (A) may be extended for not more than 15 additional days if the consumer reporting agency receives information from the consumer during that 30-day period that is relevant to the reinvestigation.

(C) **Limitations on extension of period to reinvestigate**.—Subparagraph (B) shall not apply to any reinvestigation in which, during the 30-day period described in subparagraph (A), the information that is the subject of the reinvestigation is found to be inaccurate or incomplete or the consumer reporting agency determines that the information cannot be verified.

(2) **Prompt notice of dispute to furnisher of information**.—

(A) **In general**.—Before the expiration of the 5-business-day period beginning on the date on which a consumer reporting agency receives notice of a dispute from any consumer or a reseller in accordance with paragraph (1), the agency shall provide notification of the dispute to any person who provided any item of information in dispute, at the address and in the manner established with the person. The notice shall include all relevant information regarding the dispute that the agency has received from the consumer or reseller.

(B) **Provision of other information**.—The consumer reporting agency shall promptly provide to the person who provided the information in dispute all relevant information regarding the dispute that is received by the agency from the consumer or the reseller after the period referred to in subparagraph (A) and before the end of the period referred to in paragraph (1)(A).

(3) **Determination that dispute is frivolous or irrelevant**.—

(A) **In general**.—Notwithstanding paragraph (1), a consumer reporting agency may terminate a reinvestigation of information disputed by a consumer under that paragraph if the agency reasonably determines that the dispute by the consumer is frivolous or irrelevant, including by reason of a failure by a consumer to provide sufficient information to investigate the disputed information.

(B) **Notice of determination**.—Upon making any determination in accordance with subparagraph (A) that a dispute is frivolous or irrelevant, a consumer reporting agency shall notify the consumer of such determination not later than 5 business days after making such determination, by mail or, if authorized by the consumer for that purpose, by any other means available to the agency.

(C) **Contents of notice.**—A notice under subparagraph (B) shall include—

(i) the reasons for the determination under subparagraph (A); and

(ii) identification of any information required to investigate the disputed information, which may consist of a standardized form describing the general nature of such information.

(4) **Consideration of consumer information.**—In conducting any reinvestigation under paragraph (1) with respect to disputed information in the file of any consumer, the consumer reporting agency shall review and consider all relevant information submitted by the consumer in the period described in paragraph (1)(A) with respect to such disputed information.

(5) **Treatment of inaccurate or unverifiable information.**—

(A) **In general.**—If, after any reinvestigation under paragraph (1) of any information disputed by a consumer, an item of the information is found to be inaccurate or incomplete or cannot be verified, the consumer reporting agency shall—

(i) promptly delete that item of information from the file of the consumer, or modify that item of information, as appropriate, based on the results of the reinvestigation; and

(ii) promptly notify the furnisher of that information that the information has been modified or deleted from the file of the consumer.

(B) **Requirements relating to reinsertion of previously deleted material.**—

(i) **Certification of accuracy of information.**—If any information is deleted from a consumer's file pursuant to subparagraph (A), the information may not be reinserted in the file by the consumer reporting agency unless the person who furnishes the information certifies that the information is complete and accurate.

(ii) **Notice to consumer.**—If any information that has been deleted from a consumer's file pursuant to subparagraph (A) is reinserted in the file, the consumer reporting agency shall notify the consumer of the reinsertion in writing not later than 5 business days after the reinsertion or, if authorized by the consumer for that purpose, by any other means available to the agency.

(iii) **Additional information.**—As part of, or in addition to, the notice under clause (ii), a consumer reporting agency shall provide to a consumer in writing not later than 5 business days after the date of the reinsertion—

(I) a statement that the disputed information has been reinserted;

(II) the business name and address of any furnisher of information contacted and the telephone number of such furnisher, if reasonably available, or of any furnisher of information that contacted the consumer reporting agency, in connection with the reinsertion of such information; and

(III) a notice that the consumer has the right to add a statement to the consumer's file disputing the accuracy or completeness of the disputed information.

(C) Procedures to prevent reappearance.—A consumer reporting agency shall maintain reasonable procedures designed to prevent the reappearance in a consumer's file, and in consumer reports on the consumer, of information that is deleted pursuant to this paragraph (other than information that is reinserted in accordance with subparagraph (B)(i)).

(D) Automated reinvestigation system.—Any consumer reporting agency that compiles and maintains files on consumers on a nationwide basis shall implement an automated system through which furnishers of information to that consumer reporting agency may report the results of a reinvestigation that finds incomplete or inaccurate information in a consumer's file to other such consumer reporting agencies.

(6) Notice of results of reinvestigation.—

(A) In general.—A consumer reporting agency shall provide written notice to a consumer of the results of a reinvestigation under this subsection not later than 5 business days after the completion of the reinvestigation, by mail or, if authorized by the consumer for that purpose, by other means available to the agency.

(B) Contents.—As part of, or in addition to, the notice under subparagraph (A), a consumer reporting agency shall provide to a consumer in writing before the expiration of the 5-day period referred to in subparagraph (A)—

(i) a statement that the reinvestigation is completed;

(ii) a consumer report that is based upon the consumer's file as that file is revised as a result of the reinvestigation;

(iii) a notice that, if requested by the consumer, a description of the procedure used to determine the accuracy and completeness of the information shall be provided to the consumer by the agency, including the business name and address of any furnisher of information contacted in connection with such information and the telephone number of such furnisher, if reasonably available;

(iv) a notice that the consumer has the right to add a statement to the consumer's file disputing the accuracy or completeness of the information; and

(v) a notice that the consumer has the right to request under subsection (d) that the consumer reporting agency furnish notifications under that subsection.

(7) Description of reinvestigation procedure.—A consumer reporting agency shall provide to a consumer a description referred to in paragraph (6)(B)(iii) by not later than 15 days after receiving a request from the consumer for that description.

(8) Expedited dispute resolution.—If a dispute regarding an item of information in a consumer's file at a consumer reporting agency is resolved in accordance with paragraph (5)(A) by the deletion of the disputed information by not later than 3 business days after the date on which the agency receives notice of the dispute from the consumer in accordance with paragraph (1)(A), then the agency shall not be required to comply with paragraphs (2), (6), and (7) with respect to that dispute if the agency—

(A) provides prompt notice of the deletion to the consumer by telephone;

(B) includes in that notice, or in a written notice that accompanies a confirmation and consumer report provided in accordance with subparagraph (C), a statement of the consumer's right to request under subsection (d) of this section that the agency furnish notifications under that subsection; and

(C) provides written confirmation of the deletion and a copy of a consumer report on the consumer that is based on the consumer's file after the deletion, not later than 5 business days after making the deletion.

(b) Statement of Dispute.—If the reinvestigation does not resolve the dispute, the consumer may file a brief statement setting forth the nature of the dispute. The consumer reporting agency may limit such statements to not more than one hundred words if it provides the consumer with assistance in writing a clear summary of the dispute.

(c) Notification of Consumer Dispute in Subsequent Consumer Reports.—Whenever a statement of a dispute is filed, unless there is reasonable grounds to believe that it is frivolous or irrelevant, the consumer reporting agency shall, in any subsequent consumer report containing the information in question, clearly note that it is disputed by the consumer and provide either the consumer's statement or a clear and accurate codification or summary thereof.

(d) Notification of Deletion of Disputed Information.—Following any deletion of information which is found to be inaccurate or whose accuracy can no longer be verified or any notation as to disputed information, the consumer reporting agency shall, at the request of the consumer, furnish notification that the item has been deleted or the statement, codification or summary pursuant to subsection (b) or (c) of this section to any person specifically designated by the consumer who has within two years prior thereto received a consumer report for employment purposes, or within six months prior thereto received a consumer report for any other purpose, which contained the deleted or disputed information.

(e) Treatment of Complaints . . . —
  (1) In general.—The Bureau shall—
    (A) compile all complaints that it receives that a file of a consumer that is maintained by a consumer reporting agency described in section 1681a(p) contains incomplete or inaccurate information, with respect to which, the consumer appears to have disputed the completeness or accuracy with the consumer reporting agency or otherwise utilized the procedures provided by subsection (a); and
    (B) transmit each such complaint to each consumer reporting agency involved. . . .
  (3) Agency responsibilities.—Each consumer reporting agency described in section 1681a(p) that receives a complaint transmitted by the Bureau pursuant to paragraph (1) shall—
    (A) review each such complaint to determine whether all legal obligations imposed on the consumer reporting agency under this title (including any obligation imposed by an applicable court or administrative order) have been met with respect to the subject matter of the complaint;
    (B) provide reports on a regular basis to the Bureau regarding the determinations of and actions taken by the consumer reporting agency, if any, in connection with its review of such complaints; and
    (C) maintain, for a reasonable time period, records regarding the disposition of each such complaint that is sufficient to demonstrate compliance with this subsection. . . .

§ 1681j. Charges for Certain Disclosures

(a) Free Annual Disclosure.—
  (1) Nationwide consumer reporting agencies.—
    (A) In general.—All consumer reporting agencies described in subsections (p) and (w) of section 1681a shall make all disclosures pursuant to section 1681g once during any 12-month period upon request of the consumer and without charge to the consumer. . . .
(b) Free Disclosure After Adverse Notice to Consumer.—Each consumer reporting agency that maintains a file on a consumer shall make all disclosures pursuant to section 1681g without charge to the consumer if, not later than 60 days after receipt by such consumer of a notification pursuant to section 1681m, or of a notification from a debt collection agency affiliated with that consumer reporting agency stating that the consumer's credit rating may be or has been adversely affected, the consumer makes a request under section 1681g. . . .
(d) Free Disclosures in Connection with Fraud Alerts.—Upon the request of a consumer, a consumer reporting agency described in section 1681a(p) shall make all disclosures pursuant to section 1681g without charge

to the consumer, as provided in subsections (a)(2) and (b)(2) of section 1681c-1, as applicable.

(e) Other Charges Prohibited.—A consumer reporting agency shall not impose any charge on a consumer for providing any notification required by this Act or making any disclosure required by this Act, except as authorized by subsection (f) of this section.

(f) Reasonable Charges Allowed for Certain Disclosures.—

(1) **In general.**—In the case of a request from a consumer other than a request that is covered by any of subsections (a) through (d), a consumer reporting agency may impose a reasonable charge on a consumer—

(A) for making a disclosure to the consumer pursuant to section 1681g, which charge . . . shall be indicated to the consumer before making the disclosure; and

(B) for furnishing, pursuant to section 1681i(d), following a reinvestigation under section 1681i(a), a statement, codification, or summary to a person designated by the consumer under that section after the 30-day period beginning on the date of notification of the consumer under paragraph (6) or (8) of section 1681i(a) with respect to the reinvestigation, which charge—

(i) shall not exceed the charge that the agency would impose on each designated recipient for a consumer report; and

(ii) shall be indicated to the consumer before furnishing such information. . . .

§ 1681k. Public Record Information for Employment Purposes

(a) **In General.**—A consumer reporting agency which furnishes a consumer report for employment purposes and which for that purpose compiles and reports items of information on consumers which are matters of public record and are likely to have an adverse effect upon a consumer's ability to obtain employment shall—

(1) at the time such public record information is reported to the user of such consumer report, notify the consumer of the fact that public record information is being reported by the consumer reporting agency, together with the name and address of the person to whom such information is being reported; or

(2) maintain strict procedures designed to insure that whenever public record information which is likely to have an adverse effect on a consumer's ability to obtain employment is reported it is complete and up to date. For purposes of this paragraph, items of public record relating to arrests, indictments, convictions, suits, tax liens, and outstanding judgments shall be considered up to date if the current public record status of the item at the time of the report is reported. . . .

§ 1681l. Restrictions on Investigative Consumer Reports.—

Whenever a consumer reporting agency prepares an investigative consumer report, no adverse information in the consumer report (other than information which is a matter of public record) may be included in a subsequent consumer report unless such adverse information has been verified in the process of making such subsequent consumer report, or the adverse information was received within the three-month period preceding the date the subsequent report is furnished.

§ 1681m. Requirements on Users of Consumer Reports

(a) Duties of Users Taking Adverse Actions on the Basis of Information Contained in Consumer Reports.—If any person takes any adverse action with respect to any consumer that is based in whole or in part on any information contained in a consumer report, the person shall—

(1) provide oral, written, or electronic notice of the adverse action to the consumer;

(2) provide to the consumer written or electronic disclosure—

(A) of a numerical credit score as defined in section 1681g(f)(2)(A) used by such person in taking any adverse action based in whole or in part on any information in a consumer report; and

(B) of the information set forth in subparagraphs (B) through (E) of section 1681g(f)(1);

(3) provide to the consumer orally, in writing, or electronically—

(A) the name, address, and telephone number of the consumer reporting agency (including a toll-free telephone number established by the agency if the agency compiles and maintains files on consumers on a nationwide basis) that furnished the report to the person; and

(B) a statement that the consumer reporting agency did not make the decision to take the adverse action and is unable to provide the consumer the specific reasons why the adverse action was taken; and

(4) provide to the consumer an oral, written, or electronic notice of the consumer's right—

(A) to obtain, under section 1681j, a free copy of a consumer report on the consumer from the consumer reporting agency referred to in paragraph (3), which notice shall include an indication of the 60-day period under that section for obtaining such a copy; and

(B) to dispute, under section 1681i, with a consumer reporting agency the accuracy or completeness of any information in a consumer report furnished by the agency.

(b) Adverse Action Based on Information Obtained from Third Parties Other Than Consumer Reporting Agencies.—

(1) **In general.**—Whenever credit for personal, family, or household purposes involving a consumer is denied or the charge for such credit is increased either wholly or partly because of information obtained from a person other than a consumer reporting agency bearing upon the consumer's credit worthiness, credit standing, credit capacity, character, general reputation, personal characteristics, or mode of living, the user of such information shall, within a reasonable period of time, upon the consumer's written request for the reasons for such adverse action received within sixty days after learning of such adverse action, disclose the nature of the information to the consumer. The user of such information shall clearly and accurately disclose to the consumer his right to make such written request at the time such adverse action is communicated to the consumer.

(2) **Duties of person taking certain actions based on information provided by affiliate.**—

(A) **Duties, generally.**—If a person takes an action described in subparagraph (B) with respect to a consumer, based in whole or in part on information described in subparagraph (C), the person shall—

(i) notify the consumer of the action, including a statement that the consumer may obtain the information in accordance with clause (ii); and

(ii) upon a written request from the consumer received within 60 days after transmittal of the notice required by clause (i), disclose to the consumer the nature of the information upon which the action is based by not later than 30 days after receipt of the request.

(B) **Action described.**—An action referred to in subparagraph (A) is an adverse action described in section 1681a(k)(1)(A), taken in connection with a transaction initiated by the consumer, or any adverse action described in clause (i) or (ii) of section 1681a(k)(1)(B).

(C) **Information described.**—Information referred to in subparagraph (A)—

(i) except as provided in clause (ii), is information that—

(I) is furnished to the person taking the action by a person related by common ownership or affiliated by common corporate control to the person taking the action; and

(II) bears on the credit worthiness, credit standing, credit capacity, character, general reputation, personal characteristics, or mode of living of the consumer; and

(ii) does not include—

(I) information solely as to transactions or experiences between the consumer and the person furnishing the information; or

(II) information in a consumer report.

(c) **Reasonable Procedures to Assure Compliance.**—No person shall be held liable for any violation of this section if he shows by a preponderance of the evidence that at the time of the alleged violation he maintained reasonable procedures to assure compliance with the provisions of this section. . . .

(f) Prohibition on Sale or Transfer of Debt Caused by Identity Theft.—
(1) In general.—No person shall sell, transfer for consideration, or place for collection a debt that such person has been notified under section 1681c-2 has resulted from identity theft. . . .
(h) Duties of Users in Certain Credit Transactions.—
(1) In general.—[I]f any person uses a consumer report in connection with an application for, or a grant, extension, or other provision of, credit on material terms that are materially less favorable than the most favorable terms available to a substantial proportion of consumers from or through that person, based in whole or in part on a consumer report, the person shall provide an oral, written, or electronic notice to the consumer in the form and manner required by regulations prescribed in accordance with this subsection. . . .

§ 1681n. Civil Liability for Willful Noncompliance

(a) In General.—Any person who willfully fails to comply with any requirement imposed under this Act with respect to any consumer is liable to that consumer in an amount equal to the sum of—
 (1) (A) any actual damages sustained by the consumer as a result of the failure or damages of not less than $100 and not more than $1,000; or
  (B) in the case of liability of a natural person for obtaining a consumer report under false pretenses or knowingly without a permissible purpose, actual damages sustained by the consumer as a result of the failure or $1,000, whichever is greater;
 (2) such amount of punitive damages as the court may allow; and
 (3) in the case of any successful action to enforce any liability under this section, the costs of the action together with reasonable attorney's fees as determined by the court.
(b) Civil liability for Knowing Noncompliance.—Any person who obtains a consumer report from a consumer reporting agency under false pretenses or knowingly without a permissible purpose shall be liable to the consumer reporting agency for actual damages sustained by the consumer reporting agency or $1,000, whichever is greater. . . .

§ 1681o. Civil Liability for Negligent Noncompliance

(a) In General.—Any person who is negligent in failing to comply with any requirement imposed under this Act with respect to any consumer is liable to that consumer in an amount equal to the sum of—
 (1) any actual damages sustained by the consumer as a result of the failure; and

(2) in the case of any successful action to enforce any liability under this section, the costs of the action together with reasonable attorney's fees as determined by the court. . . .

§ 1681q. Obtaining Information Under False Pretenses.—

Any person who knowingly and willfully obtains information on a consumer from a consumer reporting agency under false pretenses shall be fined under Title 18, imprisoned for not more than 2 years, or both.

§ 1681r. Unauthorized Disclosures by Officers or Employees.—

Any officer or employee of a consumer reporting agency who knowingly and willfully provides information concerning an individual from the agency's files to a person not authorized to receive that information shall be fined under Title 18, imprisoned for not more than 2 years, or both.

§ 1681s. Administrative Enforcement

(a) **Enforcement by Federal Trade Commission.**—
(1) **In general**.—The Federal Trade Commission shall be authorized to enforce compliance with the requirements imposed by this Act under the Federal Trade Commission Act, with respect to consumer reporting agencies and all other persons subject thereto, except to the extent that enforcement of the requirements imposed under this title is specifically committed to some other Government agency . . . .
(b) **Enforcement by Other Agencies.**—
(1) **In general**.—[Industry-specific regulators (e.g., the federal banking agencies, the Securities and Exchange Commission, and the Commodity Futures Trading Commission) and the Bureau shall enforce this Act under their respective enforcement statutes.]
(c) **State Action for Violations.**—
(1) **Authority of States**.—In addition to such other remedies as are provided under State law, if the chief law enforcement officer of a State, or an official or agency designated by a State, has reason to believe that any person has violated or is violating this Act, the State—
    (A) may bring an action to enjoin such violation in any appropriate United States district court or in any other court of competent jurisdiction;
    (B) subject to [except in the case of information furnishers' duty to provide accurate information and to have reasonable policies and

procedures for dealing with identity theft], may bring an action on behalf of the residents of the State to recover—

(i) damages for which the person is liable to such residents under sections 1681n and 1681o as a result of the violation;

(ii) in the case of a violation described in any of paragraphs (1) through (3) of section 1681s-2(c), damages for which the person would, but for section 1681s-2(c), be liable to such residents as a result of the violation; or

(iii) damages of not more than $ 1,000 for each willful or negligent violation; and

(C) in the case of any successful action under subparagraph (A) or (B), shall be awarded the costs of the action and reasonable attorney fees as determined by the court. . . .

(e) Regulatory authority.—

(1) In general.—The Bureau shall prescribe such regulations as are necessary to carry out the purposes of this Act, except with respect to sections 1681m(e) and 1681w. The Bureau may prescribe regulations as may be necessary or appropriate to administer and carry out the purposes and objectives of this Act, and to prevent evasions thereof or to facilitate compliance therewith. . . .

§ 1681s-2. Responsibilities of Furnishers of Information to Consumer Reporting Agencies

(a) Duty of Furnishers of Information to Provide Accurate Information.—

(1) Prohibition.—

(A) Reporting information with actual knowledge of errors.—A person shall not furnish any information relating to a consumer to any consumer reporting agency if the person knows or has reasonable cause to believe that the information is inaccurate.

(B) Reporting information after notice and confirmation of errors.—A person shall not furnish information relating to a consumer to any consumer reporting agency if—

(i) the person has been notified by the consumer, at the address specified by the person for such notices, that specific information is inaccurate; and

(ii) the information is, in fact, inaccurate. . . .

(D) Definition.—For purposes of subparagraph (A), the term "reasonable cause to believe that the information is inaccurate" means having specific knowledge, other than solely allegations by the consumer, that would cause a reasonable person to have substantial doubts about the accuracy of the information.

(2) **Duty to correct and update information.**—A person who—

(A) regularly and in the ordinary course of business furnishes information to one or more consumer reporting agencies about the person's transactions or experiences with any consumer; and

(B) has furnished to a consumer reporting agency information that the person determines is not complete or accurate,

shall promptly notify the consumer reporting agency of that determination and provide to the agency any corrections to that information, or any additional information, that is necessary to make the information provided by the person to the agency complete and accurate, and shall not thereafter furnish to the agency any of the information that remains not complete or accurate.

(3) **Duty to provide notice of dispute.**—If the completeness or accuracy of any information furnished by any person to any consumer reporting agency is disputed to such person by a consumer, the person may not furnish the information to any consumer reporting agency without notice that such information is disputed by the consumer.

(4) **Duty to provide notice of closed accounts.**—A person who regularly and in the ordinary course of business furnishes information to a consumer reporting agency regarding a consumer who has a credit account with that person shall notify the agency of the voluntary closure of the account by the consumer, in information regularly furnished for the period in which the account is closed.

(5) **Duty to provide notice of delinquency of accounts.**—

(A) **In general.**—A person who furnishes information to a consumer reporting agency regarding a delinquent account being placed for collection, charged to profit or loss, or subjected to any similar action shall, not later than 90 days after furnishing the information, notify the agency of the date of delinquency on the account, which shall be the month and year of the commencement of the delinquency on the account that immediately preceded the action.

(B) **Rule of construction.**—For purposes of this paragraph only, and provided that the consumer does not dispute the information, a person that furnishes information on a delinquent account that is placed for collection, charged for profit or loss, or subjected to any similar action, complies with this paragraph, if—

(i) the person reports the same date of delinquency as that provided by the creditor to which the account was owed at the time at which the commencement of the delinquency occurred, if the creditor previously reported that date of delinquency to a consumer reporting agency;

(ii) the creditor did not previously report the date of delinquency to a consumer reporting agency, and the person establishes and follows reasonable procedures to obtain the date of delinquency from the creditor or another reliable source and reports that date to a consumer reporting agency as the date of delinquency; or

(iii) the creditor did not previously report the date of delinquency to a consumer reporting agency and the date of delinquency cannot be reasonably obtained as provided in clause (ii), the person establishes and follows reasonable procedures to ensure the date reported as the date of delinquency precedes the date on which the account is placed for collection, charged to profit or loss, or subjected to any similar action, and reports such date to the credit reporting agency. . . .

(7) Negative information.—

(A) Notice to consumer required.—

(i) In general.—If any financial institution that extends credit and regularly and in the ordinary course of business furnishes information to a consumer reporting agency described in section 1681a(p) furnishes negative information to such an agency regarding credit extended to a customer, the financial institution shall provide a notice of such furnishing of negative information, in writing, to the customer.

(ii) Notice effective for subsequent submissions.—After providing such notice, the financial institution may submit additional negative information to a consumer reporting agency described in section 1681a(p) with respect to the same transaction, extension of credit, account, or customer without providing additional notice to the customer.

(B) Time of notice.—

(i) In general.—The notice required under subparagraph (A) shall be provided to the customer prior to, or no later than 30 days after, furnishing the negative information to a consumer reporting agency described in section 1681a(p). . . .

(C) Coordination with other disclosures.—The notice required under subparagraph (A)—

(i) may be included on or with any notice of default, any billing statement, or any other materials provided to the customer; and

(ii) must be clear and conspicuous.

(D) Model disclosure.—

(i) Duty of Bureau.—The Bureau shall prescribe a brief model disclosure that a financial institution may use to comply with subparagraph (A), which shall not exceed 30 words. . . .

(E) Use of notice without submitting negative information.—No provision of this paragraph shall be construed as requiring a financial institution that has provided a customer with a notice described in subparagraph (A) to furnish negative information about the customer to a consumer reporting agency.

(F) Safe harbor.—A financial institution shall not be liable for failure to perform the duties required by this paragraph if, at the time of the failure, the financial institution maintained reasonable policies and procedures to comply with this paragraph or the financial institution reasonably believed that the institution is prohibited, by law, from contacting the consumer.

(G) Definitions.—For purposes of this paragraph, . . . "negative information" means information concerning a customer's delinquencies, late payments, insolvency, or any form of default. . . .

(8) Ability of consumer to dispute information directly with furnisher.—

(A) In general.—The Bureau shall prescribe regulations that shall identify the circumstances under which a furnisher shall be required to reinvestigate a dispute concerning the accuracy of information contained in a consumer report on the consumer, based on a direct request of a consumer. . . .

(D) Submitting a notice of dispute.—A consumer who seeks to dispute the accuracy of information shall provide a dispute notice directly to such person at the address specified by the person for such notices that—

(i) identifies the specific information that is being disputed;

(ii) explains the basis for the dispute; and

(iii) includes all supporting documentation required by the furnisher to substantiate the basis of the dispute.

(E) Duty of person after receiving notice of dispute.—After receiving a notice of dispute from a consumer pursuant to subparagraph (D), the person that provided the information in dispute to a consumer reporting agency shall—

(i) conduct an investigation with respect to the disputed information;

(ii) review all relevant information provided by the consumer with the notice;

(iii) complete such person's investigation of the dispute and report the results of the investigation to the consumer before the expiration of the period under section 1681i(a)(1) within which a consumer reporting agency would be required to complete its action if the consumer had elected to dispute the information under that section; and

(iv) if the investigation finds that the information reported was inaccurate, promptly notify each consumer reporting agency to which the person furnished the inaccurate information of that determination and provide to the agency any correction to that information that is necessary to make the information provided by the person accurate. . . .

(b) Duties of Furnishers of Information upon Notice of Dispute.—

(1) In general.—After receiving notice pursuant to section 1681i(a)(2) of a dispute with regard to the completeness or accuracy of any information provided by a person to a consumer reporting agency, the person shall—

(A) conduct an investigation with respect to the disputed information;

(B) review all relevant information provided by the consumer reporting agency pursuant to section 1681i(a)(2);

(C) report the results of the investigation to the consumer reporting agency;

(D) if the investigation finds that the information is incomplete or inaccurate, report those results to all other consumer reporting agencies to which the person furnished the information and that compile and maintain files on consumers on a nationwide basis; and

(E) if an item of information disputed by a consumer is found to be inaccurate or incomplete or cannot be verified after any reinvestigation under paragraph (1), for purposes of reporting to a consumer reporting agency only, as appropriate, based on the results of the reinvestigation promptly—

(i) modify that item of information;

(ii) delete that item of information; or

(iii) permanently block the reporting of that item of information.

(2) Deadline.—A person shall complete all investigations, reviews, and reports required under paragraph (1) regarding information provided by the person to a consumer reporting agency, before the expiration of the period under section 1681i(a)(1) within which the consumer reporting agency is required to complete actions required by that section regarding that information. . . .

(d) Limitation on Enforcement.—The provisions of law described in paragraphs (1) through (3) of subsection (c) (other than with respect to the exception described in paragraph (2) of subsection (c)) shall be enforced exclusively as provided under section 1681s by the Federal agencies and officials and the State officials identified in section 1681s. . . .

§ 1681s-3. Affiliate Sharing

(a) Special Rule for Solicitation for Purposes of Marketing.—

(1) Notice.—Any person that receives from another person related to it by common ownership or affiliated by corporate control a communication of information that would be a consumer report, but for clauses (i), (ii), and (iii) of section 1681a(d)(2)(A), may not use the information to make a solicitation for marketing purposes to a consumer about its products or services, unless—

(A) it is clearly and conspicuously disclosed to the consumer that the information may be communicated among such persons for purposes of making such solicitations to the consumer; and

(B) the consumer is provided an opportunity and a simple method to prohibit the making of such solicitations to the consumer by such person. . . .

(4) **Scope**.—This section shall not apply to a person—

(A) using information to make a solicitation for marketing purposes to a consumer with whom the person has a pre-existing business relationship;

(B) using information to facilitate communications to an individual for whose benefit the person provides employee benefit or other services pursuant to a contract with an employer related to and arising out of the current employment relationship or status of the individual as a participant or beneficiary of an employee benefit plan;

(C) using information to perform services on behalf of another person related by common ownership or affiliated by corporate control, except that this subparagraph shall not be construed as permitting a person to send solicitations on behalf of another person, if such other person would not be permitted to send the solicitation on its own behalf as a result of the election of the consumer to prohibit solicitations under paragraph (1)(B);

(D) using information in response to a communication initiated by the consumer;

(E) using information in response to solicitations authorized or requested by the consumer; or

(F) if compliance with this section by that person would prevent compliance by that person with any provision of State insurance laws pertaining to unfair discrimination in any State in which the person is lawfully doing business. . . .

§ 1681t. Relation to State Laws

(a) **In General**.—Except as provided in subsections (b) and (c), this Act does not annul, alter, affect, or exempt any person subject to the provisions of this Act from complying with the laws of any State with respect to the collection, distribution, or use of any information on consumers, or for the prevention or mitigation of identity theft, except to the extent that those laws are inconsistent with any provision of this Act, and then only to the extent of the inconsistency.

(b) **General Exceptions**.—No requirement or prohibition may be imposed under the laws of any State—

(1) with respect to any subject matter regulated under—

(A) subsection (c) or (e) of section 1681b, relating to the prescreening of consumer reports;

(B) section 1681i, relating to the time by which a consumer reporting agency must take any action, including the provision of notification to a consumer or other person, in any procedure related to the disputed accuracy of information in a consumer's file . . . ;

(C) subsections (a) and (b) of section 1681m, relating to the duties of a person who takes any adverse action with respect to a consumer;

(D) section 1681m(d), relating to the duties of persons who use a consumer report of a consumer in connection with any credit or insurance transaction that is not initiated by the consumer and that consists of a firm offer of credit or insurance;

(E) section 1681c, relating to information contained in consumer reports . . . ;

(F) section 1681s-2, relating to the responsibilities of persons who furnish information to consumer reporting agencies . . . ;

(G) section 1681g(e), relating to information available to victims under section 1681g(e);

(H) 1681s-3, relating to the exchange and use of information to make a solicitation for marketing purposes; or

(I) section 1681m(h), relating to the duties of users of consumer reports to provide notice with respect to terms in certain credit transactions;

(2) with respect to the exchange of information among persons affiliated by common ownership or common corporate control . . . ;

(3) with respect to the disclosures required to be made under subsection (c), (d), (e), or (g) of section 1681g, or subsection (f) of section 1681g relating to the disclosure of credit scores for credit granting purposes, except that this paragraph— . . .

(C) shall not be construed as limiting, annulling, affecting, or superseding any provision of the laws of any State regulating the use in an insurance activity, or regulating disclosures concerning such use, of a credit-based insurance score of a consumer by any person engaged in the business of insurance;

(4) with respect to the frequency of any disclosure under section 1681j(a) . . . ; or

(5) with respect to the conduct required by the specific provisions of—

(A) section 1681c(g) [truncating credit card and debit card numbers];

(B) section 1681c-1 [preventing identity theft];

(C) section 1681c-2 [blocking information resulting from alleged identity theft];

(D) section 1681g(a)(1)(A) [truncating Social Security numbers];

(E) section 1681j(a) [providing free annual disclosure];

(F) subsections (e), (f), and (g) of section 1681m [guidelines for detecting identity theft; no sale of debt resulting from identity theft];

(G) section 1681s(f) [consumer reporting agencies' procedures for investigating alleged identity theft];

(H) section 1681s-2(a)(6) [information furnishers' procedures for responding to alleged identity theft]; or

(I) section 1681w [properly disposing of consumer records]. . . .

§ 1681x. Corporate and Technological Circumvention Prohibited

The Bureau shall prescribe regulations . . . to prevent a consumer reporting agency from circumventing or evading treatment as a consumer reporting agency described in section 1681a(p) for purposes, including—

(1) by means of a corporate reorganization or restructuring, including a merger, acquisition, dissolution, divestiture, or asset sale of a consumer reporting agency; or

(2) by maintaining or merging public record and credit account information in a manner that is substantially equivalent to that described in paragraphs (1) and (2) of section 1681a(p), in the manner described in section 1681a(p).

GRAMM-LEACH-BLILEY ACT

§ 6701. Operation of State Law

(a) State Regulation of the Business of Insurance.—The Act entitled "An Act to express the intent of Congress with reference to the regulation of the business of insurance" and approved March 9, 1945 (commonly referred to as the "McCarran-Ferguson Act") remains the law of the United States.

(b) Mandatory Insurance Licensing Requirements.—No person shall engage in the business of insurance in a State as principal or agent unless such person is licensed as required by the appropriate insurance regulator of such State in accordance with the relevant State insurance law, subject to subsections (c), (d), and (e).

(c) Affiliations.—

(1) **In general.**—Except as provided in paragraph (2), no State may, by statute, regulation, order, interpretation, or other action, prevent or restrict a depository institution, or an affiliate thereof, from being affiliated directly or indirectly or associated with any person, as authorized or permitted by this Act or any other provision of Federal law.

(2) **Insurance.**—With respect to affiliations between depository institutions, or any affiliate thereof, and any insurer, paragraph (1) does not prohibit—

(A) any State from—

(i) collecting, reviewing, and taking actions (including approval and disapproval) on applications and other documents or reports concerning any proposed acquisition of, or a change or continuation of control of, an insurer domiciled in that State; and

(ii) exercising authority granted under applicable State law to collect information concerning any proposed acquisition of, or a change or continuation of control of, an insurer engaged in the business of insurance in, and regulated as an insurer by, such State;

during the 60-day period preceding the effective date of the acquisition or change or continuation of control, so long as the collecting, reviewing, taking actions, or exercising authority by the State does not have the effect of discriminating, intentionally or unintentionally, against a depository institution or an affiliate thereof, or against any other person based upon an association of such person with a depository institution;

(B) any State from requiring any person that is acquiring control of an insurer domiciled in that State to maintain or restore the capital requirements of that insurer to the level required under the capital regulations of general applicability in that State to avoid the requirement of preparing and filing with the insurance regulatory authority of that State a plan to increase the capital of the insurer, except that any determination by the State insurance regulatory authority with respect to such requirement shall be made not later than 60 days after the date of notification under subparagraph (A); or

(C) any State from restricting a change in the ownership of stock in an insurer, or a company formed for the purpose of controlling such insurer, after the conversion of the insurer from mutual to stock form so long as such restriction does not have the effect of discriminating, intentionally or unintentionally, against a depository institution or an affiliate thereof, or against any other person based upon an association of such person with a depository institution.

(d) **Activities**.—

(1) **In general**.—Except as provided in paragraph (3), and except with respect to insurance sales, solicitation, and cross marketing activities, which shall be governed by paragraph (2), no State may, by statute, regulation, order, interpretation, or other action, prevent or restrict a depository institution or an affiliate thereof from engaging directly or indirectly, either by itself or in conjunction with an affiliate, or any other person, in any activity authorized or permitted under this Act and the amendments made by this Act.

(2) **Insurance sales**.—

(A) **In general**.—In accordance with the legal standards for preemption set forth in the decision of the Supreme Court of the United States in Barnett Bank of Marion County N.A. v. Nelson, 517 U.S. 25 (1996), no State may, by statute, regulation, order, interpretation, or other action, prevent or significantly interfere with the ability of a depository institution, or an affiliate thereof, to engage, directly or indirectly, either by itself or in conjunction with an affiliate or any other person, in any insurance sales, solicitation, or cross marketing activity.

(B) **Certain state laws preserved**.—Notwithstanding subparagraph (A), a State may impose any of the following restrictions, or restrictions that are substantially the same as but no more burdensome or restrictive than those in each of the following clauses:

(i) Restrictions prohibiting the rejection of an insurance policy by a depository institution or an affiliate of a depository institution, solely because the policy has been issued or underwritten by any person who is not associated with such depository institution or affiliate when the insurance is required in connection with a loan or extension of credit.

(ii) Restrictions prohibiting a requirement for any debtor, insurer, or insurance agent or broker to pay a separate charge in connection with the handling of insurance that is required in connection with a loan or other extension of credit or the provision of another traditional banking product by a depository institution, or any affiliate of a depository institution, unless such charge would be required when the depository institution or affiliate is the licensed insurance agent or broker providing the insurance.

(iii) Restrictions prohibiting the use of any advertisement or other insurance promotional material by a depository institution or any affiliate of a depository institution that would cause a reasonable person to believe mistakenly that—

(I) the Federal Government or a State is responsible for the insurance sales activities of, or stands behind the credit of, the institution or affiliate; or

(II) a State, or the Federal Government guarantees any returns on insurance products, or is a source of payment on any insurance obligation of or sold by the institution or affiliate;

(iv) Restrictions prohibiting the payment or receipt of any commission or brokerage fee or other valuable consideration for services as an insurance agent or broker to or by any person, unless such person holds a valid State license regarding the applicable class of insurance at the time at which the services are performed, except that, in this clause, the term "services as an insurance agent or broker" does not include a referral by an unlicensed person of a customer or potential customer to a licensed insurance agent or broker that does not include a discussion of specific insurance policy terms and conditions.

(v) Restrictions prohibiting any compensation paid to or received by any individual who is not licensed to sell insurance, for the referral of a customer that seeks to purchase, or seeks an opinion or advice on, any insurance product to a person that sells or provides opinions or advice on such product, based on the purchase of insurance by the customer.

(vi) Restrictions prohibiting the release of the insurance information of a customer (defined as information concerning the premiums, terms, and conditions of insurance coverage, including expiration dates and rates, and insurance claims of a customer contained in the records of the depository institution or an affiliate thereof) to any person other than an officer, director, employee, agent, or affiliate of a depository institution, for the purpose of soliciting or selling insurance, without the express consent of the customer, other than a provision that prohibits—

>(I) a transfer of insurance information to an unaffiliated insurer in connection with transferring insurance in force on existing insureds of the depository institution or an affiliate thereof, or in connection with a merger with or acquisition of an unaffiliated insurer; or

>(II) the release of information as otherwise authorized by State or Federal law.

(vii) Restrictions prohibiting the use of health information obtained from the insurance records of a customer for any purpose, other than for its activities as a licensed agent or broker, without the express consent of the customer.

(viii) Restrictions prohibiting the extension of credit or any product or service that is equivalent to an extension of credit, lease or sale of property of any kind, or furnishing of any services or fixing or varying the consideration for any of the foregoing, on the condition or requirement that the customer obtain insurance from a depository institution or an affiliate of a depository institution, or a particular insurer, agent, or broker, other than a prohibition that would prevent any such depository institution or affiliate—

>(I) from engaging in any activity described in this clause that would not violate §§ 1971-1978 of title 12, as interpreted by the Board of Governors of the Federal Reserve System; or

>(II) from informing a customer or prospective customer that insurance is required in order to obtain a loan or credit, that loan or credit approval is contingent upon the procurement by the customer of acceptable insurance, or that insurance is available from the depository institution or an affiliate of the depository institution.

(ix) Restrictions requiring, when an application by a consumer for a loan or other extension of credit from a depository institution is pending, and insurance is offered or sold to the consumer or is required in connection with the loan or extension of credit by the depository institution or any affiliate thereof, that a written disclosure be provided to the consumer or prospective customer indicating that the customer's choice of an insurance provider will not affect the credit decision or credit terms in any way, except that the depository institution may impose reasonable requirements concerning the credit worthiness of the insurer and scope of coverage chosen.

(x) Restrictions requiring clear and conspicuous disclosure, in writing, where practicable, to the customer prior to the sale of any insurance policy that such policy—

(I) is not a deposit;

(II) is not insured by the Federal Deposit Insurance Corporation;

(III) is not guaranteed by any depository institution or, if appropriate, an affiliate of any such institution or any person soliciting the purchase of or selling insurance on the premises thereof, and

(IV) where appropriate, involves investment risk, including potential loss of principal.

(xi) Restrictions requiring that, when a customer obtains insurance (other than credit insurance or flood insurance) and credit from a depository institution, or any affiliate of such institution, or any person soliciting the purchase of or selling insurance on the premises thereof, the credit and insurance transactions be completed through separate documents.

(xii) Restrictions prohibiting, when a customer obtains insurance (other than credit insurance or flood insurance) and credit from a depository institution or an affiliate of such institution, or any person soliciting the purchase of or selling insurance on the premises thereof, inclusion of the expense of insurance premiums in the primary credit transaction without the express written consent of the customer.

(xiii) Restrictions requiring maintenance of separate and distinct books and records relating to insurance transactions, including all files relating to and reflecting consumer complaints, and requiring that such insurance books and records be made available to the appropriate State insurance regulator for inspection upon reasonable notice.

(C) Limitations.—

(i) OCC deference.—Section 6714(e) of this title does not apply with respect to any State statute, regulation, order, interpretation, or other action regarding insurance sales, solicitation, or cross marketing activities described in subparagraph (A) that was issued, adopted, or enacted before September 3, 1998, and that is not described in subparagraph (B).

(ii) Nondiscrimination.—Subsection (e) does not apply with respect to any State statute, regulation, order, interpretation, or other action regarding insurance sales, solicitation, or cross marketing activities described in subparagraph (A) that was issued, adopted, or enacted before September 3, 1998, and that is not described in subparagraph (B).

(iii) Construction.—Nothing in this paragraph shall be construed—

(I) to limit the applicability of the decision of the Supreme Court in Barnett Bank of Marion County N.A. v. Nelson, 517 U.S. 25

(1996) with respect to any State statute, regulation, order, interpretation, or other action that is not referred to or described in subparagraph (B); or

(II) to create any inference with respect to any State statute, regulation, order, interpretation, or other action that is not described in this paragraph.

(3) Insurance activities other than sales.—State statutes, regulations, interpretations, orders, and other actions shall not be preempted under paragraph (1) to the extent that they—

(A) relate to, or are issued, adopted, or enacted for the purpose of regulating the business of insurance in accordance with the Act entitled "An Act to express the intent of Congress with reference to the regulation of the business of insurance" and approved March 9, 1945 (commonly referred to as the "McCarran-Ferguson Act");

(B) apply only to persons that are not depository institutions, but that are directly engaged in the business of insurance (except that they may apply to depository institutions engaged in providing savings bank life insurance as principal to the extent of regulating such insurance);

(C) do not relate to or directly or indirectly regulate insurance sales, solicitations, or cross marketing activities; and

(D) are not prohibited under subsection (e).

(4) Financial activities other than insurance.—No State statute, regulation, order, interpretation, or other action shall be preempted under paragraph (1) to the extent that—

(A) it does not relate to, and is not issued and adopted, or enacted for the purpose of regulating, directly or indirectly, insurance sales, solicitations, or cross marketing activities covered under paragraph (2);

(B) it does not relate to, and is not issued and adopted, or enacted for the purpose of regulating, directly or indirectly, the business of insurance activities other than sales, solicitations, or cross marketing activities, covered under paragraph (3);

(C) it does not relate to securities investigations or enforcement actions referred to in subsection (f); and

(D) it—

(i) does not distinguish by its terms between depository institutions, and affiliates thereof, engaged in the activity at issue and other persons engaged in the same activity in a manner that is in any way adverse with respect to the conduct of the activity by any such depository institution or affiliate engaged in the activity at issue;

(ii) as interpreted or applied, does not have, and will not have, an impact on depository institutions, or affiliates thereof, engaged in the activity at issue, or any person who has an association with any such depository institution or affiliate, that is substantially more adverse than its impact on other persons engaged in the same activity that are not depository institutions or affiliates thereof, or persons who do not have an association with any such depository institution or affiliate;

(iii) does not effectively prevent a depository institution or affiliate thereof from engaging in activities authorized or permitted by this Act or any other provision of Federal law; and

(iv) does not conflict with the intent of this Act generally to permit affiliations that are authorized or permitted by Federal law.

(e) Nondiscrimination.—Except as provided in any restrictions described in subsection (d)(2)(B), no State may, by statute, regulation, order, interpretation, or other action, regulate the insurance activities authorized or permitted under this Act or any other provision of Federal law of a depository institution, or affiliate thereof, to the extent that such statute, regulation, order, interpretation, or other action—

(1) distinguishes by its terms between depository institutions, or affiliates thereof, and other persons engaged in such activities, in a manner that is in any way adverse to any such depository institution, or affiliate thereof;

(2) as interpreted or applied, has or will have an impact on depository institutions, or affiliates thereof, that is substantially more adverse than its impact on other persons providing the same products or services or engaged in the same activities that are not depository institutions, or affiliates thereof, or persons or entities affiliated therewith;

(3) effectively prevents a depository institution, or affiliate thereof, from engaging in insurance activities authorized or permitted by this Act or any other provision of Federal law; or

(4) conflicts with the intent of this Act generally to permit affiliations that are authorized or permitted by Federal law between depository institutions, or affiliates thereof, and persons engaged in the business of insurance.

(f) Limitation.—Subsections (c) and (d) shall not be construed to affect—

(1) the jurisdiction of the securities commission (or any agency or office performing like functions) of any State, under the laws of such State—

(A) to investigate and bring enforcement actions, consistent with § 77r(c) of this title, with respect to fraud or deceit or unlawful conduct by any person, in connection with securities or securities transactions; or

(B) to require the registration of securities or the licensure or registration of brokers, dealers, or investment advisers (consistent with § 80b-3a of this title), or the associated persons of a broker, dealer, or investment adviser (consistent with such § 80b-3a); or

(2) State laws, regulations, orders, interpretations, or other actions of general applicability relating to the governance of corporations, partnerships, limited liability companies, or other business associations incorporated or formed under the laws of that State or domiciled in that State, or the applicability of the antitrust laws of any State or any State law that is

similar to the antitrust laws if such laws, regulations, orders, interpretations, or other actions are not inconsistent with the purposes of this Act to authorize or permit certain affiliations and to remove barriers to such affiliations.

(g) **Definitions**.—For purposes of this section, the following definitions shall apply:

(1) **Affiliate**.—The term "affiliate" means any company that controls, is controlled by, or is under common control with another company.

(2) **Antitrust laws**.—The term "antitrust laws" has the meaning given the term in the first section of the Clayton Act [§ 12(a) of this title], and includes § 45 of this title (to the extent that such § 45 relates to unfair methods of competition).

(3) **Depository institution**.—The term "depository institution"—

(A) has the meaning given the term in § 1813 of title 12; and

(B) includes any foreign bank that maintains a branch, agency, or commercial lending company in the United States.

(4) **Insurer**.—The term "insurer" means any person engaged in the business of insurance.

(5) **State**.—The term "State" means any State of the United States, the District of Columbia, any territory of the United States, Puerto Rico, Guam, American Samoa, the Trust Territory of the Pacific Islands, the Virgin Islands, and the Northern Mariana Islands.

§ 6711. Functional Regulation of Insurance

The insurance activities of any person (including a national bank exercising its power to act as agent under the eleventh undesignated paragraph of section 13 of the Federal Reserve Act [*uncodified provision, parallel to 12 U.S. Code § 92, authorizing national banks to act as insurance agents in towns of 5000 or fewer persons*] shall be functionally regulated by the States, subject to § 6701 of this title.

§ 6712. Insurance Underwriting in National Banks

(a) **In General**.—Except as provided in § 6713 of this title, a national bank and the subsidiaries of a national bank may not provide insurance in a State as principal except that this prohibition shall not apply to authorized products.

(b) **Authorized Products**.—For the purposes of this section, a product is authorized if—

(1) as of January 1, 1999, the Comptroller of the Currency had determined in writing that national banks may provide such product as principal, or national banks were in fact lawfully providing such product as principal;

(2) no court of relevant jurisdiction had, by final judgment, overturned a determination of the Comptroller of the Currency that national banks may provide such product as principal; and

(3) the product is not title insurance, or an annuity contract the income of which is subject to tax treatment under § 72 of title 26.

(c) Definition.—For purposes of this section, the term **"insurance"** means—

(1) any product regulated as insurance as of January 1, 1999, in accordance with the relevant State insurance law, in the State in which the product is provided;

(2) any product first offered after January 1, 1999, which—

(A) a State insurance regulator determines shall be regulated as insurance in the State in which the product is provided because the product insures, guarantees, or indemnifies against liability, loss of life, loss of health, or loss through damage to or destruction of property, including, but not limited to, surety bonds, life insurance, health insurance, title insurance, and property and casualty insurance (such as private passenger or commercial automobile, homeowners, mortgage, commercial multiperil, general liability, professional liability, workers" compensation, fire and allied lines, farm owners multiperil, aircraft, fidelity, surety, medical malpractice, ocean marine, inland marine, and boiler and machinery insurance); and

(B) is not a product or service of a bank that is—

(i) a deposit product;

(ii) a loan, discount, letter of credit, or other extension of credit;

(iii) a trust or other fiduciary service;

(iv) a qualified financial contract (as defined in or determined pursuant to § 1821(e)(8)(D)(i) of title 12); or

(v) a financial guaranty, except that this subparagraph (B) shall not apply to a product that includes an insurance component such that if the product is offered or proposed to be offered by the bank as principal—

(I) it would be treated as a life insurance contract under § 7702 of title 26; or

(II) in the event that the product is not a letter of credit or other similar extension of credit, a qualified financial contract, or a financial guaranty, it would qualify for treatment for losses incurred with respect to such product under § 832(b)(5) of title 26, if the bank were subject to tax as an insurance company under § 831 of that title; or

(3) any annuity contract, the income on which is subject to tax treatment under § 72 of title 26.

(d) Rule of Construction.—For purposes of this section, providing insurance (including reinsurance) outside the United States that insures, guarantees, or indemnifies insurance products provided in a State, or that indemnifies an insurance company with regard to insurance products provided in a State, shall be considered to be providing insurance as principal in that State.

§ 6713. Title Insurance Activities of National Banks and Their Affiliates

(a) **General Prohibition**.—No national bank may engage in any activity involving the underwriting or sale of title insurance.

(b) **Nondiscrimination Parity Exception**.—

(1) **In general**.—Notwithstanding any other provision of law (including § 6701 of this title), in the case of any State in which banks organized under the laws of such State are authorized to sell title insurance as agent, a national bank may sell title insurance as agent in such State, but only in the same manner, to the same extent, and under the same restrictions as such State banks are authorized to sell title insurance as agent in such State.

(2) **Coordination with "wildcard" provision**.—A State law which authorizes State banks to engage in any activities in such State in which a national bank may engage shall not be treated as a statute which authorizes State banks to sell title insurance as agent, for purposes of paragraph (1).

(c) **Grandfathering with Consistent Regulation**.—

(1) **In general**.—Except as provided in paragraphs (2) and (3) and notwithstanding subsections (a) and (b), a national bank, and a subsidiary of a national bank, may conduct title insurance activities which such national bank or subsidiary was actively and lawfully conducting before November 12, 1999.

(2) **Insurance affiliate**.—In the case of a national bank which has an affiliate which provides insurance as principal and is not a subsidiary of the bank, the national bank and any subsidiary of the national bank may not engage in the underwriting of title insurance pursuant to paragraph (1).

(3) **Insurance subsidiary**.—In the case of a national bank which has a subsidiary which provides insurance as principal and has no affiliate other than a subsidiary which provides insurance as principal, the national bank may not directly engage in any activity involving the underwriting of title insurance.

(d) **"Affiliate" and "Subsidiary" Defined**.—For purposes of this section, the terms "affiliate" and "subsidiary" have the same meanings as in § 1841 of title 12.

(e) **Rule of Construction**.—No provision of this Act or any other Federal law shall be construed as superseding or affecting a State law which was in effect before November 12, 1999, and which prohibits title insurance from being offered, provided, or sold in such State, or from being underwritten with respect to real property in such State, by any person whatsoever.

§ 6714. Expedited and Equalized Dispute Resolution for Federal Regulators

(a) **Filing in Court of Appeals**.—In the case of a regulatory conflict between a State insurance regulator and a Federal regulator regarding insurance issues, including whether a State law, rule, regulation, order, or interpretation regarding any insurance sales or solicitation activity is properly treated as preempted under Federal law, the Federal or State regulator may seek expedited judicial review of such determination by the United States Court of Appeals for the circuit in which the State is located or in the United States Court of Appeals for the District of Columbia Circuit by filing a petition for review in such court.

(b) **Expedited Review**.—The United States Court of Appeals in which a petition for review is filed in accordance with subsection (a) shall complete all action on such petition, including rendering a judgment, before the end of the 60-day period beginning on the date on which such petition is filed, unless all parties to such proceeding agree to any extension of such period.

(c) **Supreme Court Review**.—Any request for certiorari to the Supreme Court of the United States of any judgment of a United States Court of Appeals with respect to a petition for review under this section shall be filed with the Supreme Court of the United States as soon as practicable after such judgment is issued.

(d) **Statute of Limitation**.—No petition may be filed under this section challenging an order, ruling, determination, or other action of a Federal regulator or State insurance regulator after the later of—

(1) the end of the 12-month period beginning on the date on which the first public notice is made of such order, ruling, determination or other action in its final form; or

(2) the end of the 6-month period beginning on the date on which such order, ruling, determination, or other action takes effect.

(e) **Standard of Review**.—The court shall decide a petition filed under this section based on its review on the merits of all questions presented under State and Federal law, including the nature of the product or activity and the history and purpose of its regulation under State and Federal law, without unequal deference.

§ 6715. Certain State Affiliation Laws Preempted for Insurance Companies and Affiliates

Except as provided in § 6701(c)(2), no State may, by law, regulation, order, interpretation, or otherwise—

(1) prevent or significantly interfere with the ability of any insurer, or any affiliate of an insurer (whether such affiliate is organized as a stock

company, mutual holding company, or otherwise), to become a financial holding company or to acquire control of a depository institution;

(2) limit the amount of an insurer's assets that may be invested in the voting securities of a depository institution (or any company which controls such institution), except that the laws of an insurer's State of domicile may limit the amount of such investment to an amount that is not less than 5 percent of the insurer's admitted assets; or

(3) prevent, significantly interfere with, or have the authority to review, approve, or disapprove a plan of reorganization by which an insurer proposes to reorganize from mutual form to become a stock insurer (whether as a direct or indirect subsidiary of a mutual holding company or otherwise) unless such State is the State of domicile of the insurer. . . .

§ 6801. Protection of Nonpublic Personal Information

(a) Privacy Obligation Policy.—It is the policy of the Congress that each financial institution has an affirmative and continuing obligation to respect the privacy of its customers and to protect the security and confidentiality of those customers' nonpublic personal information.

(b) Financial Institutions Safeguards.—In furtherance of the policy in subsection (a), each agency or authority described in § 505(a) shall establish appropriate standards for the financial institutions subject to their jurisdiction relating to administrative, technical, and physical safeguards—

(1) to insure the security and confidentiality of customer records and information;

(2) to protect against any anticipated threats or hazards to the security or integrity of such records; and

(3) to protect against unauthorized access to or use of such records or information which could result in substantial harm or inconvenience to any customer.

§ 6802. Obligations with Respect to Disclosures of Personal Information

(a) Notice Requirements.—Except as otherwise provided in this subchapter [i.e., §§ 6801-6809, relating to disclosure of nonpublic personal information], a financial institution may not, directly or through any affiliate, disclose to a nonaffiliated third party any nonpublic personal information, unless such financial institution provides or has provided to the consumer a notice that complies with § 503.

(b) Opt Out.—

(1) In general.—A financial institution may not disclose nonpublic personal information to a nonaffiliated third party unless—

(A) such financial institution clearly and conspicuously discloses to the consumer, in writing or in electronic form or other form permitted by the regulations prescribed under § 504, that such information may be disclosed to such third party;

(B) the consumer is given the opportunity, before the time that such information is initially disclosed, to direct that such information not be disclosed to such third party; and

(C) the consumer is given an explanation of how the consumer can exercise that nondisclosure option.

(2) Exception.—This subsection shall not prevent a financial institution from providing nonpublic personal information to a nonaffiliated third party to perform services for or functions on behalf of the financial institution, including marketing of the financial institution's own products or services, or financial products or services offered pursuant to joint agreements between two or more financial institutions that comply with the requirements imposed by the regulations prescribed under § 504, if the financial institution fully discloses the providing of such information and enters into a contractual agreement with the third party that requires the third parry to maintain the confidentiality of such information.

(c) Limits on Reuse of Information.—Except as otherwise provided in this subchapter, a nonaffiliated third party that receives from a financial institution nonpublic personal information under this section shall not, directly or through an affiliate of such receiving third party, disclose such information to any other person that is a nonaffiliated third party of both the financial institution and such receiving third party, unless such disclosure would be lawful if made directly to such other person by the financial institution.

(d) Limitations on the Sharing of Account Number Information for Marketing Purposes.—A financial institution shall not disclose, other than to a consumer reporting agency, an account number or similar form of access number or access code for a credit card account, deposit account, or transaction account of a consumer to any nonaffiliated third party for use in telemarketing, direct mail marketing, or other marketing through electronic mail to the consumer.

(e) General Exceptions.—Subsections (a) and (b) shall not prohibit the disclosure of nonpublic personal information—

(1) as necessary to effect, administer, or enforce a transaction requested or authorized by the consumer, or in connection with—

(A) servicing or processing a financial product or service requested or authorized by the consumer;

(B) maintaining or servicing the consumer's account with the financial institution, or with another entity as part of a private label credit card program or other extension of credit on behalf of such entity; or

(C) a proposed or actual securitization, secondary market sale (including sales of servicing rights), or similar transaction related to a transaction of the consumer;

(2) with the consent or at the direction of the consumer;

(3) (A) to protect the confidentiality or security of the financial institution's records pertaining to the consumer, the service or product, or the transaction therein;

(B) to protect against or prevent actual or potential fraud, unauthorized transactions, claims, or other liability;

(C) for required institutional risk control, or for resolving customer disputes or inquiries;

(D) to persons holding a legal or beneficial interest relating to the consumer; or

(E) to persons acting in a fiduciary or representative capacity on behalf of the consumer;

(4) to provide information to insurance rate advisory organizations, guaranty funds or agencies, applicable rating agencies of the financial institution, persons assessing the institution's compliance with industry standards, and the institution's attorneys, accountants, and auditors;

(5) to the extent specifically permitted or required under other provisions of law and in accordance with the Right to Financial Privacy Act of 1978, to law enforcement agencies (including the Bureau of Consumer Financial Protection, a Federal functional regulator, the Secretary of the Treasury with respect to [certain requirements to keep records about financial transactions], a State insurance authority, or the Federal Trade Commission), self-regulatory organizations, or for an investigation on a matter related to public safety;

(6) (A) to a consumer reporting agency in accordance with the Fair Credit Reporting Act, or

(B) from a consumer report reported by a consumer reporting agency;

(7) in connection with a proposed or actual sale, merger, transfer, or exchange of all or a portion of a business or operating unit if the disclosure of nonpublic personal information concerns solely consumers of such business or unit; or

(8) to comply with Federal, State, or local laws, rules, and other applicable legal requirements; to comply with a properly authorized civil, criminal, or regulatory investigation or subpoena or summons by Federal, State, or local authorities; or to respond to judicial process or government regulatory authorities having jurisdiction over the financial institution for examination, compliance, or other purposes as authorized by law.

§ 6803. Disclosure of Institution Privacy Policy

(a) **Disclosure Required**.—At the time of establishing a customer relationship with a consumer and not less than annually during the continuation of such relationship, a financial institution shall provide a clear and conspicuous disclosure to such consumer, in writing or in electronic form or other form permitted by the regulations prescribed under § 6804, of such financial institution's policies and practices with respect to—

(1) disclosing nonpublic personal information to affiliates and nonaffiliated third parties, consistent with § 6802, including the categories of information that may be disclosed;

(2) disclosing nonpublic personal information of persons who have ceased to be customers of the financial institution; and

(3) protecting the nonpublic personal information of consumers.

(b) Regulations.—Disclosures required by subsection (a) shall be made in accordance with the regulations prescribed under § 6804.

(c) Information to Be Included.—The disclosure required by subsection (a) shall include—

(1) the policies and practices of the institution with respect to disclosing nonpublic personal information to nonaffiliated third parties, other than agents of the institution, consistent with § 6802, and including—

(A) the categories of persons to whom the information is or may be disclosed, other than the persons to whom the information may be provided pursuant to § 6802(e); and

(B) the policies and practices of the institution with respect to disclosing of nonpublic personal information of persons who have ceased to be customers of the financial institution;

(2) the categories of nonpublic personal information that are collected by the financial institution;

(3) the policies that the institution maintains to protect the confidentiality and security of nonpublic personal information in accordance with § 6801; and

(4) the disclosures required, if any, under § 1681a(d)(2)(A)(iii) [Fair Credit Reporting Act].

(d) Exemption for Certified Public Accountants.—

(1) In general.—The disclosure requirements of subsection (a) do not apply to any person, to the extent that the person is—

(A) a certified public accountant;

(B) certified or licensed for such purpose by a State; and

(C) subject to any provision of law, rule, or regulation issued by a legislative or regulatory body of the State, including rules of professional conduct or ethics, that prohibits disclosure of nonpublic personal information without the knowing and expressed consent of the consumer.

(2) Limitation.—Nothing in this subsection shall be construed to exempt or otherwise exclude any financial institution that is affiliated or becomes affiliated with a certified public accountant described in paragraph (1) from any provision of this section. . . .

(e) Model Forms.—

(1) In general.—The agencies referred to in § 6804(a)(1) shall jointly develop a model form which may be used, at the option of the financial institution, for the provision of disclosures under this section.

(2) Format.—A model form developed under paragraph (1) shall—

(A) be comprehensible to consumers, with a clear format and design;

(B) provide for clear and conspicuous disclosures;

(C) enable consumers easily to identify the sharing practices of a financial institution and to compare privacy practices among financial institutions; and

(D) be succinct, and use an easily readable type font. . . .

(4) Safe harbor.—Any financial institution that elects to provide the model form developed by the agencies under this subsection shall be deemed to be in compliance with the disclosures required under this section.

§ 6804. Rulemaking

(a) Regulatory Authority.—

(1) Rulemaking.—The Federal banking agencies, the National Credit Union Administration, the Secretary of the Treasury, the Securities and Exchange Commission, and the Federal Trade Commission shall each prescribe, after consultation as appropriate with representatives of State insurance authorities designated by the National Association of Insurance Commissioners, such regulations as may be necessary to carry out the purposes of this subchapter with respect to the financial institutions subject to their jurisdiction. . . .

(2) Coordination, consistency, and comparability.—Each of the agencies and authorities required under paragraph (1) to prescribe regulations shall consult and coordinate with the other such agencies and authorities for the purposes of assuring, to the extent possible, that the regulations prescribed by each such agency and authority are consistent and comparable with the regulations prescribed by the other such agencies and authorities.

(b) Authority to Grant Exceptions.—The regulations prescribed under subsection (a) may include such additional exceptions to subsections (a) through (d) of § 6802 of this title as are deemed consistent with the purposes of this subchapter.

§ 6805. Enforcement

(a) In General.—This subchapter and the regulations prescribed thereunder shall be enforced by the Federal functional regulators, the State insurance authorities, and the Federal Trade Commission with respect to financial institutions and other persons subject to their jurisdiction under applicable law, as follows:

(1) Under § 1818 of title 12, in the case of

(A) national banks, Federal branches and Federal agencies of foreign banks, and any subsidiaries of such entities (except brokers, dealers, persons providing insurance, investment companies, and investment advisers), by the Office of the Comptroller of the Currency;

(B) member banks of the Federal Reserve System (other than national banks), branches and agencies of foreign banks (other than Federal branches, Federal agencies, and insured State branches of foreign banks), commercial lending companies owned or controlled by foreign banks, organizations operating under §§ 601-604a or §§ 601-604a of title 12, and bank holding companies and their nonbank subsidiaries or affiliates (except brokers, dealers, persons providing insurance, investment companies, and investment advisers), by the Board of Governors of the Federal Reserve System;

(C) banks insured by the Federal Deposit Insurance Corporation (other than members of the Federal Reserve System), insured State branches of foreign banks, and any subsidiaries of such entities (except brokers, dealers, persons providing insurance, investment companies, and investment advisers), by the Board of Directors of the Federal Deposit Insurance Corporation; and

(D) savings associations the deposits of which are insured by the Federal Deposit Insurance Corporation, and any subsidiaries of such savings associations (except brokers, dealers, persons providing insurance, investment companies, and investment advisers), by the Director of the Office of Thrift Supervision.

(2) Under the Federal Credit Union Act, by the Board of the National Credit Union Administration with respect to any federally insured credit union, and any subsidiaries of such an entity.

(3) Under the Securities Exchange Act of 1934, by the Securities and Exchange Commission with respect to any broker or dealer.

(4) Under the Investment Company Act of 1940, by the Securities and Exchange Commission with respect to investment companies.

(5) Under the Investment Advisers Act of 1940, by the Securities and Exchange Commission with respect to investment advisers registered with the Commission under such Act.

(6) Under State insurance law, in the case of any person engaged in providing insurance, by the applicable State insurance authority of the State in which the person is domiciled, subject to § 6701 of this title.

(7) Under the Federal Trade Commission Act, by the Federal Trade Commission for any other financial institution or other person that is

not subject to the jurisdiction of any agency or authority under paragraphs (1) through (6) of this subsection. . . .

(b) Enforcement of § 6801 of This Title.—

   (1) In general.—Except as provided in paragraph (2), the agencies and authorities described in subsection (a) shall implement the standards prescribed under § 6801(b) of this title in the same manner, to the extent practicable, as standards prescribed pursuant to § 1831p-1(a) of title 12 are implemented pursuant to such section.

   (2) Exception.—The agencies and authorities described in paragraphs (3), (4), (5), (6), and (7) of subsection (a) shall implement the standards prescribed under § 6801(b) of this title by rule with respect to the financial institutions and other persons subject to their respective jurisdictions under subsection (a).

(c) Absence of State Action.—If a State insurance authority fails to adopt regulations to carry out this subchapter, such State shall not be eligible to override, pursuant to § 1831x(g)(2)(B)(iii) of title 12, the insurance customer protection regulations prescribed by a Federal banking agency under § 1831x(a) of title 12.

(d) Definitions.—The terms used in subsection (a)(1) that are not defined in this subchapter or otherwise defined in § 1813(s) of title 12 shall have the same meaning as given in § 3101 of title 12.

§ 6821. Privacy Protection for Customer Information of Financial Institutions

(a) Prohibition on Obtaining Customer Information by False Pretenses.—It shall be a violation of this subchapter [i.e., §§ 6821-6827, relating to fraudulently obtaining financial information] for any person to obtain or attempt to obtain, or cause to be disclosed or attempt to cause to be disclosed to any person, customer information of a financial institution relating to another person—

   (1) by making a false, fictitious, or fraudulent statement or representation to an officer, employee, or agent of a financial institution;

   (2) by making a false, fictitious, or fraudulent statement or representation to a customer of a financial institution; or

   (3) by providing any document to an officer, employee, or agent of a financial institution, knowing that the document is forged, counterfeit, lost, or stolen, was fraudulently obtained, or contains a false, fictitious, or fraudulent statement or representation.

(b) Prohibition on Solicitation of a Person to Obtain Customer Information from Financial Institution Under False Pretenses.—It shall be a violation of this subchapter to request a person to obtain customer information of a financial institution, knowing that the person will obtain, or attempt to obtain, the information from the institution in any manner described in subsection (a).

(c) Nonapplicability to Law Enforcement Agencies.—No provision of this section shall be construed so as to prevent any action by a law enforcement agency, or any officer, employee, or agent of such agency, to obtain customer information of a financial institution in connection with the performance of the official duties of the agency.

(d) Nonapplicability to Financial Institutions in Certain Cases.—No provision of this section shall be construed so as to prevent any financial institution, or any officer, employee, or agent of a financial institution, from obtaining customer information of such financial institution in the course of—

(1) testing the security procedures or systems of such institution for maintaining the confidentiality of customer information;

(2) investigating allegations of misconduct or negligence on the part of any officer, employee, or agent of the financial institution; or

(3) recovering customer information of the financial institution which was obtained or received by another person in any manner described in subsection (a) or (b).

(e) Nonapplicability to Insurance Institutions for Investigation of Insurance Fraud.—No provision of this section shall be construed so as to prevent any insurance institution, or any officer, employee, or agency of an insurance institution, from obtaining information as part of an insurance investigation into criminal activity, fraud, material misrepresentation, or material nondisclosure that is authorized for such institution under State law, regulation, interpretation, or order.

(f) Nonapplicability to Certain Types of Customer Information of Financial Institutions.—No provision of this section shall be construed so as to prevent any person from obtaining customer information of a financial institution that otherwise is available as a public record filed pursuant to the securities laws (as defined in § 78c(a)(47) of this title).

(g) Nonapplicability to Collection of Child Support Judgments.—No provision of this section shall be construed to prevent any State-licensed private investigator, or any officer, employee, or agent of such private investigator, from obtaining customer information of a financial institution, to the extent reasonably necessary to collect child support from a person adjudged to have been delinquent in his or her obligations by a Federal or State court, and to the extent that such action by a State-licensed private investigator is not unlawful under any other Federal or State law or regulation, and has been authorized by an order or judgment of a court of competent jurisdiction.

SELECTED PROVISIONS OF THE CODE OF FEDERAL REGULATIONS

12 C.F.R., PART 1—INVESTMENT SECURITIES

§ 1.1. Authority, Purpose, Scope, and Reservation of Authority

. . .

(b) Purpose.—This part prescribes standards under which national banks may purchase, sell, deal in, underwrite, and hold securities, consistent with the authority contained in 12 U.S.C. § 24 (Seventh) and safe and sound banking practices.

(c) Scope.—The standards set forth in this part apply to national banks and Federal branches of foreign banks. Further, pursuant to 12 U.S.C. § 335, State banks that are members of the Federal Reserve System are subject to the same limitations and conditions that apply to national banks in connection with purchasing, selling, dealing in, and underwriting securities and stock. In addition to activities authorized under this part, foreign branches of national banks are authorized to conduct international activities and invest in securities pursuant to 12 C.F.R. part 211.

(d) Reservation of Authority.—The OCC may determine, on a case-by-case basis, that a national bank may acquire an investment security other than an investment security of a type set forth in this part, provided the OCC determines that the bank's investment is consistent with 12 U.S.C. § 24 (Seventh) and with safe and sound banking practices. The OCC will consider all relevant factors, including the risk characteristics of the particular investment in comparison with the risk characteristics of investments that the OCC has previously authorized, and the bank's ability effectively to manage such risks. The OCC may impose limits or conditions in connection with approval of an investment security under this subsection. Investment securities that the OCC determines are permissible in accordance with this paragraph constitute eligible investments for purposes of 12 U.S.C. § 24.

§ 1.2. Definitions

(a) Capital and surplus means:

(1) A bank's Tier 1 and Tier 2 capital calculated under the OCC's risk-based capital standards set forth in appendix A to 12 C.F.R. part 3 (or comparable capital guidelines of the appropriate Federal banking agency) as reported in the bank's Consolidated Report of Condition and Income filed under 12 U.S.C. § 161 (or under 12 U.S.C. § 1817 in the case of a state member bank); plus

(2) The balance of a bank's allowance for loan and lease losses not included in the bank's Tier 2 capital, for purposes of the calculation of risk-based capital described in paragraph (a)(1) of this section, as reported in the bank's Consolidated Report of Condition and Income filed under 12

U.S.C. § 161 (or under 12 U.S.C. § 1817 in the case of a state member bank).

(b) General obligation of a State or political subdivision means:

(1) An obligation supported by the full faith and credit of an obligor possessing general powers of taxation, including property taxation; or

(2) An obligation payable from a special fund or by an obligor not possessing general powers of taxation, when an obligor possessing general powers of taxation, including property taxation, has unconditionally promised to make payments into the fund or otherwise provide funds to cover all required payments on the obligation.

(c) Investment company means an investment company, including a mutual fund, registered under 15 U.S.C. § 80a-8.

(d) Investment grade means a security that is rated in one of the four highest rating categories by:

(1) Two or more NRSROs; or

(2) One NRSRO if the security has been rated by only one NRSRO.

(e) Investment security means a marketable debt obligation that is not predominantly speculative in nature. A security is not predominantly speculative in nature if it is rated investment grade. When a security is not rated, the security must be the credit equivalent of a security rated investment grade.

(f) Marketable means that the security:

(1) Is registered under the Securities Act of 1933;

(2) Is a municipal revenue bond exempt from registration under the Securities Act of 1933, 15 U.S.C. § 77c(a)(2);

(3) Is offered and sold pursuant to Securities and Exchange Commission Rule 144A, 17 C.F.R. § 230.144A, and rated investment grade or is the credit equivalent of investment grade; or

(4) Can be sold with reasonable promptness at a price that corresponds reasonably to its fair value.

(g) Municipal bonds means obligations of a State or political subdivision other than general obligations, and includes limited obligation bonds, revenue bonds, and obligations that satisfy the requirements of § 142(b)(1) of the Internal Revenue Code of 1986 issued by or on behalf of any State or political subdivision of a State, including any municipal corporate instrumentality of 1 or more States, or any public agency or authority of any State or political subdivision of a State.

(h) NRSRO means a nationally recognized statistical rating organization.

(i) Political subdivision means a county, city, town, or other municipal corporation, a public authority, and generally any publicly-owned entity that is an instrumentality of a State or of a municipal corporation.

(j) Type I security means:

(1) Obligations of the United States;

(2) Obligations issued, insured, or guaranteed by a department or an agency of the United States Government, if the obligation, insurance, or

guarantee commits the full faith and credit of the United States for the repayment of the obligation;

(3) Obligations issued by a department or agency of the United States, or an agency or political subdivision of a State of the United States, that represent an interest in a loan or a pool of loans made to third parties, if the full faith and credit of the United States has been validly pledged for the full and timely payment of interest on, and principal of, the loans in the event of non-payment by the third party obligor(s);

(4) General obligations of a State of the United States or any political subdivision thereof; and municipal bonds if the national bank is well capitalized as defined in 12 C.F.R. § 6.4(b)(1);

(5) Obligations authorized under 12 U.S.C. § 24 (Seventh) as permissible for a national bank to deal in, underwrite, purchase, and sell for the bank's own account, including qualified Canadian government obligations; and

(6) Other securities the OCC determines to be eligible as Type I securities under 12 U.S.C. § 24 (Seventh).

(k) Type II security means an investment security that represents:

(1) Obligations issued by a State, or a political subdivision or agency of a State, for housing, university, or dormitory purposes that would not satisfy the definition of Type I securities pursuant to paragraph (j) of § 1.2;

(2) Obligations of international and multilateral development banks and organizations listed in 12 U.S.C. § 24 (Seventh);

(3) Other obligations listed in 12 U.S.C. § 24 (Seventh) as permissible for a bank to deal in, underwrite, purchase, and sell for the bank's own account, subject to a limitation per obligor of 10 percent of the bank's capital and surplus; and

(4) Other securities the OCC determines to be eligible as Type II securities under 12 U.S.C. § 24 (Seventh).

(*l*) Type III security means an investment security that does not qualify as a Type I, II, IV, or V security. Examples of Type III securities include corporate bonds and municipal bonds that do not satisfy the definition of Type I securities pursuant to paragraph (j) of § 1.2 or the definition of Type II securities pursuant to paragraph (k) of § 1.2.

(m) Type IV security means:

(1) A small business-related security as defined in 15 U.S.C. § 78c(a)(53)(A), that is rated investment grade or is the credit equivalent thereof, that is fully secured by interests in a pool of loans to numerous obligors.

(2) A commercial mortgage-related security that is offered or sold pursuant to section 4(5) of the Securities Act of 1933, 15 U.S.C. § 77d(5), that is rated investment grade or is the credit equivalent thereof, or a commercial mortgage-related security as described in section 3(a)(41) of the Securities Exchange Act of 1934, 15 U.S.C. § 78c(a)(41), that is

rated investment grade in one of the two highest investment grade rating categories, and that represents ownership of a promissory note or certificate of interest or participation that is directly secured by a first lien on one or more parcels of real estate upon which one or more commercial structures are located and that is fully secured by interests in a pool of loans to numerous obligors.

(3) A residential mortgage-related security that is offered and sold pursuant to section 4(5) of the Securities Act of 1933, 15 U.S.C. § 77d(5), that is rated investment grade or is the credit equivalent thereof, or a residential mortgage-related security as described in section 3(a)(41) of the Securities Exchange Act of 1934, 15 U.S.C. § 78c(a)(41)), that is rated investment grade in one of the two highest investment grade rating categories, and that does not otherwise qualify as a Type I security.

(n) Type V security means a security that is:

(1) Rated investment grade;

(2) Marketable;

(3) Not a Type IV security; and

(4) Fully secured by interests in a pool of loans to numerous obligors and in which a national bank could invest directly.

§ 1.3. Limitations on Dealing in, Underwriting, and Purchase and Sale of Securities

(a) Type I Securities.—A national bank may deal in, underwrite, purchase, and sell Type I securities for its own account. The amount of Type I securities that the bank may deal in, underwrite, purchase, and sell is not limited to a specified percentage of the bank's capital and surplus.

(b) Type II Securities.—A national bank may deal in, underwrite, purchase, and sell Type II securities for its own account, provided the aggregate par value of Type II securities issued by any one obligor held by the bank does not exceed 10 percent of the bank's capital and surplus. In applying this limitation, a national bank shall take account of Type II securities that the bank is legally committed to purchase or to sell in addition to the bank's existing holdings.

(c) Type III Securities.—A national bank may purchase and sell Type III securities for its own account, provided the aggregate par value of Type III securities issued by any one obligor held by the bank does not exceed 10 percent of the bank's capital and surplus. In applying this limitation, a national bank shall take account of Type III securities that the bank is legally committed to purchase or to sell in addition to the bank's existing holdings.

(d) Type II and III Securities; Other Investment Securities Limitations.—A national bank may not hold Type II and III securities issued by any one obligor with an aggregate par value exceeding 10 percent of the bank's capital and surplus. However, if the proceeds of each issue are to be used to acquire and lease real estate and related facilities to economically and legally separate industrial tenants, and if each issue is payable solely from and secured by a first lien on the revenues to be derived from rentals paid by the lessee under net noncancellable leases, the bank may apply the 10 percent investment limitation separately to each issue of a single obligor.

(e) Type IV Securities.—

(1) **General.**—A national bank may purchase and sell Type IV securities for its own account. Except as described in paragraph (e)(2) of this section, the amount of the Type IV securities that a bank may purchase and sell is not limited to a specified percentage of the bank's capital and surplus.

(2) **Limitation on small business-related securities rated in the third and fourth highest rating categories by an NRSRO.**—A national bank may hold small business-related securities, as defined in section 3(a)(53)(A) of the Securities Exchange Act of 1934, 15 U.S.C. 78c(a)(53)(A), of any one issuer with an aggregate par value not exceeding 25 percent of the bank's capital and surplus if those securities are rated investment grade in the third or fourth highest investment grade rating categories. In applying this limitation, a national bank shall take account of securities that the bank is legally committed to purchase or to sell in addition to the bank's existing holdings. No percentage of capital and surplus limit applies to small business related securities rated investment grade in the highest two investment grade rating categories.

(f) Type V Securities.—A national bank may purchase and sell Type V securities for its own account provided that the aggregate par value of Type V securities issued by any one issuer held by the bank does not exceed 25 percent of the bank's capital and surplus. In applying this limitation, a national bank shall take account of Type V securities that the bank is legally committed to purchase or to sell in addition to the bank's existing holdings.

(g) Securitization.—A national bank may securitize and sell assets that it holds, as a part of its banking business. The amount of securitized loans and obligations that a bank may sell is not limited to a specified percentage of the bank's capital and surplus.

(h) Pooled Investments.—

(1) **General.**—A national bank may purchase and sell for its own account investment company shares provided that:

(i) The portfolio of the investment company consists exclusively of assets that the national bank may purchase and sell for its own account; and

(ii) The bank's holdings of investment company shares do not exceed the limitations in § 1.4(e).

(2) **Other issuers.**—The OCC may determine that a national bank may invest in an entity that is exempt from registration as an investment

company under [15 U.S.C. § 80a-3(c)(1)], provided that the portfolio of the entity consists exclusively of assets that a national bank may purchase and sell for its own account.

(3) **Requirements**.—Investments made under this paragraph (h) must comply with § 1.5 of this part, conform with applicable published OCC precedent, and must be:

(i) Marketable and rated investment grade or the credit equivalent of a security rated investment grade, or

(ii) Satisfy the requirements of § 1.3(i).

(i) Securities Held Based on Estimates of Obligor's Performance.—

(1) Notwithstanding §§ 1.2(d) and (e), a national bank may treat a debt security as an investment security for purposes of this part if the security is marketable and the bank concludes, on the basis of estimates that the bank reasonably believes are reliable, that the obligor will be able to satisfy its obligations under that security.

(2) The aggregate par value of securities treated as investment securities under paragraph (i)(1) of this section may not exceed 5 percent of the bank's capital and surplus.

12 C.F.R., PART 32—LENDING LIMITS

§ 32.1. Authority, Purpose, and Scope

. . .

(b) Purpose.—The purpose of this part is to protect the safety and soundness of national banks by preventing excessive loans to one person, or to related persons that are financially dependent, and to promote diversification of loans and equitable access to banking services.

(1) In general; loans to affiliates.—This part applies to all loans and extensions of credit made by national banks and their domestic operating subsidiaries. This part does not apply to loans made by a national bank and its domestic operating subsidiaries to the bank's "affiliates," as that term is defined in 12 U.S.C. § 371c(b)(1) and (e), as implemented by § 223.2(a) of Regulation W, to the bank's operating subsidiaries, or to Edge Act or Agreement Corporation subsidiaries.

(2) Relationship to investment limits.—The lending limits in this part are separate and independent from the investment limits prescribed by 12 U.S.C. § 24 (Seventh), and a national bank may make loans or extensions of credit to one borrower up to the full amount permitted by this part and also hold eligible securities of the same obligor up to the full amount permitted under 12 U.S.C. § 24 (Seventh) and 12 C.F.R. part 1.

(3) Insider lending.—Extensions of credit to executive officers, directors and principal shareholders of national banks, and their related interests are subject to limits prescribed by 12 U.S.C. §§ 375a and 375b in addition to the lending limits established by 12 U.S.C. § 84 and this part.

(4) Overarching safety and soundness requirement.—In addition to the foregoing, loans and extensions of credit made by national banks and their domestic operating subsidiaries must be consistent with safe and sound banking practices.

§ 32.2. Definitions

(a) Borrower means a person who is named as a borrower or debtor in a loan or extension of credit, or any other person, including a . . . or guarantor, who is deemed to be a borrower under the "direct benefit" or the "common enterprise" tests set forth in § 32.5.

(b) Capital and surplus means—

(1) A bank's Tier 1 and Tier 2 capital calculated under the OCC's risk-based capital standards . . . ; plus

(2) The balance of a bank's allowance for loan and lease losses not included in the bank's Tier 2 capital, for purposes of the calculation of risk-based capital. . . .

(d) Consumer means the user of any products, commodities, goods, or services, whether leased or purchased, but does not include any person who purchases products or commodities for resale or fabrication into goods for sale.

(e) Consumer paper means paper relating to automobiles, mobile homes, residences, office equipment, household items, tuition fees, insurance premium fees, and similar consumer items. Consumer paper also includes paper covering the lease (where the bank is not the owner or lessor) or purchase of equipment for use in manufacturing, farming, construction, or excavation.

(f) Contractual commitment to advance funds.—

(1) **Items included.**—The term includes a bank's obligation to—

(i) Make payment (directly or indirectly) to a third person contingent upon default by a customer of the bank in performing an obligation and to make such payment in keeping with the agreed upon terms of the customer's contract with the third person, or to make payments upon some other stated condition;

(ii) Guarantee or act as surety for the benefit of a person;

(iii) Advance funds under a qualifying commitment to lend, as defined in paragraph (m) of this section, and

(iv) Advance funds under a standby letter of credit as defined in paragraph (s) of this section, a put, or other similar arrangement.

(2) Items excluded.—The term does not include commercial letters of credit and similar instruments where the issuing bank expects the beneficiary to draw on the issuer, that do not guarantee payment, and that do not provide for payment in the event of a default by a third party.

(g) Control is presumed to exist when a person directly or indirectly, or acting through or together with one or more persons—

(1) Owns, controls, or has the power to vote 25 percent or more of any class of voting securities of another person;

(2) Controls, in any manner, the election of a majority of the directors, trustees, or other persons exercising similar functions of another person; or

(3) Has the power to exercise a controlling influence over the management or policies of another person.

(h) Current market value means the bid or closing price listed for an item in a regularly published listing or an electronic reporting service. . . .

(j) Financial instrument means stocks, notes, bonds, and debentures traded on a national securities exchange, OTC margin stocks as defined in Regulation U, 12 C.F.R. part 221, commercial paper, negotiable certificates of deposit, bankers' acceptances, and shares in money market and mutual funds of the type that issue shares in which banks may perfect a security interest. Financial instruments may be denominated in foreign currencies that are freely convertible to U.S. dollars. The term "financial instrument" does not include mortgages.

(k) Loans and extensions of credit means a bank's direct or indirect advance of funds to or on behalf of a borrower based on an obligation of the borrower to repay the funds or repayable from specific property pledged by or on behalf of the borrower.

(1) Items included.—Loans or extensions of credit for purposes of 12 U.S.C. § 84 and this part include—

(i) A contractual commitment to advance funds, as defined in paragraph (f) of this section;

(ii) A maker or endorser's obligation arising from a bank's discount of commercial paper;

(iii) A bank's purchase of securities subject to an agreement that the seller will repurchase the securities at the end of a stated period, but not including a bank's purchase of Type I securities, as defined in part 1 of this chapter, subject to a repurchase agreement, where the purchasing bank has assured control over or has established its rights to the Type I securities as collateral;

(iv) A bank's purchase of third-party paper subject to an agreement that the seller will repurchase the paper upon default or at the end of a stated period. The amount of the bank's loan is the total unpaid balance of the paper owned by the bank less any applicable dealer reserves retained by the bank and held by the bank as collateral security. Where the seller's obligation to repurchase is limited, the bank's loan is measured by the total amount of the paper the seller may ultimately be obligated to repurchase. A bank's purchase of third party paper without direct or indirect recourse to the seller is not a loan or extension of credit to the seller;

(v) An overdraft, whether or not prearranged, but not an intra-day overdraft for which payment is received before the close of business of the bank that makes the funds available;

(vi) The sale of Federal funds with a maturity of more than one business day, but not Federal funds with a maturity of one day or less or Federal funds sold under a continuing contract; and

(vii) Loans or extensions of credit that have been charged off on the books of the bank in whole or in part, unless the loan or extension of credit—

(A) Is unenforceable by reason of discharge in bankruptcy;

(B) Is no longer legally enforceable because of expiration of the statute of limitations or a judicial decision; or

(C) Is no longer legally enforceable for other reasons, provided that the bank maintains sufficient records to demonstrate that the loan is unenforceable.

(2) Items excluded.—The following items do not constitute loans or extensions of credit for purposes of 12 U.S.C. § 84 and this part—

(i) Additional funds advanced for the benefit of a borrower by a bank for payment of taxes, insurance, utilities, security, and maintenance and operating expenses necessary to preserve the value of real property securing the loan, consistent with safe and sound banking practices, but only if the advance is for the protection of the bank's interest in the collateral, and provided that such amounts must be treated as an extension of credit if a new loan or extension of credit is made to the borrower;

(ii) Accrued and discounted interest on an existing loan or extension of credit, including interest that has been capitalized from prior notes and interest that has been advanced under terms and conditions of a loan agreement;

(iii) Financed sales of a bank's own assets, including Other Real Estate Owned, if the financing does not put the bank in a worse position than when the bank held title to the assets;

(iv) A renewal or restructuring of a loan as a new "loan or extension of credit," following the exercise by a bank of reasonable efforts, consistent with safe and sound banking practices, to bring the loan into conformance with the lending limit, unless new funds are advanced by the bank to the borrower (except as permitted by § 32.3(b)(5)), or a new borrower replaces the original borrower, or unless the OCC determines that a renewal or restructuring was undertaken as a means to evade the bank's lending limit;

(v) Amounts paid against uncollected funds in the normal process of collection; and

(vi) Qualifying loan participation.—

(A) That portion of a loan or extension of credit sold as a participation by a bank on a nonrecourse basis, provided that the participation results in a pro rata sharing of credit risk proportionate to the respective interests of the originating and participating lenders. Where a participation agreement provides that repayment must be applied first to the portions sold, a pro rata sharing will be deemed to exist only if the agreement also provides that, in the event of a default or comparable event defined in the agreement, participants must share in all subsequent repayments and collections in proportion to their percentage participation at the time of the occurrence of the event.

(B) When an originating bank funds the entire loan, it must receive funding from the participants before the close of business of its next business day. If the participating portions are not received within that period, then the portions funded will be treated as a loan by the originating bank to the borrower. If the portions so attributed to the borrower exceed the originating bank's lending limit, the loan may be treated as nonconforming subject to § 32.6, rather than a violation, if:

(1) The originating bank had a valid and unconditional participation agreement with a participating bank or banks that was sufficient to reduce the loan to within the originating bank's lending limit;

(2) The participating bank reconfirmed its participation and the originating bank had no knowledge of any information that would permit the participant to withhold its participation; and

(3) The participation was to be funded by close of business of the originating bank's next business day. . . .

(m) Qualifying commitment to lend means a legally binding written commitment to lend that, when combined with all other outstanding loans and qualifying commitments to a borrower, was within the bank's lending limit when entered into, and has not been disqualified.

(1) Loan participations.—In determining whether a commitment is within the bank's lending limit when made, the bank may deduct from the amount of the commitment the amount of any legally binding loan participation commitments that are issued concurrent with the bank's commitment and that would be excluded from the definition of "loan or extension of credit" under paragraph (k)(2)(vi) of this section.

(2) Commitments exceeding limit.—If the bank subsequently chooses to make an additional loan and that subsequent loan, together with all outstanding loans and qualifying commitments to a borrower, exceeds the bank's applicable lending limit at that time, the bank's qualifying commitments to the borrower that exceed the bank's lending limit at that time are deemed to be permanently disqualified, beginning with the most recent qualifying commitment and proceeding in reverse chronological order. When a commitment is disqualified, the entire commitment is disqualified and the disqualified commitment is no longer considered a "loan or extension of credit." Advances of funds under a disqualified or non-qualifying commitment may only be made to the extent that the advance, together with all other outstanding loans to the borrower, do not exceed the bank's lending limit at the time of the advance, calculated pursuant to § 32.4.

(n) Readily marketable collateral means financial instruments and bullion that are salable under ordinary market conditions with reasonable promptness at a fair market value determined by quotations based upon actual transactions on an auction or similarly available daily bid and ask price market. . . .

(q) Sale of Federal funds means any transaction between depository institutions involving the transfer of immediately available funds resulting from credits to deposit balances at Federal Reserve Banks, or from credits to new or existing deposit balances due from a correspondent depository institution. . . .

(t) Standby letter of credit means any letter of credit, or similar arrangement, that represents an obligation to the beneficiary on the part of the issuer:

(1) To repay money borrowed by or advanced to or for the account of the account party;

(2) To make payment on account of any indebtedness undertaken by the account party; or

(3) To make payment on account of any default by the account party in the performance of an obligation.

§ 32.3. Lending Limits

(a) Combined General Limit.—A national bank's total outstanding loans and extensions of credit to one borrower may not exceed 15 percent of the bank's capital and surplus, plus an additional 10 percent of the bank's capital and surplus, if the amount that exceeds the bank's 15 percent general limit is fully secured by readily marketable collateral, as defined in § 32.2(n). To qualify for the additional 10 percent limit, the bank must perfect a security interest in the collateral under applicable law and the collateral must have a current market value at all times of at least 100 percent of the amount of the loan or extension of credit that exceeds the bank's 15 percent general limit.

(b) Loans Subject to Special Lending Limits.—The following loans or extensions of credit are subject to the lending limits set forth below. When loans and extensions of credit qualify for more than one special lending limit, the special limits are cumulative. . . .

(2) Discount of installment consumer paper.—

(i) A national bank's loans and extensions of credit to one borrower that arise from the discount of negotiable or nonnegotiable installment consumer paper, as defined at § 32.2(e), that carries a full recourse endorsement or unconditional guarantee by the person selling the paper, may not exceed 10 percent of the bank's capital and surplus in addition to the amount allowed under the bank's combined general limit. An unconditional guarantee may be in the form of a repurchase agreement or separate guarantee agreement. A condition reasonably within the power of the bank to perform, such as the repossession of collateral, will not make conditional an otherwise unconditional guarantee.

(ii) Where the seller of the paper offers only partial recourse to the bank, the lending limits of this section apply to the obligation of the seller to the bank, which is measured by the total amount of paper the seller may be obligated to repurchase or has guaranteed.

(iii) Where the bank is relying primarily upon the maker of the paper for payment of the loans or extensions of credit and not upon any full or partial recourse endorsement or guarantee by the seller of the paper, the lending limits of this section apply only to the maker. The bank must substantiate its reliance on the maker with—

(A) Records supporting the bank's independent credit analysis of the maker's ability to repay the loan or extension of credit, maintained by the bank or by a third party that is contractually obligated to make those records available for examination purposes; and

(B) A written certification by an officer of the bank authorized by the bank's board of directors or any designee of that officer, that the bank is relying primarily upon the maker to repay the loan or extension of credit.

(iv) Where paper is purchased in substantial quantities, the records, evaluation, and certification must be in a form appropriate for the class and quantity of paper involved. The bank may use sampling techniques, or other appropriate methods, to independently verify the reliability of the credit information supplied by the seller. . . .

(5) Additional advances to complete project financing pursuant to renewal of a qualifying commitment to lend.—A national bank may renew a qualifying commitment to lend, as defined by § 32.2(m), and complete funding under that commitment if all of the following criteria are met—

(i) The completion of funding is consistent with safe and sound banking practices and is made to protect the position of the bank;

(ii) The completion of funding will enable the borrower to complete the project for which the qualifying commitment to lend was made; and

(iii) The amount of the additional funding does not exceed the unfunded portion of the bank's qualifying commitment to lend.

(c) Loans Not Subject to the Lending Limits.—The following loans or extensions of credit are not subject to the lending limits of 12 U.S.C. § 84 or this part.

(1) Loans arising from the discount of commercial or business paper.—

(i) Loans or extensions of credit arising from the discount of negotiable commercial or business paper that evidences an obligation to the person negotiating the paper. The paper—

(A) Must be given in payment of the purchase price of commodities purchased for resale, fabrication of a product, or any other business purpose that may reasonably be expected to provide funds for payment of the paper; and

(B) Must bear the full recourse endorsement of the owner of the paper, except that paper discounted in connection with export transactions, that is transferred without recourse, or with limited recourse, must be supported by an assignment of appropriate insurance covering the political, credit, and transfer risks applicable to the paper, such as insurance provided by the Export-Import Bank.

(ii) A failure to pay principal or interest on commercial or business paper when due does not result in a loan or extension of credit to the maker or endorser of the paper; however, the amount of such paper thereafter must be counted in determining whether additional loans or extensions of credit to the same borrower may be made within the limits of 12 U.S.C. § 84 and this part. . . .

(3) Loans secured by U.S. obligations.—

(i) In general.—Loans or extensions of credit, or portions thereof, to the extent fully secured by the current market value of:

(A) Bonds, notes, certificates of indebtedness, or Treasury bills of the United States or by similar obligations fully guaranteed as to principal and interest by the United States;

(B) Loans to the extent guaranteed as to repayment of principal by the full faith and credit of the U.S. government, as set forth in paragraph (c)(4)(ii) of this section.

(ii) To qualify under this paragraph, the bank must perfect a security interest in the collateral under applicable law.

(4) Loans to or guaranteed by a Federal agency.—

(i) Loans or extensions of credit to any department, agency, bureau, board, commission, or establishment of the United States or any corporation wholly owned directly or indirectly by the United States.

(ii) Loans or extensions of credit, including portions thereof, to the extent secured by unconditional takeout commitments or guarantees of any of the foregoing governmental entities. The commitment or guarantee—

(A) Must be payable in cash or its equivalent within 60 days after demand for payment is made;

(B) Is considered unconditional if the protection afforded the bank is not substantially diminished or impaired if loss should result from factors beyond the bank's control. Protection against loss is not materially diminished or impaired by procedural requirements, such as an agreement to pay on the obligation only in the event of default, including default over a specific period of time, a requirement that notification of default be given within a specific period after its occurrence, or a requirement of good faith on the part of the bank.

(5) Loans to or guaranteed by general obligations of a State or political subdivision.—

(i) A loan or extension of credit to a State or political subdivision that constitutes a general obligation of the State or political subdivision, as defined in part 1 of this chapter, and for which the lending bank has an opinion of counsel or the opinion of that State Attorney General, or other State legal official with authority to opine on the obligation in question, that the loan or extension of credit is a valid and enforceable general obligation of the borrower; and

(ii) A loan or extension of credit, including portions thereof, to the extent guaranteed or secured by a general obligation of a State or political subdivision and for which the lending bank has an opinion of counsel or the opinion of that State Attorney General, or other State legal official with authority to opine on the guarantee or collateral in question, that the guarantee or collateral is a valid and enforceable general obligation of that public body.

(6) Loans secured by segregated deposit accounts.—Loans or extensions of credit, including portions thereof, to the extent secured by a segregated deposit account in the lending bank, provided a security interest in the deposit has been perfected under applicable law.

(i) Where the deposit is eligible for withdrawal before the secured loan matures, the bank must establish internal procedures to prevent release of the security without the lending bank's prior consent.

(ii) A deposit that is denominated and payable in a currency other than that of the loan or extension of credit that it secures may be eligible for this exception if the currency is freely convertible to U.S. dollars.

(A) This exception applies to only that portion of the loan or extension of credit that is covered by the U.S. dollar value of the deposit.

(B) The lending bank must establish procedures to periodically revalue foreign currency deposits to ensure that the loan or extension of credit remains fully secured at all times.

(7) Loans to financial institutions with the approval of the Comptroller.—Loans or extensions of credit to any financial institution or to any receiver, conservator, superintendent of banks, or other agent in charge of the business and property of a financial institution when an emergency situation exists and a national bank is asked to provide assistance to another financial institution, and the loan is approved by the Comptroller. For purposes of this paragraph, financial institution means a commercial bank, savings bank, trust company, savings association, or credit union.

(8) Loans to the Student Loan Marketing Association.—Loans or extensions of credit to the Student Loan Marketing Association.

(9) Loans to industrial development authorities.—A loan or extension of credit to an industrial development authority or similar public entity created to construct and lease a plant facility, including a health care facility, to an industrial occupant will be deemed a loan to the lessee, provided that—

(i) The bank evaluates the creditworthiness of the industrial occupant before the loan is extended to the authority;

(ii) The authority's liability on the loan is limited solely to whatever interest it has in the particular facility;

(iii) The authority's interest is assigned to the bank as security for the loan or the industrial occupant issues a promissory note to the bank that provides a higher order of security than the assignment of a lease; and

(iv) The industrial occupant's lease rentals are assigned and paid directly to the bank.

(10) Loans to leasing companies.—A loan or extension of credit to a leasing company for the purpose of purchasing equipment for lease will be deemed a loan to the lessee, provided that—

(i) The bank evaluates the creditworthiness of the lessee before the loan is extended to the leasing corporation;

(ii) The loan is without recourse to the leasing corporation;

(iii) The bank is given a security interest in the equipment and in the event of default, may proceed directly against the equipment and the lessee for any deficiency resulting from the sale of the equipment;

(iv) The leasing corporation assigns all of its rights under the lease to the bank;

(v) The lessee's lease payments are assigned and paid to the bank; and

(vi) The lease terms are subject to the same limitations that would apply to a national bank acting as a lessor. . . .

§ 32.5. Combination Rules

(a) General Rule.—Loans or extensions of credit to one borrower will be attributed to another person and each person will be deemed a borrower—

(1) When proceeds of a loan or extension of credit are to be used for the direct benefit of the other person, to the extent of the proceeds so used; or

(2) When a common enterprise is deemed to exist between the persons.

(b) Direct Benefit.—The proceeds of a loan or extension of credit to a borrower will be deemed to be used for the direct benefit of another person and will be attributed to the other person when the proceeds, or assets purchased with the proceeds, are transferred to another person, other than in a bona fide arm's length transaction where the proceeds are used to acquire property, goods, or services.

(c) Common Enterprise.—A common enterprise will be deemed to exist and loans to separate borrowers will be aggregated:

(1) When the expected source of repayment for each loan or extension of credit is the same for each borrower and neither borrower has another source of income from which the loan (together with the borrower's other obligations) may be fully repaid. An employer will not be treated as a source of repayment under this paragraph because of wages and salaries paid to an employee, unless the standards of paragraph (c)(2) of this section are met;

(2) When loans or extensions of credit are made—

(i) To borrowers who are related directly or indirectly through common control, including where one borrower is directly or indirectly controlled by another borrower; and

(ii) Substantial financial interdependence exists between or among the borrowers. Substantial financial interdependence is deemed to exist when 50 percent or more of one borrower's gross receipts or gross expenditures (on an annual basis) are derived from transactions with the other borrower. Gross receipts and expenditures include gross revenues/expenses, intercompany loans, dividends, capital contributions, and similar receipts or payments;

(3) When separate persons borrow from a bank to acquire a business enterprise of which those borrowers will own more than 50 percent of the voting securities or voting interests, in which case a common enterprise is deemed to exist between the borrowers for purposes of combining the acquisition loans; or

(4) When the OCC determines, based upon an evaluation of the facts and circumstances of particular transactions, that a common enterprise exists.

(d) Special Rule for Loans to a Corporate Group.—

(1) 50 percent limit.—Loans or extensions of credit by a bank to a corporate group may not exceed 50 percent of the bank's capital and surplus. This limitation applies only to loans subject to the combined general limit [see § 32.3(a)]. A corporate group includes a person and all of its subsidiaries. For purposes of this paragraph, a corporation or a limited liability company is a subsidiary of a person if the person owns or beneficially owns directly or indirectly more than 50 percent of the voting securities or voting interests of the corporation or company.

(2) **Combination rules**.—Except as provided in paragraph (d)(1) of this section, loans or extensions of credit to a person and its subsidiary, or to different subsidiaries of a person, are not combined unless either the direct benefit or the common enterprise test is met.

(e) **Special Rules for Loans to Partnerships, Joint Ventures, and Associations**.—

(1) **Partnership loans**.—Loans or extensions of credit to a partnership, joint venture, or association are deemed to be loans or extensions of credit to each member of the partnership, joint venture, or association. This rule does not apply to limited partners in limited partnerships or to members of joint ventures or associations if the partners or members, by the terms of the partnership or membership agreement, are not held generally liable for the debts or actions of the partnership, joint venture, or association, and those provisions are valid under applicable law.

(2) **Loans to partners**.—

(i) Loans or extensions of credit to members of a partnership, joint venture, or association are not attributed to the partnership, joint venture, or association unless either the direct benefit or the common enterprise tests are met. Both the direct benefit and common enterprise tests are met between a member of a partnership, joint venture or association and such partnership, joint venture or association, when loans or extensions of credit are made to the member to purchase an interest in the partnership, joint venture or association.

(ii) Loans or extensions of credit to members of a partnership, joint venture, or association are not attributed to other members of the partnership, joint venture, or association unless either the direct benefit or common enterprise test is met.

(f) **Loans to Foreign Governments, Their Agencies, and Instrumentalities**.—

(1) **Aggregation**.—Loans and extensions of credit to foreign governments, their agencies, and instrumentalities will be aggregated with one another only if the loans or extensions of credit fail to meet either the means test or the purpose test at the time the loan or extension of credit is made.

(i) **Means test**.—The means test is satisfied if the borrower has resources or revenue of its own sufficient to service its debt obligations. If the government's support (excluding guarantees by a central government of the borrower's debt) exceeds the borrower's annual revenues from other sources, it will be presumed that the means test has not been satisfied.

(ii) **Purpose test**.—The purpose test is satisfied if the purpose of the loan or extension of credit is consistent with the purposes of the borrower's general business. . . .

§ 32.6. Nonconforming Loans

(a) **In General**.—A loan, within a bank's legal lending limit when made, will not be deemed a violation but will be treated as nonconforming if the loan is no longer in conformity with the bank's lending limit because—

(1) The bank's capital has declined, borrowers have subsequently merged or formed a common enterprise, lenders have merged, the lending limit or capital rules have changed; or

(2) Collateral securing the loan to satisfy the requirements of a lending limit exception has declined in value.

(b) **Reasonable Efforts Required**.—A bank must use reasonable efforts to bring a loan that is nonconforming as a result of paragraph (a)(1) of this section into conformity with the bank's lending limit unless to do so would be inconsistent with safe and sound banking practices.

(c) **Decline in Value of Collateral**.—A bank must bring a loan that is nonconforming as a result of circumstances described in paragraph (a)(2) of this section into conformity with the bank's lending limit within 30 calendar days, except when judicial proceedings, regulatory actions or other extraordinary circumstances beyond the bank's control prevent the bank from taking action. . . .

§ 32.8. Temporary Funding Arrangements in Emergency Situations

In addition to the amount that a national bank may lend to one borrower under § 32.3 of this part, an eligible bank with the written approval of the OCC may make loans and extensions of credit to one borrower subject to a special temporary lending limit established by the OCC, where the OCC determines that such loans and extensions of credit are essential to address an emergency situation, such as critical financial markets stability, will be of short duration, will be reduced in amount in a timeframe and manner acceptable to the OCC, and do not present unacceptable risk. In granting approval for such a special temporary lending limit, the OCC will impose supervisory oversight and reporting measures that it determines are appropriate to monitor compliance with the foregoing standards as set forth in this paragraph.

Made in the USA
Lexington, KY
21 January 2016